the message of

PSALMS 73 – 150

Songs for the people of God
Revised edition

Michael Wilcock

INTER-VARSITY PRESS
36 Causton Street, London SW1P 4ST, England
Email: ivp@ivpbooks.com
Website: www.ivpbooks.com

First published 2001, reprinted with minor alterations September 2001. Reprinted 2002, 2005, 2007, 2008, 2009, 2011
This edition published 2023

British Library Cataloguing-in-Publication Data
A catalogue record for this book is available from the British Library.

ISBN: 978–1–78974–417–0
eBook ISBN: 978–1–78359–622–5

Set in 9.5/13pt Karmina
Typeset in Great Britain by CRB Associates, Potterhanworth, Lincolnshire
Printed and bound in Great Britain by Ashford Colour Press Ltd, Gosport, Hampshire

Produced on paper from sustainable sources.

Inter-Varsity Press publishes Christian books that are true to the Bible and that communicate the gospel, develop discipleship and strengthen the church for its mission in the world.

IVP originated within the Inter-Varsity Fellowship, now the Universities and Colleges Christian Fellowship, a student movement connecting Christian Unions in universities and colleges throughout Great Britain, and a member movement of the International Fellowship of Evangelical Students. Website: www.uccf.org.uk. That historic association is maintained, and all senior IVP staff and committee members subscribe to the UCCF Basis of Faith.

Bible
Speaks
today

the message of

PSALMS 73 – 150

Series editors:
Alec Motyer (OT)
John Stott (NT)
Derek Tidball (Bible Themes)

In affectionate memory of
Joseph Cort McPhail
who loved words
and
Frederick Henry Pickering
who loved the Word

Contents

Book III
(Psalms 73 – 89)

Psalms 73 – 83

1. The Asaph Collection

Three famous David psalms (15, 24 and 68) have already drawn our attention to the great day when God's ark was brought to its final home in God's city. Together with an account of the event, 1 Chronicles 15 and 16 give details of how David planned the worship of the sanctuary for that day and for later times. He appointed three men, one from each of the three clans of the tribe of Levi, to supervise its music: Heman and Ethan at Gibeon, where the altar of sacrifice was, and Asaph at Jerusalem.[1] When Solomon's temple was completed, reuniting ark and altar, the three musicians too were reunited to serve the now-centralized Jerusalem cultus (cf. 2 Chr. 5:12).

Of these three men, Asaph is the one of chief interest in Book III of the Psalter. While each of the others is connected with one psalm at the end of the book (88 is 'of Heman', 89 'of Ethan'), no fewer than eleven are psalms 'of Asaph'. Another that we have considered already (50) is placed between the first Korah Collection and the second David Collection, in the middle of Book II. They are a magnificent group, covering a wide range of themes.

We cannot help noticing that at least two relate to the destruction of Jerusalem in 587 BC. How is it that we find psalms 'of Asaph', who lived in the time of David at the beginning of the monarchy, lamenting something that took place four hundred years later, at the end of it?

It so happened that on the day I was writing this the oratorio *Belshazzar's Feast*, by William Walton, was broadcast from Leeds Town Hall,

---

[1] Cf. 1 Chr. 16:37–42 (Jeduthun = Ethan).

one of the great centres of the musical life of the north of England; and the performers included the Leeds Festival Chorus. The work, which incidentally quotes an Asaph psalm (81), had been premiered nearly seventy years earlier, from the same concert hall, *by the same choir.* 'What unbelievably long-lived singers,' you say! Well, no. The organization outlasts the individuals who form it at any one time. Though the parallel is not exact, the 'Asaph Choir' in a similar way long outlived the original Asaph, and presumably kept up his tradition and style. So did the family music ministries begun by Ethan (later known as Jeduthun) and Heman. All three names are still significant in the reigns of Hezekiah and Josiah, three and four hundred years after David (cf. 2 Chr. 29:13; 35:15).

There are even more frequent mentions of Asaph alone, stretching over an even longer period.[2] In fact not only Israel's downfall but also her exile are already history when Nehemiah 12 brings together two points of interest: the reminder that 'long ago, in the days of David *and Asaph,* there had been directors for the musicians', and the choice of one of his descendants for just such a post (Neh. 12:35, 46).

It is not surprising then to find in the psalms that bear his name a broad overview spanning the whole period of the monarchy. Indeed it ranges not only further on, beyond the exile to the restoration, but further back, beyond the judges to the exodus, and sees the Lord's activity throughout. Like the Korah and David Collections of Book II, these psalms use the word 'God' far more often than the word 'LORD'. But the God of the Asaph Collection is repeatedly a God who judges, as he did in Egypt; who speaks, as he did at Sinai; and who over the years constantly shepherds his people. In other words, he is the Elohim who by his acts shows himself very clearly to be Yahweh – the Lord, the God of Israel.

As to why these psalms should have been placed where they are in the Psalter, the remarkable Psalm 73, standing at the head of the main collection, may at once begin to yield clues.

Psalm 73

Apart from the isolated example in the middle of Book II, this is the first of the Asaph psalms, and one of great importance.

---

[2] In the times of Jehoshaphat (2 Chr. 20:14), Ezra (2:41; 3:10) and Nehemiah (7:44).

What will lead us through it step by step is the psalmist's train of thought, rather than a division into stanzas or some other poetic device. Even so, a significant word we have noticed elsewhere reappears here, and acts as a marker, whether intentionally or not, at the beginning of each of three logical sections. It is the Hebrew word *'ak*, meaning (as we saw in Ps. 62)[3] 'truly' or 'only', 'surely' or 'really', and having an effect not unlike that of italics in English. The opening line of Psalm 73 demonstrates this.

1. The psalmist's problem (73:1–12)

Surely God is good to Israel. He really is. The word is not here a meaningless filler, as it sometimes can be ('We *really* want to thank you, Lord': why, who needs convincing? If we want to, let's get on and do it, without the aid of windy adverbs). No; verse 1 is a creed. Like the negatives of the first psalm, it defines what Israel believes: not this, but that. Over against the other faiths and the other gods of Bible times, she believes that her God *really is* what he claims to be.

But is he? What we see in the world seems to contradict what we say in church. According to our creed, it is to those who are right with him that God is good, whereas the wicked 'are like chaff that the wind blows away' (Ps. 1 again). But the evidence of our eyes tells us otherwise. The word *surely* takes on a very different tone – 'Oh, *surely* you remembered!', meaning you almost certainly didn't – and the psalmist cries out in distress, 'Surely, Lord, you are supposed to be good to Israel, aren't you? Because it doesn't look much like it to me.'

He sees *the prosperity of the wicked* (3), the very *shalom* that Psalm 72 promised not to them but to God's own people. How can those who have no interest in God be so healthy, strong and carefree (4–5)? How can they be so arrogant and malicious (6–9), and get away with it? And why are they allowed to lead so many others astray (10–11)? 'My people turn to them and lap up all they say, asking, "How will God find out?"'[4]

Hence the psalmist's doubts and questions. It is not that his faith is slipping into unbelief; 'doubt is something only a believer can experience, for you can only doubt what you believe. Doubt is to unbelief what temptation is to sin. A test, but not yet a surrender.'[5] But something is slipping: his confidence, his assurance, his peace of mind (2–3).

---

3 See p. 1.221. Ps. 39 is another example of the multiple use of *'ak*.

4 Verses 10–11 JB. The verse is a very difficult one, but this is as good a translation as any.

5 Clements, p. 74.

2. The psalmist's crisis (73:13–17)

Surely in vain I have kept my heart pure. What is the point of trying to do right when it is those who do wrong who thrive? The point is sharpened for the psalmist when he himself begins to be *afflicted* and experience *punishments* – when the righteous receives what the wicked deserves. 'If we are honest we have to admit that for most of us innocent suffering remains a purely academic problem, until we become the suffering innocent in question.'[6]

Over against his grievance, however, is the awareness that to say publicly what he feels privately would be a terrible let-down for the fellowship of believers to which he belongs (15). Some might find it a real stumbling block: 'If *he* reckons the game isn't worth the candle, we too might as well give up.'

Trying to work through these questions on his own gets him nowhere (16). But he is not on his own. He has just been reminded that he belongs to 'the family of God' (15 NEB). That thought in turn leads him to *the sanctuary of God* (17). It is in the temple that his questions will be answered. We have no idea how; to speculate about God's methods (a prophetic word? a mystical experience?) is to miss the point. The fact is that the temple was where God called his people to meet with him and with one another, to hear his word and to respond in praise and prayer and self-offering. In that God-centred fellowship each is at the service of the rest, and each is attentive and obedient to what God says to all. The church today, like the temple in former days, should provide such a fellowship, and there the things that puzzle and confuse begin to fall into place, even if we do not get the kinds of answers we were asking for.

3. The psalmist's answer (73:18–28)

Surely you place them on slippery ground. Scandalized by the prosperity of these crooks, the psalmist has felt as though his feet were slipping (2); but their feet really will.

The first thing that becomes clear to him is the truth about the arrogant wicked (18–20). A psalm in Book I (37) and one in Book II (49) have already touched on what God has in store for them. From prosperity they will come to *ruin*, success stories which show no signs of decline will one day end *suddenly* and *completely*, and power which seemed so real, and the

---

[6] Ibid., p. 77.

people who wielded it, God will *despise . . . as fantasies*, an unpleasant dream that vanishes at daybreak.

Equally clear becomes the truth about the doubting believer (21–24). First, the psalmist's grievance may have been understandable, but it was even so a *senseless and ignorant* reaction, with a good deal of envy and self-pity in it. When he is, so to speak, 'in the sanctuary', the facts come into focus. He realizes that even in his bitterest moments the grace of God unfailingly surrounds him. Distress of mind is not the same thing as loss of faith.

Then in verses 23–24 a sermon outline leaps off the page – Grasped, Guided, Glorified! Kidner, noting this, clarifies it with a sequence of tenses (God has grasped, does guide and will glorify his servant), and a reminder of the New Testament parallel in Romans 8:29–30.[7] As in earlier psalms that have raised the question of the afterlife, verse 24 may have a double focal length, having in view possibly honour in this world, but much more probably glory in the next.[8] In describing how God 'took' Enoch at the end of his earthly life, Genesis 5:24 uses the same word as the psalmist does here.

The closing verses (25–28) make clear the truth about spiritual values. To listen to the wicked, you would think they controlled heaven and earth (9); but those who have God with them really do have the best of both (25). The end of the arrogant will be final and complete, as we have seen, but when the life of the believer comes to an end (so v. 26 literally), God continues to be his or her *portion*. The nub of the matter is whether one is *near* God or *far from* him (27–28). The former is the real and lasting good that has been there all the time in the little creed of verse 1 – little, but infinitely great: *multum in parvo*.

More than one commentator quotes Lewis's powerful words concerning the two destinies. 'We can be left utterly and absolutely *outside* – repelled, exiled, estranged, finally and unspeakably ignored. On the other hand, we can be called in, welcomed, received, acknowledged.'[9] That final distinction will answer all the psalmist's questions.

4. Psalm 73 in the Psalter

As with other parts of the Bible, much of the academic study of the Psalter for much of the twentieth century was along the lines of 'form criticism'.

---

[7] Kidner, p. 263.

[8] See p. 1.44.

[9] C. S. Lewis, 'The Weight of Glory', in *Transposition and Other Addresses* (London: Bles, 1949), p. 30.

That is, it asked, 'What form of poetry is such-and-such a psalm?' and in effect rearranged the book of Psalms, classifying them as laments or hymns, as royal or individual or cultic or wisdom or 'law' poems.

More recently attention has turned back to the book as it stands, 150 psalms in Bible order. It is in that shape, after all, that it has been recognized from the beginning as part of the written Word of God. Brevard Childs, for example, entitled his influential 1979 book 'Introduction to the Old Testament *as Scripture*'. It is as though, in the world of horticulture, after a spate of encyclopaedias of garden plants the experts were now publishing studies of actual gardens in which the plants grow. Why were these flowers planted at this end of the garden, those halfway along, and that third kind at the far end?

Walter Brueggemann asks this question about Psalm 73.[10] His answer is that being placed practically at the midpoint of the Psalter it is a 'linkage' or 'threshold', not simply between Books II and III, but between the two halves of the larger book. The Psalter moves 'From Obedience to Praise, from Duty to Delight' (to quote one of his section headings), that is, from the obedience of Psalm 1 to the praise of Psalm 150. Where Psalm 1 says that if we walk in God's way God will be good to us, the psalms that follow in Books I and II repeatedly complain that such an idea is far too simple. Life is not like that. Yet as we go on through the Psalter we find, equally often, a sense that, in spite of all, God *will* be good to his people; till the final psalms come to a climax of unalloyed praise.

It is obvious that Psalm 73 follows just this pattern. Verse 1 corresponds to Psalm 1: *God is good* to the *pure in heart*. Verses 2–12 represent what Brueggemann calls the 'painful candour' with which the pure in heart expostulate: But God, you're not! We suffer, and the wicked flourish! Verses 13–17 are the 'threshold', where they are brought to see things from God's standpoint. Thereupon verses 18–26 express 'grateful hope', which leads to the final verses of the psalm, corresponding to the final psalms of the book.

5. Psalm 73 in the Bible

This understanding of the Psalter, and of our present psalm within it, is clearly a matter of orientation.[11] Those who look at the world with what seems to them the simple, innocent perspective of Psalm 1 (and of Ps. 73:1)

---

10 Brueggemann, pp. 189–213.

11 See ibid., pp. 8–15.

will be disoriented by the hard experience of real life, which seems to contradict it. They need then to be reoriented – to be turned so as to see these confusing facts from a different point of view. That new orientation will bring them ultimately to Psalm 150 (and to Ps. 73:27–28), and to the recognition that in a deeper sense than they had realized 'God surely *is* good to Israel.'

When the form critics classify 73 as a wisdom psalm, they have in mind some parallels in Proverbs (e.g. 23:17–18), but chiefly the book of Job. What we find there, however, is considerably more than mere 'wisdomspeak' parallels. Psalm 73 is 'the book of Job in a nutshell'.[12] The orientation of Job 1:1–5 is plain: here is a man greatly blessed by God because he is 'blameless and upright'. Like the little girl in Saki's short story, he would no doubt have 'won several medals for goodness'.[13] Then unexpected and undeserved tragedy turns his moral world upside down, and nearly thirty-seven chapters describe his disorientation. A personal encounter with God (chs. 38–41) finally reorients him, even though his questions do not receive answers as such, and at the end he is blessed 'twice as much as . . . before' (42:10).

Can we not go further? Is not this the pattern of the entire Bible story? Psalm 1, and Psalm 73:1, and Job 1:1–5, all reflect the first two chapters of Genesis. At the beginning, all that Adam has to do is to obey, and Eden will be his in perpetuity. But that is not how things work out; and a world disoriented by sin needs reorientation before it has any hope of re-discovering Eden. And in fact it will never do so. The discovery that God really is good cannot be a mere reversion to the old innocence, for that is a virginity lost for ever. The way back to Eden is barred by a flaming sword; there is only the long hard way forward. The glories of Psalm 73:24–26, and Psalm 150, and Job 42, and the last two chapters of Revelation, are the glories of Paradise, and Paradise is not Eden. You can get there only by way of Psalm 73:17, which in New Testament terms is the encounter with God in Christ at Calvary.

Psalm 74

As we have seen, the final editors of the Psalter might well have intended Psalm 73 to be the hinge between its two halves. But this does not mean

---

12 Clements, p. 75.

13 'The Story-Teller', in *Beasts and Super-Beasts* (1914).

that every psalm in the first half is disoriented, complaining that God has got things wrong, or that every psalm in the second half has been reoriented, serenely trusting that in spite of appearances God has got things right. The very next poem in the book – this one, Psalm 74 – is one of its bitterest complaints, arising from one of Israel's bitterest experiences: the destruction of Jerusalem in 587 BC, which brought the Hebrew kingdoms to an end.

We could derive a possible shape for the poem from the tenses of its verbs, as Tate does.[14] But with headings based on its themes rather than its grammar, this is the chiastic structure that results:

An appeal: remember us (1–3);
    a reminder: what they have done (4–9);
        an appeal: destroy them (10–11);
    a reminder: what you have done (12–17);
an appeal: vindicate yourself (18–23).

1. An appeal: remember us (74:1–3)

Most versions of verse 1a beg a question. *Why have you rejected us for ever?* assumes that it *is* for ever, which in the nature of things the psalmist could not know. Perhaps he was really asking, '*Is* it for ever?' (NEB), 'Have you finally rejected us?' (JB).

The fall of God's own holy city must certainly have seemed final. It was the end of an age. From that end, with the breadth of vision characteristic of the Asaph psalms, our psalmist looks right back to the beginning of Hebrew history. It is the people of Abraham, the chosen (Gen. 18:19), who are now rejected – the flock whose Shepherd God had been since the days of Jacob (Gen. 48:15), the nation redeemed from Egypt in the days of Moses, the kingdom established on Mount Zion in the days of David.

The Jerusalem Bible speaks of Zion's 'endless ruins'. But graphic though the image is, they are not so much 'endless' as 'everlasting', in that the psalmist cannot imagine them ever being rebuilt; and God is probably being asked, not to 'pick [his] way through' them, as the JB says, but to come quickly, to see the catastrophe for himself. As so often in the Bible, his 'remembering' is far more than a jogging of the memory; it is the taking of action. What he did when his people were slaves in Egypt – 'I have

---

[14] Tate, p. 245, following G. F. Sharrock.

indeed seen . . . I have heard . . . I have come down to rescue them' (Exod. 3:7–8) – the psalmist is asking him to do again. Not that he is ever absent; but he wants his people to want him with them in their trouble.

2. A reminder: what they have done (74:4–9)

'What they have done' can scarcely refer to anything other than the events of 587 BC,[15] and *they* are the Babylonian armies of Nebuchadnezzar. With a string of verbs in the perfect tense the psalmist tells God not so much the story as the outcome of it: this is what they *have done*, and you can see the results for yourself.

They have been here, with their war cries in the very temple where your voice used to be heard, their insignia replacing yours, their axes hacking your house to pieces and their torches burning it to the ground. They have destroyed every vestige of your worship (there was only one worship centre at that time, but verse 8b means either the last of the series of places where the ark had been housed in its long history, or else every possibility of meeting in that place). No signs of God's presence, no words through his prophets: this above all is what the psalmist deplores. So does the book of Lamentations, dating from the same period, especially in 2:5–9.

Why should God want to be told all this? He knows it already; indeed, he himself set the tragedy in motion. Is such a reminder, then, one of those foolish and otiose prayers which seem to assume that he needs information ('Lord, doubtless thou hast seen in the papers . . .')?

Not at all. It is a proper response to the Shepherd-Redeemer of verses 1–2, and his unspoken invitation: 'Tell me all about it.'

3. An appeal: destroy them (74:10–11)

The double question which seemed to be exercising the psalmist in verse 1 ('Why is it? And is it for ever?') is explicit in these two verses. Sometimes even the staunchest believer finds that the two really mystifying things about the way God works are his reasons and his timetable. Our psalmist will find in due course that the 'how long' has a limit, and the 'why' an answer.[16] In the meantime he does not hesitate to express his mystification to God.

---

[15] It has occasionally been argued, not very convincingly, that Pss 74 and 79 relate to an assault on Jerusalem in 359–358 BC by Artaxerxes III of Persia (perhaps the background to the apocryphal book of Judith), or to the desecration of the temple in 167 BC by Antiochus IV of Syria.

[16] See Kidner, p. 267.

Nor is there any hesitation in verse 11b about telling God what to do! Some translators find this line odd, and amend one or two of the words, but we can accept the Hebrew as it stands, even though 'the text is abrupt: "from the midst of Thy bosom! destroy!"'[17] The violence of *Destroy them!* may be distasteful, but we have had to face imprecations of this kind before,[18] and this one makes very good sense when we realize what is in the psalmist's mind. He is thinking once more of the exodus. It is alluded to in the redemption-language of verse 2, it will come to the fore in verses 12–15, and here at the midpoint of the psalm it is seen in the stretching out of God's right hand to do again exactly what he did, according to Exodus 15:12, when he destroyed the Egyptian army at the Red Sea. Now in 587 BC, as then centuries earlier, the survival of God's chosen people is at stake.

> A holy war his servants wage,
>> Mysteriously at strife;
> The powers of heaven and hell engage
>> For more than death or life.[19]

It is inconceivable that the church should perish; so since this is a fight to the bitter end, it must be the enemy who is destroyed.

4. A reminder: what you have done (74:12–17)

These six verses are the counterpart of verses 4–9. Again we have a series of verbs in the perfect tense, describing something that has actually happened; again a reiterated pronoun, not now 'they, they, they' but an emphatic 'you, you, you'; again a historic event – in this case, two – with continuing effects, in the earlier passage the enemy's destruction of Jerusalem and in this one God's creation both of his people and of the world they live in.

In reminding God repeatedly here that *It was you who . . .* , the psalmist is also encouraging himself. His God parted the Red Sea and defeated Egypt (13–14), provided for Israel in the desert and brought her across Jordan into the Promised Land (15). All this was both astonishing in itself,

---

[17] Cohen, p. 238.

[18] See on Pss 35; 40; 58; 69.

[19] James Montgomery, 'Lift up your heads, ye gates of brass' ('Psalm 24 turned into a war cry': Watson, p. 318).

and miraculous in forging what turned out to be an indestructible nation. And what he had already done much earlier was in some respects even more astonishing, and so miraculously permanent that we easily overlook it. He had brought into being at the beginning of time the whole structure of day and night, sea and land, summer and winter, which is the setting for all the dramas of history, and which as Genesis 8:22 tells us will last 'as long as the earth endures'.

This is the God to whom the psalmist has been appealing at a time when his world has crashed in ruin. The chaos wrought by Nebuchadnezzar is closer and therefore looms larger. But he knows that the creating and recreating power of God is in fact infinitely greater.[20]

5. An appeal: vindicate yourself (74:18–23)

In the appeals of verses 1–3 and verses 10–11 the psalmist both questioned and pleaded. Here the questions are all behind him, and his prayer is all pleas: *Remember, Rise up*, do this, don't do that. Anyone can ask God questions, but if you are going to tell him to do things, you have to be pretty sure of yourself – or of him!

But then the psalmist *is* sure of him. We notice that where his first cry to God was 'Remember *us*' and his second was 'Destroy *them*', he is now concerned for **your** name, **your** covenant, **your** cause. And he is well aware what these phrases imply. He knows who and what the God of Israel is, and something of how he works. That has been shown by the psalm's repeated harking back to what this God has done in the past. Again, although the name LORD appears only once (18), this recital of his acts is its equivalent.

It is a case of taking back to God in prayer what history – we should call it Bible history – teaches about these things. Every servant of God can do the same. In the psalmist's case he is saying that because God's name and covenant are what they are, his reputation is bound up with his people's fortunes. He is supposed to be a Saviour, specifically *their* Saviour, and instead of saving them he has lost them! So at any rate *foolish people* will say. As we know, they, the 'fools', are not the stupid but the rebellious,[21] and would not want to think differently anyway. But, Lord, says the psalmist, why should you even give them the excuse to mock?

---

[20] Contrast the setting of Nebuchadnezzar's activity ('in the midst of thy holy place', v. 4 RSV) with that of God's ('in the midst of the earth', v. 12 RSV).

[21] See Pss 14 in Book I and 53 in Book II.

With hindsight, we know that the Lord is going to vindicate his name. The terrible events of the sixth century BC will turn out to be not a failure on the part of his power and love, but something necessary to a much greater plan than the psalmist can yet see. They are like the movement of a piston in a steam locomotive; the engine is moving in one direction, and the piston, seen in close-up at one particular moment, is moving in the other. 'It's going *backwards*! Why is it going *backwards*?' Because it has to; otherwise the locomotive will not move forwards. That is the way it is designed.

But if the psalmist's view is limited, his heart is true. His prayer will be answered, though in a manner far more complex, thorough and slow than he can at present imagine.

Psalm 75

Who says what in this psalm? As can happen in the world of biblical studies, the various opinions are at once very decided and mutually exclusive. In verse 1, *we* is presumably the congregation, and in verses 2–3 God speaks. But is he speaking also in verses 4–5? And in verse 10? And are we to visualize a temple ceremony in which parts are taken by the king, or a prophet, or a 'worship leader' of some kind?

The NIV underlines the obvious by inserting two words between the first two verses: *God . . . You say, 'I choose . . .'* The Hebrew text does not do that. It leaves us to draw our own conclusions. It draws attention less to how the psalm might have been used as liturgy, more to what it actually says. The theme is an Asaph speciality, God the Judge, made vivid by a series of striking pictures in verses 2–8.

1. The pillars of the earth (75:2–3)

Whether the pillars were literal or metaphorical (the pagans no doubt thought the first, the Hebrews the second), they meant the stability of the world we see around us, not only earth and sky but also the social and political structures of the human race. When these are shaken, from one point of view God himself is responsible, as in Job 9:6 and 26:11; from another, the forces of evil do the shaking, while he continues to hold the deeper framework steady, as here (and as in the previous psalm, vv. 16–17). The day will come when, as Haggai 2:6 predicts and Hebrews 12:26–27 endorses, God himself will shake to pieces the entire created order, 'so that what cannot be shaken may remain'. Meanwhile, however, his people can have confidence that none of the turmoils of history is beyond his control.

It seems that the psalmist and his contemporaries have recently emerged from just such a time of upheaval. God has not failed his people. A number of parallels with the relevant parts of Isaiah suggest that again, as in earlier psalms, it is the thwarted invasion of Judah by the Assyrians, in the time of Hezekiah, for which the psalmist is giving thanks (e.g. Isa. 10:5–19; 30:27–31; 37:21–23).

With a breadth of vision typical of the Asaph psalms, the psalmist hears the God who set these pillars in place on the day of creation declaring that it is he who will also decide *the appointed time* for the day of judgment. He means of course in the first instance the limited judgment of Sennacherib of Assyria. But what prophets and apostles say about the final shaking is equally true of the final judging.

2. The horns of arrogance (75:4–5)

These verses are of course the psalmist's words; perhaps he means them to be understood also as God's words, continuing after the *selah* break, or as those of a prophet, or as those of the congregation, speaking for Israel, as it were, with a single voice. All would agree that God's opponents needed to hear this message.

Horns are another Bible metaphor. The horns of powerful animals, the bull and the ram and the he-goat, are in mind, and in a neutral sense they mean power, whether bad or good. Hence verse 10 promises that the wicked will be defeated and the righteous come out on top. In a bad sense, the horns mean power that is pushy, thrusting, self-willed: in a word, arrogant. The 'stiff neck' of verse 5 (see AV) is similarly that of a wilful animal refusing to be bridled or tamed.

'So it must be God who speaks these words,' we may say. 'If these "horns of arrogance" are people of that kind, they are unlikely to listen to any voice less compelling than God's. What would be the point of someone like me bleating "Do not lift your horns against heaven"? Are the great ones of the earth going even to hear me, let alone listen to me, still less do what I tell them?'

True, if these were the words of mortals, those mortals would have to be prophets. They would have to have the mind of God, and the call of God to let it be known, even in the corridors of worldly power. But then God's New Testament servants do 'have the mind of Christ' (1 Cor. 2:16), and in democratic countries today the opportunity to speak it where powerful people will hear it. And might not the opportunity be itself the call?

3. The wheel of fortune? (75:6–7)

Fortuna was one of the lesser gods of classical mythology. She was often portrayed in charge of a great wheel; mortal men and women found themselves around the rim of it, at the top or at the bottom or anywhere between, according to their position in life, entirely at her whim.

The arrogant wicked didn't believe in her, of course. They saw themselves as having clawed their own way to the top. An innocent paganism, on the other hand, took it that the greater gods must have smiled on them. A more sophisticated, cynical or envious paganism asked what could possibly make the gods favour such unpleasant people, and told themselves that this was merely Fortune spinning her wheel.

Our psalm does not use the metaphor of the wheel, as it does those of the pillars and the horns and the cup. But it has the Bible's answer to all such questions. When the Prayer Book version says, 'Promotion cometh neither from the east, nor from the west', it may sound old-fashioned, but it speaks to a situation as real today as it ever was. When people get to the top, the ultimate cause is neither their own ability, nor the favour of some supposed 'higher power', nor even the turning of Fortune's wheel; it is God.

Of two aggressors who attacked Old Testament Jerusalem, Psalm 75 probably celebrates the bringing down of the first, the Assyrian king Sennacherib. History tells of the exalting of the other, the Babylonian king Nebuchadnezzar, just over a century later. God was in control of both; and according to the book of Daniel the latter too had to learn this lesson. 'Walking on the roof of the royal palace . . . he said, "Is not this the great Babylon I have built . . . by my mighty power and for the glory of my majesty?"' Immediately, 'even as the words were on his lips', the doom of insanity fell upon him, until he came to 'acknowledge that the Most High is sovereign over all kingdoms on earth and gives them to anyone he wishes' (Dan. 4:29–32).

4. The cup of wrath (75:8)

The wheel may not be a biblical metaphor,[22] but the cup certainly is. Like the horns, it can be good or bad. We have seen that the psalmist's 'cup

---

[22] The wheels in Ezek. 1 have a different function; they are a symbol rather than a metaphor.

overflows' with the Lord's blessing in 23:5, and shall find him taking the 'cup of salvation' in 116:13. On the other hand, the prophets speak often of the cup of God's wrath.[23] In the New Testament too that cup awaits the wicked at the end of the age, though Christ drained it on his people's behalf when he went to the cross.[24]

The God of Psalm 75, who holds in place the moral pillars of the world, condemns the horned arrogance of the wicked and turns the wheel of so-called 'fortune', will bring down those who lift themselves up, and compel them to drink this cup of punishment. Ironically, it is full of top-quality wine, rich and strong – nothing but the best for such deserving people!

For they do deserve it. We are presented here, as so often in Scripture, with the paradox of divine sovereignty and human responsibility. It was God who had raised up Sennacherib in the 700s, as he would raise up Nebuchadnezzar a century later, and as he had raised up the pharaoh of the exodus hundreds of years earlier, to 'show you my power, and to make my name resound through all the earth' (Exod. 9:16 NRSV; see Amos 6:14; Hab. 1:6). Yet they would not hesitate to claim that they had themselves 'lifted up their horns', and he would be quite justified in punishing them for their pride.

Verses 1 and 9 frame the psalm with thanks and praise, each linked with the telling of what God has done. Perhaps the *selah* was the point for a reading from the story of the exodus, or from 1 Samuel 2 (Hannah's song). The Magnificat, Mary's song, would be their New Testament counterpart – 'He has performed mighty deeds with his arm; he has scattered those who are proud in their inmost thoughts. He has brought down rulers from their thrones but has lifted up the humble' (Luke 1:51–52). And perhaps verse 10 is a final reassurance from the Lord God of Israel, or else a promise from the Davidic king. (With the coming of Christ, in whom Lord and King turn out to be the same person, these amount of course to the same thing.) We could well understand the compilers placing this psalm of encouragement about the defeat of one enemy immediately after a psalm of distress about the temporary triumph of another.

---

[23] E.g. Isa. 51:17, 22; Jer. 25:15; 49:12; Ezek. 23:31–33; Hab. 2:16.

[24] Rev. 14:10; 16:19; Matt. 26:39ff. and parallels; John 18:11.

Psalm 76

With *selah* twice, an emphatic *You* twice, and four times a verb form that is in effect a title of God (such as 'the Shining One'),[25] Psalm 76 has a certain symmetry about it. For example, we might reasonably see each half halved again by a *selah*. The first quarter begins with God as the Self-revealing One in verse 1, and the second quarter begins with him as the Shining One in verse 4. The second half begins and ends (7 and 12) with him as the Awe-inspiring One. Furthermore, the second and third quarters answer to each other, beginning respectively with 'You the Illustrious' and 'You the Terrible' (4 and 7 JB).

Like the previous psalm, these four stanzas of three verses each may celebrate the deliverance of Jerusalem from the Assyrian invader in the reign of Hezekiah. If so, 2 Kings 18 – 19 and Isaiah 36 – 37 are again the background.

1. The Self-revealing One (76:1–3)

Psalms 46 – 48 in the first Korah Collection talk the same language as this one. There too God is great (47:2; 48:1), makes himself known as his people's defence (48:3) and destroys the weapons of war (46:9).

It is a particular place and people that witness to his revealing of himself. Down the ages many supposedly Christian nations have despised, if not persecuted, the Jews, often in the name of God. Yet all the time this psalm was reminding them that (to quote the Prayer Book version) 'in Jewry is God known'. They would know nothing of their own Christian God were it not for Israel and Judah, Salem and Zion. There and there alone our Christian heritage, with all its ramifications, has its roots. 'Salvation' above all, its central trunk, 'is from the Jews' (John 4:22).

God makes himself known also in a particular way. The words here translated *tent* (*sōk*) and *dwelling-place* (*mĕ'ônâ*) are regularly used elsewhere in the Old Testament for the lair or den of a lion (e.g. Ps. 10:9; Jer. 25:38 – *sōk*; Job 38:39–40; Ps. 104:22 – *mĕ'ônâ*). There too, and in the New Testament as well, the lion is a powerful image of the Lord himself.[26]

---

[25] John 1 has two striking examples of the Greek equivalent of this verb form. Jesus is 'the Lamb of God, who takes away the sin of the world' (29) and 'the one who will baptise with the Holy Spirit' (33). The phrases are literally 'taking away sin' and 'baptizing with the Holy Spirit'; he is the Sin-removing One and the Spirit-baptizing One.

[26] Frequently in the prophets; and see Rev. 5:5.

It may be in the psalmist's mind in stanza 2 also, as we shall see, and even perhaps in stanzas 3 and 4.

2. The Shining One (76:4–6)

The creator of Narnia, C. S. Lewis tells us, is 'a Lion' who appears at the very beginning of the story 'huge, and shaggy, *and bright*'.[27] When the psalmist says in verse 4a 'It is you who are the Shining One', he could have in mind the Bible's divine Lion; for of the several possible readings of verse 4b, one which sticks closely to the Hebrew text describes his returning majestically 'from the mountains of prey' (RV).

In this case the prey looks remarkably like the army of Sennacherib. What God had said was that arrow and shield would have no place in the siege of Jerusalem (2 Kgs 19:32 = Isa. 37:33; cf. v. 3). What he did was to send his angel to 'put to death a hundred and eighty-five thousand in the Assyrian camp. When the people got up the next morning – there were all the dead bodies!' (2 Kgs 19:35 = Isa. 37:36).

If the lion's spring was there a metaphor for the overthrow of a literal army, both lion and army can be metaphors for the God who comes to the aid of his people. How often does he spring on their enemies in ways that no-one expected! How often does he outflank their foes by some stratagem for which both sides are entirely unprepared! It is human nature for us to tell God how to help us; it is divine wisdom to recognize that he may well achieve the same ends by quite different means.

3. The Awe-inspiring One: i (76:7–9)

Where stanza 1 began with the Self-revealing One, and stanza 2 with the Shining One, stanzas 3 and 4 are framed by an inclusio: the combination of the two begins (7a) and ends (12b) with the Awe-inspiring One. So in this quarter, stanza 3, verse 7 may still have in mind the awesome picture of the Lion, verse 8 the Assyrian army in its *last sleep* (5), and verse 9 the whole episode of 2 Kings 19 and Isaiah 37 as a prime example of God judging and saving.

Three facts open up a broader vision. The afflicted of the land can equally be the afflicted of the earth – not just Israel but the world. The verbs that describe what God has already done can equally be 'prophetic perfects', describing what from some future standpoint we shall see he

---

[27] C. S. Lewis, *The Magician's Nephew* (London: Penguin, 1963), p. 96.

has done. And the awed Old Testament cry *Who can stand . . . ?* is equally that of the 'kings of the earth' in Revelation 6:15–17, when at the end of time they are confronted by the wrath of the Lamb, who is also the Lion, our Lord Jesus Christ (cf. Rev. 5:5–6).

Thus what is in the first instance a song of praise for something that has already happened is also a song of confidence about something that has yet to happen. We are intended to see both layers of meaning in it, and can readily grasp how to make use of both.

4. The Awe-inspiring One: ii (76:10–12)

Verse 10 speaks to God. As the differences between the translations show, it is difficult to work out exactly what the psalmist was saying. The RSV comes very close to the Hebrew text: 'Human wrath serves only to praise you, when you bind the last bit of your wrath around you.' If for the psalmist the fury of the Egyptians was the prototype, and that of the Assyrians the latest example, for us likewise this is a reassuring message: every assault that the world makes upon God and his people and his stand-ards he will turn around so that it redounds to his own glory. Every last bit of it he can take up and use for his own purposes.

Verse 11 speaks to the church. *The One to be feared* is a divine title, but not of the verbal kind we have been noting; it is simply a noun, the Fear. Other Old Testament scriptures remind us that the Lord is 'the Fear' of Israel, that is, he whom she reveres,[28] so verse 11b probably parallels verse 11a: as it is his own people who are urged to make vows to the Lord their God, it is they too (now described as 'all who are around him', NRSV), rather than *all the neighbouring lands* (NIV), who are urged to bring him gifts.

Verse 12 proclaims to all that this is again the Awe-inspiring One, who will in the end overcome every assault that the powers of this world can mount against him.

Psalm 77

Form criticism[29] classifies this as another lament, which may or may not have a happy ending. It is, however, more than that. As an Asaph psalm,

---

[28] 'Let [the LORD of hosts] be your fear' (Isa. 8:13 AV, correctly). He is also called 'the Fear of Isaac' (Gen. 31:42), though with a different Hebrew word.

[29] See pp. 2.5–6.

one of the group headed by the momentous Psalm 73, it turns out to be something rather special.

1. Two problems

There is a type of problem in Scripture which you notice only when you set different translations side by side. Sometimes it has to do with the tenses of verbs; Psalm 18 provided a case in point.[30] Sometimes it has to do simply with the words in the text.[31]

With regard to the former, verse 1 begins with *I cried* in the NIV, but with 'I cry' in the NRSV, and in each case half the psalm follows suit. But wait, we say: which should it be? A past distress, with the second half telling us how the psalmist has come out of it? Or a present distress, with the second half telling us his intentions but not necessarily God's solutions? Surely these are two quite different readings of the psalm?

With regard to the latter, a central verse here contains not one but two problematic words. Is verse 10a about an *appeal*, or about a 'grief' or an 'infirmity'? And is verse 10b about the *years* of God's right hand (that is, of his power), or about a 'change' in it? Of the various permutations the NIV opts for 'appeal + years', the AV/RV for 'infirmity + years' and the NRSV for 'grief + change'. As Motyer says, the first of these is 'a translation well suited to the context'.[32] Since we soon realize as we work through the psalm that this must be a key verse in it, we may think it strange that its meaning should be so uncertain. But the psalm as a whole will enable us to see what kind of hinge verse 10 is meant to be, and therefore what it is likely to mean.

2. Two moods

Verses 1–9 are indeed a lament, like many others we have come across as far back as Psalm 3. What makes this one distinctive?

In his mood of wretchedness, the psalmist looks back to *the years of long ago*, and to one historic occasion in particular. At Mount Sinai God promised Moses, 'I will proclaim my name, the LORD, in your presence', and the following day he did so: 'The LORD, the LORD, the compassionate

---

[30] See on Psalm 18.

[31] V. 6 raises a third translation problem. Is it about songs-in-the-night being remembered (cf. Job 35:10), or about songs being remembered-in-the-night? The point is of no great significance; the psalmist is certainly remembering them in gloom, but they might also have been night songs in the first place.

[32] Motyer, p. 535.

and gracious God . . . abounding in love' (Exod. 33:19; 34:6). But instead of finding comfort in those ever-memorable words, and telling God that in spite of all he still believes them, the psalmist fears the promise has failed, the compassion is withheld, the grace has been forgotten and the love has vanished (8–9).

What has so sapped his faith? A rejection that seems final (*for ever*). Surely the fall of Jerusalem is the background of this psalm, as of 74. Brueggemann highlights the collision between what he calls 'canonical memory', the Bible story that the psalmist has always believed in, and 'concrete pain', the present experience which seems to contradict it.[33] There could be no sharper clash than that between the great words God had said on Mount Sinai and the disaster the psalmist has witnessed on Mount Zion.

Thus we have here a 'worst case' scenario to illustrate the principle of Psalm 73. To use Brueggemann's terms, the psalmist began with an orientation towards faith in the God of Sinai. But what he has since had to see and endure has disoriented him. Like 73:17, however, 77:10 is the point at which he is reoriented. Somehow he finds he is seeing things differently. In verse 5 it was cold comfort to recall *the years of long ago*; but now he knows them to be *the years when the Most High stretched out his right hand*, a right hand as powerful today as it ever was.

So the mood of the psalm's second half is in great contrast to that of its first half. The key to the change must be 'the turn from self to God'.[34] *I* am the focus of verses 1–9. They are full of *my* misery, *my* complaints, *my* assumptions – a preoccupation with self such as our modern culture has revived with great success and feeds assiduously. But verses 10–20 are all about *you, your power, your path*, a willingness to *consider all your works and meditate on all your mighty deeds*. If there is a change, it is not in God, as perhaps the psalmist has been tempted to think ('The right hand of the Most High has changed', 10 NRSV); it has to be in his own attitude.

3. Two scriptures

From Exodus came the creed he at first took for granted and then began to question. To Exodus he now returns for this serious meditation. The particular passage in his mind must be Moses' song after the crossing of

---

[33] Quoted in Tate, p. 276.
[34] Brueggemann's ch. 13 (pp. 258–267) is entitled 'Ps. 77: The Turn from Self to God'.

the Red Sea, especially Exodus 15:11–18, to which he alludes in some detail, and which could be a *selah* reading after verse 15. In fact he now sets about considering the whole story of the exodus, from the plagues of Egypt (14; Exod. 9:16), through the crossing of the sea (16) and the meeting with God at Sinai (17–18), to the arrival at the very borders of the Promised Land (20). This pondering on Scripture, in breadth and in depth, is light years away from a mere formal repetition of a creed, however biblical, and it equips the believer to cope with the most desperate circumstances.

For the exodus story is only one example, although an outstanding one, of a God who has power over everything he has made. The waters of the Red Sea represent the chaos upon which the Creator imposed order at the beginning; and of course a God of that sort always has that sort of power, even when it is our present world (and our faith) that seems to be disintegrating.

The other closely related scripture is the prophecy of Habakkuk. There too God is the Holy One (1:12), as in Psalm 77:13 and Exodus 15:11; so he is, of course, in countless other scriptures, but the special interest of this one is that Habakkuk is coming to this God with the same question, about the same event, as the psalmist. In his case Jerusalem has not yet fallen, but as a prophet he has been shown that it will soon do so. The Babylonians, 'that bitter and hasty nation' (1:6 AV), are on their way. How can a holy God, who has made such promises to his people, allow such an evil?

In the prayer which forms his third chapter Habakkuk shows that he too has been pointed back to the exodus. His language is full of allusions to it. He has been directed to a God who really is totally and ultimately in control of all that happens. William Cowper paraphrases the prophet's closing verses:

Though vine nor fig tree neither
    Their wonted fruit should bear,
Though all the fields should wither,
    Nor flocks nor herds be there,
Yet God the same abiding,
    His praise shall tune my voice,
For, while in him confiding,
    I cannot but rejoice.[35]

---

[35] William Cowper, 'Sometimes a light surprises'.

Is not this holy God 'from everlasting?' asks Habakkuk (1:12). Yes, he is. He is 'God the same abiding', whether or not the psalmist was tempted to imagine a change in him.

Psalm 78

Book III here brings us the longest of all the psalms except 119. A fine and thought-provoking contribution to the Asaph group, it echoes other collections too.

1. Asaph, Korah and David

Like the Asaph psalms generally, 78 is about a God who acts and speaks. *His deeds* and *his commands* (7) are the subject of much of the psalm. Furthermore, he shepherds his people, and he judges their enemies (and them too); both themes have figured in the last few psalms. He thus again shows himself to be the kind of God who can properly be called the Lord, though once more the actual name is seldom used here.

Among the Korah psalms, 49:1–4 parallels this one's invitation to hear and listen as the psalmist sets forth parables and things hidden (1–2).[36] Both psalms are speaking as the opening verses of the book of Proverbs speak. And 44:1 assumes the custom that 78:3–6 describes in detail, the passing on by word of mouth from one generation to the next the great facts of the faith. All this links both the Asaph and Korah Collections with the wisdom books of the Old Testament.

A feature common to these two collections and to the David psalms as well is the use of certain titles for God: the *Most High* (here in vv. 35 and 56) and the *Rock* (v. 35, and most often elsewhere in that great David celebration, Ps. 18). But for all its links with other psalms, 78 as a whole is unlike any that we have so far come across.

2. A ramble with landmarks

It leads us through perhaps five centuries of Israel's history, from the time of Moses to that of David.[37] But it is not a steady march through nine books of the Bible, from Exodus to 2 Samuel. It lingers at some points and

---

[36] In 49:4 the NIV translates the same Hebrew words as 'proverb' and 'riddle'.

[37] The exodus is believed to have taken place in either the fifteenth or the thirteenth century BC. David reigned in the early tenth century. See *The New Bible Commentary* (Leicester: IVP, 1994), pp. 22–27, 234–235.

bypasses others, and after forty verses we are to our surprise back where we started, only to find ourselves then, quite suddenly, on the homeward stretch. Not so much a journey; more a ramble, it seems.

Yet as poetry the psalm is not nearly so unstructured as this overview might lead us to think. A hint of its careful composition peeps through near the end, in the masterly chiasmus of verses 67–68 – in fact in the order of the Hebrew text a double chiasmus:

> Then he rejected
> > the tents of Joseph,
> > the tribe of Ephraim
> he did not choose;
> but he chose
> > the tribe of Judah,
> > Mount Zion,
> which he loved.

This sure 'instinct for form', as Manning calls it,[38] is writ large in the psalm as a whole. Motyer's outline demonstrates this clearly. After an eight-verse introduction, a three-verse preface to the first half (9–11) centres on the words *They forgot*; a parallel preface to the second half (40–42) says *They did not remember*. Then in each half of the psalm four sections follow. What the psalmist says about God's *redemption* of his people (12–14) is much amplified the second time round (43–53). In each part a couple of verses (15–16, then 54–55) set out his *provision* for them. His *judgment* on them is covered at greater length (17–33 and 56–64), and his *love* for them in spite of their rebellious forgetfulness completes each sequence (34–39 and 65–72).

God led Israel out of Egypt and through the desert in the time of Moses: that is the theme of part one, verses 9–39, which often echoes the language

---

[38] The same pattern is shown by four well-known lines from the hymn 'Jesu, Lover of my soul'. Manning (pp. 21–23) quotes them as an example of 'the literary power and skill and instinct for form that lie behind [Charles] Wesley's success as a verse maker':
> Just and holy
> > is Thy Name,
> I am
> all unrighteousness;
> false and full of sin
> > I am,
> > Thou art
> full of truth and grace.

of Exodus. Part two, verses 40–72, brings the story down to the time of David. It reminds us that God's care for his people had been that of a shepherd (52), and explains that with the setting up of the monarchy it was to David – who better? – that he had delegated this role (70–72).

His choice of David, of the southern tribe of Judah, meant the rejection of Saul, who though a Benjaminite was closely identified with the northern tribes and territories, here given the umbrella name of Ephraim (cf. 1 Sam. 9:1–4; 2 Sam. 2:8–9). On this showing, the death of the rebellious and disobedient Saul in the battle of Gilboa, when 'the Israelites fled before' the Philistines (1 Sam. 31:1ff.), would account for the otherwise puzzling verses 9–11. They establish at the outset of the main part of the psalm (9–72) what the goal of its argument is going to be (67–68).

3. The object of the exercise

Psalm 78 is not therefore a mere historical ramble for those who like that sort of thing. Nor is it a history lesson in the normal sense. The introduction, verses 1–8, makes two things very clear. First, the psalmist's narrative is a matter of parables and things hidden, of proverbs and riddles, because 'by itself the record of the past is a tangle of events, an enigma . . . needing interpretation'.[39] So he selects his facts, and by making the right emphases and the right connections he brings out what they really mean, and the implications of it.

At the same time his hearers have to have a willing spirit. Matthew quotes verse 2 in respect of the parables of Jesus (Matt. 13:35), which made sense to the teachable but remained riddles to the self-willed. 'Who can tell the pleasure,' wrote Sir Henry Baker, 'Who recount the treasure, / By thy word imparted / To the simple-hearted?'[40]

Second, God expects his people to be well acquainted with this sort of history. From Exodus 10:2 onwards each generation has been urged to pass on to the next the heritage of Scripture truth, Bible facts with Bible interpretations. Exodus and 1 Samuel plus Psalm 78, as here, provide only one of countless examples.

This is now, as ever, an encouragement to preachers who feel they have run dry, and a challenge to parents who are inclined to leave the job to 'specialists'. For the object is that as the successive generations grasp

---

[39] Motyer, p. 535.
[40] H. W. Baker, 'Lord, thy word abideth'.

these ever-fresh truths, they should *put their trust in God*, and *not forget his deeds*, but *keep his commands* (7). This is of course precisely the warning of the two little prefaces. The first looks ahead to Saul, who wilfully *forgot* what God had done (11). The second looks back to the Israelites in the wilderness, who in an equally rebellious spirit *did not remember* his power (42).

We saw in the last psalm how remembering can at first seem a profitless exercise, producing nothing but groans and complaints (77:3, 6–9). But far from dismissing the idea, the psalmist there applied himself with determination to doing it properly: 'I will remember the deeds of the LORD; yes, I will remember your miracles of long ago. I will consider all your works and meditate on all your mighty deeds' (77:11–12). That is just what Psalm 78 makes us do.

4. The first time round: redemption and provision

Verses 12–14 sum up God's redemption of his people from Egypt in three tremendous sentences. God acted: he brought about the miraculous plagues; he divided the sea; he came down in the pillar of cloud and fire. His people knew it: they witnessed the plagues, walked through the sea, followed the moving pillar. They had a testimony as real as that of John, who perhaps had verse 3a in mind as he began his first letter: 'That which was from the beginning, which we have heard, which we have seen with our eyes, which we have looked at and our hands have touched – this we proclaim' (1 John 1:1).

Verses 15–16 focus on God's provision of water for the Israelites in the desert. Two different Hebrew words identify the *rocks* as those of Exodus 17 and the *crag* as that of Numbers 20. On the other hand, only one Hebrew word lies behind the *divided* sea and the *split* rock. Neither English word really suits both actions,[41] but we could follow the RV and picture the Lord 'cleaving' the rock as he 'cleft' the sea, thus showing himself in control not only of both earth and sea but also of both the decisive event and the continuing need.

5. The first time round: judgment and love

Verses 17–33 are a composite picture of two or three incidents in Exodus 16 and Numbers 11. These were connected with God's providing of food

---

[41] *Pace* Tate, who has the rather infelicitous phrase 'He split the sea' (p. 278).

25

as well as water, but are mentioned chiefly because of the carping, unbelieving spirit in which the people *put God to the test*. Significantly, the words from this passage which are quoted in the New Testament are a slightly garbled version of verse 24, found on the lips of Jesus' questioners in John 6:30–31. 'What sign then will you give that we may see it and believe you? What will you do? Our ancestors ate the manna in the wilderness; as it is written: "He gave them bread from heaven to eat."' Their attitude is very like that of their ancestors; they are well on their way to falling under God's judgment, as that earlier generation had done.

Finally verses 34–39 show the greatness of his love for them. For what was their sin? First, that though he had redeemed them, they would not trust him; then that when he punished their unbelief, not only were they not repentant, but they had the gall to pretend they were. And still he loved them!

6. The second time round: redemption and provision

The psalmist now takes us back to Egypt. As before, in verses 12–14, the section that describes Israel's redemption (43–53) begins there, with the miracles God did *in the region of Zoan*.[42] Here too it goes on to the bringing out of Israel 'under the cloud' and 'through the sea'. But between Egypt and Zoan on the one hand and the cloud and the sea on the other is a rapid sequence of terrifying pictures, showing what fearful things these miracles were.

Why at this point should God's people be taken back to the deeds of God *in Egypt*, when the psalmist has already been telling *how often they rebelled against him **in the wilderness*** (40)? Surely because they needed reminding of his power (42) – what he could quite properly do, and in their own experience actually had done, to those who persistently rebel against him. *They did not remember*, they did not choose to remember, that even while some were being redeemed, others were being *struck down*: so the little preface runs straight into this first section, from verse 42 to verse 43.

All this is a flashback. The storyline has by now reached a point forty years further on. God has *brought them to the border of his holy land*, and his provision for them here takes the form of settling them in the territory he has prepared for them; verses 54–55 echo Exodus 15:17, the conclusion of Moses' song after the crossing of the Red Sea.

---

[42] Zoan was a great Egyptian city in the Nile Delta, not mentioned in Exodus.

7. The second time round: judgment and love

In the space of just two verses the 'provision' section of the second half has brought us into the period covered by Judges and 1 Samuel. There the second 'judgment' section, verses 56–64, is set. Israel's sins are no longer those of the desert, but those of Canaan (58); she has graduated from merely mistrusting God to replacing him with more biddable alternatives. God's punishment is to have the ark captured by the Philistines, its priests slaughtered (1 Sam. 4) and its shrine at Shiloh destroyed (Jer. 7:12–14; 26:6, 9). He removes every sign of his presence among his people. Words could not say more plainly, 'If you don't want me, you shall not have me.'

Yet the extraordinary message of the final section (65–72) is that in spite of all he still loves them. *His enemies*, and theirs, are not to have the last word. He himself mobilized the Philistines; he will now *put them to everlasting shame* (66). He *wakes*, and his people's nightmare is ended – at any rate for the time being.

And the time is the time of David. We are now at the end of 1 Samuel. God's choice of David's tribe, Judah, means the rejection of the northern tribes (67–68), which must be represented, as we have seen, by the rejected king Saul. It is not yet a matter of their being actually disinherited; it is the leadership of the nation that has passed to Judah, as ancient prophecy said it would (Gen. 49:8–10).

8. The sanctuary and the shepherd

So this stirring review of perhaps half a millennium of Bible history draws to a close. We imagine ourselves looking back from the early days of the monarchy, for that surely was the period when Psalm 78 was written, with the heading *of Asaph* meaning in this case 'by Asaph'. What do we see standing firm as the turbulence dies down?

Two magnificent facts. First, the *sanctuary* (69): not necessarily yet Solomon's temple, but at least the shrine where the ark had been reinstated by David, the great event we have already seen celebrated in Psalms 24 and 68. 'Ichabod' may have been written over the house of God in Shiloh: 'The Glory has departed from Israel, for the ark of God has been captured' (1 Sam. 4:21–22). But God had now raised up Zion in its place, a sanctuary *built . . . like the heights, like the earth that he established for ever*. His glory was back among his people.

Second, the *shepherd* (70–72). The powerful, loving care of the God who had *brought his people out like a flock* at the time of the exodus (52;

27

Ps. 77 ended on the same note) was now embodied in his servant David. The occupation in which the new king had grown up – he knew all about *tending the sheep* – converged with God's own centuries-old occupation, the tending of his own 'perverse and foolish' flock.[43] *And David shepherded them with integrity of heart; with skilful hands he led them.*

We should meditate on Psalm 78 with humility, shame and penitence. It is a powerful picture of our own sinfulness. But the two images that complete it are immensely encouraging. It will not escape us that both of them persist into the New Testament. The Gospels tell us that Christ is himself the tabernacle and the temple where God dwells among his people,[44] and the shepherd who cares for them (John 10:11ff.; Heb. 13:20; 1 Pet. 5:4); and the book of Revelation shows us that even in the world to come Christ will still be both temple and shepherd (Rev. 7:17; 21:22).

Perhaps a psalm like 78 is what the chronicler had in mind when he said that 'Asaph . . . prophesied under the king's supervision' (1 Chr. 25:2). What a grasp of truth was given to these two men – a vision even broader than those we normally associate with this present collection!

Psalm 79

The compilers of the Asaph Collection must have seen the irony of placing this psalm alongside the previous one. In 78 David has come to the throne, and his rule as shepherd king promises an end to centuries of folly and evil. In 79 four more centuries have gone by, and the Davidic monarchy has itself come to an end, mired in the selfsame folly and evil it was supposed to remedy. At the close of 78 God's sanctuary has been 'established for ever' on Mount Zion; at the start of 79 the holy temple is defiled and the holy city is in ruins.

1. What we lament

Among the Asaph psalms 79 is a close companion to 74. What both lament is the fall of Jerusalem in 587 BC, an event which seems both real and recent to the psalmist. He may have been a survivor of the disaster; but even if he is writing a considerable time after it, the psalm has the vividness, the sense of horror and outrage, of an eyewitness account.

---

[43] H. W. Baker again, 'The King of love my Shepherd is'.

[44] John 1:14 ('made his dwelling' = 'tabernacled', RV mg.) and 2:19–21; 1 Cor. 3:16.

It is yet another liturgy enabling people to put their feelings into words, and in verses 1–4, at any rate, to 'tell God all about it'. Of course he knows all about it already; but it is good to remind ourselves once more that talking to God, whatever the subject, is a good habit to get into.

As to what 'it' may be, information technology brings so many lamentable things to our attention every day that it is hard to know where to begin to be horrified. So perhaps it is worth remembering that the truest application of a psalm like this one is to a disaster overtaking the church of Christ. It is primarily about God's people being crushed by the powers of evil, or shamed in the eyes of the watching world.

2. What we admit

Talking to God about the horrors of earthquake or genocide is a proper and important thing to do; but it is not the theme of this psalm. Here, *we are objects of contempt* (4); it is about *us*. Church troubles that are on our minds may be taking place in some distant land, but we identify with God's people there. And as at verse 5 prayer turns from telling to asking, and continues so for eight verses, that identification becomes something more than just lamenting the misfortunes of others. It looks beyond the trouble to its possible cause, and begins to confess sin – *the sins of past generations* (8), *our sins* (9).

Great and good men in Bible times have been prepared to do this. Job is himself suffering, up to his eyes in trouble; he knows of no particular sin that would account for it, yet bows before God to 'repent in dust and ashes' (Job 42:6). Nehemiah and Daniel, both in affluent surroundings far from the scenes of misery, identify not just with the sufferers but with their sin. 'I confess the sins we Israelites, including myself and my father's family, have committed against you,' says the one. 'We have sinned and done wrong,' says the other. 'We have been wicked and have rebelled; we have turned away from your commands and laws' (Neh. 1:6; Dan. 9:5). Or are we more like Jeremiah, aware that we are ourselves in a Jerusalem that is about to fall? Or, still worse, like Zedekiah, whose deliberate sins contributed to its fall, royal son of David though he was (Jer. 37:6–8; 52:1–11)? One way or another, we all have something to admit, something to confess, when the church is in trouble.

3. What we don't understand

When the anger of God, which we know made itself felt in the old days (78:59, 62), is poured out on the church in our own day (79:5), an honest admission of guilt does not necessarily solve all the questions. There remains in particular the matter of the name of God (9). Yahweh is a God of faithfulness and justice. So when his people not only suffer but go on suffering, and when his enemies not only go unpunished but go on being unpunished, doesn't that reflect on his good name? He is supposed to have pledged himself to care for the former and to deal with the latter, and he seems unable to do either. Isn't he laying himself open to the derision of the nations around (10, 12)?

As so often, the question is at bottom to do with God's timing. In terms of the catastrophe of 587, we can understand the punishment of Judah, the victory of Babylon, and the jeers of a malicious onlooker like Edom (cf. Obad. 10–14). What we find hard to understand is why all this seems to go on so long (5).

4. What we promise

Even without having the question answered, the psalmist, together with those who join him in his prayer, still clings to his faith that God really is the Lord, a God of faithfulness and justice. Hence the prayer of verse 10, that he will make himself known as such. The psalmist expects it to happen publicly, *among the nations*; he would like it to happen soon – *before our eyes* probably means 'while we are still here to see it'. But he is certain it will happen one day.

That is why the telling of verses 1–4 and the asking of verses 5–12 are followed by the promising of a response of praise, sooner or later, from us *your people* (13). From *the sheep of your pasture*, we should say – this being an Asaph psalm![45] Even if the dynasty of David, the shepherd king, no longer rules in Jerusalem, God's own shepherd care of his flock will follow them, even through the valley of the shadow of death, says the most famous of all the David psalms; and they will dwell in the house of the Lord, recounting his praise, for ever (Ps. 23:4, 6).

Psalm 80

In one more shepherd psalm, the Asaph Collection brings us yet another example of its breadth of vision and depth of insight.

---

[45] The phrase in v. 13 is repeated from 74:1; cf. also 77:20; 78:52, 70–72.

1. I am the good shepherd

Two pictures dominate Psalm 80, and instantly remind Christian readers of two of the great claims of Jesus in John's Gospel: 'I am the good shepherd' and 'I am the true vine' (John 10:11, 14; 15:1). Equally striking is the fact that in this Old Testament scripture the shepherd represents Yahweh and the vine represents Israel, yet in the New Testament Jesus is both. He is both God the Lord, and the true Israel, God's Son. It is one aspect of his being at once both God and man, the paradox that lies at the heart of the Christian faith.

While the psalmist concentrates much more on Israel as the vine, what Jesus says about himself as the shepherd in John 10, especially in verse 16, will provide us with a helpful framework.

Like 76, a psalm that may have been written at the same time (as we shall see), 80 addresses God by titles based on verbs: the Shepherding One, the Guiding One, the Enthroned One. These direct our attention at once to the special concern of this psalm. Within the first two verses we call him the *Shepherd of Israel*, we speak to him as the God who guides Joseph, and we pray that from his throne between the cherubim he will shine upon Ephraim, Benjamin and Manasseh. Most of these are unfamiliar names in the Asaph psalms. Israel and Judah yes, and Salem and Zion, where the Asaph ministry was based; but all we have heard of these others is that though Joseph was redeemed from Egypt (77:15), Ephraim 'did not keep God's covenant' (78:9–10), and so God 'rejected the tents of Joseph' and 'did not choose the tribe of Ephraim' (78:67).

2. I have other sheep

That rejection had to do only with the nation's leadership, the replacement of King Saul by King David. But eighty years later the grievance boiled over, and destroyed the nation's unity. For these names represent the ten tribes that became the breakaway northern kingdom.[46] That is the 'Israel' on whose behalf the psalmist appeals for God's shepherd care.

---

[46] Benjamin's position is unclear. What was curious about Ahijah's prophecy of the nation's break-up was that he tore his cloak into twelve pieces, representing the tribes of Israel, gave ten to Jeroboam, and kept *one* for Rehoboam (1 Kgs 11:29–32). Perhaps it really was 'only the tribe of Judah' that 'remained loyal to the house of David' (1 Kgs 12:20), while Benjamin, as a small 'buffer state' (in which moreover Rehoboam's capital was situated), was pressed into service with Judah 'to go to war against Israel and to regain the kingdom for Rehoboam' (1 Kgs 12:21) – unwillingly, since as Saul's tribe it would have little sympathy with David's. 'Joseph' (i.e. Ephraim and Manasseh) and Benjamin had the closest of ties: see Gen. 35:24; 48:5; Num. 2:18–24, and the note on Saul's personal contacts, which seem to have been of the same kind. So it is natural to suppose that Benjamin was one of the ten, and belonged in principle if not always in fact to the north (1 Kgs 15:22). The missing 'piece of the cloak' would then be the southernmost tribe Simeon, already absorbed into Judah (Josh. 19:9).

Renegades though the northern tribes were, it was not as inappropriate as we might think for a plea like Psalm 80 to be addressed to God for them. None of the tribes of Israel would ever have forgotten the prophecies spoken of them by their father Jacob. 'Benjamin is a ravenous wolf': that certainly came true (Gen. 49:27; Judg. 19 – 20; 1 Chr. 12:1ff.). But 'Joseph is a *fruitful vine* . . . because of the *Shepherd* . . . your father's God' (Gen. 49:22ff.) – was that to come to nothing?

For it was all twelve tribes that were the vine brought out of Egypt, transplanted to Canaan, and flourishing from Sinai to Lebanon, from the Euphrates to the Mediterranean, in the days of David and Solomon (8–11). When the psalmist speaks of the destruction of the northern tribes' vine (12–16), he surely means the events of 722 BC, when the northern kingdom was overrun and its capital Samaria fell to the invading Assyrians.

3. That are not of this sheepfold

Good people in the south, even godly kings advised by their prophets, differed in their attitudes to the northerners. In Asa's time there were hostilities, in Jehoshaphat's there were alliances. Uzziah seems to have ignored them, while after the disaster of 722 BC Hezekiah showed great concern for the survivors.[47]

Were they or were they not part of the flock of God? An equivalent question has often exercised the church. We, naturally, are theological southerners – it is among us that the true worship of God is to be found! We are not so sure about the people up the road. They talk a language similar to ours, perhaps even the same one, but do they mean the same things by it? Can you be at home in the sanctuaries of Bethel and Dan and have fellowship with us of Jerusalem? In fact, can you even survive spiritually without moving down here to Jerusalem and joining with us? Yet Elijah and Elisha, Amos and Hosea continue to live up there.

Paul puts his finger on the real issue in Romans 2:28–29. True faith is a question of whether we belong to God's people 'only outwardly', or 'inwardly . . . [in] the heart'. Is the heart right with God? That does not mean that the words and the forms of worship don't matter; if the heart

---

[47] Cf. 1 Kgs 15:16ff.; 2 Chr. 16:1ff. (Asa); 1 Kgs 22:1–40; 2 Chr. 18 (Jehoshaphat); 2 Kgs 15:1–7; 2 Chr. 26 (Uzziah); 2 Chr. 30 (Hezekiah).

is right, it will obey the word of God and discern between the good and the bad in such things. But it does mean that sometimes we can tell, sometimes we cannot, whether a person or a group of people really do belong to 'the sheep of his pasture' (Ps. 100:3; cf. 74:1; 79:13). They may not be 'of this sheepfold', but that is a different question. What is called for is an attitude towards theological northerners, if we may call them that, which is neither dismissive nor naïve, but concerned; especially when over there the vine seems to be in such a desperate state.

4. I must bring them also

Reading the psalm as a poem, we notice that it has a refrain, a verse repeated at intervals, though with variations. *Restore us*, we pray (3, 7, 19), *make your face shine on us, that we may be saved.* It is parallel to Psalm 67:1, and an echo of Aaron's blessing in Numbers 6:24–26.

Certainly the devastated north needs to be restored. But the plea goes deeper than a desire merely to have things put right. The RV gives us a better word than 'restore', one which also highlights a marker verse we might otherwise miss. By this marker the poem is thus divided into four roughly equal stanzas, with similar endings:

Turn us, O God (3)
Turn us, O God Almighty (7)
Turn to us, O God Almighty (14)
Turn us, O Lord God Almighty (19)

The psalmist asks God not just to restore, nor yet to return, as if he had gone away, but to *turn round*, so that his face will once more shine on us. And at the same time we are praying that he will *turn us round*. We have turned our backs on him, so he has turned his back on us.

This new turning, however, works differently. It is not a case of 'If we turn away he will turn away, so if we turn back we can make him turn back.' No; it is the paradox of salvation: if I am lost, it is my doing; but if I am saved, it is his doing. I can cause him to turn his back on me, but I cannot make him turn round again, because unaided I cannot first turn myself. Verse 14 is thus the crux of the psalm: a plea that in his mercy he will look on me again, and thus do for me something I cannot do for myself. In one sense of course I do convert, I do repent; in a deeper sense

I have to be converted, he has to 'bring [me] repentance' (Acts 5:31). He must bring the straying sheep back, for they will never come back of their own accord.

5. There shall be one flock

We are brought at last to the questions of date and authorship. Not so dull as they may sound! The compilers have gathered Asaph psalms, all with a recognizable family likeness, from widely spaced points in history. From perhaps 1000 BC comes 78; from 701 BC, 75 and 76; from 587 BC, 74 and 77 and 79. Now with 80 the destruction of Ephraim, Benjamin and Manasseh in 722 BC seems in view.

Was the psalm written by an eyewitness? Or by another northern psalmist some time after the event? The author certainly speaks as one who himself needs to be saved from a dire situation.

On the other hand, we recall the concern of southerners like Hezekiah for the war-ravaged north: 'Turn again unto the LORD,' he pleads with the survivors in just the words of Psalm 80; '[he] will not turn away his face from you' (2 Chr. 30:9 AV/RV). Later, in the darkest days of the southern capital, shortly itself to be laid waste, the Lord commissions Jeremiah with a similar appeal: literally, 'Proclaim toward the north, "Turn, faithless Israel"'; and in due course he hears Ephraim's response: 'Turn thou me, and I shall be turned' (Jer. 3:12; 31:18 AV/RV).

Ezekiel was to see in the acted parable of two sticks joined into one the eventual reunion of Ephraim and Judah (Ezek. 37:15–28); and already that solidarity was being expressed by southerners like these. As in Psalm 79 we were reminded of Nehemiah and Daniel identifying with others far away in their prayers of confession, so here we could imagine an Asaph psalmist in the south writing this heartfelt poem as if he himself could feel the deep need of northern Israel.

And there is in the end only one flock. We may have the deepest misgivings about some who reckon themselves God's people. We may deplore some of the beliefs and practices that flourish under the name of the church of Christ. But wherever the inheritance of biblical truth may still be found, there is the one 'Israel of God', and we must pray for 'peace and mercy to all who follow this rule' (Gal. 6:16).

Dare I quote in this connection a visitor to this country eighty years ago, one keenly aware of the common heritage of two nations faced at that time by a common foe?

I am American bred,
I have seen much to hate here – much to forgive,
But in a world where England is finished and dead,
I do not wish to live.[48]

For America, read Judah; for England, read Israel. Or, in our own time, any 'us' and 'them' in the Christian church.

Psalm 81

Here is good cheer, beginning with music (2) and ending with fine food (16). Here too, between the tambourines and harps and lyres on the one hand and the wheat and honey on the other, is a challenge like that of the Asaph psalm in Book II and the familiar Venite in Book IV (50 and 95).

1. Two knotty verses

We should recognize at the outset that verses 5 and 10 are not quite straightforward. The mention of Egypt (5) takes us back yet again to the time of the exodus. There, as older versions of the NIV had it, 'we heard a language we did not understand', meaning, on the face of it, that we, the Israelites, were strangers in an alien land. It should be 'I', not 'we', but that need not change the meaning; it could still be 'I', the nation of Israel personified, who had to get used to living among foreigners.

Literally, though, verse 5c reads 'I heard a voice I did not know', and could well mean 'I began to hear a voice I had not heard before.' Even then it might be Israel hearing the Egyptians. But so momentous in the story of the Hebrews was the new chapter that began with the exodus that a different interpretation is more likely. The new voice is not that of Egypt; this is either Israel hearing God, or God hearing Israel. For God had never before heard his people crying out to be rescued; and they had never before heard him speak as a rescuer – as a Redeemer, to use the classic Bible term. The great words of redemption, which brought judgment to Egypt and deliverance to Israel, were the essence of his name Yahweh. That is why he could tell Moses that though Abraham, Isaac and Jacob had used that name, they could not in the nature of things have grasped what it really meant (Exod. 6:1–8).

---

[48] Alice Duer Miller, *The White Cliffs* (London: Methuen, 1941).

If it is God hearing a cry his people have never before needed to utter, then verse 5 corresponds to verses 10 and 16, each completing one-third of the psalm with words of God about himself: I hear, I fill, I satisfy. It will also imply, in answer to a secondary question, that verse 5a means what it says in the NIV: God *went out against Egypt* (even though the words are practically the same as those of Gen. 41:45, describing how '*Joseph* went out *over* the land of Egypt' [RSV]).

Verse 10 also may have more to it than we think. *Open wide your mouth and I will fill it* could be a promise of food. But that is explicitly the promise of verse 16; and generally in the Old Testament the 'opening' and 'filling' of the mouth is not about food but about speech. The whole of this section, verses 6–10, is God speaking, and pleading with his people to hear and listen. If only they will open their ears to him, they will find their mouths filled too, also with words – responses of praise and prayer and proclamation.

2. Water and light (81:1–5)

If this is the right way to read two debatable verses, the psalm falls simply into three parts, each ending with an 'I' statement by God. And when he speaks like this, he is concerned as much in verse 5 as in verses 10 and 16 with his people's open mouth. Here it utters a cry of distress, which is, as we have seen, the distress of an enslaved people. For as in other Asaph psalms, we are back in the days of the exodus. This is clearly a liturgical psalm, for a congregation meeting to recall those days; and since along with the rescue itself the psalmist commemorates also the lawgiving at Sinai and God's provision for his people in the desert, it must be a hymn for the feast of Tabernacles. This was the grand harvest festival, beginning with the full moon at the end of September (as we should say) and preceded by the feast of Trumpets at the new moon two weeks earlier (3).[49]

Only after Israel was settled in the Promised Land, of course, did Tabernacles celebrate harvest. As the festival of water and light, it praised God then for his gifts of sunshine and rain, and was the background to Jesus' 'living water' and 'light of the world' proclamations in John 7 and 8. But originally, during the forty years of wandering in the wilderness, there had been no such thing as a harvest. The water there was not rain, but miraculous streams that burst from the rocks; that was God's *providence*.

---

[49] Cf. Lev. 23:23–25, 33–36, 39–43; Deut. 16:13–15.

And the light? Too much of it, they might have said – this tyrannous desert sun, 'nothing is hidden from its heat'! Yet these words in Psalm 19 (NRSV) see in that sunlight a picture of the light of God's *revelation*. Here it is in verse 4: every *decree* and *ordinance* in the law of God, the life-giving, soul-satisfying word of God of which the second and third parts of our psalm also speak, is God's gift of illumination to the darkened mind of humankind.

3. Water: the acts of God (81:6–10)

Part two is taken up with the acts of God on behalf of his people in those formative days. Verses 6–10 are full of allusions to the accounts of the period in Exodus and Deuteronomy, as any good set of cross-references will show.[50] These were the practical things, the evidences, which showed plainly that he was Yahweh, the rescuing God he claimed to be. He had brought to an end the slavery of the brickfields. He had come down in the cloud to destroy the host of Egypt in the sea and to inspire the camp of Israel at the mountain. All of this nobody could deny. When they tested him at Meribah (Exod. 17:7) he was really testing them. The water that gushed from the rock typified everything he had done for his people; they had seen it all; surely they could not be so crass as to withhold their trust from such a God.

These divine acts were acts of grace. They had not been earned and could not be bought. The proper response to them was one of thanks-giving and love, the first of the two great themes of the related Psalm 50. *No foreign god* (9) operated in this way; such gods had to be placated or cajoled or bribed. The same is true of their modern equivalents. We hear on all hands the complacent belief of our neighbours that they expect somehow to contrive to keep on the right side of their 'God'. By contrast, you can tell those who have listened to the God of Psalm 81: they stand agape at the astonishing mercy and goodness of God to such undeserving sinners as them, and he fills those open mouths with gratitude and testimony.

4. Light: the words of God (81:11–16)

The festival that focused on God's practical goodness was the occasion, once every seven years, for an important extra. This was the public

---

50 Those of the RV are outstandingly thorough. See pp. 1.96–97.

reading of the law given to Israel at Sinai (Deut. 31:9–13). We should readily agree that God's word is a precious gift to his people, yet even so we might think it odd if we found a Bible set in the place of honour among the fruit and vegetables at a harvest festival! The Old Testament church saw perhaps more clearly than many Christians do that the word is not only just as much a provision for our welfare as the harvest is, but is also equally practical, and even more necessary. 'I have treasured the words of his mouth', says Job, 'more than my daily bread' (Job 23:12).

The Israelites may have understood this, but they did not always act on it, any more than we do. There is a sharp irony about their later enjoyment of Tabernacles. Seven days' al fresco living in 'booths', or shelters made of branches, in effect an annual camping holiday, was no doubt good fun. Forty years' living in tents in a desert, which was what it commemorated, had been no fun at all. And it had been entirely their own fault, for precisely the reason given here in verse 11. They *would not listen*, they *would not submit*, to the word of God. They wanted their own way instead of his. So he gave them what they wanted; the principle is laid down here in verse 12, and in the New Testament in Romans 1:24, 26 and 28. 'Be careful what you want,' said Spurgeon, 'because you're sure to get it.'[51]

So it was a matter of disobedient people and a long journey, when it might have been obedient people and a short journey. But in either case the grace and truth of God would make themselves known, and there would be his unfailing provision to celebrate at Tabernacles. The difference was, and still is, that those who do listen and follow (13) find God to be their strength: so verses 14–15 pick up verse 1. And they find their mouths are filled, no longer with a cry of distress (5), and not simply with a testimony of praise (10), but with new and even greater blessings (16). Manna was miracle enough, but he has in store for us the finest of wheat; and not just water, but honey, from the rock.

Psalm 82

This, the last but one of the Asaph psalms, characteristically portrays God as Judge. The inclusio of his giving *judgment among the 'gods'* (1) and being

---

called to *judge the earth* (8) frames some of the strangest and most hotly debated lines in the Psalter. We did not leave the knotty problems of the psalms behind when we moved from 81 to 82.

1. Another knot (82:1)

Seen in imagination or in vision, the dramatic picture of God presiding over a council or assembly is not unique to this poem. The book of Job depicts something similar, so does the prophet Micaiah, and so do the New Testament's descriptions of the day of judgment (Job 1:6–12; 2:1–7; 1 Kgs 22:19–23; Matt. 25:31; 2 Thess. 1:6–10; Jude 14–15). The big question here is the identity of the *gods* among whom judgment is being given. Broadly, there are four kinds of answer.

One suggestion is that they are what the psalm says they are, namely gods – the gods of heathendom. As with the previous psalm we might find a parallel in 95:3, where the Lord is 'the great God, the great King above all gods'.

Another suggestion is that they are what Paul calls the principalities and powers (cf. Eph. 6:12 AV/RV/RSV), angelic spirit beings, good or bad, whom Scripture does sometimes call 'sons of God' (e.g. in the Job references just noted), and who in some way preside over, or at least influence, human affairs.

A third is that they are human beings, the rulers or judges or priests of Israel, to whom God delegated just the kind of task set out in verses 3–4 (cf. Exod. 21:6; 22:8, 9, 28; and mg. in each case).

A fourth is that they are the people of Israel themselves, *all sons of the Most High* even if the Old Testament does not actually call them 'gods'.

The commentaries go into these possibilities in detail, and each generally opts for one or other of them. We shall return to the question when we reach verses 6–7.

2. A thread to follow (82:2–5)

Whoever these *gods* are, it is clear from verse 2 what they have been doing, and from verses 3–4 what they ought to have been doing instead. There is no doubt what God expects of them. The *cause of the poor* and the *oppressed* are dear to his heart, and should be to theirs also.

Thus far they do seem to be the judges of Israel, reckoned to be falling down on the job, subjected to an enquiry, and due (7) for dismissal. It looks as though they will not have the chance to mend their ways; verses 3–4 are not so much a renewed briefing as a reminder of the original briefing, which they have failed to carry out.

Verse 5 brings further uncertainties. Is it the unjust authorities or their victims who know and understand nothing? Which of the two groups is it that walks about in darkness? Either way, God's action in calling wrongdoers to account has exposed things that are very wrong in the structures of society.

The sequel (6–8) will show that he does not intend either to leave these unworthy *gods* in control, or to get rid of them and leave the needy without any framework of justice. He will show that he is himself the one who can be relied on to 'rule the peoples with equity and guide the nations of the earth', as we recall from an earlier psalm, 67:4. If this present psalm really is at first about the judges of Israel, it ends with a far wider view of the just government God intends to set up eventually. When today cracks appear in the integrity of those who make, administer and enforce law in our own society, we must be as disturbed by it as the psalmist is; and we too must look to God to do something about it.

3. Tied tighter – or beginning to unravel? (82:6–7)

We have already followed the obvious thread of the argument through to the end. But it does not in fact run smoothly. Verses 6–7 are the really knotty passage in the psalm, much more so than the first mention of the *gods* in verse 1.

Verse 7 is the lesser problem. Does dying *like mere mortals* imply that they are *not* human (and therefore gods or angels), or that they *are* human, that is, that they will die like the mere mortals they are? Does 'fall like any prince' (NRSV) mean that they are themselves 'princes' or 'rulers', as in the NRSV margin, or that they are not?

If these questions have no answer, perhaps they also have no great importance. Verse 6 on the other hand raises questions of very great importance. It appears in the New Testament, as more than just an allusion, and more even than a quotation. Jesus appeals to it, citing its exact words, at a crucial point in one of the key controversies between him and his opponents. The account is in John 10:31–39: 'Again his Jewish opponents picked up stones to stone him', because (they said)

> 'You, a mere man, claim to be God.' Jesus answered them, 'Is it not
> written in your Law, "I have said you are 'gods'"? If he called them "gods",

to whom the word of God came – and the Scripture cannot be set aside – what about the one whom the Father set apart as his very own and sent into the world? Why then do you accuse me of blasphemy because I said, "I am God's Son"?'

I referred in passing to Carson's acute comment on these words in connection with part of an earlier psalm, 45:6.[52] As he points out, 82:6 shows, according to Jesus, 'that the word "god" is legitimately used to refer to others than God himself'. And since it is God, no less (the 'I' is emphatic), who here in Scripture is calling others 'gods', 'on what biblical basis should anyone object when Jesus says, *I am God's Son?*'[53]

Since Jesus' understanding of the psalm is obviously of supreme interest, we should note two other phrases of his. First, he says the title 'god' is applied to those 'to whom the word of God came'. Second, he says that if it was proper to use it of them, it is even more properly used of 'the one whom the Father set apart as his very own and sent into the world'. We are back at Sinai yet again. Who at Sinai received the word of God? Who was sanctified ('set apart') and commissioned ('sent into the world')? It was Israel – not its leaders, its judges, but the whole nation.

That is surely the real point of Jesus' argument. He is not cheapening the word 'god' and saying it is not as special as we thought. He is highlighting the name 'Israel' as one even more special than we thought, since it is in him alone, the true Israel, that we find what the name is really meant to signify.

4. A knot worth struggling with (82:8)

This is the point that Carson makes – convincingly, in my view. *God presides in the great assembly* (1), not in a council of angels or judges; the word is the one used dozens of times in Exodus and Numbers for the whole gathering of Israel, as well as here at the outset of the Psalms in the keynote 1:5. The people of Israel are *all sons of the Most High*, for according to Exodus 4:22 the nation itself 'is my firstborn son'; and among them ('among the gods') God is on this occasion targeting their unjust judges.

What will happen when he removes them, these faithless leaders – for die they will, like the *mere mortals* they are?

---

[52] See p. 1.158 n. 24.

[53] D. A. Carson, *The Gospel according to John* (Leicester: IVP, 1991), p. 397. The whole section on John 10:34–36 / Ps. 82 is worth pondering.

Two things. He will in the end reveal himself as the ultimate Judge, and not of their nation only, but of all nations; then all the evils of verses 2–5 will finally be swept away. And Israel itself will be reborn, for one of the 'gods' will turn out to be in the fullest sense 'God'. One out of all those *sons of the Most High* – the angel of the annunciation uses the very words to Mary – 'will be called *the* Son of the Most High' (Luke 1:32). That is to say, the unthinkable will happen, as with Yahweh the shepherd and Israel the vine in Psalm 80: the parallel lines, divine and human, will converge, and God 'will judge the world with justice by the man he has appointed' (Acts 17:31). Once more the Psalter intrigues us with an enigma whose complete solution is disclosed only in the New Testament and by the miracle of the incarnation.

Psalm 83

Although its neighbours are so noteworthy, 82 for its strangeness and 84 for its familiarity, 'this little-read psalm'[54] does have a special interest of its own. It was after all chosen by the editors of the Psalter as the completion of their Asaph Collection, and that is more likely to mean a climax than an unimportant tailpiece.

1. The what and the how

We look first at the content of the poem as a whole, and at the way the psalmist has shaped it.

The *selah* after verse 8 could be intended as a midpoint marker; we notice that a string of proper nouns in the verses immediately before it is balanced by another in the verses following it. They are practically all names of Israel's enemies, known from other parts of the Old Testament.

Before the earlier group, her current enemies (5–8), words of theirs are quoted (*Let us destroy*), and before that the psalm has begun with Israel's own words to God, a dismayed prayer for help in the face of the attackers' threats. The later group of names (9–12) is drawn from earlier history, and ends with another quote from the enemy (*Let us take possession*). The psalm ends with another cry to God, this time a defiant prayer in which Israel fully expects his deliverance.

---

[54] Tate, p. 349. ('One is tempted not to bother with the message of this little-read psalm'!)

Seen in this way, the poem is structured as a very obvious chiasmus:

A dismayed prayer (1–4)

['*Let us destroy,' they say*]

because of present enemies (5–8);

because of past enemies (9–12)

['*Let us take possession,' they said*];

a defiant prayer (13–18).

2. A dismayed prayer (83:1–4)

Enemies figured often in Book I, the first David Collection. The account of David's life includes many examples of the antagonism that was felt towards him personally, by individuals whom Scripture names. Sometimes he prays simply to be rescued from them. At other times he prays for their downfall, in the imprecatory psalms, of which 35 was the first we considered in detail. One important point about those psalms is that David, knowing himself to be God's chosen king, sees attacks on him as attacks on God.

In this psalm, written long after his time (Assyria is by now looming on the horizon, v. 8), the opposition is similarly seen as opposition to God: these are *your* enemies, says the psalmist, *your foes* (2). They are not now individuals, as in David's time, but nations; and Israel *as a nation* is the object of their threats, *your* people, *those you* cherish (3–4).

The agreed policy of these neighbouring states has an unpleasantly modern ring to it: *Let us destroy them as a nation, so that Israel's name is remembered no more.* Just such tensions have often recurred in the Middle East since the founding of the state of Israel in 1948. But though the wording of the threats may be identical, the two situations, ancient and modern, are not. The phrase 'the people of God' took on a whole new meaning with the coming of Christ. In fact what the psalmist was pleading for his nation, that we should plead, not for our nation nor for the Jewish nation, but for *the church* – God's nation, that is; God's church. The prayer was squarely based on the promises of God (a kind of praying always to be encouraged), because God had said that these were his people, and this was where he wanted them to be. So it was those promises that were under threat, and surely for the sake of his own reputation he could not *remain silent.*

Therefore, as the nations have spoken in threat, and the psalmist has spoken in dismay, now let God speak in answer.

3. Present enemies (83:5–8)

When is all this happening? We have only to find a time in the history of Israel when the nations represented by the eleven names here formed an alliance against her. The problem is that no such time is known. We do know of hostile alliances between different groupings of these nations in twos and threes, but not of one that brings them all together. As with Procrustes' bed in the old legend, the body will not fit: if we do find such a list of allies in the histories, either the list in verses 6–8 has to be lopped to tally with it, or it has to be stretched to tally with the one here.

It seems more likely that the psalmist is looking back over the centuries and presenting a poetic picture of the many enemies that have arisen against Israel at various times, from the earliest (Amalek, Exod. 17:8) to the latest (Assyria, 2 Kgs 15:19). It may be that verse 6 portrays her 'nearest and dearest'(!), closely related peoples with long-cherished grudges: Edom descended from Jacob's brother Esau, the Ishmaelites from Isaac's half-brother, and Moab from Abraham's great-nephew, Lot's son.[55] If 'Gebal' (cf. NRSV) is the Phoenician port of *Byblos* (as in NIV), a neighbour and ally of Tyre, verse 7 looks like a circle of nations which had at different times been a thorn in the flesh for Israel: Gebal to the north, Ammon to the east, Amalek to the south, Philistia to the west, and back to the north with Tyre. Verse 8 only makes sense if Assyria is shaking hands across the centuries with Moab and Ammon, whose beginnings are recorded as far back as Genesis 19.

Such a montage, historical figures placed side by side in a non-historical setting, is not unique to this psalm. The books of Chronicles sometimes use a similar technique.[56] Such a stylized tableau helps readers like ourselves, in another time and place, to see corresponding patterns in what is happening in our own experience as God's people. We too can recognize ancient attacks renewed, enemies on every side, the promises of God concerning his church called in question. We can make the psalm our own prayer.

4. Past enemies (83:9–12)

In his plea to God, the psalmist harks back to the days of the judges. All the proper nouns in verses 9–12 are well known from that period of Israel's

---

[55] The Hagrites may or may not be 'descendants of Hagar' (= Ishmaelites), as in the NIV's first edition.

[56] See my *The Message of 1 and 2 Chronicles* (London: IVP, 2022), pp. 88–90.

history, and all of them (except of course the place names Kishon and Endor) are Israel's antagonists. In other words, our psalm focuses not on Deborah, Barak, Jael or Gideon, the nation's deliverers in the two sections of Judges referred to, but on the Canaanite king and his general from chapters 4–5 and the Midianite kings and their generals from chapters 6–8.

These are the old-time equivalents of the enemies menacing Israel in the psalmist's portrayal of her present situation. They said, *Let us take posses-sion of the pasture-lands of God*, just as the new enemies are saying, *Let us destroy . . . Israel's name*. They, that is the Canaanites and the Midianites, more than any other of Israel's foes in those days, came with weight of numbers to overwhelm the newcomers and prevent their settling in the land God had promised them (Judg. 4:1–3; 6:1–6; see also Josh. 11:1–10).

This may be why the psalmist appeals to God's deliverances at that time rather than others at other times earlier or later. For a new thing was happening: what Psalm 80 earlier described as the transplanting of God's vine from Egypt to its intended vineyard in Canaan. It was indeed brought out of Egypt; it did indeed take root in new soil. Hence the psalmist's prayer, with its biblical basis: what God has so triumphantly taken in hand cannot now be allowed to fail. *Do to them*, our present assailants, *as you did to Midian*. Psalm 83 expresses the same confidence as Philippians 1:6, and for the same reason – since God has rescued this people, his honour is bound up in the preserving of them: 'He who began a good work in you will carry it on to completion until the day of Christ Jesus.'

5. A defiant prayer (83:13–18)

Wind and fire are the classic symbols of God's power, as the experience of Moses and Elijah and the first Christians will tell us (cf. 1 Kgs 19:11–12; Heb. 12:18–21; Acts 2:1–3). The psalmist is entirely confident that God's enemies will be blown away like *chaff* or *tumble-weed* (how could we ever have understood v. 13 before American movies introduced us to tumble-weed?[57]), or consumed as in a forest fire.

The second half of this rather longer section, verses 16–18, tells us what the psalmist wants, over and above the mere removal of the threat. We should always be prepared to have God probe the motives and objectives that lie behind our prayers. If he were ever to say, 'Why exactly are you asking this?', would we have a defensible answer?

---

[57] We took it to refer to thistledown, or whirling dust, or a wheel!

Our psalmist has half a dozen ends in view as the purpose of his praying. Certainly he wants Israel to be delivered from her enemies. He also wants, as a matter of justice, that having done dismaying things to others they should themselves be *dismayed*; and if that sounds merely vindictive (it should not, in view of biblical principles to which earlier psalms have directed us), that they should be brought to feel dismay *at their own doings*, that is, *shame*. It is presumably not the ashamed, but the hardened, that he prays may *perish*. We are permitted to think in such extreme terms, of course, only of those who persist to the end in opposing God.

According to verse 16b he wants their downfall to be an object lesson to others, who may because of it be brought to seek and to acknowledge the Lord. But throughout these three verses he may have alternatives in mind for the enemies themselves. If they refuse to recognize the Lord, then they must perish. In this he is saying no more than God himself has said; again this is a prayer based on the word. But if dismay leads to shame, shame may lead even these hostile people to seek and finally to know the Lord.

Psalms 84 – 89

2. The second Korah Collection

To entitle the remaining psalms of Book III 'the second Korah Collection' is a matter of convenience rather than accuracy. Only four of the six are headed 'Of the Sons of Korah'; the others bear the names of David and Ethan, and one of the Korah psalms is additionally labelled 'of Heman'. We recall these less familiar names from the introduction to the Asaph Collection. All are connected with the temple cultus in Jerusalem, and the families of musicians appointed by David to lead it.

At this point Book III reverts to the practice of Book I in regularly using the name Yahweh, 'the Lord', where the intervening psalms have used Elohim, 'God', much more often. When we realize, as we shall in due course, that two or three of the Korah psalms here seem to run parallel to those that begin Book II, we may suspect that the Sons of Korah have left us two alternative liturgies in these two different idioms, though the poems in both sets are equally powerful and memorable. On the whole they lack perhaps the wide-ranging historical background of the Asaph psalms, but they are more objective and less tied to the particular experiences of an individual than many of the David psalms.

Psalm 84

The first of this supplementary Korah group is as well known and well loved as any psalm in the Psalter. Two metrical English versions of it are still to be found in standard hymn books: Isaac Watts's 'Lord of the worlds above', dating from 1719, and Henry Lyte's 'Pleasant are thy courts above', of 1834.

1. A long way from home

The love of an Israelite for Israel's holy place, God's sanctuary, shines out in a number of psalms. We have seen it in Books I and II, in both David Collections (27:4 and 63:1–2), and shall find it again in Book V (122:1; 137:5–6). Here it begins the second Korah Collection, as it began the first, for this pilgrim song is a companion to the combined Psalms 42 and 43. In each case we have a poem which expresses a longing to be worshipping God in his temple, and which opens a sequence of psalms that seem to have been intended for people travelling to Jerusalem for one of the great festivals, most likely the feast of Tabernacles.

Both its three-stanza shape, and its description of pilgrims eager to appear before the living God in his dwelling-place, are features that 84 shares with 42 – 43. There are also differences. In the earlier psalm the psalmist seemed a long way from his own home, let alone God's; and wherever he may have been physically, he was emotionally very far adrift from his moorings. In 84 the singer is not in that distracted state of mind. He is simply away from Jerusalem, which is where he would like to be.

For an occasion like Tabernacles, people would set out on pilgrimage from every part of the country. Their own homes might be a long way from God's home on Zion, but they had every intention of getting there, and our psalm reads as though its author would have been among them.

2. The second Korah pilgrim song

The *selahs* at the end of verses 4 and 8 provide the simplest and most obvious way of dividing the psalm. It falls into three stanzas of four verses each, which then turn out to be related in ways that are not quite so simple.

The point about God's *lovely* dwelling-place (1) is not that it is beautiful, but that it is beloved.[1] So the first and last verses of the psalm make a chiastic inclusio that frames the rest: How beloved the house, O Lord Almighty; O Lord Almighty, how blessed the person. And might the other two 'blesseds', in verses 4 and 5, be part of the poem's design? They might indeed; one ends stanza 1, the other begins stanza 2, on either side of the first *selah*. When we then notice that two other related phrases bridge the gap at the second *selah*, we see a pattern which can hardly be accidental:

---

[1] Cf. GNB, JB, NEB.

How beloved the house, O Lord Almighty (1)
    [*in love with the house, 2–3*] –
how blessed the dwellers (4)!
    [*Selah*]
How blessed the pilgrims (5)
    [*En route for the house, 6–7*] –
Listen, O God (8)!
    [*Selah*]
Look, O God (9)
    [*At home in the house, 10–11*] –
O Lord Almighty, how blessed the person (12)!

In love with the house (stanza 1): that certainly describes the psalmist. He is totally taken up with it. He envies the birds who are able at will to make their home there. But he loves the house only because of the one whose house it is: he is crying out for the living God, so clearly it is not so much for the *courts* of the Lord, as for the courts of the LORD, that he yearns. And the altar, above all, is in his mind's eye, for there the sacrifice is offered which deals with his sin and puts him right with God.

En route for the house (stanza 2), the pilgrims do not have an easy journey, but God gives strength to the feeble, refreshment to the thirsty, blessings (rather than *pools*, though there may be an intentional play on words in the Hebrew) on the way, and the promise of meeting him at the end.

At home in the house (stanza 3), they find awaiting them every imaginable good. The best obtainable anywhere else is as nothing compared to this.

3. A close look at Old Testament details

Psalm 84 has more than its share of puzzles. In four verses in particular the meaning is not obvious to modern readers, though no doubt it was in Old Testament times.

Verse 5 ends with 'in whose heart are the ways', and has the translators struggling. Even the RV, normally sticking so closely to the Hebrew text, feels the need to suggest an explanation: 'the high ways *to Zion*'. The word for 'ways' may carry the idea of pilgrimage, as in NIV, and be the biblical equivalent of the medieval route to the shrine of Thomas à Becket at Canterbury, marked even on today's maps as the 'Pilgrims' Way'. The

French translation of Louis Segond makes an attractive suggestion. In their hearts the pilgrims find '*des chemins tout tracés*', ways ready mapped out; where real desire for God is, there too is a Spirit-given homing instinct as to how to reach him.

Verse 6 may refer to an actual place, *the Valley of Baka*. Perhaps it was the Valley of Rephaim, leading up to Jerusalem from the west, whose poplar trees are noted in 2 Samuel 5:22–25. In the psalm it is a particularly arid stretch of one of the pilgrim routes, 'but faith turns it into a place of springs, finding refreshment under the most untoward circumstances'.[2]

Verse 9 in av/rv says 'Behold, O God our shield', while more recent translations add a comma, as it were, saying in effect 'Behold, O God, our shield.' In the latter case, *shield* is a metaphor or title for the king, and that is probably correct in this verse, even though the same title is given to God in verse 11; for here *our shield* is parallel to *your anointed one*.

The first half of verse 10 looks more straightforward than it really is, but the niv conveys the sense well enough. The oddity of its second half is that it seems to contrast being an unimportant person in God's house with being an important person among the wicked, whereas to be a doorkeeper in the temple was not a menial position at all, but an honoured one. In fact our psalmist probably has in mind not a person with an official position, but simply someone who has to stand near the door. Better 'standing room only' in this theatre than a seat in the stalls at that one!

4. A broad view of New Testament principles

It is a great thing to be able to say concerning a psalm like 84, 'I will sing with my spirit, but I will also sing with my understanding' (1 Cor. 14:15). With a little background knowledge, we can at least grasp something of what an Old Testament believer would have meant by it.

But how does it, in Isaac Watts's words, 'speak the common sense of a Christian'? What sort of continuity between Old Testament and New enables us to sing it to the praise of Christ?

We note three points, one in each stanza.

In respect of verses 1–4, it may be that we have to adjust our focus. The psalmist is in love not so much with the beloved house of God, as with God himself; and, dare we say it, there is something he loves even more than

---

[2] Kirkpatrick, p. 507.

that. For what does he envy the sparrow and the swallow? For their habitual closeness to the altar of sacrifice. His heart is set not simply on the living God, but on the *loving* God, the one who has provided the way to forgiveness and renewal by the shedding of blood. In Christian terms, the Pilgrims' Way has the cross in view from the outset.

In respect of verses 5–8, in what sense are New Testament pilgrims like us en route for the house? John Bunyan's hero was on his way to the Celestial City, and that is a classic Christian understanding of the journey. Even the many for whom this life is a real 'vale of tears'[3] may yet find that grace enables them to go *from strength to strength* till they reach the joy of heaven.

On the other hand, 'Pleasant are thy courts below, / In this land of sin and woe,' as Lyte puts it; 'How fair . . . Thine earthly temples are,' says Watts. Both hymn writers recognize that God's house is accessible here as well as hereafter. It is anywhere that God's people congregate in his presence. The pilgrimage need mean nothing more exotic than regular churchgoing – a determination not to 'give up meeting together, as some are in the habit of doing' (Heb. 10:25), seduced by the modern cult of individualism, leisure, mobility and lack of commitment.

In respect of verses 9–12, finding oneself finally at home in the house of God is somehow connected with the prayers at the second *selah*. Verse 10 should begin as verse 11 does with the word 'for' or 'because'. So why should Israelite pilgrims pray for the king (9)? *Because* (10) of the surpassing value of meeting God in his house. In other words, firm strong government in Israel ensures the safety of travellers and the security of the temple, and facilitates the meeting. And we Christians know that God does indeed *look with favour on* [his] *anointed one*. Under the kingship of Christ our access to God's presence is guaranteed.

Why then is it so good to enjoy such access? *Because* (11) *God is a sun and shield* (so '*guide* and *guard* my erring heart', says Lyte); and because he showers *favour and honour* upon those who seek him. Again the Old Testament language acquires new depths with the coming of Christ: in the fullest sense, grace, glory and every good thing are given to *those whose way of life is blameless* (11) because it is a walk of faith (12).

---

[3] The possibility that *Baka* might mean 'weeping' (balsam trees 'weeping' gum?) prompted Watts, Lyte and many others to see this life as a 'vale of tears', or a 'vale of woe'. We may have been fortunate enough for this metaphor to seem somewhat extreme; we should remember that millions have not.

Psalm 85

Although 85 is in many ways a characteristically Korah psalm, it recalls features of the Asaph and David Collections too. Besides matters of form and style we cannot miss its spiritual power.

1. A Korah liturgy

Again the Sons of Korah seem to be providing a liturgy, and again the second collection parallels the first. As in 42 – 43, so in 84, pilgrims set out for the festival in Jerusalem; as in 44, so now in 85, they arrive.

For these psalms, 44 and 85, are very much the approach to temple worship. 'Lament' or 'complaint' is the standard label for part, at any rate, of these psalms, though form criticism itself recognizes that there is more to them than that. They are in fact what is usually called in Anglican liturgy the 'penitential introduction' to a service.

While there is, in Goulder's words, an 'extensive . . . web of relatedness' between 85 and 44,[4] a simple outline in three parts is enough to show the relationship. Each psalm first recalls what God has done for his people in the past, things they neither could have done themselves nor deserved to have done for them (44:1–8; 85:1–3). Each then recognizes that now, in the present, all is not well. God's favour and renewal are needed once more (44:9–16; 85:4–7). Each finally looks for just such a renewal of his blessing, one with some distress (44:17–26), the other with great confidence (85:8–13).

2. An Asaph connection

On what past acts of God's favour is Israel's present appeal based? He *restored the fortunes of Jacob* (1) most obviously when he brought the nation's exile in Babylon to an end, in the sixth century BC. In fact that is the event regularly called 'the restoration', and most commentators hold that Psalm 85 was written after it and is looking back to it in these opening verses.

It is conceivable, even so, that the *land* means Canaan at the time of the original settlement, and that the sins covered and the wrath set aside belong to the days of the wilderness journey. At several points our psalm recalls the wording of Exodus 32 – 34. If it were that that our psalmist had

---

[4] Goulder, *Korah*, p. 86.

in mind, it would be very much in the Asaph style, spanning great stretches of Israel's history to show the greatness of Israel's God.

Whether or not this is so, something else here certainly does hark back to a recent Asaph psalm. The link between 85 and 80 is a verb which appears, usually in disguise in the NIV, four or five times in each of these psalms. Unlike a famous British politician of the 1980s, neither of our authors could ever say, 'The psalmist's not for turning.' They are very much for it. Turning and being turned, both on God's part and on Israel's, are for them a necessity.

As in 80, the word is here translated *restore* and 'return', and it is also concealed behind *revive us again* (6). In the remembering of verses 1–3, God has in the past *turned* the fortunes of Jacob and has himself *turned* away from his fierce anger. In the pleading of verses 4–7, he is asked to *turn* Israel again, and to *turn* to revive her. In the listening of verses 8–9, his promises of peace are heard, provided Israel does not *turn* again to folly. In the expecting of verses 10–13, there is a vision of a new age in which no more turning will be needed.[5]

We should already have taken to heart what Psalm 80 has said about all this. In its context, as the second in a pilgrimage sequence, our present psalm reminds us of a further fact. 'Turning' may be a dictionary definition of conversion, and we may say, 'Oh, I don't need to "turn"; I was converted long ago.' But it is also a very good definition of repentance, and that is required of us every time we (so to speak) arrive at the temple.

3. A David picture

When all the turning is done, God's salvation and glory become real to us (9). A beautiful picture of what that means now emerges. There are passages like this elsewhere in the Psalter; we have already noticed at least two, both in David psalms.[6]

The cartoon-like description of 55:9–11 personifies a range of evils that are corroding the life of the city.[7] We could picture these characters, labelled with capital letters: Lies the politician and Threats the businessman, Destruction the civil servant, Violence and Strife the thugs on the street corner; even a couple of respected citizens called Malice and Abuse.

---

[5] The headings 'remembering', 'pleading', 'listening' and 'expecting' are those of Motyer's commentary, p. 541.

[6] Others are 40:11; 57:3, 10; 61:7 (all David psalms); 89:14 (the Ethan psalm).

[7] See p. 1.197.

A much earlier, and better-known, David psalm personifies much pleasanter truths. In 23:6 he who has the Lord as his shepherd can say, 'Surely your goodness and love will follow me all the days of my life.' An Israelite cartoonist is not likely to have portrayed these as a couple of sheepdogs, as an English one might be tempted to do! But Alexander Maclaren's picture is not so wide of the mark: 'Two bright-faced angels walk behind him as his rear-guard.'[8]

So it is here in 85:10–13. We see Faithfulness and Covenant Love meeting, Righteousness and Peace embracing, and are thus shown that heaven and earth are in harmony, as God intended. Righteousness in particular is the herald of his coming, whether he comes at the end of the age or into the present life of the repentant people of God; for where sinners turn to him in penitence and faith, they find that he is both 'just and the one who justifies' (Rom. 3:26).

4. But the style is that of the Sons of Korah

Verses 1–3 remember how God has shown himself in the past to be one who forgives and restores. Are they alluding to the return from exile, or to the exodus centuries before that? Verses 10–13 expect renewed blessing; but does that imply a good harvest after a bad one (12), whereas the parallel Psalm 44 implied restoration after a political disaster?

If we wish the psalmist had been more specific, we may be missing the point he wants to make. Like the liturgies produced by Cranmer and his fellow Reformers of the Church of England, the Korah psalms are designed to be a Book of *Common* Prayer: specific and personal enough to be heartfelt, general enough for everyone to use, and to use repeatedly. No doubt psalms like 44 and 85 grew out of a particular 'single occasion', as Goulder puts it; but he sees them then, 'in stylised form, being repeated year after year, to lay before God whatever defeats have been incurred'.[9]

This is the style of Watts rather than that of Wesley, the difference we noted when beginning to study the first Korah Collection.[10] To revert to the section themes noted earlier, any believer, even today, can with the first three verses *remember* some personal experience of the spiritual turnaround without which none of us enjoys the Lord's blessing. All of us

[8] A. Maclaren, *The Psalms*, Expositor's Bible (London: Hodder & Stoughton, 1893), vol. 1, p. 231.

[9] Goulder, *Korah*, pp. 85–86.

[10] See pp. 1.147–148.

have often to *plead*, with the next four, for a renewal of it, a 'turn for the better' in restoration and revival. Again today we may *listen* (8 and 9) to his promises of peace, salvation and glory to those who for their part pledge not to *turn to folly*. The four final verses put into words for us the blessings we may *expect* when the relationship is right.

In all probability Israel of old used the Korah psalms annually at Tabernacles; in Christian churches where the Psalter is sung as a monthly cycle, they come round that much more frequently; but in fact they lend themselves to the need of all believers at any time when the Spirit of God moves them to repentance, to a turning from sin, and to a yearning for a renewal of old mercies.

Psalm 86

Nearly all of Book I and the greater part of Book II were taken up with David psalms. The first three-quarters of Book III have so far been quite different, consisting of Asaph and Korah psalms. A single David psalm at this juncture is rather unexpected, especially in a collection which seems to have been made (as Ps. 74 in particular has shown) at least four hundred years after David's time.

1. The unexpectedness of Psalm 86

As well as the surprise of finding a David psalm here at all, two other features of it may catch our attention. If we think we recognize parts of it, we may be remembering them from our own recent reading. There are allusions, sometimes exact quotations, that point us back to earlier psalms, and not to the psalms only. Nearly the whole of this one turns out to be a mosaic of fragments pieced together from others, and from related Old Testament scriptures. Kirkpatrick imagines 'some pious soul whose mind was steeped with the scriptures already in existence, and who recast reminiscences of them into a prayer to suit his own particular needs'.[11] It might in that case be reckoned a David psalm, though written long after David's time, because so much of it recalls verses from four of the first David Collection (Pss 25 – 28) and four of the second (Pss 54 – 57).

In the NIV, as in many English versions, the other unexpected thing has to do with the way God's name is printed. 'LORD' represents Yahweh, 'Lord'

---

[11] Kirkpatrick, p. 515.

represents Adonai. Since the latter was less venerable, to many in Israel it came to seem, paradoxically, more respectful; in such circles, as we have seen, the Four Letters were too holy to be uttered, and where YHWH was printed, Adonai would be read.[12]

We should be wrong to assume on that account that Adonai was not in itself a name of any great significance. It means Sovereign, or Master,[13] and it figures here in Psalm 86 no fewer than seven times, more often than either 'LORD' or 'God'.

2. The Master and his servant (86:1–6)

The prayer of the opening verses is addressed to Yahweh, as the inclusio of verses 1 and 6 says. But he, the God of covenant love (5), is also Adonai. That is what the psalmist calls him three times in this section. The relationship between them colours its prayers.

Three things are implied in verse 2 by the fact that God is his Master. He is devoted to him; not in the 'feely' sense of a spaniel-eyed fawning, but in the robustly practical sense of something earmarked or assigned ('the money will be devoted to the building scheme'). He serves him; if one is master, the other is obviously servant. He trusts him; if he fulfils the servant's role responsibly, he can rely on the master to take care of the larger issues.

The following verses give three more reasons why the psalmist can pray with confidence. They are indicated by the word *For* which appears in verses 3 and 4 and which should appear also at the beginning of verse 5. He believes he will be answered and blessed *because* his prayer is constant; *because* it is heartfelt and single-minded; and *because* his Adonai is also Yahweh, kind, forgiving and abounding in covenant love (cf. Exod. 34:5–6).

3. The Master and his power (86:7–13)

Most English translations understand the verb in verse 13b to be in the past (*you have delivered*), but it can mean 'you will deliver', and the future also makes very good sense. Its effect is to give the second section, like the

---

[12] Hence, as we have seen, the imaginary name Jehovah; see p. 1.147 n. 2.

[13] The words of Jesus to his disciples, 'Ye call me Master and Lord: and ye say well; for so I am' (John 13:13 AV), are not a claim to be Adonai and Yahweh, although the latter was soon, and rightly, going to be read into the Greek word *kyrios*. (*Kyrios* in itself means no more than 'Sir', but was used to translate 'Yahweh' in the LXX.) 'Master' in John 13:13 means 'Teacher' (so NIV, NRSV).

first, an inclusio, framing the rest between two expressions of confidence: *When I am in distress . . . you answer me* (7); *You have delivered me from the depths, from the realm of the dead* (13).

Within that, verses 8–10 praise the power and greatness of the Master. From Exodus 15:11 onwards many scriptures celebrate the incomparable God. In the heavenly realm (8a) there is none like him.[14] In the world of creation, no-one else's 'works' (8b NRSV) can compare with his; in the world of humankind all nations will bow to him (9); in the events of history his deeds, unlike anyone else's, have repeatedly been miraculous (10).

Verses 11–13 bring that power to bear on the psalmist's situation. He is praying not so much against his enemies, who are to be introduced in verse 14, as for himself. Both halves of his actual petition, verse 11, are memorable, even though the first is, we might say, recycled from 27:11. Kidner makes the important point that this prayer to learn God's way and to walk in God's truth is 'about forming the right habits . . . rather than making the right moves'.[15] It has to do with the development of a whole mindset whose decisions will increasingly be in line with God's.

On the other hand, verse 11b is not recycled from anywhere. It is unique, and a gem. I was struck by its grammatical oddity years before I realized its spiritual profundity. 'Unite my heart to fear thy name,' said the AV/RV – how could anyone unite something that was already a unity, a singular noun?

Three of the great hymn writers understood. Philip Doddridge remembered the 'happy day that fixed [his] choice' on Christ as his Saviour:

> Now rest, my long-divided heart,
> Fixed on this blissful centre, rest.[16]

Charles Wesley knew a continuing need:

> I want a true regard,
> A single steady aim.[17]

---

[14] Whether *the gods* are the heathen gods (who are not, of course, real) or the angels (who are).

[15] Kidner, p. 312.

[16] Philip Doddridge, 'O happy day, that fixed my choice'.

[17] Charles Wesley, 'Jesus, my strength, my hope'.

Thomas Ken, a hundred years earlier, had spelt out the practical implications:

> Direct, control, suggest, this day,
> All I design, or do, or say,
> That all my powers, with all their might,
> In thy sole glory may unite.[18]

4. The Master and his enemies (86:14–17)

As so often in the David psalms, we are to take it for granted that David's enemies are God's enemies: the *ruthless people* that *are trying to kill me* have *no regard for you* (14). The direct quotation from Exodus 34:6 (15) shows that the Master is the covenant-keeping Lord of Sinai. Adonai is indeed Yahweh. Each term has its distinctive meaning, but even so, all that can be said of either is equally true of the other.

If in this case we have a psalm not only of, but by, David, the *ruthless people* could well be the conspirators who gathered round Absalom. We know from 2 Samuel 15 – 18 what a traumatic time the great rebellion was for David. Yet there is no trace of self-pity in these closing verses. Much folly on his part had contributed to his dire predicament, but he faces it with fortitude and honesty.

For example, the prayer for mercy may be recognizing not merely his need but his sin; the enemies may be in the wrong, but he does not pretend that he is without blame. The prayer for strength shows that he is not spineless or defeatist. The prayer for a sign is not for something that will reassure him, like Gideon's fleece (Judg. 6:36–40), but for something that will expose and confound his, and his Master's, enemies.

Patchwork the fabric of Psalm 86 may be. But David himself would have found that it fitted him well enough, and what he would own, we ought not to call common.

Psalm 87

The last but one of the Korah psalms is in some ways an enigma. Even so, its clarities outweigh its obscurities, as in so much of the Psalter.

---

[18] Thomas Ken, 'Awake, my soul, and with the sun'.

1. Psalm 87 and the liturgist

Many a guess could be hazarded as to how this intriguing psalm might have figured in the temple cultus in Jerusalem. How did the Sons of Korah envisage its being used as liturgy?

If once more the *selah*-pauses were intended for Scripture readings, it would not be hard to propose suitable passages. Something inspiring from Jerusalem's history could follow verse 3, something prophetic about the ingathering of the nations could follow verse 6.

Verse 7 would then of course be left as a curious tailpiece. It is by any reckoning a very strange verse. The suggestion has even been made that it is not part of the poem, as such, at all, but a rubric or stage direction: 'At this point the singers and dancers will perform *All my fountains are in you*'! As if to balance that, verse 1 looks more like a title than a first line. Literally, it reads simply 'His foundation on the holy mountains.'

All this is speculation. We are on firmer ground in noticing again the link between the two Korah Collections, and the possibility that both were intended for pilgrimages to a festival in Jerusalem. Psalm 84, like 42 – 43, would have been for the departure from home; 85, like 44, for the arrival at the capital. After the David psalm 86 in the second collection, and three extras in the first collection, 87 corresponds to 48 as a song about Zion. In particular, verses 1 and 8 of the earlier psalm are echoed in this one: 'The city of our God, his holy mountain . . . As we have heard, so we have seen in the city of the Lord Almighty, in the city of our God: God makes her secure for ever.'

2. Psalm 87 and the hymn writer

The planning of church services today, which should include the use of psalms in some form or other more regularly than tends to be the case, ought also to involve the choice both of appropriate scriptures and of related hymns and songs.

With this last in view, whose eye would not be caught by verse 3? John Newton's certainly was, and the av gave him the first line of a new hymn practically ready-made: 'Glorious things are spoken of thee, O city of God.'

The psalm and the famous hymn will not in fact bear close comparison. That memorable line provided a launching pad from which Newton took off in an exhilarating flight of fancy (always on a scriptural course, be it said), touching down again in Psalm 87 only in his final verse. The city's rock foundation came from the Gospels (Matt. 7:24–25; 16:18), its walls of salvation from the prophets (Isa. 26:1; 60:18). He found its streams of living water in Psalm 46:4; Ezekiel 47; and John 7:38. Then, unexpectedly, his mention of manna and the pillar of cloud and fire takes us away from the city to the desert, and back from Psalms to Exodus, though admittedly to pilgrims on a journey which will eventually end in Jerusalem.[19]

Finally, 'of Zion's city I *through grace* a member am': at last we are back with our psalm.[20] If it is about anything, it is about the grace that brings in undeserving outsiders, and blesses them with the privileges of citizenship.

3. The song of the city (87:1–3)

The mountain in verse 1 is literally 'mountains', either the range on which the city is situated, or the hills within its boundary (like the seven hills of Rome), or a singular hill referred to by an 'intensive' plural (as when we speak of the skies or the seas).[21] It means of course Jerusalem.

The point of verse 1 is that God is its founder. It existed already in the time of Abraham,[22] and exists still today. But when God appointed it as David's capital, that was in effect a new foundation. For the next thousand years, from the time of David to the time of Christ, it was in a very special sense God's city (cf. Ps. 78:67–72; 132:13–18; John 4:21–24). As its meaning for today becomes clear we shall realize where and when it is that God says to us 'The place where you are standing is holy ground' (Exod. 3:5).

Verse 2 indicates what is so special about it. Why should God love it *more than all the other dwellings of Jacob*? Is not the whole of Israel his, holy and beloved? Yes; but this is the place (like Sinai before it; Deut. 4:10) where he calls his people together, for praise and prayer and the hearing of his word, centred on the one altar of sacrifice for the forgiveness of sins. That is the very reason for the pilgrimage, as 84:1–3 has recently reminded us.

No wonder that the city, with all that it stands for, has inspired those who love it as God does, and has moved them to utter *glorious things* (3) in their singing and preaching. They are celebrating the church: not a denomination, however historic, and certainly not a building, however fine, but the gathering of the people of God, here and hereafter. A key New

---

[19] See on Ps. 24.

[20] Besides the four verses referred to here, Newton's original text included one about the 'blest inhabitants of Zion' and their status as kings and priests (Rev. 1:6 AV).

[21] Cf. Gen. 1:1–2, 'the heavens . . . the waters'.

[22] See p. 1.161 n. 32.

Testament scripture to which earlier psalms have pointed us, Hebrews 12:22–24, puts the doctrine in a nutshell. How good if that divinely planned reality can be well and truly earthed in our own regular, local gathering! How much in the spirit of 87:3 if *glorious things* can be said about *that*!

4. The song of the citizens (87:4–7)

The most astonishing part of Psalm 87 is yet to come. A cluster of proper nouns in verses 4–7 represents notable nations of Old Testament times. What unites them is that they are all very definitely not Israelite! *Rahab* means Egypt (cf. Isa. 30:7; 51:9), and Egypt and Babylon were the first and last great enemies of Israel in the Old Testament. Philistia and Tyre were her near neighbours, the one an incessant thorn in the flesh and the other proudly independent. Cush, or Ethiopia, was simply a long way away – the ends of the earth, where Israel was concerned.

Yet it is such people whom God says he will draw to Zion. And not just as visitors. Three things are said about them in verse 4, and each is reiterated. The Lord will *record* them: that is, as verse 6 explains, he will write them down *in the register of the peoples*. Well, of course he will; that is plainly where they belong, in the register of the *peoples*, not in that of God's own people. Ah, but they will be recorded there as belonging with *those who **acknowledge** me*. Acknowledging the Lord means knowing him personally, the special privilege of his people Israel. Perhaps that is what verse 7 is about: these non-Israelites will abandon their old beliefs, and recognize that in Israel's God alone is the source of all good and all joy.

So they are to be honorary members, as it were? Yes, and more. They will be registered as having been *born* in Zion. Again verse 6 repeats an amazing fact: they will be reckoned not just as citizens but as natives of the city of God, whatever their race or nationality, their place of origin or religious background.

'It cannot escape our notice that to know God, to acquire a second, spiritual, citizenship, and to be born again, are all New Testament descriptions of a profound change in the human heart (John 17:3; Phil. 3:20; John 3:3, 7).'[23] None, Jew or Gentile, who has refused to be saved by grace through faith, can expect admission to the city of God. But all, of any race, in whom his grace does bring about that change, will be welcomed there.

---

[23] My *The Message of 1 and 2 Chronicles*, p. 73.

61

Psalm 88

Although we are not yet quite at the end of Book III, this is the last of the Korah psalms. In some respects it harks back to 42 – 43, the first of them, a pairing which frames the combined Korah Collections. In others it recalls 49, and thus completes the parallels we have noticed as we set the two collections side by side, rather than end to end: 42 – 43 with 84, 44 with 85, 48 with 87, and now 49 with 88.

1. Praying in darkness

Psalm 88 is, as we can see at a glance, a prayer. Form criticism classifies it as an 'individual lament'. How the psalmist himself might label it is plain from the way he speaks to God, three times over: *I cry out to you . . . I call to you . . . I cry to you*. The whole psalm is one long, desperate cry. It may be divided with these words as three section headings.

Day and night I cry out to you (1). Very true to experience is the way he can address the Lord as *the God who saves me*, and yet feel that he has to implore this God to listen to him (2). The next three verses are full of his troubles, and real and terrible they are. The fear of imminent death is in every line. It does seem to be death itself, rather than the process of dying, that he fears. As we have seen often elsewhere, there is an Old Testament hope of life beyond death, but of that hope he has quite lost sight.

The reference to the dead *whom you remember no more* switches the focus from the psalmist to God. The repeated *I* of verses 3–5 is followed by a string of accusations directed at *You* in verses 6–8. By verse 9a these protests about his treatment at God's hands have reverted, in their turn, to one more bitter cry about his own misery: first I, I, I, you; then you, you, you, I.

I call to you, LORD, every day (9). This prayer, this 'spreading out of the hands', consists of half a dozen questions. All the psalmist has experienced of God's doing great things for men and women and of their giving heartfelt thanks to God, all his awareness of God's love and faithfulness, of God's *wonders* and *righteous deeds*, belongs naturally to this life and this world. He cannot begin to imagine how such things could be real in Sheol where the dead go, in Abaddon where creation is unmade, in *the place of darkness* and *the land of oblivion*. In other words, the assumption that I shall go to some supposedly better place when I die is a mere foolish fancy. I shall be leaving my present troubles for something considerably worse.

These verses, 10–12, really amount to a single question, a rhetorical one, since the psalmist reckons he already knows the answer. I'm right, Lord, aren't I? Yes. Well, then?

Yet his prayers continue. *I cry to you for help, LORD* (13). The final section, verses 13–18, completes the picture of his abject misery. A sense of rejection by God, prolonged affliction, overwhelming terror, and abandonment by his nearest and dearest, are crowned by one of the most despairing cries in the Psalter (if the NIV is correct): *darkness is my closest friend.* The words recall the horror of 49:14: 'Like sheep they are appointed for Sheol; Death shall be their shepherd' (NRSV). That verse describes the fate of unbelievers. The link suggests that the writer of 88:18 has not after all lost sight of the hope that God's covenant love continues beyond this life. Rather, he recognizes it only too well, and *believes that he has forfeited it.*

2. Praying in total darkness

'My soul is in deep anguish,' says one of the earliest David psalms. 'Among the dead no one proclaims your name. Who praises you from his grave?' (6:3, 5). Many such so-called 'laments' have appeared in the Psalter, from that point to this. Many other psalms have shown their authors in peril of their lives, though when 30:3, for example, speaks of the danger of 'going down to the pit', it is to thank God for having rescued the psalmist from it.

In one respect 88 stands out from all these. The threat of death and the fear of death create in it a gloom which is practically unbroken. No other prayer in the Psalter is quite as desperate as this one. The God-forsaken cry of 22:1–2 is perhaps even more terrible, but then that psalm turns to praise two-thirds of the way through; whereas in 88 darkness literally has the last word. Scarcely a gleam of hope has lightened the psalm at any point. Almost the only positive thing in its eighteen verses is the address in the opening line to *the God who saves me.* And since it seems more than possible that the psalmist fully expected not to be saved, either from death or after death, even those brave words may have sounded to him, in the very act of uttering them, a meaningless formula.

In a moment we must ask when, where and by whom Psalm 88 might have been sung originally. But what congregation could sing it today with any degree of sincerity? What modern song or hymn would pretend to be an adequate version of it? Cowper's last poem, quite different from the hymns he wrote for the people of Olney to sing, at least echoes it. He describes the drowning of a seaman in an Atlantic gale, and likens it to his own descent into depression and insanity.

> No voice divine the storm allay'd,
>> No light propitious shone,
> When, snatch'd from all effectual aid,
>> We perish'd, each alone;
> But I beneath a rougher sea,
> And whelm'd in deeper gulfs than he.[24]

Hardly a song for congregational worship, then, and we might need to find a meaning for *selah* other than the point at which music is played or Scripture is read in a temple liturgy. But many an individual will know well what 88 is about.

3. Who, when, where?

As for an individual in Old Testament times who might have been through such a 'dark night of the soul' and put it into poetry, there has been no shortage of suggestions. King Uzziah's leprosy removed him from society, *confined* him in separate quarters, and would have *made [him] repulsive* to his friends (8, 18). The words for *set apart* in verse 5 and for Uzziah's 'separate house', his isolation ward, in 2 Chronicles 26:21 are closely related. But his illness came only at the end of a long and successful reign, and that does not tally with verse 15. King Hezekiah too 'became ill', we are told. Not only was he 'at the point of death', but he was also poet enough to write a psalm, after his miraculous recovery, describing his experience (Isa. 38:1–22). That psalm resembles the one before us in a number of ways; but Hezekiah never suffered the isolation of our psalmist.

The prophet Jeremiah, reckoned to be a disturber of the peace, was *confined* (8) in King Zedekiah's guardroom and other unpleasant places, including a literal *pit* (6; Jer. 32:1–3; 38:4–13). He might well have said, *From my youth I have suffered* (15; Jer. 1:1–19), though he was never quite deserted by friends. Equally close to the thought of Psalm 88, though in a different way, is the book of Job, a man *made . . . repulsive* (8) to all but the four companions he could have done without, and crying out to God repeatedly (1) for answers that never came (Job 19:1–19).

---

[24] William Cowper, 'The Castaway'.

Yet another parallel is the third chapter of Lamentations, where we find the affliction, the darkness, *all day long*, the pain, the confinement and the unanswered prayer. The 'depths of the pit' and the overwhelming waters are there too (Lam. 3:1–9, 53–55). But in the end the prayer is heard, and at the chapter's heart is the great reassurance 'His compassions never fail. They are new every morning' (Lam. 3:22–23, 56–58). These laments over the destruction of Jerusalem (Lam. 1:1, 3, 6, 9–10) point to a further possibility: that our psalmist is writing not as an individual, but as the representative of the entire mourning nation. To that idea we shall return in a moment.

There remains the heading which the compilers gave to 88. Perhaps it means just what it says, and the author is none of the above, but Heman, either the musician, the colleague of Asaph and Ethan, or the celebrated sage of Solomon's time (cf. 1 Kgs 4:31). Delitzsch even suggests that the latter Heman, one of 'the wise' with whom the wisdom books are associated, might have 'made a passage of his own life, suffering, and conflict of soul, a subject of dramatic treatment', and written not only this psalm but also the book of Job.[25]

4. A long way from home

An intriguing, quite different, suggestion about the psalm's background comes from Goulder. The mountains and surging waters of 46:3 introduced us to his theory that the Korah Collections were not originally Jerusalem psalms at all. They make best sense, he thinks, if we understand them to have come from the temple worship at Dan, in the far north of the northern kingdom. Up there Hermon is a proper mountain, and the upper Jordan a proper river, as in 42:6–7, and these could account for much of the language of 88.

The words *mahalath leannoth* in the heading are obscure – the [something] of affliction? – but the first of them is not unlike the word for 'holes in the ground' in Isaiah 2:19. That, says Goulder, could be exactly where the psalmist was; or rather, not the psalmist himself, but the person for whom the psalm was written. The *lowest pit* and the *darkest depths* were some fearful pothole into which the foaming waters of Jordan, newly sprung from Mount Hermon not as a trickle but as a cataract, disappeared again. *Confined* in the claustrophobic *terrors* of such a place, the afflicted

---

25 Delitzsch, vol. 3, p. 24.

one cried out to God, *You have overwhelmed me with all your waves . . . Your wrath has swept over me* (6–8, 16).

And had the Lord caused him to fall in? Not at all. The picture is that of a ceremony – need one add, a man-made ceremony – in which the king, or the high priest, or some other representative of the nation, was expected to *go down to the pit* and submit to the wrath of God on his people's behalf. He would of course be pulled out again *in the morning* (13). That would be the 'resurrection', as it were, which would show that God had accepted the 'offering'.

This is perhaps the most elaborate attempt to explain Psalm 88 by providing it with a real historical background. To do Goulder credit, he sees it as a pointer to Christ.

> It speaks of the redemptive suffering of the innocent to heal the sin of society. It is not for nothing that the Church has selected it as one of the psalms for Good Friday, when one held to be God's son . . . was counted with them that go down into the pit; and whose prayer came before the God of his salvation in the morning.[26]

Dan, however, is a long way from Jerusalem, and such a ceremony is a long way from Heman's liturgies in the temple on Zion. The whole theology of the northern kingdom's shrines, based on nothing more than the political schemes of its first king, Jeroboam, is very far removed from the covenant given to Moses and renewed to David and his descendants in the southern kingdom.

5. Very close to home

Goulder's focus on Christ, praiseworthy in itself, in fact misses the point. It arises from his imaginary setting for the psalm, not from the psalm itself. Like every other possible background that we have noted, it is little more than guesswork. Brueggemann, rightly in my view, points us in just the opposite direction in order to see the value and the role of Psalm 88. If there were unmistakable connections between it and other scriptures, they would be saying to us, 'Read the psalm against *this* background, and all will stand out in clear relief.' But there are not; and in the best Korah tradition[27]

---

[26] Goulder, *Korah*, p. 210.
[27] See p. 1.157.

it tells us that we do not need to identify the who, the when and the where. In fact we are better off not knowing.

For, to use Brueggemann's terms, here is a psalmist who is totally disoriented, and a psalm which speaks to us when we are totally disoriented.

> The truth of the matter is that the listener to such a psalm *in a time of actual dislocation* will have no doubt as to the meaning of the references and will find such exegetical speculation both unnecessary and distracting.[28]

In other words, reconstructions like those above will merely make you impatient if you already know perfectly well what your own *lowest pit* and 'overwhelming waves' are. Psalm 88 has already come home to you.[29]

It is true that Christ himself came down this way, and was lifted out again. But here he is concerned to reach back, through his word and through the servants who know his word, to the soul that is stuck in the depths. This can happen to a believer, he says; it does not mean you are lost. It can happen to someone who does not deserve it; it does not mean you have strayed. It can happen at any time, as long as this world lasts; only in the next will such things be done away. And it can happen without your knowing why. There are answers, there is a purpose, and one day you will know.

Psalm 89

A *maskil* of Ethan the Ezrahite completes Book III. As we noted in connection with Psalms 32 and 47, the Hebrew word may have something to do with 'understanding', and 89 grapples with a question very hard to understand. Like every major question of Scripture it finds its ultimate answer in the cross of Christ, though when the psalm was written it would have seemed insoluble.

Whichever Ethan is meant (there were two of them),[30] 89 as it stands must have been composed long after his time. Verses 1–37 look back to the

---

28 Brueggemann, p. 12. My italics.

29 Similarly, Paul's omitting to tell us what exactly his thorn in the flesh was (2 Cor. 12:7) enables us to identify that much more readily with his pain.

30 As with the two Hemans, one was of the tribe of Levi, and a colleague of Asaph's in directing the music at the Jerusalem sanctuary; the other was a wise man, not a Levite, famous in the time of Solomon (1 Kgs 4:31; 1 Chr. 6:31–33, 39, 44).

palmy days of David and Solomon, but the rest, if not the whole, must date from the other end of the monarchy, four hundred years later. It is an 'Ethan psalm' in the sense that 74, for example, is an 'Asaph psalm',[31] belonging to the tradition and the choir that bore his name.

1. Getting to grips with a long psalm

In the first half of Book III the Asaph Collection has a *maskil* even longer than this one. These are among the biggest psalms in the Psalter, 78 with seventy-two verses, 89 with fifty-two. In contrast to a short one like 1 or 23, where it is easy to grasp the poem in its entirety and to see the end from the beginning, 78 showed the value of dividing a long poem into logical sections. An analytical outline is a map that enables us to look ahead and see where the psalmist is leading us.

First we should note that Ethan's *maskil* really has fifty-one verses, not fifty-two, since the closing words are a doxology for Book III as a whole. Then it is obvious that a violent change of tone at verse 38 sets the last fourteen of those fifty-one apart from the rest. Next we observe a possible break after the first fourteen verses, when the theme of the Lord's greatness is followed by that of his people and their king. The Hebrew text would tell us, and the length of the verses even in English may hint at it, that the metre of the poetry also changes at about that point.

Then as a matter of mere counting, we note that every verse has two lines, except verse 19 which has four; that the poem is thus 104 lines long; and that 104 is a multiple of eight. Alec Motyer's analysis relates not only to all this, but also to the development of the themes and to the positions of all but one of the *selahs*, and most importantly makes very good sense. It divides the 104 lines into three main sections, as follows:

Three and a half eight-line stanzas (1–14):
    The supreme God and his wonders;
Six eight-line stanzas (15–37):
    The covenant-making God and his promises;
Three and a half eight-line stanzas (38–51):
    The terrible God and his contradictions.

---

[31] See pp. 2.1–2.

2. The supreme God and his wonders (89:1–14)

Verses 1–4, the first stanza, are firmly rooted in the great seventh chapter of 2 Samuel. There the Lord speaks to David at the beginning of his reign. His message through Nathan the prophet is about his choosing and building up of David and his kingdom, about David's throne and his descendants, and about a promise which will hold good for ever. Verses 3–4 of our psalm use just this language,[32] and ground it in the Lord's covenant love and faithfulness, each acclaimed twice in verses 1–2.

Verses 5–8 show this God, the Lord, supreme among the *holy ones*. 'Angels' is perhaps the best general name for the myriads of *heavenly beings* who throng the supernatural world. Very dimly do our eyes perceive that world, those who inhabit it, and who belongs where in their spiritual hierarchies. It is by contrast perfectly obvious to the hosts of heaven how incomparably great the Lord is among them. Moses and Micah saw it too (cf. Exod. 15:11; Mic. 7:18), and so do the psalmists (cf. Pss 35:10; 71:19; 86:8).

Verses 9–12 remind us that we can, all the same, see something of his greatness. As Paul would put it long afterwards, 'God's invisible qualities – his eternal power and divine nature – have been clearly seen, being understood from what has been made' (Rom. 1:20). The reiterated *you* and *your* in these verses show that both the original creation of land, sea and sky, and the continuing control of them, are evidences of the supremacy of God in the world that we do know, as well as in the world above that we don't. He is sovereign in nature as well as in supernature. And he is sovereign in history, since Rahab, the name of the original chaos monster, was applied also to Egypt when the Lord tamed her too at the time of the exodus (cf. 87:4; Job 26:12–13). 'Who did all this, Lord? Why, you did.'

Verses 13–14 take us back to the covenant love and faithfulness of verse 1. How could such a God, with all the wonders he has done, possibly fail to keep his promises to David?

3. The choice of a people; the choice of a king (89:15–21)

The six central stanzas begin with a picture of the people who are the object of the Lord's covenant love (15–18). They would even today be the envy of the nations. The first word of the stanza is *Blessed*, and it goes on

---

[32] These passages in 2 Sam. 7 and Ps. 89 should be compared. They are intimately connected, though the NIV sometimes obscures the linking Heb. words (e.g. 'offspring' in 2 Sam. = *line* in the Ps.).

to describe their joy under the righteous rule of God's chosen king, who is their *horn* of power and *shield* of protection.

God's choice of them is tied in with their response to him. His favour has not become their automatic right; they are people who have *learned to acclaim* him, and who walk in his light. In the words of Priscilla Owens' hymn, based on the AV of verse 15, they 'have heard the joyful sound', which in Christian terms means the shout of praise that 'Jesus saves', and rejoicing in his salvation they determine to live in obedience to his commands.

The nation is of course Israel, named in the last line of this stanza. So we are led into the next one, which reminds us that the king is David.

The eight lines of verses 19–21 take us back to verse 3, and not just to the covenant that God made with David through Nathan in 2 Samuel 7, but to his anointing by an even greater prophet in 1 Samuel 16, long before he acceded to the throne. 'Samuel took the horn of oil and anointed him . . . and from that day on the Spirit of the LORD came powerfully upon David' (1 Sam. 16:13).

The one to whose hands God has entrusted the government of his people is David his *servant*. David is spoken of in this way repeatedly in 2 Samuel 7; in Psalm 78:70 and often elsewhere in the Psalter; and in prophecies by Jeremiah and Ezekiel, significantly, as the Davidic monarchy came to an end (Jer. 33:19–26; Ezek. 34:23–24; 37:24–25). The New Testament takes up the same phrase in Zechariah's prophecy in Luke 1:69 and in the united prayer of the church in Acts 4:25; and Paul, quoting 1 Samuel 13:14, explains it as God saying of David, 'he will do everything I want him to do' (Acts 13:22).

The enduring interest of verse 20 is that the servant is anointed: that is, he is chosen to be king. As time went by and the great days of the monarchy became a distant memory, the prophetic figure of the Servant of the Lord was seen increasingly as one whose service meant suffering (cf. Isa. 42 – 55). This figure and the very different one of the King who would one day come to put all things to rights seemed two quite distinct personages. It was hard for a Jew of Jesus' time to think otherwise. 'They crucified him; *but* we had hoped that he was the one who was going to redeem Israel' (Luke 24:20–21). If he was the one, he couldn't be the other. The fact was, nevertheless, that Jesus was both at once – the Servant King; and the idea that the two might be combined had been there from the outset in the person of David.

4. The king exalted; the covenant eternal (89:22–29)

The third stanza, verses 22–25, sets out the kind of king that the Lord will make of David. This is where the choosing and anointing of 1 Samuel 16 are followed by the covenant promises of 2 Samuel 7. The eight lines are a poetic version of God's words in verses 9–11 there, practically quoting verse 10b in *The wicked will not oppress him* (22b here). Earlier royal psalms such as 2 and 21 have spoken in a similar way.

The exalting of the king's majesty and power, his *horn*, is regularly to be seen in the histories of Kings and Chronicles, when David and his descendants put themselves under the same discipline that verse 15 has already enjoined on their people – when, that is, they *walk in the light of your presence, LORD*. No wonder the triumphs of a king were expected from Jesus, the Son of David, since he so obviously walked in the light. Even more important than the king's obedience was God's *faithful love*, literally his faithfulness and his covenant love, with which verse 24 underpins the psalm's adaptation of the three verses in 2 Samuel.

The fourth stanza, verses 26–29, confirms the terms of the covenant between the Lord and the king, and then confirms that it is eternal. Here at the midpoint of the psalm is the crucial fact, the nub of the matter. God sets out the two sides of the agreement: 'He, the king, binds himself to me as his Father, God, Rock and Saviour; I, his God, "appoint him my firstborn", the greatest of all kings.' The resounding words hark back to 2:7–9, to much of 18, and to other psalms besides. They point forward to the New Testament, notably to Revelation 1:5.

But the key point here is that four successive lines emphasize that this covenant *will never fail*. Hidden behind the English translation are, yet again, the psalm's motto words, for *love* is covenant love, and the quality of 'never failing' is faithfulness. These ensure that the promises will hold good *for ever*, he says – *as long as the heavens endure*.

5. Temporary discipline; permanent promises (89:30–37)

Earlier psalms, including 88, the most recent, have touched on what we might call the Job question: why bad things happen to good people. It is a big question, but we ought not to let it loom so large that it obscures a simpler fact – that when bad things happen to us it may be due to our being bad people. The Bible makes no bones about this. It tells us not just that sin abounds, but that sin rebounds.

Far from being exempt from the rule, the great ones of the earth stand under greater judgment; *noblesse oblige* – nobility has its obligations. Hence the warnings of verses 30–33, the fifth stanza. If the kings of David's line utter the 'joyful sound' and call God their Saviour, they must also be careful to walk in his light, as we saw in verse 15. If they do not, they will find not only that their sin has automatic effects, but also that God is quite prepared to allow those effects to take their course; more, that he will himself actively punish the wrongdoer. Scripture, not noted for its political correctness, does not hesitate to speak of punishment, to describe it as something painful, and to use the metaphor of 'the rod'.[33]

We should heed such warnings. If men like David and Solomon needed them, how much more may we. If we have learned from Scripture not to be surprised by undeserved pain, how much less should we expect to be spared it when we deserve it.

But even so, says the Lord, making the same point as before and using the same words as before, my servants must not imagine that when I discipline them they have forfeited my covenant love or my faithfulness. Just the reverse, as Old and New Testaments agree (Heb. 12:5–11, quoting Prov. 3:11–12).

And the last stanza of the central section, verses 34–37, underlines this truth. The fifth and sixth stanzas both grow out of 2 Samuel 7:14–15: 'When he does wrong, I will punish him with a rod wielded by men . . . But my love will never be taken away from him.' These final eight lines could not hammer home more powerfully the unalterable promise (34–35) of an unending kingship (36–37).[34]

6. The terrible God and his contradictions (89:38–51)

The *But* of verse 38 represents an agonizing turnaround in the flow of the psalm.

Whoever the Davidic king was at the time, verses 38–41 lament the capture of his city and the loss of his crown. Much the most likely period is the reign of Zedekiah, from 597 BC to 587 BC. Zedekiah will not himself be the one of whom the psalm speaks; he is the puppet king installed by the Babylonians in place of his nephew Jehoiachin, whom they have taken

---

[33] 'Do not withhold discipline from a child; if you punish them with the rod, they will not die' (Prov. 23:13).

[34] *Like the sun . . . like the moon* echoes the Solomon psalm, as does *all generations* in vv. 1 and 4 (72:5, 7, 17). We cannot be sure what the *faithful witness* is. The moon, the sun, the rainbow, the laws of nature, God himself, have all been suggested; something at any rate which testifies to the constancy of his promises.

into exile. Verses 42–45 picture the royal eighteen-year-old dethroned and clad in *a mantle of shame*; the very last paragraph of the books of Kings portrays him still wearing 'prison clothes' in Babylon thirty-seven years later (2 Kgs 25:27–30). The exalting of the Lord's right hand, in verse 13, has been contradicted by the exalting of his enemies' right hand, in verse 42.

Perhaps Psalm 89 had two authors. Perhaps verses 1–37 were a song of praise from a happier time (in the heading, as in those of so many earlier psalms, we might naturally take *of* to mean 'by', and in this case Ethan, David's contemporary, to be the writer) and four hundred years afterwards they were adapted for use in that last terrible decade of Judah's history. If this is so, 'the adapter allows the old hymn to run its majestic course',[35] and then contrives a new ending for it. Astonishingly (though we have seen examples of this remarkable ability before), he makes verses 38–51 an exact counterpart of verses 1–14, and the whole becomes a composite poem of beautiful symmetry, yet one which is as passionate as it is ingenious.

For with verse 38 the psalm begins to accuse God. You, you, you, a dozen times: you, Lord, you who made all these promises, you who stressed how solid and permanent they were – it is you, of all people, who have now broken your word. Well, it asks in the last long stanza (46–49), are we *ever* to see the promises made good? And the great words that opened the psalm (the older psalm?) are thrown back at the Lord as a challenge: where is the faithfulness, and where is the covenant love? In fact verse 49 takes up the exact wording of verse 1, where *great love* should be the 'loves' of the Lord, in the plural: the manifold 'commitments of changeless love'.[36] Where are they all? *Remember, Lord*, says the psalmist, greatly daring, in his final four lines (50–51), 'this is the kind of thing that gets you a bad name'.

7. The sure mercies of David?

How might God respond to the Ethan musicians who first composed and sang Psalm 89 – that is, the psalm as we have it?

He would not be harsh, for all their harsh words to him; they were a group of bewildered believers, to whom it genuinely seemed that he had

---

[35] Goulder, *Korah*, p. 230.

[36] Motyer, p. 544.

let them down. He would understand that. All the same, they were wrong. They were disoriented and needed to be set right. They had to grasp that David's royal line really would survive the wreck of an earthly kingdom. They had themselves sung of the difference between punishment in verse 32 and rejection in verse 33. They were indignant at the sight of the young king being marched into captivity, *mocked* at *every step* by the enemy (51). They assumed that this was rejection, and in verse 38 they said so. But it was rejection only of the wickedness in Israel that Jehoiachin represented, not of Israel herself. For her it was disciplinary punishment.

The unusual phrase at the beginning and the end of our psalm, the plural 'covenant loves', appears also in a famous passage in Isaiah. 'All . . . who are thirsty' are invited to 'come to the waters', and as you 'come to me' and 'listen', God says, 'I will make an everlasting covenant with you, my *unfailing kindnesses* promised to David' – so the NIV's first edition reflected the 'sure mercies of David', as the AV had called them. It is then that the Lord makes the memorable declaration: 'As the heavens are higher than the earth, so are my ways higher than your ways and my thoughts than your thoughts.' Often and often you will not be able to understand my methods or my timing, but my ultimate intentions you know, and I shall never abandon them. 'My word that goes out from my mouth . . . will not return to me empty, but will accomplish what I desire and achieve the purpose for which I sent it' (Isa. 55:1, 3, 9, 11).

Psalm 48 brought to our attention the Hebrew notion that the past is in front of us and the future is behind us.[37] An idea so alien to Western culture is worth thinking about. Our generation is busily editing history out of its educational system, and is besotted with hopes and fears, plans and projections for the future. But the word of the Lord insists that concerning the future we know *nothing*, except the single fact that one day we shall meet him, either at our death or at his return. By contrast, the past in all its glittering variety he spreads before those who are prepared to learn from it as a comprehensive guide to living in the meantime.

Old Testament prophecy, so extensive and so varied, all points to the same single fact, though from one stage further back: that 'God is working his purpose out.' Everything that happens, however mystifying, he weaves into the fulfilling of his covenant with the line of David, which is the line of Christ. He speaks to the psalm-singers of old as he speaks to us: 'Learn

---

[37] See p. 1.169 n. 45.

from the blessings of David's and Solomon's reigns something of what the sure mercies of David will mean to those who obey me. Learn from the miseries of Jehoiachin's and Zedekiah's reigns something of what is in store for those who flout me.'

Book IV
(Psalms 90 – 106)

Psalms 90 – 106
3. The first Exodus Collection

Few of the psalms of Book IV carry a heading, and of those that do, none mentions any of the names associated with the temple choirs, Asaph or Korah, Heman or Ethan. Yet more than any of the first three books, this one has the feel of an integrated song book. We can readily imagine congregations gathered in the temple at Jerusalem singing or hearing these psalms. A comparatively large number of them have passed into regular use in Christian worship, either as they stand, as canticles, or adapted as hymns.

Since we cannot attach to them a label like 'Korah Collection' or 'Asaph Collection', is there any title which might usefully unify them?

One intriguing fact that emerges as we read through the seventeen poems is at least a pointer to such a title.[1] Psalm 90, the first of them, has been given (for whatever reason)[2] the heading 'A prayer of Moses the man of God'. Psalm 95 is one of three that refer explicitly to Moses' time, and to the account of Israel's journey through the desert to Sinai; verses 8–9 speak of 'Meribah . . . [and] Massah in the wilderness, where your ancestors tested [and] tried me', practically quoting Exodus 17:7. In the next of the three, we have a more general reference: 'Moses and Aaron . . . called on the Lord and he answered them. He spoke to them from the pillar of cloud' (99:6–7). Perhaps here Exodus 24 is the chapter in the forefront of the psalmist's mind. Third, Psalm 103:7–8 begins, 'He [the Lord] made known

---

[1] What follows is one aspect of a theory worked out in great detail in Goulder, 'Fourth Book'. It is perhaps rather more elaborate than the text warrants, but of great interest.

[2] I.e. the phrase does not necessarily mean that Moses wrote it. See p. 1.8.

his ways to Moses', and then quotes Exodus 34:6, where the Lord is doing just that, proclaiming his name and its meaning. Psalm 105 is a very positive summing up of the whole exodus story, looking back from it to the time of Abraham and on from it to the conquest of Canaan. Psalm 106 traces the same story from Egypt, through the journey and the conquest, to the time of the judges, now with an almost wholly negative tone.

In answer to the question of when liturgical psalms would have been used in Israel, scholars have suggested a variety of special occasions, sometimes with very little, if any, basis in Scripture. But there was one such occasion, touched on in earlier psalms (most recently 81),[3] about which the Bible tells us a lot. This was the feast of Tabernacles, which as well as celebrating the completion of the harvest included every seventh year a reading of the law God gave through Moses (Deut. 31:9–13), and recalled every year the time when God brought his people out of Egypt and through the wilderness (Lev. 23:39–43).

So, on the one hand, a real, not hypothetical, festival draws thousands of worshippers to Jerusalem and over an eight-day period commemorates the exodus. On the other hand, a collection of seventeen psalms (two for each day of the festival, and one extra either to begin it or to round it off?) not only reflects the exodus story frequently, but at certain points connects with it in detail and in order – Psalm 95 with Exodus 17; Psalm 99 with Exodus 24; and Psalm 103 with Exodus 34. In fact it is possible, as we shall see, to plot correspondences between all seventeen psalms and a sequence, in order, of readings from Exodus.

It seems not unreasonable, therefore, to think of Book IV as a collection for use at Tabernacles; or, given that that is only a theory, at least to call it an Exodus Collection.

Psalm 90

According to its heading, the psalm that introduces Book IV is *A prayer of Moses the man of God*. In that, and in other respects too, it is unique in the Psalter; and even in the rest of the Old Testament, perhaps only Isaiah 40 matches its opening verses for their awe-inspiring contrast between the greatness of God and the littleness of human beings. From them comes

---

[3] See pp. 2.35ff.

one of the best known of all English hymns, Isaac Watts's 'O God, our help in ages past'.[4]

1. Man frail, and God eternal (90:1–6)

'Man frail, and God eternal' was the title Watts gave to the first part of his hymn. Its nine stanzas, six of which are in common use today, are for once a real paraphrase. Their lines are woven from the Old Testament text as it stands, without the New Testament gloss that their author so often adds, as for example when he turns Psalm 72 into 'Jesus shall reign'.[5]

With the phrase 'from generation to generation' the NEB reflects the Hebrew of verse 1 – the sweep of the ages from our point of view, Watts's 'Our help in ages past, / Our hope for years to come'. It is balanced by *from everlasting to everlasting* (2), the same thing from God's point of view. The nine stanzas of the hymn, covering only verses 1–6, stress the reassurance of verse 1 ('Under the shadow of thy throne / Thy saints have dwelt secure'), returning to it at the end with 'our eternal home'. The psalm as a whole has a darker tone. It stresses not the continuity of all the generations, but the transience of each of them, in a series of striking pictures.

Dust does not figure in the Hebrew of verse 3b, but the NIV is probably right to repeat it from verse 3a.[6] Thus reinforcing each other, the two lines look back to Genesis 2:7 and 3:19: 'God formed a man from the dust . . . "Dust you are and to dust you will return."'[7]

The thousand years of verse 4 are not exactly Watts's 'thousand ages in thy sight . . . like an evening gone', though what he says is true enough. The psalmist's theme is the brevity, not of time itself, but of human life, and he surely has in mind the extraordinary ages of the people of antiquity recorded in Genesis 5, several of which exceeded nine hundred years. 'Even those whose life-span was near-millennial . . . came to death like all others.'[8]

A flood is the first picture in verse 5: 'Time like an ever-rolling stream / Bears all its sons away.' Watts found it explicit in his AV, and it is implicit

---

4 So most modern hymn books print its first line. This was John Wesley's alteration of the original '*Our God, our help*'. Watts wrote another paraphrase of the same psalm, in a different metre, whose first line is 'Lord, what a feeble piece'! So it is when compared to this one, perhaps Watts's finest.

5 See p. 1.252.

6 Less likely is the view of some that, when 'God causes one generation to die off', i.e. to turn to dust, v. 3a, 'He calls another into being', i.e. to turn back, v. 3b (so Luther; and see Delitzsch, vol. 3, p. 51).

7 In Genesis the word for 'dust' is different, but the word for 'return' is the same.

8 Motyer, p. 545.

in the NIV's verb 'to sweep away'. The second picture is sleep, whether we are meant to think of a day that is ended by sleep, or 'a dream' that 'dies with the opening day'. The third, following through into verse 6, is the grass of the Middle Eastern countryside, not the evergreen plant of temperate climates but one that can both spring up and wither in the space of a few hours.

The psalmist speaks considerably more about the frailty of human beings than about the eternity of God. We may say readily enough that we believe God is eternal, but we need to be reminded repeatedly that our life in this world is not. For every advance in medical or environmental technology helps to reinforce the illusion that it could be. It is easy to snigger at the maudlin deathbed scenes of Victorian fiction, but as someone once said (the modern world has forgotten who), 'Blessed are those who mourn' (Matt. 5:4). Every death is a little undermining of humanity's pride in this respect.

2. People are sinful, and God wrathful (90:7–11)

There is a reason for the shortness of human life, the burden of verses 3–6. 'You turn us back to dust . . . *For* we are consumed by your anger' (3, 7 NRSV). The little word *for* throws a narrow but intense beam of light on a range of Bible questions – the great age of Methuselah among them! Why does the story of the Garden of Eden seem so unreal to the modern mind, the stuff of legend? Why is such a steep decline in life expectancy noted at the beginning of Scripture? Indeed, why do human beings die at all?

The Bible's answer is summed up here in Psalm 90. We are mortal because God is angry, and God is angry because we are sinful. When we say that men and women are creatures of dust, we mean not simply that they were made of it but also that they return to it (3). Genesis 3:19, which recorded the pronouncement of this doom, is the background to that verse; and Genesis 3:17, which records the reason (Adam's disobedience), is the background to verse 8: *You have set our iniquities before you, our secret sins in the light of your presence.*

The effect of God's wrath at the sinfulness of humanity is that *our days pass away* under it. Even more to the point, they 'decline', as the verb might be translated – the word is the one Jeremiah uses as the destruction of Jerusalem draws near: 'Woe to us, for the day declines, for the shadows of evening lengthen!' (Jer. 6:4 NRSV) – as though human life passed its noontide when Adam fell, and has ever since been growing steadily darker and more chilly.

That long, long descent may be exactly the reason why our psalmist says, *Our days may come to seventy years.* What a decline from the thousand years of verse 4, which the old patriarchs only just missed! The curve has levelled out, we still have our threescore years and ten, *yet the best of them are but trouble and sorrow*, and they still lead inexorably downward to the grave.

Such are the wages of sin (Rom. 6:23). Verse 11b is difficult, but may well mean that God's wrath towards men and women is proportionate to the reverence they fail to show towards him. That, at bottom, is what sin is.

3. People praying, and God answering (90:12–17)

The psalmist has already accepted that he is a part of sinful humanity, as guilty as anyone else. Now he puts into the words of six prayers, one for each remaining verse, the response that every humble penitent should make to the God of eternity, once it is grasped that he is also a God of wrath.

First, *Teach us.* The numbering of days is a lesson not in elementary arithmetic but in life-changing theology. Teach us not how many days we have lived so far, still less how many may be left to us, but *why* it is that our years are so comparatively few (why seventy, and not a thousand – why, indeed, the patriarchs were limited even to a thousand), and why they are so beset with trouble. In the words of Augustine, noted in connection with Psalm 32, the beginning of knowledge is to know yourself a sinner. That is why. That is the heart of wisdom.

Second, *Relent. Turn* and *return* in verse 3 and *relent* in verse 13 all represent the same word. It was a key word in two of the psalms of Book III, 80 and 85.[9] God will continue to turn sinners back to dust, as it were – that is, to bring about the death which is the consequence of sin – and only a repentant sinner, one who turns from his or her sin, has any hope of seeing God turn from the course of inexorable justice.

But there is that hope. It is based on the covenant love of God, it looks forward to a new morning after this 'long day's journey into night',[10] and therefore it can pray, third, that he will *satisfy* the penitent with joy

---

[9] See pp. 2.33 and 2.53.
[10] The title of Eugene O'Neill's play of 1940.

and gladness. So is the declining day of verse 9 to be followed by another morning, after all? And will it be in this life or the next? Either way, there is some remarkable insight here.

Fourth, *Make us glad* with blessings in proportion to our afflictions. A daring prayer! Yet it falls short of the great New Testament promise; for 'our light and momentary troubles are achieving for us an eternal glory that far outweighs them all' (2 Cor. 4:17).

The last two prayers, for God to reveal to us both himself and his deeds and for his favour to rest on us, belong together. They show a humble grasp of the fact that there is something even greater than his wrath. In New Testament terms it is the grace that meets the demands of justice and righteousness and can therefore bless sinners in spite of their sin. Here too the gospel was to bring a richer meaning to the psalmist's words. He no doubt had in mind that his work might turn out to be of value, and not wasted, in this life. But it is the resurrection life that Paul has in mind when he assures us, 'You know that your labour in the Lord is not in vain' (1 Cor. 15:58).

4. People captive, and God rescuing

Few commentators reckon that the heading *A prayer of Moses* means that Moses was actually the author of Psalm 90. Most would place it, like so many similar psalms, in the time of the exile. Likenesses between it and some of the words of Moses in Exodus 32 and Deuteronomy 32 and 33 are not in themselves sufficient reason to date it in his time.

Those who think he did write it generally hold that it belongs to 'the wearisome years of divine alienation' in the desert of Sinai;[11] those who do not, that Israel was at that time a new nation soon to conquer a new country, whereas the psalm is about a people in decline, tired and time-worn.

But push the date back forty years, and a different picture emerges. Moses is an exile in Midian, or even, perhaps, still a prince in Egypt. Israel is indeed not yet a nation, but she has long been a people; God has already been her dwelling-place through all the generations since Abraham. Moses at forty has been educated as an Egyptian, but knows himself to be an Israelite, and when he goes 'out to where his own people [are] and [watches] them at their hard labour' (Exod. 2:11), the fact that they have

---

[11] Motyer, p. 545.

been 'enslaved and ill-treated' for four hundred years (Gen. 15:13) is quite enough to account for the agonized soul-searching of Psalm 90. 'Israel is still in the night of trouble,' says Kirkpatrick,[12] and the morning of verse 14 – the morning when she is going to see the host of Egypt washed up dead on the shore of the Red Sea (Exod. 14:23–31) – is as yet in the unimaginable future.

Read the psalm in that light, and verse after verse falls into place. We begin to grasp that the Egypt of Moses, which we think of as 'Ancient Egypt', was the *New* Kingdom, and that eighteen dynasties of its kings had already passed away. Israel's Sovereign, Adonai (1, 17; we recall from 81:5[13] that she had not yet experienced him as Yahweh the Rescuer, though the name was in use, as in v. 13), was surely greater than any of them. Well, was he? We see in the sufferings of the brickfields the misery of verses 7–11 and the afflictions of verse 15, and the longing expressed in verse 17 that there might be something better to show for all this toil than a couple of Egyptian store cities.

It is hard to see why *Moses the man of God* should not be the one who first prayed this prayer. In any case the compilers chose well in prefacing Book IV with a psalm that sits so aptly alongside the first two chapters of Exodus. It would be, and perhaps it was, a fine and solemn introduction to the feast of Tabernacles.

Psalm 91

Few psalms could be at once as encouraging and as thought-provoking as this one, paraphrased for modern church use as Timothy Dudley-Smith's 'Safe in the shadow of the Lord' and Henry Lyte's 'There is a safe and secret place'. The sense of security which is incidental in 90 ('Under the shadow of thy throne / Thy saints have dwelt secure') is the main thrust of 91; but it is not cheaply won.

1. A motto unfolded

I shall not be the only reader to whom verse 1 in its AV form has long been familiar yet slightly mystifying: 'He that dwelleth in the secret place of the most High shall abide under the shadow of the Almighty.' But 'dwell' and

---

12 Kirkpatrick, p. 552.
13 See pp. 2.35–36.

'abide', neither of them in common use today, surely mean roughly the same thing? Parallelism is all very well (as in v. 13, *You will tread on the lion and the cobra; you will trample the great lion and the serpent*), but to declare that the person who lives in God's shelter will live in God's shelter is not poetic, merely fatuous. Perhaps it means that line 1 is what you have to do, and line 2 is what you discover when you do it: in other words, take refuge in him, and you will find safe lodging.[14]

This opening verse is the text or motto for the rest of the psalm, which unfolds in two nearly equal sections what is implied in it. In each the psalmist first claims that the Lord is his own refuge, and then turns at once to his fellow believer[15] and encourages him or her likewise to take the implications to heart. *He is* **my** *refuge . . . Surely he will save* **you** (2–3); *The* LORD *. . . is* **my** *refuge*, and *If . . . you make the Most High* **your** *dwelling . . . no harm will overtake* **you** (9–10).[16]

Each half then sets forth a series of vivid pictures of the perils that can beset God's people and the protection he provides for them.

2. A comprehensive insurance policy

Seven such perils are listed in verses 3–8. The memorable quartet in the middle, *the terror of night . . . the arrow that flies by day . . . the pestilence that stalks in the darkness . . . the plague that destroys at midday*, are flanked by snares and slanders in verse 3[17] and the *fall* of many in verse 7. The list is pervaded with the assurance that none of these things need be feared, and includes two splendid pictures of the Lord's care, 'the warm protectiveness of a parent bird' and 'the hard, unyielding strength of armour' (4).[18]

In verses 9–16 it is the ways in which God promises his care that provide the framework, and two further kinds of peril, the stumbling foot and the dangerous beast, that are included. At beginning and end of the psalm the care is exercised by God himself; but here, perhaps in case he might seem remote, it is also delegated to angels, the spirits who serve him by serving 'those who will inherit salvation' (Heb. 1:14). And according to

---

[14] The word is the same as 'endure' in 49:12; see p. 1.174, and Kirkpatrick, p. 555.

[15] The *you* is singular throughout.

[16] Reversing the two lines of the NIV of v. 9 gets closer to the original Hebrew, and makes good sense of a difficult verse. Cf. the RV.

[17] Many commentators follow the LXX in reading the Hebrew not as *pestilence*, which appears in v. 6, but as 'word' (same consonants; different vowel-pointing).

[18] Kidner, pp. 332–333.

verse 11, not just one guardian angel apiece, either – *angels* (plural) *to guard you* (singular)!

Take them in the literal sense, and any of these troubles could happen to any of us. They are representative of the things people fear. Take them metaphorically, and they stand for an even wider range of ills; they are then in effect a comprehensive list, intended to tell us that there is nothing at all God's people need to fear. There are no exclusions in this insurance policy, hidden away in the small print.

3. What Moses said

Its very comprehensiveness makes 91 a psalm for use at any time, and one that could have been written at any time too. (*Most High* and *Almighty* in v. 1 are names that go back at least to the days of Abraham; Gen. 14:18ff.; 17:1). Those who give it a late date and presume that it belongs to the days of the exile see it as an encouragement to Israelites who might be caught up in the fall of Babylon, as Daniel was (Dan. 5:29–30).

There is no reason why it could not be equally well placed at the other end of Israel's national history, in the time of Moses. Like the previous psalm, this one has several reminiscences of Exodus and Deuteronomy – for example, the 'wings' of God (Exod. 19:4; Deut. 32:11), the finding of refuge (Deut. 32:37), the guardian angel (Exod. 23:20), protection from illness and the promise of long life (Exod. 23:25–26). But it is not simply coincidences of words that catch our attention. It is the correspondence between the psalm and the exodus storyline. Whether or not all five books from Genesis to Deuteronomy are the words of Moses, he was certainly a prophet who spoke to his contemporaries, and more than once reminded them of all that had happened in their lifetime. Better than any other Scripture background, what Moses said about those events fits Psalm 91, and fits it like a glove.

See how both tell the same story. Israel was trapped in Egypt, a victim of the pharaoh's deadly word, which had commanded her enslavement (3). By the end of the plagues the Israelites had seen thousands brought low all around them by a destruction from which they had been preserved (7), and had witnessed the punishment of the wicked (8; Exod. 8:22–23; cf. Exod. 9:4–7, 26; 10:23). And all this had fulfilled what the Lord had earlier said to Moses in the sevenfold promise of Exodus 6:6–8, which is extraordinarily like the majestic sequence of 'I wills' that closes Psalm 91.

4. What Jesus said

The one New Testament quotation from this psalm is found in the account of Jesus' temptation, in Matthew 4 and Luke 4, spoken not by Jesus but by the devil.

Jesus had responded to the devil's first temptation as he would respond to the other two, by quoting from Deuteronomy. Thus he showed himself to be the true Israel (and indeed the true Adam), by his inflexible will to obey the law by which God had said his people (in fact humanity as a whole) were to live. As Shakespeare's Merchant says, 'The Devil can cite Scripture for his purpose',[19] and here he made shift to turn the tables on Jesus by himself quoting the word of God. Standing with him

> on the highest point of the temple . . . he said, 'Throw yourself down. For it is written: "He will command his angels concerning you, and they will lift you up in their hands, so that you will not strike your foot against a stone."'
> (Matt. 4:5–6, quoting Ps. 91:11–12)

What is the fallacy in the tempter's reasoning? Simply this, as Dick France well puts it: that the 'suggestion was of an artificially created crisis, not of trusting God in the situations which result from obedient service'.[20] Satan is manipulating Psalm 91 to make it apply where it does not apply. The insurance policy is invalid in cases of wilful misuse. The promise does not give Jesus – or the psalmist's contemporaries, or us – carte blanche to embark on any project that he, or they, or we, may dream up, believing that it will be automatically covered by the policy. Rather, it is for those who love, acknowledge and call upon God (14–15), and who in that spirit of devotion and submission want only to go his way and not their own. Those are the terms to which the insured party has to agree. To ignore them and then to expect his protection is, as Jesus said, a foolish and wicked attempt to put God to the test (cf. Matt. 4:7, quoting Deut. 6:16).

5. What Paul said

The great words of Romans 8:35–37, beginning, 'Who shall separate us from the love of Christ?', include a quotation from another psalm, 44:22,

---

[19] William Shakespeare, *The Merchant of Venice*, I.iii.99.

[20] R. T. France, *Matthew*, TNTC (Leicester: IVP, 1985), p. 99.

and they may seem to be saying something rather different from the promises of 91. Here the psalmist says plainly *No harm will overtake you* (10); Paul says that no harm will 'separate us from the love of Christ', which of course implies that it will befall us.

Yet the two passages are making practically the same point. The crucial thing is what follows after Paul's citation of the earlier psalm. 'In all these things we are more than conquerors through him who loved us' (8:37). *In* all these things: we are not saved from them; we are saved in them. The negatives are transmuted into positives; by a divine alchemy the lead turns to gold.

When therefore we stumble at 91:9–10 and protest, 'But harm *does* befall God's people, however trustingly and obediently they take refuge in him', we do well to ponder Spurgeon's comment on these verses. I have quoted it elsewhere, but it is so full of insight that this exposition would be incomplete without it:

> It is impossible that any ill should happen to the man who is beloved of the Lord . . . Ill to him is no ill, but only good in a mysterious form. Losses enrich him, sickness is his medicine, reproach is his honour, death is his gain.

The earlier words of Paul, in Romans 8:28, are in the great preacher's mind as he explains, 'No evil in the strict sense can happen to him, for everything is overruled for good.'

Psalm 92

The compilers called it a song for the Sabbath day; Isaac Watts paraphrased it as the hymn 'Sweet is the work, my God, my King'; the psalmist wrote it as a chiastic psalm of praise.

1. There and back again

When we first came across chiasmus, in Psalm 6,[21] it may have seemed a very artificial way of writing poetry, peculiar enough to kill any real feeling. In fact the ABCDCBA shape of a chiastic poem is as natural as going for a walk and returning by the same route. We set out from A and

---

[21] See pp. 1.88, 1.135.

pass B and C on our way to D, then come back via C and B, home to A again.

In the case of Psalm 92, D represents verse 8, which is very clearly the poem's midpoint: the middle Yahweh of seven, the middle verse of fifteen, the middle line of thirty-one. A is the 'constant worship' of verses 1–3 and 12–15. B tells 'what the Lord has done for me' in verses 4–5 and 10–11. C is about 'seeing and not seeing' in verses 6–7 and 9. Those phrases will be our headings. The pattern may be set out as follows:

The Lord, the Most High –
we proclaim his covenant love and faithfulness
in day-long praise.
    'I am gladdened by your deeds!
        Some do not see,
            supreme Lord;
        but some do see.
    I am strengthened by your victories!'
In lifelong fruitfulness
we proclaim his uprightness and straightforwardness –
the Lord, the Rock.

2. Constant worship

The psalmist, and all his fellow Israelites too, he implies, love to *make music* morning and night to the praise of God (1–3). No doubt their music would sound as strange to us as ours would to them. But there are words set to it, with which (in translation!) we find ourselves very much at home, since they proclaim God's covenant love and faithfulness, that perennial theme of the church's praise in both Old Testament and New.

To a parallel proclamation the end of the psalm returns (12–15). The theme is similar, but it is celebrated in different words and in a different way. We want to 'show forth thy praise', God's people might tell him in the words of the Prayer Book's General Thanksgiving, 'not only with our lips, but in our lives; by giving up ourselves to thy service, and by walking before thee in holiness and righteousness all our days'. They appreciate the metaphor of the palm tree, ever fresh, flourishing and above all fruit-bearing, even to *old age*. They recognize that worship is service rather than services, fruitfulness rather than tunefulness; and it is lifelong, not just day-long.

3. What the Lord has done for me

The psalmist is gladdened by the deeds of the Lord (4–5) and strengthened by his victories (10–11).

He can sing for joy at what he knows of the deeds and works and thoughts of God. Most obviously this means the created world visible around him. Being a believer, he is aware also of the acts of God in history and in his own experience. And as a humble listener to God's own explanations of these things, he knows at least a little of the deep and complex plans that underlie them.

The horn and the oil in verse 10 are familiar symbols of strength and blessing. Here too a wide range of benefits could be in mind, but the particular thing the psalmist's *eyes have seen* and his *ears have heard* (11) is God's overcoming of his enemies. Even that has many possible applications. Gatherings of God's people on any number of occasions across almost the whole span of Old Testament history – certainly from the exodus onwards – could have praised God in these terms. The NEB is wrong to use the word 'gloat' in translating verse 11; it is in the Lord's power to destroy evil and to preserve those who trust him that Israel rejoices.

4. Seeing and not seeing

The fools of verse 6 are, as always, not those who are stupid but those who ignore God. What is underlined here is their lack of perception. It may be that the verse looks back to what precedes it, so that the greatness of God's works and the profundity of his thoughts are the things fools do not understand. It may be on the other hand that the NIV is correct in linking verse 6 with what follows: fools do not understand that the flourishing wicked are on 'slippery ground' and on their way 'down to ruin' (73:18). In practice both are true. Fools cannot see either the greatness of God or the littleness of humanity, in particular the brevity and the pointlessness of the life of the wicked.

The psalmist, however, can see these things very well. For the corresponding verse on the other side of the pivotal verse 8 also speaks of the destruction of the wicked, and twice has the old-fashioned word 'Lo':[22] 'Look, Lord – your enemies perishing and evildoers scattered!' (9).

---

[22] So AV/RV/RSV, rather than NIV's *surely*.

The mention just now of Psalm 73, with which Book III and the second half of the Psalter began, will remind us of the major reorientation of which that psalm speaks. The psalmist here, like the contributors to Book IV in general, is not perplexed by the prosperity of the wicked. He has already 'entered the sanctuary of God' and 'understood their final destiny'. He may in the past have been disoriented by the problem, but now he sees it from God's point of view.

5. The first Sabbath of Tabernacles?

The psalmist's perception is even more clearly in evidence in verse 11 than in verse 9: *My eyes have seen the defeat of my adversaries; my ears have heard the rout of my wicked foes.* It reads like a thanksgiving for a particular deliverance, and would have made the psalm a suitable choice on many occasions in Old Testament history, as we have already noted.

But might there be some further pointer to its Old Testament use, something that arises from its position in the Psalter? In the preface to Book IV, I referred to the possible link between this book and the feast of Tabernacles. If its seventeen psalms were spread over the eight days of Tabernacles, we could reasonably imagine 90, standing a little apart as a 'prayer of Moses', being sung before the festival began. With the rest then following in sequence, two per day, 92 would be (as its heading says) one of those appointed *for the Sabbath day*, the first of the eight.

Were this the rationale of the compiling of the fourth book of the Psalter, there would be no mystery about what the singers of 92 would have in mind as they chanted 'I sing for joy at the work of your hands' (as older versions of the NIV translated v. 4). If 90 were the lament of Moses, against the background of Exodus 1 – 2, and if 91 reflected Israel's experience during the plagues of Egypt, against the background of Exodus 3 – 12, *the* 'work' of 92:4 would surely be, among all the multitudinous works of God, the deliverance of Israel from her enslavement.

We must not get ahead of ourselves; we know that she would not be completely free from Egypt till the sea was crossed and the Egyptian army was destroyed. But we have not yet reached Exodus 14 – 15. The night of Passover was the actual night of deliverance, when 'all the LORD's divisions left Egypt . . . On this night all the Israelites are to keep vigil to honour the LORD for the generations to come' (Exod. 12:41–42). Throughout those generations the feast of Unleavened Bread, in the spring, would focus exclusively on the Passover. But the feast of Tabernacles, in the autumn, would commemorate the whole great exodus-event from Egypt to Canaan, and would thus include the Passover.

For the moment, therefore, what Israel sees as the defeat of her adversaries is the capitulation of Pharaoh, at last, to the demand 'Let my people go.' No other victory in the story of Israel can compare with this; until the great deliverance of which it is a prefiguring is brought about at Calvary.

Psalm 93

The next eight psalms are often thought of as a group. Most of them praise the Lord explicitly as king, and all of them celebrate his rule and authority. Special occasions for which they may have been intended, such as ceremonies re-enacting the enthronement of Israelite kings, are largely the fruit of learned guesswork. Something Scripture does say, however, relates to the future day when 'the Lord will be king over the whole earth'. Those words come from the climax of the prophecy of Zechariah, which sees people from 'all the nations' going up 'year after year to worship the King, the Lord Almighty, and to celebrate the Festival of Tabernacles' (Zech. 14:9, 16). So it may be that this is more than just a series of 'royal psalms'. As in 90 – 92, so in 93 – 100, we may find the real possibility of a Tabernacles connection.

1. The Lord: the world: the seas: the statutes

Its many repetitions – *robed in majesty . . . robed in majesty, lifted up . . . lifted up, mightier . . . mightier* – do not impede the flow of Psalm 93; rather, they drive it along with a punchy rhythm,[23] although scarcely are we caught up by its momentum before it comes to a sudden end. No complex structure here!

First the Lord is acclaimed, with his majesty and strength and his unshakeable throne. The created world is unshakeable too, though not in the same sense. Significantly, the two lines that say so are enclosed within the five that praise God's greatness. Its firmness is derivative; it stands firm only because its Creator has made it so. Certainly it has been there for uncountable ages; but he is *from all eternity.*

Seas are 'floods' in the earlier English versions, and are literally 'rivers'. It is the power of the waters in any form that so perturbs most people in

---

[23] See p. 1.90.

Bible times, and not them only. You may recognize that the seas are no more independent of their Maker than the earth is, and yet at the same time see them as a proper metaphor for all that rises against him in rebellion. Even so they, like the earth, are contained within the all-embracing control of the mighty Lord.

The unexpected shift from the seas to the statutes in verse 5 will puzzle only those who have forgotten the similar shift from sunlight to law in Psalm 19. There is a correspondence between the Lord himself, his attributes and his works which makes the transition easy between one sort of reality and another. The world the Lord has created, his own inherent greatness and the laws he has uttered may all be described, with equal truth, as *established, firm and secure*. When God's Spirit reshapes people's lives according to those laws, the result is a holiness that is equally permanent, and will adorn God's house *for endless days*.

2. An act, not just a fact: but when?

It was not only in school on weekdays that I used to be confronted by Latin verbs. The ancient titles of the Psalms faced me every Sunday in the Prayer Book, telling me in the case of 93 (and 97 and 99) that *Dominus regnavit*. I knew the verb to be in the perfect tense, and wondered why in Latin the psalm was saying, 'The Lord *has reigned.*' Had he since abdicated?

No; the Latin perfect translated a Hebrew perfect, which meant something like 'The Lord has proclaimed himself king.' As Kirkpatrick says, the series of perfects in verse 1 indicate 'not merely a fact . . . but an act'.[24]

This sort of concept is what has led many scholars to envisage the enthronement rituals mentioned above. The king re-enacts his original coronation service, they think, and in doing so he represents the Lord as doing the same. Scripture does not actually tell us of any such addition to the original 'church calendar' set out in the books of Moses; so perhaps it was an integral part of Tabernacles, as the Zechariah passage might suggest.

Since all this is conjecture, might these enthronement psalms have been composed not for repeated use but for some particular occasion? Were there not times in Israel's history when the Lord's rule seemed to have been eclipsed, and then in due course reasserted itself? An obvious example would be the restoration after the exile. True, there is no longer

---

[24] Kirkpatrick, p. 564.

any Davidic king, Nehemiah or Ezra might have said, but clearly the Lord has regained *his* throne, as the repatriation of his people shows.

There is one major problem with that theory. The leaders of restoration Israel knew very well that what had just happened was not the Lord seating himself once more on his royal throne, for the simple reason that he had never been off it. When, indeed, *did* he actually sit down and proclaim himself king? *Your throne was established long ago*, is the answer of our psalm; in fact you, the Lord, the King, *are from all eternity.*

3. The once and future King

Perhaps there are just two occasions on which it might be truly said, 'The Lord has become king.' One is at the creation of the world. 'By the seventh day God had finished the work he had been doing; so on the seventh day he rested from all his work' (Gen. 2:2). Although in one sense his throne had already stood from all eternity, in another sense it was only then that he sat down to begin his reign over the world, because before that there had been no world for him to be king of.

The other such occasion is at the other end of history and the other end of Scripture: 'The kingdom of the world has become the kingdom of our Lord and of his Messiah' (Rev. 11:15). Here too a new domain has come into being. There is a new creation, and he who is from all eternity now takes the throne from which 'he will reign for ever and ever'.

Between those two enthronements he has never not been king. If one theme more than another runs through the whole of Psalm 93 it is *permanence.*

All the same, we for our part can do with regular reminders of the fact. We need to hear the *Dominus regnavit* of creation; he has been on the throne all the time. This psalm fits into the Tabernacles sequence just at the point where the Lord brings *the thunder of the great waters* (4) down upon the armies of the king of Egypt, and as his own people walk through on dry ground he shows that he himself is the true and eternal king. He is highly exalted, they sing, and *majesty* in verse 1 echoes their words (Exod. 15:1, 18–19, 21).

We need too the encouragement of the *Dominus regnavit* at the end of history, the 'prophetic perfect' which takes us forward to the glorious day when in heaven we shall say, 'He has taken his throne, and reigns!' No wonder what is sung there is 'the song of God's servant Moses' as well as 'of the Lamb', and no wonder it sings the praise of the 'King of the ages' (Rev. 15:3 NIV mg.).

Psalm 94

Without saying so in as many words, 94 chimes with the rest of this group of psalms in proclaiming that the Lord is king.

We notice from the outset ways of thinking and turns of phrase that seem familiar. At a number of points we ask ourselves, Have we not come across this sort of thing earlier in the Psalter?

1. Five sections

Verses 1–7 are what is often labelled a 'lament'. A fiercer term would be more apt here: complaint, at least, or indignant appeal. The arrogant wicked – we have met them before – are in control, making life hard for God's people, and assuming that God (if he exists) can safely be ignored. So the psalmist appeals to God to reveal himself as the universal Judge. There is little point in trying to blunt the sharp talk of vengeance since, whatever word we use, it is a matter of determined evildoers being paid in their own coin and getting their deserts (2).

Verses 8–11 have a prophetic ring to them. They rebuke the foolish, point to a God who hears and sees and knows, and make it plain that all nations are God's concern. Verse 10 sounds like the first two chapters of Amos, and looks ahead to the first two chapters of Romans. From the start these verses expect to be heeded and acted upon.

Verses 12–15 recall wisdom books like Proverbs, and earlier psalms in the same style. Half the section is addressed to the Lord, the other half is about him, and both assume confidently that he overrules all things for the eventual blessing of his people.

Verses 16–19 are a testimony to the Lord as the only rescuer. Elsewhere, Psalms 18:31–32 and 73:25–26 (like many others) speak similarly, and these two also have in mind the occasions when the psalmist has almost lost his footing.[25]

Verses 20–23 bring the poem to an end with the ferocious confidence that the Lord who is the refuge of the psalmist will be the destroyer of his enemies. This final section is pervaded by the spirit of the imprecatory

---

[25] Cf. 73:2; and 'sustains' in 18:35 is the same word as *supported* in 94:18. See the AV.

psalms, which we noticed as far back as 7, and considered at length in 35, in the first David Collection. It is the David psalms too that speak often of the Lord as refuge, rock and fortress.

Each of the five sections, then – a complaint section, a prophetic section, a wisdom section, a testimony, a triumph – represents a type of psalm that is familiar enough. To see what binds them together as a whole, we look first at the links both within Psalm 94 and between it and its predecessors, and then at the most likely historical setting for it.

2. The ties that bind

Word links between the five parts help to unify the poem. The paying back of the wicked is mentioned near the start of the opening prayer and near the end of the closing praise (2 and 23), and forms an inclusio for the whole. The phrase *takes . . . notice* in verse 7, at the end of the first section, and in verse 8, at the beginning of the second, connects these two; as the NEB neatly puts it, 'They say, ". . . The God of Jacob pays no heed." Pay heed yourselves, most brutish of the people!' Verse 5, part of the distressed cry of complaint, is answered by verse 14, part of the calm response of wisdom: the Lord's people, his inheritance, are being crushed and oppressed by their enemies, but they will never be rejected or forsaken by him.

As the second of the eight kingship psalms, 94 grows out of 93. The 'rising up' of the Judge in 94:2 quells the 'lifting up' of the waves in 93:3, and the *proud* in 94:2 are matched by the Lord's 'majesty' in 93:1; each pair of Hebrew words is related. Without duplicating the kingship language, 94 shows that if Yahweh as king controls the 'pounding' waves, it means that as judge he can deal with those who are 'crushing' (the same word in 94:5 as in 93:3) his people. Present discipline (94:10, 12) and future judgment (94:15, 23) are aspects of the Lord's rule in 93. The divine throne of 93:2 will outlast every *corrupt throne* (94:20) that aims to rival it.

Looking back beyond 93, we find links between 94:8 and 92:6 (the senseless and the fools), and between the *corrupt throne* of 94:20 and the 'deadly pestilence' of 91:3. With regard to the connection with 92, the foolish, as we know, means the wilful rather than the stupid; but they are fit companions for the senseless, who really are stupid, because they have no sense of spiritual values. The great Dr Johnson compared a 'brutish' person (the word he would have found in the AV of 94:8) to a bull that one might imagine saying, 'Here I am with this cow and this grass', and believing that no creature could possibly be happier.[26] No, no! The psalms of Book IV will not allow such bovine mindlessness. They demand that we *think*.

With regard to the connection with 91, these psalms also join in promising deliverance from the throne of 94:20 and the pestilence of 91:3. The words *corrupt* and 'deadly' are the same; here it is a throne of destruction, there the phrase probably means, as we recall, a word of destruction. That connection brings us to the question of the setting of Psalm 94.

3. When and where

Ears attuned to the voice of the Old Testament will hear in verse 1 the words of Moses in Deuteronomy: the avenging God (32:35) who shines forth (33:2). Verse 2 will take them even further back, to hear Abraham in Genesis speaking to the Judge of all the earth (18:25).

If Book IV is indeed intended for use at Tabernacles, and if therefore it is pointing us back to Israel's beginnings, at least to the exodus narratives, what are we to make of Psalm 94?

In that context 93 must be related to the Lord's commanding the waters to part for the rescue of Israel and to come crashing back for the destruction of the Egyptians. Then 94 must be looking back across the sea, so to speak, to review all that has happened up to now. At once we realize that verses 1–7 are, as it were, in inverted commas. They are the cry of an enslaved nation, arising from the interminable years of 'trouble and sorrow', as the prayer of Moses has put it in introducing this Exodus Collection (90:10). That time, more than any later one, saw the Lord's people crushed and oppressed (94:5), and the oppressor caring nothing for their God (94:7): 'Who is the LORD,' said Pharaoh, 'that I should obey him and let Israel go?' (Exod. 5:2).

The Exodus account is very frank about the *senseless ones among the people*, in verses 8–11, who would not listen to Moses and heard only the words of Pharaoh as he aggravated their misery and hardened his heart (Exod. 5:19ff.; 6:9). In fact the Lord knew exactly what he was doing, and Pharaoh's plans were futile (11). As verses 12–15 put it, a pit was being dug for the wicked. The Lord would keep his promise to his people, and set all things to rights.

---

[26] Quoted by Kidner, p. 335.

We should read the first words of verses 16–19 as another quotation. This was the cry of Israel: *Who will rise up for me against the wicked?* But by the time the sea was crossed, she knew the answer, and had the rest of that fourth section as a testimony. Verses 20–23 put in a nutshell the story so far. The 'throne of destruction' corresponds to the 'word of destruction' in 91:3 (we noted above the parallel phrases *corrupt throne* and 'deadly pestilence'), the rule of Pharaoh that *brings on misery by its decrees*. But the Lord who has hitherto permitted it now puts an end to it. The repayment of the arrogant wicked, a prayer in verse 2, is a fact by verse 23.

4. A psalm for today

As a commemoration of the exodus, these psalms are as valuable to us as to any other generation of the people of God. Old Testament Israelites may have regarded Tabernacles as a festive season, but it was important for them to recapture also something of the terrible reality of the evil from which their ancestors had been redeemed. Here (1–7) they were given words to express a proper hatred of all that Egypt had stood for. We with the same words may pray as we ought for the overthrow of evil, especially of the ultimate evil from which the greater redemption of Calvary has rescued us.

The remainder of verses 8–11 is sobering as well, in a different way. While Egypt deserved punishment, Israel needed rebuke; there were plenty of *senseless ones among the people* who were too obtuse and unbelieving to see or to trust what the Lord was doing as he exposed the futility of the pharaoh's policies. This also each generation of his people has to take to heart. Certainly it is a reprimand to today's church.

Only against the dramatic background of the first two sections does the calm optimism of the third (12–15) make sense. Only when we grasp what God can do both in the once-for-all victory of getting Israel out of Egypt, and in the continuing task of getting Egyptian attitudes out of Israelite hearts – that is, only when we are right with God – can we know for ourselves that *he will never forsake his inheritance*.

Then come testimony (16–19), quoting the original cry for help and joyfully witnessing to the way the Lord has answered it; and finally triumph (20–23), with no illusions about the power and wickedness of the enemy or about his certain fate, and therefore recognizing all the more clearly the greatness of the Lord our Fortress, our Rock and our Refuge.

Psalm 95

Except for Easter Day, 'upon which another Anthem is appointed', every morning of the year should see the people of every parish in England gathering to encourage one another with the words of this psalm. *Venite, exultemus Domino* – O come, let us sing unto the Lord! That at any rate was what the English Reformers intended. Today, 450 years later, the expectation is somewhat unrealistic, but the principle is sound.

1. His most worthy praise: his most holy Word

The Prayer Book's services of Morning and Evening Prayer contain ten canticles, six of which are ancient hymns or New Testament scriptures. The remaining four are psalms. One of these, the Deus Misereatur (67), we considered in Book II. The other three are all taken from the kingship psalms of Book IV: the Venite (95), the Cantate (98) and the Jubilate (100).

Although our present psalm comes very early in Morning Prayer, an introduction has already reminded the worshippers of the object of their meeting. It is to pray to God, certainly, but also 'to set forth his most worthy praise' and 'to hear his most holy Word'. Those are the twin themes of the psalm, and divide it helpfully. In verses 1–7 we encourage one another to praise God: *Let us sing for joy to the LORD . . . Come, let us bow down in worship.* In verses 8–11 the psalmist begins to speak, though the voice quickly becomes God's voice, urging us to listen to his word.

Both parts of the psalm give reasons for these exhortations, for worship is not meant to be a mindless activity. We should sing for joy, *for the LORD is the great God* (3); we should bow in worship, *for he is our God* (7). 'Far above us in his greatness, he is yet close to us in his goodness,' said John Stott.[27] The reason why we ought to listen to his voice is a more solemn one, set out in a different way. It takes us back into Israel's history, and in due course we shall look at it in detail.

2. Sing, bow, hear

It is equally possible to divide the psalm into three sections. Setting out its twenty-five lines as 10 + 5 + 10 displays clearly both its symmetry and its key words: sing, bow, hear.

---

[27] J. R. W. Stott, *The Canticles and Selected Psalms* (London: Hodder & Stoughton, 1966), p. 18.

While the one to whom we sing is the Lord, the Rock and the Saviour, it is particularly as the great God, the great King, that we delight in him (1–5). His rule is that of the Creator and Sustainer. The mountains and the deeps are even now in his hands, just as earth and sea were formed by his hands in the first place. And though our modern world is far fuller of man-made marvels than the world of the Bible was, we should admire all the more the God who enables us to make them.

Let us sing to God, we said to one another in verse 1; now joy is succeeded by awe, as we encourage one another to bow down before him (6–7a). For this great God *is our God*. He is called our Maker here, not, probably, as the one who created the human race, but as the one who has made Israel a nation, and has brought her to be his own *flock*. The Creator is also the Redeemer.

So let us bow down. This, rather than liturgy or music or 'the cultus', is what worship is. We kneel, we are brought low, we are humbled by the realization that the God who made the universe cares about *us*. As the body is bowed, so should the mind and the will be bowed in submission to him.

Then we shall be prepared to hear (7b–11), that is, to listen and obey. The reason in this case might be summed up in the words 'Listen, for the Lord is an angry God.' The last four verses of the psalm are thought by some not to belong with the first seven, and they were not to be found in the Venite of the 1980 Alternative Services Book, which in this followed the proposed Prayer Book of 1928 (and the American Prayer Book of 1789!). It is ironic that those who sing an amputated Venite never hear what it says about the importance of hearing.

3. A liturgy for the Old Testament church

As with so many psalms, the dating of 95 has varied widely. Its use would certainly have been very appropriate at the dedication of the rebuilt temple after the exile; headings connecting 96 and 97 with that time were given to those psalms by the translators of the Greek Old Testament. It would have been equally apt at other times, even at the other end of Israel's history. There is no denying that like its neighbours 95 echoes the words of Moses, especially in Deuteronomy 32 – 33. There too God is Israel's Rock and Saviour and Maker; there too he is angry with his people, and recalls the events at Massah and Meribah (Deut. 32:6, 15, 18; 33:8).

So we come back again to Tabernacles. The place names Massah and Meribah are the first explicit reference to Exodus in these psalms since the mention of Moses in the heading of 90. With them the exodus story, the theme of Tabernacles, comes to the fore again, right on cue. The links are only suggestions, but they work: Exodus 1 and 2 with Psalm 90, the plagues in Exodus 3 – 12 with 91, Israel brought 'out of the land of slavery' (Exod. 13:3) with 92, the crossing of the sea (Exod. 14 – 15) with 93, and a review of 'the story so far' in 94.

Now the joy of 95:1 – Miriam's song by the sea, Exodus 15:20–21 – quickly gives way to the perversity of 95:8–9, the 'testing' and 'strife' which are the meanings of the two place names in Exodus 17:7.

Annually at the feast of Tabernacles, as Kidner has well said, 'Israel in holiday mood remembered the wilderness . . . and was doubtless tempted to romanticize it as an idyllic age.' What God remembered, and reminded her of in Psalm 95, was her ingratitude and unbelief and his anger and disgust. It was 'a cold douche of realism'.[28]

In fact the grumbles had begun a mere three days after the spectacular miracle at the Red Sea (Exod. 15:22–24), and continued on and off for the next forty years, to the other Meribah (Num. 20:1–13) and beyond. They bore all the marks of a chronic disease needing repeated treatment. Tabernacles might have been designed expressly to be, among other things, an annual check-up. 'Will you hear his voice *today*? Here you are, singing and bowing, but are you *listening*?'

4. A liturgy for the New Testament church

The whole point of the psalm is that the challenge to hear and heed spans the centuries. 'Today' is its keynote. I do believe that in some sense these psalms go back to the time of Moses; but what that means in the case of this one is that paradoxically its setting is precisely not the time of Moses. Psalm 95 is speaking to Israel on some occasion at least forty years – perhaps, for all we know, four hundred years – after the incident at Massah (10). That is the point. It says, 'God is speaking to you now, today, as really as he was then. You are as likely as your forebears were to harden your hearts and to refuse to listen. It is entirely possible for God to be as disgusted with you as he was with them.'

---

28 Kidner, p. 345. See on Ps. 81.

The New Testament takes up this very issue and expounds it thoroughly in the third and fourth chapters of Hebrews. The author there is warning his first-century readers of the possibility of an unbelieving, disobedient heart which hears but does not listen, and which forfeits God's blessing as a result. His argument is, 'That was what happened in Moses' time; years afterwards the psalmist said "Massah can happen again today"; so when we read his words, we realize that exactly the same thing could happen to us now, even though another thousand years may have gone by.'

And of course when we for our part read Hebrews, two thousand years later still, we see its author's 'Today' quoting the psalmist's 'Today' which is quoting Moses' 'Today', and we realize what the Holy Spirit *is saying to us* (the vivid present tense in Heb. 3:7). 'If in your own Today *you* hear his voice,' he urges us, 'do not harden *your* hearts.'

As well as that final step forward into the present, we need to take one final step back before the events at Massah. The hardness of heart, the disobedience and unbelief, which eventually barred that whole generation from arriving in the Promised Land, were an unwillingness to look back just a matter of months, even days. *Your ancestors tested me; they tried me, though they had seen what I did* (95:9). In Egypt God had done what he had said he would do, and they all knew it. But already that had become unreal. It was relegated to history. Now, they said, we think you ought to be doing such-and-such, and if you don't we shan't trust you any more.

The fact was that God's saving acts in the past were the guarantee that today he was still equally trustworthy. 'See to it, brothers and sisters, that none of you has a sinful, unbelieving heart that turns away from the living God.' And the responsibility is, as the Venite makes plain, that of the whole fellowship: 'Encourage one another daily, as long as it is called "Today", so that none of you may be hardened by sin's deceitfulness' (Heb. 3:12–13).

Psalm 96

This is 'the other' Cantate. The better-known one is 98, given by the Prayer Book as an alternative canticle to the Magnificat in Evening Prayer; 96 is its close sibling, though not its twin. Josiah Conder's finest hymn,[29] though based on a New Testament text (Rev. 19:6 AV, 'The Lord God

---

[29] Unless it is surpassed by the magnificently Christocentric 'Thou art the everlasting Word'.

omnipotent reigneth'), clearly reflects verses 10–11 here: 'The Lord is King; lift up thy voice, / O earth, and all ye heavens rejoice!'

1. New scene

Something that has so far been only hinted at in the Exodus Collection here opens up before us. The earth, whose depths and heights are, we know, in the Lord's hands (95:4), appears twice as an inclusio framing the first part of 96: *Sing to the LORD, all the earth* (1); *Tremble before him, all the earth* (9). Within the frame these verses speak four times of the *nations* or the *peoples* who inhabit the earth.[30] The second part of the psalm, verses 10–13, tells us the message to be spoken *among the nations.* In this part the earth, together with the sky and the sea and *everything in them*, is at the centre, and the world and its peoples are in the framing verses (10 and 13).

We have had glimpses of this worldwide vision elsewhere, for example in the second David Collection (66:1, 7, 8), in both Korah Collections (47:1–3 and 87), and even as far back as 9:8, where the words of 96:10c have already appeared. But a psalm whose entire background is the grand panorama that we have here is a new thing in the Psalter.

2. New singers

We knew from its opening words that 95 was a call to Israel, the psalmist's fellow worshippers, to sing to the Lord. The invitation of 96 is much wider. In fact it contains three separate exhortations, which alternate with three declarations, and they call the whole world with everything and everyone in it to praise God.

The way the NIV sets out the lines and sentences of the poem helps us to see this structure. The first part of the psalm, verses 1–9, has three sections, each of three verses (or six lines): exhorting, declaring, exhorting. The second part, verses 10–13b, also has three sections, and in this case each has three lines: declaring, exhorting, declaring. The last two lines, verse 13cd, round off both the second half and the psalm as a whole.

First, all the earth is exhorted to sing to God (1–3). That in itself would be straightforward, were it not that the singing is to be a proclamation of his salvation, and a proclamation by all the earth to all the nations. Who

---

[30] The RSV is consistent in translating the two Hebrew words 'nations' (*gôyim*) in v. 3a, 'peoples' (*'ammîm*) in vv. 3b, 5, 7.

exactly is singing what, we may wonder? Israel knows God as Saviour, but what is it about him that the earth knows and the nations don't? If there is no obvious answer, we can leave the question and return to it later – sound advice for every Bible problem.

Next comes a declaration of the Lord's greatness (4–6). As the Creator of all, surrounded by Splendour and Majesty, Strength and Glory (personified, as if they were great angels; we have seen such things in earlier psalms),[31] he altogether transcends the so-called gods of the nations.

Now a second exhortation (7–9): this time it is the nations that are called to worship the Lord. *Families of nations*[32] are less likely to mean larger groupings (Indo-European nations, Islamic nations, English-speaking nations) than subgroups, tribes within each nation: smaller divisions, so more of them. There must have been a universal change of heart for all these to be recognizing God's glory, bringing gifts, putting themselves out to come to his courts, trembling before him.

We may take all the second half to be what is proclaimed *among the nations* (10) that have heard of the Lord's salvation (2) and recognize his glory (7, 8). Its three sections are out of kilter with the verse numbers, but each is a three-line sentence in the NIV. Verse 10 is another declaration: *The LORD reigns.* As in 93:1, it seems to look back to the way his rule has held creation together from the beginning; and it seems to look forward to his universal rule over humanity too. Verses 11–12a are a final exhortation, that sky and sea as well as land should join the singers of praise; and verses 12b–13b a final declaration, that all this joy relates to his rule, the government of a true and righteous God. So the psalm's closing lines, verse 13c–d, proclaim.

3. New song

The *new song* of verse 1 looks as if it is connected with the cry *The LORD reigns* in verse 10. That, as we have seen, is 'a new and overwhelming assertion . . . rather than a timeless theological truth'.[33]

So the song would have been composed for an occasion when the reign of the Lord was being newly asserted. Commentators differ as to what that might have been. The psalm's heading in the Greek Old Testament says it

---

[31] See p. 2.54.

[32] The phrase appears also in the triumphant ending of the great 'crucifixion' psalm, 22 (v. 27).

[33] Kidner, pp. 348–349. See pp. 2.91–92. The suggestion that the *new song* is, like the Lord's compassions, 'new every morning' (Lam. 3:22–23) is therefore unlikely, though attractive.

was for use 'when the house was being built after the captivity'; with the restoration and the new temple it was again clear that God was on the throne. Or it might be placed earlier, at the time of some military victory in the period of the monarchy. Earlier still, we find it quoted almost in full in 1 Chronicles 16:23–33, as part of the celebration when David, newly enthroned in Jerusalem, brought the ark of the covenant there too.

Others believe it to be a look into the future. Isaiah 42:10 begins exactly as our psalm does, and the new song of which the prophet speaks belongs with the new things which the Lord says he is about to do (43:18–19; 48:6–7). The prophecy could be foreseeing the return from exile; or the coming of the gospel (as Calvin argues, quoting Rom. 10:14, for how can the world praise one it has had no opportunity to believe in?); or perhaps something more remote, namely the final day of the Lord.

If, however, there is a real link between the Book IV psalms generally and the themes of Exodus and Tabernacles, the key to Psalm 96 lies in the past rather than in the future. Few if any would date its composition in the time of Moses, but its themes do fit readily into an account of that time.

4. New splendour

It has been possible to parallel the psalms from 90 to 95 with readings taken in sequence from Exodus 1 to Exodus 17. Bearing in mind how 96 sees the praise of the Lord spreading outwards from Israel to the rest of the nations, we are intrigued to find Exodus 18 describing how the Israelite camp in the wilderness is visited by 'Jethro, the priest of Midian and father-in-law of Moses' (Exod. 18:1). Jethro is related to Moses not only by marriage but by their common descent from Abraham (Gen. 25:1–6). All the same, he is not an Israelite; and when he says to his son-in-law, 'Praise be to the LORD, who rescued you from the hand of the Egyptians and of Pharaoh . . . Now I know that the LORD is greater than all other gods' (Exod. 18:10–11), he is the first non-Israelite in Israel's history to speak thus.[34]

This is the new thing. *The LORD reigns* is in the perfect tense, 'The LORD has proclaimed himself king', and is therefore a one-off event and not a timeless truth. But it is not a recent event. The Lord's enthronement is no new thing, for it dates back to the beginning of time. He became king of the earth when the earth was made. What *is* new is the song that proclaims it to the nations that do not yet walk in Israel's light.

---

[34] See on Ps. 47.

In other words, the new thing, the good news of God's kingdom, is for everyone. This, the dominant theme of a far-reaching psalm, may suggest which is the most likely of several possible meanings for verse 9a. It hardly means that the nations are called to worship him in the splendour of a holy place (so JB), still less in 'array of holiness' in the sense of distinctive robes (so NEB margin)! On the other hand, it is a great gospel truth that they should do so 'in the splendour of holiness', spiritually distinctive because they have been 'clothed . . . with garments of salvation and arrayed . . . in a robe of his righteousness' (Isa. 61:10).

But perhaps the interpretation most in line with the thrust of the psalm is that all nations are summoned to worship him *in the splendour of his holiness*, just as the NIV says. For what is so holy, so special and distinctive, about him? Is it not that he has so loved the whole wicked world, and the nations sunk in sin, that he has sent his own beloved Son – first Israel, and then Jesus, the true Israel – to be the one through whom he will rescue them?

Psalm 97

Like 68, this is a psalm 'full of quotations', woven from threads drawn from other parts of the Psalter, it seems, though none the worse for that. Its author has made a tapestry that hangs well alongside its companions in this section of the book.

1. The Lord reigns (97:1)

The eight psalms of which this is the fifth have much in common. A number of phrases recur often, and so do the motifs of kingship and rejoicing. The opening words of the poems suggest that the compilers had a pattern in mind, running parallel to the development of an overall theme. From 93 to 100 the psalms begin with these eight phrases or words: The Lord reigns / the God who avenges / come / sing / the Lord reigns / sing / the Lord reigns / rejoice!

Again, *The LORD reigns* is in the perfect tense, and is an act, not just a fact. Like the other psalms in the group, 97 is not saying that the Lord has just been enthroned, either in a regular religious ceremony or in some recent deliverance of Israel's. But there have been, and will be, certain points in the Bible story when his royal majesty shines forth, and shows that it was he who ascended the throne at the beginning of all things. Only when the world recognizes this and accepts his rule of righteousness and justice (2) will it find that the machinery of life runs as it should.

2. Clouds and fire (97:2–3)

Among the psalms, 18 in particular has a spine-tingling picture of the Lord flying to his people's aid with wind and rain, hail, thunder and lightning.[35] Elsewhere in Scripture an even closer parallel calls for our attention as we read these kingship psalms. With the link between 96 and Exodus 18 fresh in our minds, we can scarcely help thinking, when 97 begins with clouds and thick darkness, lightning and fire, of Exodus 19. After the description of Jethro's visit to Moses there follows that of Israel's arrival at Sinai, and of the day when 'there was thunder and lightning, with a thick cloud over the mountain . . . Mount Sinai was covered with smoke, because the LORD descended on it in fire' (Exod. 19:16, 18). Once more, then, we are in the midst of the feast of Tabernacles, and its review of the exodus story.

'The sight was so terrifying that Moses said, "I am trembling with fear"' (Heb. 12:21). But the initial terror gave way to a combination of awe and (surprisingly) delight. That at least is what we find repeatedly to be the psalmists' attitude to the law given at Sinai. The nineteenth psalm is an outstanding example in Book I, and this one is no exception. When the awesome God of righteousness and justice makes himself known, the earth trembles (4) and yet is glad (1). Rejoicing fills the psalm, beginning, middle and end. Our own breaking of the law is a separate issue; while confessing that we are sinners, we yet long for a world under the rule of law, provided it is a law made and administered by God.

3. Zion hears (97:8)

Verses 8–9 move from Mount Sinai to Mount Zion – it is the move we may recall from 68:17[36] – and the psalm's historical background widens. We are taken back from Exodus to Genesis, to a time when Zion was called Salem, and the mysterious Melchizedek was both its king and the priest of God Most High. Just as even Moses trembled when the Lord came down on Sinai, so even Abraham bowed when Melchizedek came forth from

---

[35] Ps. 18:9–14. One commentary notes 'the prevalence of meteorological phenomena in theophanic accounts'! Not all of us, it seems, have spines that tingle.

[36] See p. 1.237.

Salem. There were no clouds or fire then; but each of these great men recognized the coming of one greater than himself (cf. Gen. 14:18–20; Heb. 7:1–7).

We are also taken forward from the days of Moses to the days of the monarchy. Verse 8 is almost exactly the same as 48:11, and we recall that earlier series of pilgrimage psalms – Tabernacles psalms? – in the first Korah Collection in Book II. They had similar roots to those of 97; the God of Abraham figured in 47:9, and the Most High in both 47:2 and 46:4. As this last verse puts it, they were centred on Jerusalem, 'the city of God, the holy place where the Most High dwells', and seem to celebrate a great deliverance, often identified with the lifting of the Assyrian siege in the reign of Hezekiah (see Pss 46; 47; 65; 66). Again, there were no 'meteorological phenomena'[37] on that occasion. But what was actual at Sinai is very good picture language for what happens wherever the enthroned Lord intervenes unmistakably in his people's affairs.

4. Worship him (97:7)

In all likelihood the words *Worship him, all you gods!* expand the Bible background still further. It is the Greek translation of either Deuteronomy 32:43 or (more probably) this verse that is quoted in Hebrews 1:6.[38] The author of Hebrews understands the *gods* of verse 7c to be not the idols of verse 7b (for 'God does not require the worship of false gods'),[39] but the angels. We have come to see in earlier psalms – 45 and 82, for instance[40] – that the Bible does speak of angels in this way.

According to this New Testament passage, it is '*when God brings his firstborn into the world*' that he says, 'Let all God's angels worship him.' In other words, just as Abraham and Hezekiah were not literally deafened or dazzled as Israel was at Sinai, but even so had a metaphorical thunder-and-lightning experience of the majesty of God, so it was when Christ was born. We may be right to sing of the 'silent stars' and the 'dark streets' of Bethlehem in Phillips Brooks's Christmas hymn,[41] but for those there who had the eyes to see and the ears to hear,

---

[37] See n. 35 above.

[38] See David Gooding, *An Unshakeable Kingdom* (Leicester: IVP, 1989), pp. 58, 79. For the opposite view, see F. F. Bruce, *Hebrews* (London: Marshall, Morgan & Scott, 1964), pp. 15–16.

[39] Gooding, p. 58.

[40] See pp. 1.158, 2.39.

[41] 'O little town of Bethlehem'.

the glory of the Lord shone around them . . . They were terrified. But the
angel said to them, 'Do not be afraid. I bring you good news that will
cause great joy' . . . Suddenly a great company of the heavenly host
appeared with the angel, praising God.
(Luke 2:9–10, 13)

So here in Psalm 97 not Sinai nor Zion nor Bethlehem only, but the
whole earth, both trembles and yet is glad, is first terrified and then
rejoicing; for of course with the birth of Jesus comes the possibility of the
worldwide harvest of which Jethro the Midianite was one of the first-
fruits. The spread of the gospel has indeed in our New Testament times
made *the distant shores rejoice* (1).

5. Friend and foe (97:3, 10)

There are pointers to one more broadening of our psalm's significance.
Would it be true to say of any of the occasions we have so far considered
that that is the point at which God's *fire . . . consumes his foes on every side*?
Well, hardly. And if such a total destruction of evil will not happen till the
end of time, will that not also be the day when having guarded *the lives of
his faithful ones* he finally, in the fullest sense, *delivers them from the hand
of the wicked*? Then the great simplicities of Psalm 1, which by the time
we get to Psalm 73 may have come to seem oversimplified and belied by
experience, will turn out to have been right after all. And on that day when
evil is vanquished and his people vindicated, it will also be in the fullest
sense that all the earth will be glad and all the peoples will see his glory.

Along with the assurances that pervade the psalm and are crystallized
in verse 10b comes the requirement of verse 10a, that *those who love the
Lord* should *hate evil. His faithful ones* are those upon whom his covenant
love rests, and who therefore covenant to love him in return. If we are called
by *his holy name* (12) we are expected to live a correspondingly holy life, and
to take seriously the pursuit of righteousness and the hatred of sin.

And the Bible writers would unanimously pour scorn on the notion that
this is a recipe for gloom. Our psalmist in particular, looking back over the
past manifestations of the kingship of Yahweh and forward to the final
one, sees everywhere cause for rejoicing. The keynote of the whole psalm
is joy, and his closing verses strike it loud and clear. 'There's no other way
/ To be happy in Jesus, / But to trust and obey.'[42]

---

[42]   J. H. Sammis, 'When we walk with the Lord'.

Psalm 98

The better known of the Cantates is the simpler and more artless of the two, both in structure and in content. It divides into three unequal parts (each has three verses, but they are of different lengths), and the development follows the sense rather than any literary pattern.

1. Sing, shout, resound

Sing, shout and *resound* are the first verbs in verses 1, 4 and 7. With them the three sections begin. Many other joyful noises, however, come tumbling out as the psalm proceeds. Between the framing shouts of verses 4 and 6, the middle section is full of music, and in verses 7–9 the resounding sea is accompanied by clapping rivers and singing mountains.

In a similar way, although we might say that the summons to praise God is addressed to Israel in the first section, to the nations in the second and to the natural world in the third, the distinctions there too are not so cut and dried. True, verses 4–6 are full of people playing instruments, but it is *the earth* that is called to rejoice. True, verses 7–9 are mostly about the world of nature, but that includes *all who live in it.*

First, the psalmist calls his fellow Israelites to sing to God. Appropriately, they are to praise him as their Saviour, for that is his special relationship to them. Each of the first three verses speaks of his salvation; that is at the heart of the meaning of his name Yahweh, the Lord, and his covenant love and faithfulness to the house of Israel have been seen chiefly in his saving them (3).

Next, the peoples of the earth are called to praise him as King. They may not know him as Saviour, but they do know that wherever a community has been under his kingly rule it becomes something infinitely desirable: a Christian society, characterized not by religious observances but by godly living, which gives the lie to the silly and ignorant notion that Christianity spoils everything it touches.

Finally, the whole creation must acclaim God as Judge, that is, as governor. Where we obey his laws and abide by his decisions, not only we but also our environment will benefit.

2. A psalm for Old Testament people

Psalm 98 can be thought of as an exodus psalm, however long after the exodus it was actually written. The ancient translation of the Old

Testament into Syriac gave it the heading 'Of the redemption of the people from Egypt', and verse 1, singing to the Lord of the salvation brought about by his right hand, is a clear echo of the song of Moses (Exod. 15:2, 6).

There were later occasions, while Israel was a monarchy, for which the public use of the psalm would have been very appropriate. *Salvation* is translated 'victory' in verse 1 in the AV and the Prayer Book, and consistently throughout the first three verses in the NRSV and the NEB; some great military success could well have been celebrated by just such a song.

The event to which many think it best suited is God's rescue of his people from exile in Babylon. That really was a victory achieved only by *his right hand and his holy arm*, with no Israelite armies involved at all. In fact it had nothing to do with any military operation. A new government and a new policy in a heathen empire beyond the Euphrates was God's instrument in bringing Israel home again. The later prophecies of Isaiah, especially chapters 44–63, speak of this, and use similar language to that of our psalm: God's hand and arm, his salvation and righteousness, singing and clapping, the joy of the natural world (cf. Isa. 44:23; 51:3; 52:9–10; 55:12; 56:1; 59:16; 63:5; etc.).

To go back to the earliest of the periods of Old Testament history just suggested, there must have been some reason why the Syrian translators linked Psalm 98 with the exodus. It would certainly slot into place alongside the reading that would follow the clouds, darkness and fire of Psalm 97 and Exodus 19. With the next four chapters of Exodus God starts to reveal his law to the people he has redeemed. 'I am the LORD your God, who brought you out of Egypt, out of the land of slavery,' he begins in Exodus 20:2. That was the classic instance of his miracles of judgment and rescue, the *marvellous things* of Psalm 98:1. And in the next breath the God of Exodus 20 is proclaiming the Ten Commandments. He who has so recently *made his salvation known* has now also *revealed his righteousness*, says the second verse of the psalm. Awesome and even frightening as the giving of the law was at the time, it was also for God's people, when they grasped its implications, an occasion to *burst into jubilant song* (98:4, as already in 97:1–2).[43]

---

[43] See pp. 2.106–107.

3. A psalm for New Testament people

For Christians the gospel of Jesus is what calls forth the new song. They realize that all the Old Testament contexts in which Psalm 98 might quite properly have been sung were pointing forward to that fulfilment.

Watts's version of its second part, beginning at verse 4, fell out of favour for some reason for a hundred years, but now appears regularly in modern hymnals among the Christmas hymns. 'Joy to the world! The Lord is come; / Let earth receive her King.' The joy of Christmas is paralleled by that of Palm Sunday, when the prophecy of Zechariah 9:9 was fulfilled: 'Shout, Daughter Jerusalem! See, your king comes to you, righteous and victorious, lowly and riding on a donkey' – another coming, with the same words (shout, king, come, righteous, victory/salvation) as in Psalm 98.

And there is of course one more coming that we are meant to have in mind when we sing the Cantate. With the incarnation of Christ and all the events of the gospel story, culminating in God's sending his Spirit to his church and his church into the world, he had in a wonderful new way *made his salvation known and revealed his righteousness to the nations* (2). But a yet more far-reaching renewal awaits us in the future, when he finally *comes to judge the earth* (9). Why should the earth, as distinct from the people who live on it, rejoice at the coming of the Lord? Why will the rivers clap and the mountains sing? Because, as Paul tells us, 'the whole creation has been groaning as in the pains of childbirth right up to the present time', and still 'waits in eager expectation' to 'be liberated from its bondage to decay'. That passage in Romans 8:18–22 shows how the present state and the future destiny of the natural world are bound up with those of humanity. Adam's sin infected not only his descendants but also his environment. Only when sin is finally done away can the world be renewed. Thus one end of Scripture answers to the other: God speaks to Adam at the beginning, in Eden, in Genesis 3:17: 'Cursed is the ground because of you.' He speaks again at the end, in Paradise, in Revelation 21:5: 'I am making everything new!'

Watts, with his characteristic breadth of vision and depth of insight, sees both of these New Testament comings, and both of the deliverances they bring, behind the new song of Psalm 98: 'He comes to make his blessings flow / Far as the curse is found.' We are right to see in the Cantate a celebration of real, effective comings in the past. We are equally right to take them as a confirmation of our future hope. 'He who testifies to these things says, "Yes, I am coming soon." Amen. Come, Lord Jesus' (Rev. 22:20).

Psalm 99

One more psalm begins with the words *The LORD reigns*. The first was immensely positive (93), the next dramatic but joyful (97); this, the third, is austere and bracing.

1. Thrice holy

The holiness of God is the theme of the threefold acclamations of heaven in both Old Testament and New: '"Holy, holy, holy is the Lord God Almighty", who was, and is, and is to come' (Rev. 4:8; cf. Isa. 6:3).

Here too it is proclaimed three times over. Verses 3, 5 and 9, each of which ends with a declaration of it, look like the refrains of three stanzas of a poem, and therefore markers for the dividing of it. On the other hand, those stanzas would obviously be very unequal. Perhaps a better-proportioned division into two is what the psalmist intended, with a longer refrain, verse 9 echoing verse 5: *Exalt the LORD our God and worship at his footstool (his holy mountain); he (the LORD our God) is holy.*

A structure different from both of these will best suit the purposes of this exposition. It is slightly more complex, though no more so than a metrical pattern familiar from a number of English hymns, usually known as 64.64.6664.[44] In this pattern the first couplet (in terms of Ps. 99, vv. 1–3) matches the second (4–5) and the fourth (8–9); the third is slightly different (6–7), providing variety, yet leading into the fourth in a natural and integrated way.

The word *holy* is the climax of the first, second and fourth sections of the psalm, and all these include words addressed directly to the Lord. They link him with the names of Zion (2), Jacob (4) and Israel (8). The third section we shall consider separately. It refers, intriguingly, not only to Moses and Aaron, whom we are not surprised to find here in this Exodus Collection, but also to an unexpected person from a later time, the prophet Samuel.

2. Your name, your deeds, your answer

What the psalmist says to the Lord in verses 1–3 concerns his *great and awesome name*. Let the nations praise it: not yet because of what he has

---

[44] E.g. Mansell Ramsey's 'Teach me thy way, O Lord', or S. D. Phelps's 'Saviour! Thy dying love'. John Bunyan's 'Who would true valour see' (or in Percy Dearmer's adaptation, 'He who would valiant be') is similar (65.65.6665).

done, that is, his name of Creator and Redeemer, but because of what he is. In a word, let them recognize his holiness.

This, it has to be said, is what the nations are so loath to accept. The fact that he is *holy* – distinctive, and supreme in his distinctiveness; unique, and demanding in his uniqueness – is seen, and responded to, only by his own holy nation. The rest of the world may be prepared to admit that he exists, that he is at least as much of a deity as all the other deities, even that he is *primus inter pares*. But holiness of this sort? No.

Yet his deeds are undeniable. In verses 4–5 the psalmist says to him, *You have established equity; in Jacob you have done what is just and right.* Even the world that ridicules Christian standards when they are labelled 'Victorian family values' will say that it respects 'the principles of the Sermon on the Mount'. When the Lord directs our lives according to those principles, we too do *what is just and right*. The holy God is producing holiness in his people, and it is apparent to every unbiased observer, as we saw in 98:4–6.[45]

We leave aside for the moment the famous servants of God named in verse 6, except to note that it is about God's response to them that the psalmist speaks in verse 8. *You answered them; you were to Israel a forgiving God, though you punished their misdeeds.* Punishment even for his own servants, yet forgiveness even for sinners, and both in strict justice; for then as now he is at the same time both just and the justifier of those who cast themselves on his mercy (cf. Rom. 3:26).

3. Moses, Aaron, Samuel

Verse 6 is another of the explicit links between the psalms of Book IV and the exodus narrative. In the latter we have arrived, in our hypothetical readings for the feast of Tabernacles, at Exodus 24. Up to now Moses alone had been summoned, several times, to meet the Lord on the cloud-capped summit of Sinai, but now the invitation was different. 'Come up to the LORD, you *and Aaron* . . .' (1). The two brothers, with Aaron's two eldest sons and seventy of the elders of Israel, climbed the mountain, and Scripture tells us that in some extraordinary way they 'saw the God of Israel' (10).

It is that access to God that the psalmist seems to focus on. Verse 6 may be setting before us first Moses, who was both prophet and priest, in the

---

[45] See p. 2.108.

sense that he represented both God to Israel and Israel to God;[46] then Aaron, the first formally appointed high priest; then Samuel, after a long interval the next prophet of Moses' stature.[47] All were intermediaries who both prayed and prophesied, spokesmen in both directions.[48]

Of each of these men it is true to say that *they called on the LORD and he answered them*, and they stand for all others who have had that experience. Of course the voice from the cloud had already called to them,[49] for God always takes the initiative, and grace always precedes faith. But as they sought him in prayer, that voice gave them in reply the *statutes and the decrees* by which they and their nation were to live. The holy God requires holiness in his people. The psalm updates the ancient story; that is after all the purpose of a festival like Tabernacles, to keep the memory of those crucial events fresh in one's mind and relevant to one's life. The call to holiness is as valid today as it ever was.

Psalm 100

For a psalm of few verses, this one has captured the imagination of a great many people down the years. Its appeal *endures*, as the Lord's covenant love and faithfulness do (5), *through all generations*.

1. In Old Testament times

Like the rest of this Exodus Collection, it looks back to the time of Moses. The words *He . . . made us* refer to the making, not of humanity, but of Israel, when God constituted her his nation at Sinai. He guided his people through the desert as *the sheep of his pasture*. He instructed them there to set up the *courts* of his tabernacle; as 99:6–7 recalls Exodus 24, so 100:4 tallies with Exodus 25 – 31.

As another 'entrance-liturgy', like 15 and 24, this psalm might well have been used regularly when worshippers arrived at the Jerusalem temple, whether Solomon's or the rebuilt one after the exile. At some stage it will

---

[46] 'A servant in all God's house', and thus a type of Jesus, as Heb. 3:1–6 points out.

[47] 'Moses, and Aaron as His priest, and Samuel as one who calls on His Name' (note the two commas): A. R. Johnson, as quoted by Anderson, p. 696.

[48] As prophets: cf. Exod. 7:1; Deut. 34:10; 1 Sam. 3:20; as intercessors: cf. Exod. 32:31–32; Num. 16:46–50; 1 Sam. 12:23.

[49] For all three of them the voice was first heard from something at least related to the pillar of cloud and fire: the burning bush (Exod. 3:1ff.), the cloud on the mountain (Exod. 24), the darkness of the sanctuary at Shiloh (1 Sam. 3:1–10).

have been fitted into its present place, with the kingship psalms, 93 – 99, then with the Exodus Collection of Book IV, 90 – 106, and finally as part of the Psalter we know. It shares much of the language of its companions, especially 95; there and elsewhere we have already seen Israel's Maker and Shepherd, and her coming into his presence with thanksgiving and joyful shout.

2. In New Testament times

The downfall of the Israelite monarchy, followed centuries later by the destruction of the second temple, meant that eventually neither the Lord's throne nor his temple courts could be taken any longer in a literal sense. But Psalm 100 has continued to be sung as enthusiastically as ever, by Jews and Christians alike, by the medieval church and then in the sixteenth century by the Reformed churches too. As the Jubilate it found itself reunited with its biblical neighbours the Venite and the Cantate in the Church of England's Prayer Book, and at the same time turned into metrical verse for the so-called 'Old Version' of the Psalter. In that form it became one of the few English hymns of the period to have a secure place still, 450 years later, in our hymnals (and to the original tune, the Old Hundredth!) – William Kethe's 'All people that on earth do dwell'.

Years afterwards Isaac Watts made his own version, which John Wesley shortened and adapted, so that it began 'Before Jehovah's awful throne'. It too survives, and deserves to. The proper response to an early date printed beside a hymn writer's name is not 'How impossibly old-fashioned', but 'There must be something special about this for it to have lasted so long.'

3. In our times

And there is something special about it. In whatever form we may be familiar with Psalm 100, we cannot miss its breadth of vision.

Three calls, to shout, to worship and to come, are followed by a statement about the Lord, telling us why we should. The pattern is repeated: we are to enter his gates, give him thanks, and praise his name, again with facts about God as the reason why.

We might say that verses 1–2 are about the expression of our words, the obedience of our deeds (*worship* here is about serving)[50] and the desire of our hearts. The common denominator in all three should be joy; and there

---

[50] Most translations before the 1984 NIV and 1989 NRSV had 'serve'.

is joy, when we know the God of verse 3. The exodus story explains the verse. It tells us that the only true God is the one who at the burning bush in Exodus 3:15 made himself known as the Lord, Yahweh, the Redeemer ('This is my name for ever, the name you shall call me from generation to generation'). He has made Israel his 'holy nation', and she is his 'treasured possession' (Exod. 19:5–6), while the picture of her as his flock of sheep has already been applied in Psalm 78:52 specifically to his leading of his people safely through the desert.

Such power! Such care! And now in his presence (4) his worshippers bring him thanks and praise, for the three great facts that underlie what we have come to know of his power and care. He has done all this out of his goodness, his covenant love and his faithfulness.

So there are six imperatives: shout, serve, come; enter, thank, praise – seven, if we include the 'know' in verse 3. But to whom are they addressed?

The psalm speaks from within the fellowship of God's people (3), where we are saying these things to one another. But it speaks to *all the earth*, and it speaks a message valid for *all generations* (1, 5). It shakes the Jew by reaching out to the Gentile. It sets before the church the challenge of the world. For the Reformers, it broke the power of an unspiritual priesthood with a gospel for '*all* people that on earth do dwell'. It holds out the hope not only of a new humanity but of new heavens and a new earth.

I am constantly amazed that out of the genteel, superficial culture of the early eighteenth century – Watts's culture – should have come such majestic stuff as this:

> Wide as the world is thy command;
> Vast as eternity thy love;
> Firm as a rock thy truth shall stand,
> When rolling years shall cease to move.

His non-Anglican congregation will never have sung the Jubilate as such. But he and they had grasped the greatness of it.

Psalm 101

As a David psalm, and one full of protestations of innocence and goodness, what is 101 doing here, so far from the others of its kind (such as 17 or 26) in Book I?

The answer turns this latest example of the psalmist's apparent self-righteousness from something obscure into something illuminating. It throws a shaft of light into a hugely important area of human life.

We note four or five significant words in it.

1. Silencing and ministering (101:5, 6, 8)

It emerges that the psalmist is one who is in a position to silence slanderers (5), indeed *all the wicked in the land* (8), and one whom others serve as his ministers (6). In Old Testament Israel this is of course the king, and Psalm 101 is by no means out of place in the company of the royal psalms 93 – 100.

As in Book I, *blameless* ought not to be thought the equivalent of 'bloodless'. On the contrary, it denotes a person of robust integrity. For the king this means (as Kidner puts it) a 'concern for a clean administration, honest from the top down'.[51] The book of Proverbs often connects practicalities and principles in this way, and it echoes our psalm at many points.[52]

The Proverbs style with its brief and pithy sentences is also here, so that the structure of the psalm is less like the organic growth of a tree than like the erection of a building, the building blocks being lines grouped in pairs or in sets of four. It has twenty-eight lines, therefore seven four-line stanzas. What follows is one way of combining these into larger units.

The opening stanza (1–2a) introduces the theme of integrity, the *blameless life*, and the covenant love and justice which as characteristics of God's rule ought to characterize the king's rule too.

The next three stanzas (2b–5; notice *blameless* again in the first of them, 2b–3a) are about the king's personal values. Here the word *heart* is the link: he covets integrity of heart, distances himself from 'perverseness of heart' (so the NRSV), and will not tolerate pride of heart.

Finally three stanzas (6–8; note the third *blameless* in v. 6) set forth his policy in public life, with regard to those he associates with himself in government. Their walk must be blameless, as his seeks to be. In the closing lines Allen pictures him as chief justice of the realm 'at his regular morning judicial sessions', expressing in his judgments 'his commitment to high moral principles'.[53]

---

[51] Kidner, p. 357.

[52] Some of the links between Prov. and the verses of Ps. 101 are 20:7 (v. 2); 11:20 (v. 4); 21:4 (v. 5); 25:5 (v. 7); 20:8 (v. 8).

[53] Allen, p. 6.

2. When? (101:2)

The question of when the psalm might originally have been composed and used has received the usual variety of answers: an annual royal ritual, a king's actual enthronement, dates as late as those of the Maccabees in the second century BC or as early as David's in the eleventh. We could imagine David uttering one of the great psalms of Book I, 'In my distress I called to the LORD . . . He parted the heavens and came down' (18:6, 9), as a thanksgiving for God's having answered his cry in this psalm, *When will you come to me?* (101:2).

But that cry cannot by itself turn 101 into the complaint of a person in distress, as a number of commentators suggest.[54] Our psalm sounds more like 15 or 24, with David newly installed in Jerusalem and eager to bring the ark of God there too, as the visible symbol of God's presence among his people. The events of 2 Samuel 6 are a fitting background for all these psalms, and an answer to the prayer *When will you come . . . ?*

That was the glad morning of David's reign. As time went by it became all too obvious that not even David could live up to the ideal he had set for himself and his successors. In many monarchies since Bible times the royal court has combined the king's household and the nation's government; *house* means the first in verse 2, the second in verse 7. David was not in fact blameless in his private life (2a–5). He did set vile things – adultery, murder – before his eyes; he failed to distance himself from his perverse son, or silence his slanders. So his public life (6–8) fell to pieces as well, and he nearly lost his kingdom, as 2 Samuel tells us at length.

But the failures of the Davidic kings were no proof that the ideal was unattainable. Rather, they pointed ahead to a future king, a Son of David yet to be born, of whom it would truly be said 'He has done everything well', and who one day would judge not Israel only, but the world, with justice (Mark 7:37; Acts 17:31).

3. Every morning (101:8)

The public face of the royal court was in Old Testament days the king's personal involvement with government and with the judiciary. In the UK we still use the term 'High Court' in connection both with parliament and with law. Verse 8 shows us David engaged *every morning* with what the

---

[54] See Allen, pp. 4–5.

Prayer Book calls 'the punishment of wickedness and vice, and . . . the maintenance of [God's] true religion, and virtue'.[55]

Since the exodus story has repeatedly come to mind throughout the psalms of Book IV, 101:8 may remind us of Exodus 18:13, and Moses going one better even than David by sitting 'to serve as judge for the people . . . from morning till evening'! (His father-in-law advised a spot of delegation before he wore himself out.) But there is something deeper here than the mere organization of a legal system. The point about the practice of government and law by David and his appointees is that he recognized his responsibilities towards his subjects. God had 'brought him to be the shepherd of his people Jacob . . . And David shepherded them with integrity of heart' (78:71–72). It was some time back, moreover, that we read Exodus 18, and our readings for Tabernacles have brought us by now to Exodus 32. What do we find there? A Moses who descends from Mount Sinai to find God's people bowing down to a golden calf, and who thereupon both administers summary justice on the sinners and pleads to God for their forgiveness.

That concern for righteousness in the community is the great burden of Psalm 101. It is a righteousness that must direct not only the life of the people but also the hearts of its leaders. What nonsense it is to claim that the private lives of politicians have no bearing on their public duties! If (for example) their spouses can't trust them, why should anybody else? But the same applies to standards in the church, and to every Christian who has any sort of responsibility for other Christians – which ought to mean all of us. We all need forgiveness for having failed in our concern for one another's righteousness, and still more for having let our own standards slip in private, where no-one but God was aware of it.

The ideal stands. The Lord can wipe the slate clean today, and the challenge is renewed.

Psalm 102

It is not only the opening of this psalm that many will find familiar, in the liturgical form 'Lord, hear our prayer, and let our cry come unto thee.' We have already come across every phrase of verses 1–2 somewhere else in the Psalter, and much of the rest of it will recall earlier psalms.

---

[55] The Prayer for the Church Militant, in the Communion Service; and see 1 Pet. 2:14.

Yet the distinctive heading introduces a psalm which taken as a whole is equally distinctive.

1. Three poems

The simplest and most obvious division of it is into three sections, verses 1–11, 12–22 and 23–28. They seem at first glance to be so different that they might almost be separate poems; though if we put our mind to suggesting titles for them in the modern fashion, we may find after all a thread that unites them.

The first eleven verses seem to be the prayer of a sick man. As keenly felt as the symptoms of his illness is his sense of isolation. Keener still is his awareness that life is slipping away; with this the section begins, with this it ends, and we might do worse than name it 'The disappearing days' (3 and 11).

The next eleven verses are about something apparently quite unrelated: the rebuilding of Zion. Nor is this a pleading prayer, like the first section. It is rather a prophecy, or at the very least a confident expectation that God is going to restore the city, to universal acclaim, at a time of his choosing. So certain is the event that we might entitle this section 'The appointed time' (13).

The final six verses, though they begin somewhat in the spirit of the first section, seem to be almost entirely about God himself, and in particular about him as the ever-living God, who brought our world into being and will one day bring it to an end. In contrast to the life of our world, still more that of our race (to say nothing of a single human life), he himself enjoys 'the endless years' of eternity; there is our third title (27).

2. Three backgrounds

We have no idea who the psalmist was, or when he lived. The first part of the psalm might almost be another version of the prayer-poem King Hezekiah wrote at the time of his near-fatal illness (Isa. 38), except that the attack on Jerusalem during his reign involved siege only, not the damage suggested by verses 14 and 16. The second part might sound more like the time of the exile – the *dust* of Zion (14) is the same word as the 'rubble' that Nehemiah found everywhere when he returned to rebuild the city (Neh. 4:2, 10) – except that the return was never a matter of condemned prisoners being released (20).

119

So the background to the composing of the psalm helps us little, since we cannot be sure what it was. Another kind of historical background, though equally uncertain, is possible, and very suggestive. That is the inclusion of Psalm 102 in Book IV of the Psalter, in a sequence that can be related to the exodus and the feast of Tabernacles.

In Exodus 32 Moses shouldered the responsibility of both executing judgment and begging mercy for Israel following her worship of the golden calf (Ps. 101). Exodus 33 shows God apparently about to abandon Israel only part-way through her journey, Moses pleading that it may not be so, and God promising him his continued favour and a new revelation of his great name Yahweh. We shall see how such themes turn out to be paralleled by Psalm 102.

Most importantly, the greater part of its third section is quoted in the New Testament, in Hebrews 1:10–12. There are no doubts at all about this parallel. The letter to the Hebrews may have been written as long after the psalm as the events of Exodus took place before it, but even so we may think of the letter as 'background', in the sense of the consistent plan of God that stands behind all Scripture. We should not imagine the Old Testament quotations in Hebrews 1 to be 'mere proof-texts wrenched out of their contexts'; as David Gooding says, 'the very opposite is true'.[56] And if the author of Hebrews has the whole of Psalm 102 in mind when he quotes three verses out of it, his Christian use of those verses must be valid background for the whole psalm.

3. The disappearing days (102:1–11)

'Fever, frailty, wasting, pain, sleeplessness, melancholy, rejection and despair' – so Kidner catalogues the symptoms of the psalmist's distress.[57] Two further effects of it are given pride of place in this, another of the psalms that succeed in combining technique and emotion. Of the psalmist's string of similes (*like*, eight times), three at the poem's centre express his isolation (6–7) and the rest at its beginning and end show how quickly his days seem to be slipping away.[58]

Since the first two sections are not in fact separate poems, being clearly and logically connected (*I wither away like grass* [11], *but you, LORD, sit*

---

[56] Gooding, p. 47.
[57] Kidner, p. 360.
[58] Counting vv. 1–2 as an introduction, note the inclusio of vv. 3–4a and 11, and the chiasmus pivoting around vv. 6–7.

enthroned for ever [12]), is the second meant to be the solution to the first? If so, it seems cold comfort: 'I am at death's door, but I suppose it's a relief to know that you at any rate will live for ever'![59]

If, however, the psalmist believes that the ever-living God is going to *rebuild Zion and appear in his glory* (the theme of section 2), but that he himself *won't be there to see it*, then whatever else may be the cause of his distress in section 1, this must be the crown of it. Earlier psalms have indicated that Old Testament believers passing through the gate of death expected to find glory on the far side (as in 73:24), but to leave behind them on this side the cherished cultus of Zion, whose very *stones [were] dear* to them (as in 6:5; the phrase is in v. 14 of our present psalm).

4. The appointed time (102:12–22)

This section also is a chiasmus, with the Lord, his name or renown, and his city of Zion at its beginning and its end, and his answering of prayer in verse 17 as its pivot. It looks forward to future events of which those who witness them will say, 'See, they have happened'; in other words, it is full of 'prophetic perfects'.

Verses 13–16, looking ahead, declare prophetically that *the appointed time has come*, and the Lord has appeared in glory and rebuilt Zion. Verses 18–20 tell us plainly that it is being *written for a future generation* that he has done these things, meaning that from the point of view of the psalmist's generation he is going to do them.

Three points should be noted about this second poem. One is the prominence of the Lord's name in it. Although the name Yahweh is used as early as Genesis 4:26, its meaning begins to be made known only in the time of Moses. When Moses first encounters God at Mount Sinai, before the exodus, he is told, 'This is my name for ever, and this is my memorial unto all generations' (Exod. 3:15 AV/RV). On his return there after the exodus, it is the name God promises to proclaim in his presence (Exod. 33:19, from our suggested Tabernacles reading). 'Name' and 'memorial' are likewise bracketed here in the psalm, in the inclusio of verses 12[60] and 21. So as something that reveals the central truth of what the Lord is, the coming restoration of Zion is on a par with the events of the exodus.

---

[59] 'The assurance of God's permanence is the answer to [the psalmist's] overwhelming sense of transience' (Allen, p. 14).

[60] RV 'memorial', where NIV has *renown*.

This brings us to the second point. Israel's rescue from Babylon was thought of as just such a parallel to her rescue from Egypt. So was that the *appointed time* of which these verses speak? No. They foresee something greater than the end of the Babylonian exile. It will be the rescue of *prisoners . . . condemned to death*, by a Lord who will *appear in his glory*. It will cause *all the kings of the earth* to revere him, *the peoples and the kingdoms* to worship him.

The third point is that this will happen in answer to prayer (17). But how that sharpens the psalmist's anguish! For his is the prayer that is here seeking an answer, and the answer is promised not to him but to *a future generation*. His days, it seems, are to *vanish like smoke*. Indeed, it is not just a case of 'Swift to its close ebbs out life's little day';[61] his grief is not so much that his life is short, as that it is to be unnaturally *shortened*. 'He has broken my strength in mid-course; he has shortened my days . . . "Do not take me away at the mid-point of my life"' (23–24 NRSV). Thus we are led into the final section of the psalm.

5. The endless years (102:23–28)

It is easy to see why so many versions and commentaries take practically the whole of this passage to be addressed by the psalmist to God. That seems to be the straightforward way of reading it. Yet one wonders what point he would be trying to make were he saying, 'Do not take me away, O my God, in the midst of my days; your years go on through all generations.' Would he be 'simply urging God not to be mean; to remember that he himself enjoys eternal life, and therefore he ought not to grudge a creature of his the few days that make up half a mortal's life'?[62]

The letter to the Hebrews, which has important things to say about other aspects of Psalm 102, illuminates this passage in particular. It adjusts the lighting, as it were, so that verse 24, which we thought we could see clearly, really does become clear. Its quotation of verses 25–27 begins like this: 'In the beginning, *Lord*, you laid the foundations of the earth' (1:10); and the whole passage from 24b to 28 is taken to be addressed, not by the psalmist to God, but by God to the Messiah.

The Christian author was not altering the Old Testament text to suit himself. It was the pre-Christian Jewish translation of the Greek Old

---

[61] Henry Lyte, 'Abide with me'.

[62] Gooding, p. 74. Gooding's section on Heb. 1:8–10 (pp. 66–77) is at the same time a penetrating exposition of the whole of Ps. 102, to which I owe much.

Testament that he was quoting, which means that already before the time of Christ there were those in Israel who understood Psalm 102 to be messianic. Its words (like those of many other psalms) were really too 'big', so to speak, to fit the Old Testament person to whom they originally applied; but when the Messiah came, they would fit him (cf. Pss 2; 16; 22; 72; etc.). The New Testament says that these Septuagint translators were right. The psalmist was speaking, and God was speaking to him, as if he were the Messiah; and the Messiah turns out to be (as New Testament theology makes crystal clear) the pre-existent Lord through whom the worlds were made.

At this point, therefore, the psalmist begins to speak unimaginably greater things than he can grasp himself. Notice that only in the first half of verse 24 is he speaking his own words; thereafter he is saying what God says to the Messiah.

> I said: 'Do not take me away, my God, in the midst of my days.' [Then he said to me:] 'Your years go on through all generations. In the beginning you laid the foundations of the earth . . . They will perish, but you remain . . . your years will never end.'

Now read the whole psalm again! See how the Old Testament poet is led to experience things, to say and to hear things, which foreshadow the story of Another, later and far greater than him. The Gospels, with the rest of the New Testament and not least the letter to the Hebrews, tell it all: as in verses 1–11, the pain, the isolation, the divine wrath (though no sin that deserved it), and the life cut short; as in verses 12–22, the new city of God and its recognition among the nations, which in his days on earth he would not see; as in verses 23–28, the anguished prayer that if it were possible he might be spared the suffering, and his Father's reassurance that both he and *the children of* [*his*] *servants* would survive not only these afflictions but even the end of the world as we know it.

So great is the plan of God for Messiah his Son, and for all who belong to him.

Psalm 103

As one of the two David psalms in Book IV, 103 belongs with 101. As a song of praise, it belongs with the three that follow, and complete this book.

As so often, it is possible to find a chiastic shape here. For example, the same words open and close the psalm, and the repeated *all* at the beginning recurs at the end, while *righteousness* in verses 6 and 17c frames the references to covenant love in verses 8 and 17b, and at the centre in verse 11. On the other hand, the poem can equally well be divided into five stanzas; that division is the basis of our own five sections. The best of Henry Lyte's metrical versions, 'Praise, my soul, the King of heaven' (see Pss 67; 84; and 91), a versification of this psalm, provides apt titles for them.

1. Ransomed, healed, restored, forgiven (103:1–5)

In spite of its heading, 103 shows less individualism than many David psalms, and in this recalls the style of the Korah Collections.[63] They, moreover, begin with the psalmist talking to himself, as he does here: in 42:5 his will is lecturing his emotions, here in 103:1–2 it is encouraging his mind. An exercise we neglect to our cost! Practising it, we may enjoy the vigour of eagles (5) – a contrast to the moping trio of pelican, owl and sparrow in 102:6–7.[64]

The words *forget not all his benefits* echo Deuteronomy (6:12; 8:11), and are the first hint that this psalm also will be pointing back to the days of Moses. Forgiveness is the first benefit, with the raw exposure of Israel's need of it in the golden calf incident in Exodus 32. Still needed repeatedly by all of us, it is given instantly to the sinner who repents.

Healing is the second, another exodus promise (cf. Exod. 15:26, and Isa. 53:4 as quoted in Matt. 8:17). The way God deals with sickness differs from the way he deals with sin. In the case of this benefit, the timing is up to him, as Scripture plainly shows; he often delays it until the total healing of the life to come. If the psalmist here is David, he knows all about this difference through the illness of the child born of his adultery with Bathsheba: 'The LORD has taken away your sin . . . But . . . the son born to you will die' (2 Sam. 12:13–14).

Through the same traumatic experience David was well aware of the third benefit. He had been redeemed *from the pit*: 'The LORD has taken away your sin,' the prophet told him; 'you are not going to die.' A look back to the rescue from Egypt, Israel 'ransomed' (to use Lyte's term) from a living death, broadens the meaning; a look forward to the New Testament,

---

[63] See p. 1.147.

[64] The AV's guess at three birds that we cannot identify for sure.

to 'the redemption that is in Christ Jesus' (Rom. 3:24 NRSV), deepens it immeasurably.

Finally the believer is 'restored', satisfied and renewed, by the Lord's covenant love and compassion, that is, the divine commitment and affection, the will and the heart of God.

2. Grace and favour to our fathers (103:6–10)

The redeeming work of God may be summed up in terms of verse 6. It is *righteousness*, rather than merely the NRSV's 'vindication': as Kidner well says, 'He puts straight not only the record . . . but the whole situation and the people concerned.'[65]

Justice for all the oppressed has in our day become the slogan of many well-meaning unbelievers. But if they wanted to know what God meant by it they would have to turn to those in Scripture to whom *he made known his ways* – in the words of the hymn, to 'our fathers in distress'. Specifically, it is the story of the exodus, of Israel in the time of Moses, that explains how God puts straight everything, and everyone, that goes wrong. And as in Book IV we arrive at Psalm 103, our parallel readings in Exodus arrive, right on cue, at chapter 34. Of several references here to the historical account,[66] the crucial one is verse 8 of the psalm. Like 86:15 before it and 145:8 after it, this quotes the proclamation before Moses, on his final ascent of Mount Sinai, of the name Yahweh, which summed up all God's 'work of righteousness' since he first came down to his people in their misery and enslavement. 'He passed in front of Moses, proclaiming, "The LORD, the LORD, the compassionate and gracious God, slow to anger, abounding in love and faithfulness"' (Exod. 34:6).

This tells us that what God was dealing with was Israel's helplessness and (still more) her sinfulness – that is, there was something in her for him to be compassionate about, and something for him to be angry about. It tells us that he is both Judge and Saviour, both accusing and rescuing. And it tells us that his justice is met and satisfied by his mercy. He is 'slow to chide and swift to bless', as the hymn puts it. He *will not always accuse*; his appearing as Judge is 'a passing mode',[67] while his character as Saviour is permanent.

---

[65] Kidner, pp. 365–366.

[66] Besides Exod. 34:6 (= v. 8), we may notice 34:7 (vv. 10–12); 34:9 (v. 3); and 34:10–11 (v. 18).

[67] Motyer, p. 553.

125

3. Well our feeble frame he knows (103:11–14)

In verses 6–10 the psalmist was concerned with the Lord's attitude to the sin and the helplessness of his people. Now in verses 11–14 he tells us how it looks from their point of view – as we might say, from our point of view.

First our *transgressions* (12), a word which picks up *sins* and *iniquities* in verse 10, and with them looks back to 32:1–2 in the Psalter and to 34:7a in Exodus.[68] His covenant love, not any atonement we might try to make, puts everything straight in this respect. For the method we look elsewhere; the psalmist is focusing on the fact. *As high as the heavens are above the earth* – how great the love that takes on the fearful task of removing our sins! *As far as the east is from the west* – how effectively it does it![69]

Contrasting with these images of distance is one of closeness. Illustrating the Lord's concern for our helplessness is the domestic picture of the loving father and his children. It is a picture not to be altered, still less abandoned, when modern opinion-makers find it quaint, unrealistic or even offensive. Such a father knows his children intimately. Although he has high ideals for them, he makes allowance for their weaknesses and their immaturity – in Lyte's words, for 'our feeble frame'.

4. Mortals rise and perish, God endures (103:15–18)

Lyte versified this stanza along with the rest, in lines that modern hymnals omit: 'Frail as summer's flower we flourish: / Blows the wind, and it is gone.' Perhaps the weakest verse of his hymn, it contains what is certainly the weakest line: 'But while mortals rise and perish, / *God endures unchanging on.*' There is no denying that the psalmist makes the positive point far more strongly: *From everlasting to everlasting the LORD's love is with those who fear him, and his righteousness with their children's children.* True, in the proclamation of the Lord's name in Exodus 34, as in both statements of the second commandment (Exod. 20:5; Deut. 5:9), it is his punishment, not his love, which is said to affect 'the third and fourth generation'. But even in those three places his love to 'thousands' may mean what in yet another place, Deuteronomy 7:9, it really does mean: that 'his covenant of love' persists,

---

[68] See AV/RV/NRSV; NIV varies its translations of the three Hebrew words.

[69] At what stage in history did people realize how much better this east–west image is than the north–south one would be? You can go only so far to the north (or south), whereas you can keep going east (or west) indefinitely. Our sins have been removed an infinite distance.

not just to three or four, but (as the NIV indicates) 'to a thousand *generations* of those who love him and keep his commandments' (cf. Exod. 20:6 RV mg.).

Compared to this, human life is ephemeral, here today and gone tomorrow. It is likened to grass or to the *flower of the field* not only in the famous passages in the prophets and in the Gospels (Isa. 40:6–8; Matt. 6:28–30), but in the first psalm of this book (90:5–6), and more recently still in 102:4, 11, as well as here.

If the contrast in the phrase 'Mortals rise and perish, God endures' was not in itself any great comfort to the psalmist in 102:11–12,[70] why should it be any different here? Yet the two psalms do differ markedly in tone. The assurance that God's love will be as real to his descendants as it is to him does here lift the psalmist's heart. Perhaps in 103 he has grasped the messianic gist of 102:23–28: that because of the death of One whose days are indeed 'cut short', but whose years nonetheless 'go on through all generations', the same paradox is true of all who belong to him. It is the resurrection doctrine which Jesus tells us was implicit already in Exodus 3:15.[71] It is what makes these verses such a powerful message of hope at countless funeral services, and points mourners to Christ. How can even death pluck *those who fear him* out of a love which is everlasting?

5. Dwellers all in time and space (103:19–22)

With the opening verse of this final stanza, 103 takes up the theme of the kingship psalms, 93 – 100. What especially stirs our psalmist is the fact that the Lord *rules over all*, that is, over everything, the entire creation. He shows at once that by this he means more than the world and the people we see around us, more than the hidden structures of the physical globe or of human society, more even than the entire universe of which our planet is such a tiny part. His mind flies at once to the angels of God, who although awesome spirit beings, *mighty ones* who inhabit a heavenly dimension outside the scope of scientific observation, are just as much the Lord's creatures as we are.

The *heavenly hosts* may be another term for the angels, or he may be moving across into the observable universe and thinking of the stars.

---

[70] See pp. 2.120–121.

[71] See p. 1.17.

They too are God's servants, in that he has planned every position and motion for them, and throughout space they *do his will*.[72] Certainly by verse 22 his call embraces every creature heavenly and earthly, 'dwellers all in time and space', and finally includes himself.

For as in an orchestra, each individual voice is as necessary as the total sound. Each and all find fulfilment in making the music the composer intends. The most heartfelt praise of any is due from those who are conscious of having been desperately out of tune, but who (to revert to the plain speaking of the first stanza) now know that all their sins are forgiven and all their afflictions are to be healed.

Psalm 104

It says something about the psalms of Book IV that they should have given rise to so many of our most enduring English hymns. Hard on the heels of 'Praise, my soul, the King of heaven' comes 'O worship the King, all glorious above.' Fine hymns both, they differ in one respect: Lyte's version of 103 works steadily through the whole of his psalm, whereas Sir Robert Grant's of 104 is subject to a sudden acceleration halfway through. His first verse represents the psalm's verse 1, his second its verses 2 and 3, his third its verses 5–9, while his fourth sums up the next twenty-one, and his fifth and sixth are his own rounding off of the whole.

1. Psalm 104 and Genesis

What Grant did with the psalm is very like what the psalmist himself had done with the biblical story of creation. That was plainly his basis, and it is striking how he follows the order of the days of creation in Genesis 1. Not, however, their proportion! Verse 2a corresponds to Day One and verses 2b–4 to Day Two; then a long section (5–18) is devoted to Day Three, five verses (19–23) to Day Four, and two (25–26) to Day Five, and only to half of it at that. What God made on Day Six, namely human beings and the animals, had already begun to appear back in verse 11.

In other words, the psalm is very far from being simply a versified form of Genesis 1. The verbs in 104:1, literally 'You *have become* great, you *have*

---

[72] George Meredith called them 'the brain of heaven', 'the army of unalterable law' ('Lucifer in Starlight').

clothed yourself with majesty', align it with the royal psalms earlier in this book, in that they too speak of the Lord who '*has become* king'. We noted in 93:1, 'The Lord reigns, he is robed in majesty', that such words describe an act, not just a fact.[73] I suggested there that the creation, and not some more recent event, was in mind, and that is explicitly the case here. Yet an account of a past event is exactly what 104 is not. Certainly it looks back to what happened at the beginning, but really it is celebrating the way creation works now. That is why its proportions differ from those of Genesis 1.

2. The marriage of form and freedom

Rhapsodic, exuberant, free: so the commentators describe the poetry which here takes flight from the picturesque but stately language of Genesis. However, we are well aware by now that for the psalmists freedom and form are in no way incompatible. Bearing in mind the related techniques of inclusio and chiasmus, and certain key words that recur in the course of the poem, we begin to see in it a shape which tallies also with our psalmist's developing themes.

First, the key words. In the diagram below, 'Blessing' represents the verb in *Praise the Lord, my soul*, in verses 1 and 35c.[74] Most, though not quite all, of the instances of the verb 'make' and the noun 'works' represent two Hebrew words which are related, and can be covered by the one word 'making'. (One of them figures in the pivotal v. 19, though there it has got lost in the NIV translation.) *Earth* is obviously a third key word, given the poem's theme, and occurs frequently.[75] The fourth is 'man', used of course in its generic sense, as in Genesis 1 (cf. NIV *people*).

Combining the evident sense of the psalm with the occurrence of these four words brings to light a remarkably well-organized chiastic structure, in which we can readily follow the psalmist's train of thought out from verse 1 to verse 19 and back again to verse 35.[76] A division into five sections, plotted against the verse numbers, may be set out as follows:

---

[73] See p. 2.110.

[74] Not, however, the *Praise* in v. 35d, which is a different word and probably belongs with 105, not 104.

[75] *'Ădāmâ* once; *'ereṣ* seven times.

[76] See pp. 1.31–32. For many of the points made here, see Allen, p. 32.

Blessing	Earth	Making	Man	
Blessing				1
		Making		4
	Earth			5
	Earth			
		Making		}13
			Man	14
		Making		19
			Man	23
		Making		}24
	Earth			
	Earth			30
		Making		31
Blessing				35

3. What God is and what he does (104:1–4)

'Bless the LORD, O my soul' (1 NRSV). Both the Greek and the Latin words for 'bless' are literally 'well-speak',[77] and though that idea is not what lies behind their Hebrew counterpart *bārak*, it is a good way of describing what in effect it means. If I 'speak well' of you, it has of course to do with good things regarding you, not with the fine way I say them! In Scripture, God first blesses us in Genesis 1:3, when he 'speaks' light into existence – something good for us. We bless him when we 'declare [his] praises' (1 Pet. 2:9) – something good about him.

So what good things does the psalmist say about this God, the Maker of light on creation's first day, and of the sky, and all that the light shows us in the sky, on its second day?

In defiance of many notions, ancient and modern, as to what God is and does, three facts converge here. First, there is the 'awesome wonder' of those who 'see the stars' and 'hear the rolling thunder', and who are moved to cry, 'How great thou art!'[78] But such a cry does not in itself imply anything about '*who* thou art'. Millions have a sort of pantheistic belief that God is somehow 'in' or 'behind' everything. But the psalmist goes much further. He is very clear about a second fact. He knows that the God who makes a garment of the light, a tent of the sky and his palace floor of the

---

[77] Gk *eulogeō*, Lat. *benedico*.
[78] Carl Boberg, tr. Stuart Hine, 'How great thou art'.

rain clouds is the One who made light and sky and clouds in the first place, the Maker of everything.

The third and most important fact is this. The God whose presence we sense in the world around us, the God whose power we believe brought it into being, is the One whom the psalmist calls 'Yahweh my God' – the God of Israel, the God of the Bible. And he is of course the God and Father of our Lord Jesus Christ. It is he 'whose robe is the light, whose canopy space'. With him, and with no other, the God of creation in both its senses – omnipresent in all things that are made, and omnipotent in the making of them – is to be identified.

4. Making and maintaining a habitable world (104:5–13)

Knowing of the widespread belief in Bible times that the natural, original state of the world was chaos, we are not surprised to find even the psalmists fearing floods and deep water (42:7; 69:1–2) and rejoicing when the Lord shows he controls them (29:10; 93:4). This he did in Genesis 1 on the second day of creation, separating the water below from the water vapour above, and on its third day, defining the boundary between sea and land. Thus he literally put the waters in their place.

What does our psalmist make of this?

He reverses the pagan picture of earth as a vulnerable island threatened by an overwhelming waste of waters. He depicts instead, in the words of Grant's hymn, the earth 'stablished . . . fast by a changeless decree, / And round it . . . cast, like a mantle, the sea'. Then, unexpectedly, he describes the sending of the waters *to the place . . . assigned for them* not with the perfect tense as a once-for-all event, but with the imperfect, the continuous tense; God is even now making sure they stay there. And best of all, in verses 10–13 he shows God actually harnessing the threat and making it serve his own ends. It becomes a blessing, in the form of springs, the waters below, and rain, the waters above.

5. People in the midst of the makings (104:14–23)

People in verse 14 and *people* in verse 23 frame this central section, and the 'making' of the moon to mark the seasons, in verse 19, is the pivot of the whole poem.[79]

---

[79] Neither *makes* (14) nor *work* (23) represents the 'making' root (*ʿāśâ/maʿăśeh*) that we are noting, whereas v. 19 does have it: 'He *made* the moon for the seasons' (NASB, sticking more closely to the Heb. than practically any other translation).

Here, the psalmist's starting point in the Genesis account is the second part of Day Three (plants and trees) and Day Four (sun and moon). Again he is updating the creation story, concerned less with what happened then than with the way things are now. So as he looks at what God made on the third and fourth days he sees a world already populated by the animals and humans made on the sixth day.

In doing so, he reveals a way of thinking that must leave even the most arrogant humanist gasping. It was not original to the psalmist, for he had found it in Genesis 1. The plants and the trees of Day Three (v. 11 of that chapter) are there, God says on Day Six, for humanity's benefit (1:29). The sun and moon of Day Four 'serve as signs to mark sacred times, and days and years' (1:14); again, for the benefit of humanity – who else would note the signs? This section of the psalm has a similar thrust. God's purpose in making trees and plants was to feed the creatures of the sixth day! His object in making a sun and a moon was to give those creatures regular cycles of dark and light, and of months and seasons! Well, it is of a piece with what the first David Collection told us, almost a hundred psalms ago, about humankind as the crown of creation (8:3–8).

For these verses do remind us that though God designed the earth for both humanity and the animal kingdom, the former is the greater. Birds and beasts *seek their food*, and their lodging too, direct *from God* (21). But humans are farmers, not just hunter-gatherers (14). God's gift to them of the three staple commodities of Bible times, wine, oil and bread (15), is in fact a gift both of the three plants, vine, olive tree and grain, and also of the ability to make something of them. Because God the Maker has made men and women in his own image, humans in their turn become makers.

6. A completion and a summary (104:24–30)

Although the third verse of Grant's hymn, about the stability of the earth, is based on verses 5–6 of the psalm, its opening line ('The earth, with its store of wonders untold') comes from verse 24. This fourth section begins, as the corresponding second section ended, with *your works*, or 'makings', and will give us our final glimpse of *your creatures*, or rather 'your riches'.[80]

It is to the sea that the psalmist turns to complete his survey. Three things at once capture our attention. As elsewhere, so here when he

---

[80] Literally, *his work* (13) is 'your works', and *creatures* (24) is 'possessions' or 'riches'.

considers the sea, he is interested more in the way creation is now than in the way it came about; for *There the ships go to and fro* – certainly a post-Eden development! Second, he will be going only as far as Day Five of the creation story, and only the first part of it, at that; for his view of creation as it now is has already noticed the birds of Day Five and the animals and humans of Day Six.

Third, the sea has become for him something almost benign. Even the Leviathan, greatest of all sea creatures (in Job 41 probably the crocodile, but here no doubt something like the whale), is almost Disneyfied,[81] an object of terror yet delight, *formed to frolic there*. The seas may still lift up their 'pounding waves' (93:3), but chaos has been tamed. Humankind, the crown of creation, actually use these waters for their own purposes: their ships 'have turned the oceans into highways instead of barriers'.[82]

Verses 27–30 are a summary of the works of the Lord, his making of the entire animal kingdom and of its environment. Again the psalmist is concerned not so much with what God did as with what he does. During their lifetimes all living creatures are sustained by him, and those lifetimes are themselves begun and terminated as he gives and then withdraws the breath of life. Significantly, the psalmist speaks not of life and death, but of death and life. His Creator is the continuing Sustainer; as each passing generation is succeeded by the next, we see him *renew the face of the ground*.

7. What endures and what vanishes (104:31–35)

In the overall structure of the psalm these verses correspond to the opening section. The works ('makings') of verse 31 and the praise ('blessings') of verse 35c mirror the blessing and making of verses 1 and 4. Of the other two key words, *earth* provides this final section with an inner frame (32 and 35a), and the *people* ('man') of the middle section, verses 14–23, figure here as the psalmist himself on the one hand, and the wicked on the other.

The believer's perspective on the world is radically different from the unbeliever's. They might agree, of course, on the impermanence of it. The psalmist believes that the God who made it so that *it can never be*

---

[81] Cf. Monstro, the whale that swallows the Jonah-like seafarers in Walt Disney's 1940 film *Pinocchio*.

[82] Kidner, p. 372.

moved (5) has only to look at it in a certain tone of voice, as they say, for it to tremble (32). He can, and one day will, unmake it. But for the believer something is permanent, and that is the glory of the Lord. And the believer's praise to the Lord will also be unending (33) – certainly lifelong, and the Psalter has suggested often enough that that life will outlast the death of the body, and indeed the death of the universe.

What a curious discord seems to be struck by verse 35a–b, *May sinners vanish from the earth and the wicked be no more!* It seems that an ancient malignity has resurfaced from Book I. Yet in the context it makes perfect sense. Something went wrong in Eden, long before ships began to go to and fro: 'Disproportion'd sin / Jarr'd against natures chime, and with harsh din / Broke the fair musick that all creatures made / To their great Lord.'[83] Sin, not the elimination of it, is the discord. That is what must not be allowed to endure. And if it is objected that the psalmist wants not just sin, but sinners, to *be no more*, God has offered a way for the one to be detached from the other, namely by repentance and forgiveness. It is those who refuse to leave their sin who cannot but be destroyed together with it. We might properly say that Psalm 104 as a whole is a picture of what creation was meant to be, and a kind of sketch of what it one day will be; and the discordant verse 35 is, ironically, a tiny pointer to the cross of Christ, through which the new creation will come into being.

8. Psalm 104 and Exodus

Have the compilers of Book IV deserted Exodus at last? Yes and no. These psalms follow that narrative no further than the proclamation of the Lord's name in Exodus 34:6, quoted in 103:8. But 104:5–18, looking back to creation's third day in Genesis 1, does look back also to Moses, being very close in its wording to the preview he gives to Israel, in Deuteronomy 8:7–9 and 11:11–15, of the Promised Land that lies before her. The springs in the valleys and hills, the grain and wine and oil, the grass for the cattle, all are there.

That perhaps is the place of 104 in a Tabernacles sequence. For Israel in Egypt the domination of sin and wickedness has seemed interminable. But the compassionate, gracious God of 103:8 has brought it to an end, and the possibility of a new life, life as God meant it to be from the beginning,

---

[83] John Milton, 'At a Solemn Musick'.

lies ahead. Compared with those coming days, 'as many as the days that the heavens are above the earth' (Deut. 11:21), the Egyptian captivity will seem in hindsight no more than a passing discord, like that single couplet at the end of our psalm's thirty-five verses.

Not that this undervalues what it costs to deal with sin. The exodus story as a whole is as we have seen a model of the New Testament story of redemption, and points in all sorts of ways to the cross. The slain Lamb will be for ever not at the periphery but at the centre of heaven. But that belongs rather to psalms like 22. This one relates to the New Testament somewhat differently.

9. Psalm 104 and the New Testament

It is quoted directly only in Hebrews 1:7: 'Of the angels [God] says, "He makes his angels winds, and his servants flames of fire"' (NRSV). Set beside its original, Psalm 104:4, the oddity of the quotation is obvious. Like God, the New Testament author is 'speaking of the angels' (see NIV), and of their being used as, or even turned into, winds; the psalmist is speaking of the winds, and of their being used as, or turned into, God's angels or messengers.[84] But in the psalm either version would make the same point, which is that with the exception of his Son, all beings, animate or inanimate, are subject to God as his creatures.

It is of that supreme greatness and power, and the never-flagging exercise of it, that the New Testament and the psalm speak with one voice. 'Since the creation of the world God's invisible qualities – his eternal power and divine nature – have been clearly seen, being understood from what has been made,' says Paul in Romans 1:20. The voice of creation speaks to all, and has a convicting power, 'so that people are without excuse'.

It also speaks particularly to believers, and to them it is a voice of encouragement. So Peter commends the teaching of a scripture like Psalm 104. Seeing how wonderfully God has made, and still maintains, this extraordinary universe, his troubled people should learn to 'commit themselves to their faithful Creator'. The implication of 1 Peter 4:19, the only place in the New Testament where he is given this title, is that he can be relied on to do even more wonderful things for them.

---

[84] Heb. 1:7 is following LXX, so the question is whether the Gk or the Heb. version of the OT is the more correct here. The debate is inconclusive and perhaps unimportant.

Frail children of dust, and feeble as frail,
In thee do we trust, nor find thee to fail;
Thy mercies how tender, how firm to the end,
Our Maker, Defender, Redeemer, and Friend!

Psalm 105

The last two psalms of Book IV are non-identical twins. Fittingly for the close of this Exodus Collection, each is a review of the exodus story, but the contrast between the positive tone of 105 and the negative tone of 106 could not be greater.

1. Form and freedom again

While short usually means simple where the structure of psalms is concerned, long does not necessarily mean complicated. The telling of a story, which is what 105 and 106 do, is a relatively straightforward process. Although the techniques of Hebrew poetry are evident here in 105 as they were in 104,[85] it is the flow of the story that chiefly determines the shape of this poem. Compared with the structure of 78, which told a similar story in a much more complex way in Book III, that of our present psalm is simple and orderly, and sticks closely (though often with considerable streamlining) to the sequence of events in the historical books from Genesis to Joshua.

As before, the combination of poetic technique and narrative flow suggests certain divisions in the poem. It seems to fall readily into four sections.

Verses 1–11 are a call to God's people to remember his great acts, beginning with *the covenant he made with Abraham*, especially the promise of a homeland for his descendants.

Verses 12–23 describe first how Abraham's family was actually living there already, but as nomadic *strangers* in the land, and then how circumstances led them to migrate to Egypt.

Genesis has provided the psalm's background up to this point. Now it moves into Exodus, and verses 24–36 cover Israel's experience in Egypt until the night of her rescue, at the time of the last of the ten plagues.

---

[85] See Allen, p. 46.

The final section, verses 37–45, follows her journey from Egypt back to Canaan, the narrative from Exodus to Joshua, and the promise from its making to its fulfilment.

2. Remember, remember (105:1–11)

'Oh yes, I remembered your birthday. I didn't do anything about it, but I did remember it!'

In Bible language, remembering (like hearing) is not just something that happens in the head. Really to remember, really to hear, implies that you do something about what has come to your memory or your ear.

The two rememberings in these verses are both cases in point. When in verse 5 Israel is urged to remember, this is the last of a string of imperatives. It sums up those that have gone before. 'Thank the Lord, proclaim his name, declare his deeds, sing, praise, tell,' says the psalmist; 'glory in him, rejoice in him, look to him, seek his face; in a word, *remember.*'

What is to be remembered is put in a nutshell in verse 5: God's wonders, miracles and judgments. It will be opened out in the rest of the psalm, and is set forth in full detail, of course, in the historical books from Genesis onwards.

In verse 8 Israel is assured that with the Lord, too, remembering is a matter of action, not just of memory. In his case, what is to be remembered is the covenant he made with the patriarchs Abraham, Isaac and Jacob, the ancestors of the nation. Genesis recounts all three incidents (Gen. 17:1–8; 26:2–5; 28:10–15).

Why, we may ask, should the psalmist concentrate on the 'land' aspect of the covenant? Perhaps it is because the promise of countless descendants is by definition not measurable; with the promise of a specific land, you know when they have got there. So 'place' provides the framework, and verses 9–11 will be fulfilled in verses 42–44, demonstrating how God actively and effectively remembers his covenant; while 'people' provide the action, as they discover in experience what it is that they are to remember in the days to come.

3. From Canaan to Egypt (105:12–23)

Verses 12–15 are a bird's-eye view of thirty chapters of Genesis (Gen. 12 – 41; vv. 14–15 allude to Gen. 12:10–20; 20:1–18; 26:1–11). Abraham, 'called to go to a place he would later receive as his inheritance', says the New Testament, 'made his home in the promised land like a stranger in a foreign country; he lived in tents, as did Isaac and Jacob, who were heirs with him of the same promise' (Heb. 11:8–9). Their travels were not aimless, and they were certainly not lost, as the word *wandered* might suggest; the psalmist's very point is that God was guiding them and keeping them. For three generations they simply adopted the nomadic life led by so many people in earlier times.

The famine of verses 16–19, which would eventually bring the family to Egypt (Gen. 42 – 50), took place some years after God 'had sent a man ahead of them' (17 NRSV) by causing Joseph to be sold as a slave by his brothers, and taken there (Gen. 37 – 40). What *came to pass*, and in doing so put an end to his enslavement, was any or all of the half-dozen significant dreams which figure in Joseph's story – his own, his fellow prisoners', the Egyptian king's – and through which *the word of the* LORD came with power to a new generation and an alien culture (Gen. 37:5–11; 40:4–23; 41:1–40).

The pharaoh's admiration for his ability to interpret these, and the consequent giddy rise from obscurity and the prison to fame and the premiership, are the theme of the last third of this section, verses 20–22, corresponding to the last nine chapters of Genesis.

Verse 23 tells us what God's objective was through these years. It says, in effect, 'That was how Israel came to be in Egypt'; and if the section is reckoned to end with this verse, it provides with verse 12 a very revealing inclusio. The people who thus moved from Canaan to Egypt had been *gērîm* when they were nomads in the one, and were still *gērîm* now that they were settlers in the other. Today we should call *gērîm* 'temporary residents' or 'resident aliens'. The New Testament brings together the words 'aliens', 'pilgrims' and 'strangers';[86] perhaps the simplest modern equivalent is 'expatriates' – apt enough, since the psalm is about the bringing of Israel to her *patria*, her homeland.

4. In Egypt (105:24–36)

Because the psalmist's declared interest is the miracles and judgments of God, verses 24–36 deal almost entirely with the final days of the Israelites' prolonged stay in Egypt, the days of the plagues. The greater part of their stay is covered in two verses, where first their becoming *fruitful* and

---

[86] Almost alone among the versions, RV translates the three Gk words consistently: 'strangers/sojourners' (Eph. 2:19), 'strangers/pilgrims' (Heb. 11:13), 'sojourners/pilgrims' (1 Pet. 2:11). These references provided New Testament 'background' to Ps. 39:12; see p. 1.134.

numerous is quoted from Exodus 1:7, and where then the changed attitude of the Egyptian government and its enslaving of them is a summary of the rest of that chapter.

Verse 26 introduces the men of the hour: Moses the Lord's servant and Aaron his chosen one, as Abraham and the sons of Jacob were in verse 6, and both of them sent by God, as Joseph was in verse 17. The sending is described at length in Exodus 3 and 4 (note 3:10; 4:10–16).

The purpose of it is that through these men the Lord should demonstrate his power in Egypt. The list of the plagues is in poetic form, neither complete nor chronological. It frames six earlier plagues between the ninth and the tenth. By the ninth (28), Pharaoh's counsellors had got the message at last and were advising him to come to terms with Israel ('they did not rebel against [God's] words' any longer,[87] after he had *turned their waters into blood* and so on). By the tenth (36), even Pharaoh saw the folly of holding out further (Exod. 10:7; 11:3, 8–10; 12:29–36). In grim counterpoint to the eighth plague, when locusts 'devoured *all* the vegetation' (35 NRSV), confirming the advice of the officials, came this last one, when God *struck down **all** the firstborn* (36), finally convincing the king.

5. From Egypt to Canaan (105:37–45)

The account of Israel's return from Egypt to Canaan is as streamlined as the rest. The next seven chapters of Exodus, or for that matter the next three or four books of the Bible, are condensed into just five verses.

What has been left out? Everything negative. There is nothing about the journey as such, nothing about its length, nothing about the sins of Israel which made it forty years longer than it need have been. Some positive things have been omitted, too: the giving of the law, the making of the tabernacle.

What on the other hand does the psalmist highlight? The wealth and well-being of the escaping slaves (37), their absolutely definite break with Egypt (38), and the provision of all they would need on their way to the Promised Land: the pillar of cloud and fire – 'light by night and shade by day,' sings John Newton[88] – and miraculous food and water (39–41).

---

[87] V. 28 NRSV mg. (cf. AV/RV), following the Heb. text, and implying pluperfects in the verbs of vv. 29–35. In fact God had sent seven plagues, and was threatening the eighth, when the Egyptian officials finally gave up rebelling against him (Exod. 10:7).

[88] John Newton, 'Glorious things of thee are spoken'.

Thus the forty gruelling years in the wilderness are both telescoped and seen in their best light. Scarcely is Israel *brought out . . . with shouts of joy* than she has reached her destination. The promise at the beginning of the psalm (6–12) and the fulfilment at the end (42–44) are described in almost identical terms: Abraham the Lord's servant receives the promise, and his people, the Lord's chosen ones, receive the fulfilment, being given the lands of the Canaanite nations as their inheritance.

6. All the constellations of the storie

Behind George Herbert's quaint seventeenth-century spelling lie great depths of perception. He compares Scripture to a starry sky; he longs to know how all its

> lights combine
> And the configurations of their glorie!
> Seeing not onely how each verse doth shine,
> But all the constellations of the storie.[89]

The outlines drawn on sky maps since ancient times, joining up the stars and making the constellations, are of course imaginary. The connections between the 'lights' of Scripture, however, are real; and as we look again at Psalm 105 with that in mind, a pattern emerges, and we discern the shape of this cluster of stars.

First and foremost, the psalm is showing us the Lord himself. He who is effectively the object of all the verbs in verses 1–6 becomes the subject of dozens more throughout the rest of the psalm. Whatever Abraham or Moses or Egypt or Israel may be doing, it is he who promises, rebukes, sends, makes, turns, speaks, brings, gives. He takes the initiative and is the moving force behind all that happens.

That means, second, that to achieve his aims he will when necessary use unpleasant means. He caused famine in order to bring Jacob's family to Egypt, where he had already sent Joseph (to slavery and prison!) so that he would be in the right place at the right time to save them. He made Israel numerous, and Egypt apprehensive, and brought about a worse slavery than Joseph's for that later generation, before sending Moses to save *them*.

---

[89] George Herbert, 'The H. Scriptures, I'.

Third, all of this is his 'remembering' of his covenant. What he has planned and promised, that he will infallibly do, however complex, protracted and puzzling his methods may seem.

7. What was it for?

A kind of inclusio frames the psalm as a whole, commands that require a response. 'Praise, proclaim, remember,' urge verses 1–5; *keep his precepts and observe his laws*, says verse 45.

This final verse expects those who first inherit Canaan to be as faithful to the Lord in their new land as he has been to them in bringing them to it. The opening verses have gone further. They expect praise as well as obedience, and that from a much later generation of Israel. They are taking for granted a sense of national solidarity down the centuries: how else can the singing, the glorying, the rejoicing, be real and heartfelt?

So too with the call to proclaim the Lord's name, as verse 1a could and perhaps should be read.[90] Israelites of every successive generation are to *make known among the nations* the deeds of God at the exodus as something *he has done* for *them*. And so with the call to remember: it concerns events that took place perhaps fifteen centuries before Christ, but ever afterwards Israel will say 'These things happened to *us*.'

Thus we find a large part of this psalm reckoned to be especially apt for the setting up of David's sanctuary in Jerusalem, and there is similar praise and thanksgiving when rebuilding begins after the exile (cf. 1 Chr. 16:4, 8–22; Ezra 3:11; Neh. 12:24).

Our culture has not yet turned its back on the past so completely as to destroy this sense of historical continuity. Some in England would say even today that 'we' won the battle of Waterloo in 1815, and must not be surprised when some in Ireland still want to avenge what 'we' did to 'them' in Cromwell's campaign of 1649, or indeed Henry II's of 1171.

But where is one to draw the line that separates us from our forebears? Whatever the answer among the nations of the twenty-first century may be, the history of Israel says, 'Nowhere.' Nowhere *at all*: together with the Israel of David and Ezra, what we might call the new Israel, that is, the Israel of God in our New Testament days, remembers the exodus not as something that happened to somebody else, but as something that happened to 'us'.

---

90 'Call on' here (NRSV, AV) is the same word as 'proclaim' in Exod. 33:19; 34:5–6.

8. Descendants of Abraham his servant

The phrase *a thousand generations*, in verse 8,[91] is considerably more startling than it seems at first glance. A figure of speech, granted, and not meant literally, but what is it intended to convey? A period not only much longer, but *many times* longer, than that which elapsed between Abraham and Christ (Matt. 1:17). It is in those terms – 30,000 years! – that Scripture thinks of the reach of the covenant. It will assuredly still be valid far, far beyond our time, if the world should last so long.

For with the coming of Christ God was remembering, not abandoning, his ancient covenant (Luke 1:68–75). He was renewing it. The meaning of the phrase 'offspring of his servant Abraham' (6 NRSV) was immeasurably widened, to include all, Gentile as well as Jew, who belong to Christ (Gal. 3:29). And the promise of the land was seen to be the promise of 'a better country – a heavenly one' (Heb. 11:16).

In this way Psalm 105 becomes our heritage as well as that of Old Testament Israel. Christians too can say concerning the events of the exodus, 'It was we who were brought out of that old life of slavery into a new life of freedom, to "keep his precepts and observe his laws".' The difference is that they can look back also on the greater rescue of which that was but a picture, their redemption through the death of Christ. The greater the debt, the greater the challenge of the psalm's opening: to proclaim and to praise, to look to his strength and to seek his face always, and actively and repeatedly to *remember the wonders he has done.*

Psalm 106

Like the last psalm, this one is a review of the exodus years. It begins later, not with Abraham but with the exodus itself and Israel's departure from Egypt, and ends later, looking ahead into the period of the judges and perhaps further.

Again the style of writing and the development of the theme combine to suggest a possible division. Praise and remembrance (1–5) precede a very condensed account of the plagues and the crossing of the Red Sea (6–12). Conversely, working backwards from the end of the psalm – it is another chiasmus – we find remembrance and praise (43–48) following an overview of events in Canaan after Israel's arrival there (34–42). This

---

[91] See on 103:15–18, and Deut. 7:9.

Canaanite section corresponds to the Egyptian section near the beginning. In between is a series of six episodes taken from the story of the desert wanderings, all of them much to Israel's discredit (13–33).

1. Praise and remembrance (106:1–5)

Of the twin psalms 105 and 106, this one is disguised; only with verse 7 will we begin to see the family resemblance, and the differences. At the outset it is not easy for form criticism to decide how to classify it. One kind of psalm is suggested by the thanks and praise of verses 1–2, another by the echo of the wisdom books in *Blessed are those who* in verse 3, another by the *Come to my aid* of verse 4.

Read to the end of the psalm, then return to the beginning, and you realize that these five verses are in no way a group of unrelated clichés. 'The long catalogue of failures which will dominate the psalm'[92] sheds light back on to the call of verse 1, and gives it a poignant depth. Israel really does have cause to thank God for his goodness and enduring love when she recognizes that she has been so undeserving. Verse 2 is no mere rhetorical question; the only people who can *fully declare his praise* are those who *always do what is right* (v. 3 echoes 15:2–5 and 24:4–5, each following a similar question) – or those who realize that they don't, and that they will never do so without his aid (4).

Psalm 1 is recalled both by the *Blessed* of verse 3 and by the balance shown in verses 4 and 5 between the individual and the community. As far back as 1:5, in the preamble to the Psalter, the 'assembly of the righteous' was introduced, and the psalmist as a member of it.[93] The author of 106 likewise has a personal relationship with the Lord, yet sees his own need and the Lord's meeting of it as being bound up with the church's need and the Lord's meeting of that. *Come to my aid when you save them* both distinguishes and identifies the one and the many. I will *share in the joy of your nation*, sings the psalmist, much as Paul will say to the Thessalonians, 'Now we really live, since you are standing firm in the Lord' (1 Thess. 3:8). *Blessed are those* who have that balance right!

2. In Egypt (106:6–12)

As the psalmist identifies with the community, so he expects the community to identify with its ancestors. Here 106 expresses the 'Waterloo

---

[92] Kidner, p. 378.
[93] See p. 1.4.

syndrome' that 105 brought to our attention.[94] *I* and *we* belong together, and *we* and *they* are the same people, and so (as Kidner puts it) an indictment becomes a confession.[95] We may not be in their situation, but if we were, we would do just what they did. In fact in equivalent ways that is exactly what we do do. This at any rate is what the psalmist confesses on behalf of his own generation, and there is no reason why the *we* should not also mean 'we of the twenty-first century'. We have sinned *like* them; much more disturbing, we have sinned *with* them (6 AV/RV). This is more than regrettable coincidence; it is inherited wilfulness.

The first exodus-event that our psalmist mentions specifically is the crossing of the Red Sea. There God saves and redeems (10) and Israel believes and praises (12). But this positive reaction is uncharacteristic, as is made plain by verse 7 and the Exodus passages that lie behind it. One could understand the Israelites' sufferings in Egypt wiping out the memory of God's *many kindnesses*, literally his acts of covenant love, showered upon their family in the days of Abraham, Isaac and Jacob. They might possibly have been excused for discounting the early miracles which were Moses' credentials (cf. Exod. 4:1–17, 29–31; 5:19–21; 6:9–12). But by the time they reached the frontier, the seashore, they had seen Egypt brought to its knees and Moses totally vindicated, and yet *they rebelled* at the first sign of danger (cf. Exod. 14:10–12).

So the psalmist is not ignoring what had happened before the crossing of the sea. Where 105 devotes its first thirty-six verses to those years as a long tale of Yahweh's blessing, 106 sums them up in a single verse as evidence already of Israel's ingrained unbelief.

3. In the desert: craving (106:13–15)

This unbelief has many facets. With great insight the psalmist selects points in the wilderness journey which will illustrate six of them. Not surprisingly, since these are cardinal sins, the New Testament comments on them too; the first one, for example, reminds us of another wilderness, and Christ's temptations there.

Practically from the start of their journey through the desert God had provided his people miraculously with food, meat in the form of quail and bread in the form of manna (Exod. 16). The manna was a constant supply

---

[94] See p. 2.141.
[95] Kidner, p. 379.

over the next forty years, but the quail were apparently a one-off bonus, and by Numbers 11:4–6 Israel was saying, 'If only we had meat to eat! . . . We never see anything but this manna!'

Verse 14 shows that the sins exposed were on the one hand the *craving*, the selfish desire, and on the other the attitude which would measure God by how he met it. Hoping to find the same weaknesses in Jesus, the devil suggested that he too should first satisfy his own need for food by a miracle, and then see whether God would rise to a test proposed to him (Matt. 4:1–7).

The effect in Israel's case (15) was dramatic. It revealed how fundamental this sin is – why, perhaps, it comes first in the series. Numbers tells us that the Lord became so 'exceedingly angry' that even 'Moses was troubled'. The people were told that they would have what they wanted, for a month on end, until they were sick of it; and into the bargain, the Lord 'struck them with a severe plague' (Num. 11:10, 18–20, 31–34).

Why was the penalty so severe for what might seem mere greed?

The cause of their sin (13) was something that explains the Lord's anger. They would not look to the past with eagerness to find what kind of God he had shown himself to be, and therefore would not look to the future with trust as he worked out his *plan*, his plan for their welfare. They wilfully detached themselves from the perfect pattern he had been, and was still, weaving for them, and told him that what really mattered was what they wanted there and then.

An earlier psalm (81) has already brought to mind a dictum of Spurgeon's: 'Be careful what you want, because you're sure to get it.' What God wants is infinitely more important, even from our own selfish point of view: '*E'n la sua volontade è nostra pace,*' says Dante; 'in his will is our peace'.[96] Both preacher and poet were well aware of what Jesus had said long before: 'My food . . . is to do the will of him who sent me'; 'Not my will, but yours be done' (John 4:34; Luke 22:42).

4. In the desert: envy (106:16–18)

Numbers 16 provides the second of these 'negative archetypes', as Allen calls them,[97] classic instances of sin during Israel's desert journey. Dathan and Abiram of the tribe of Reuben, and the Levite Korah, with whose name

---

[96] Dante Alighieri, *The Divine Comedy: Paradiso*, iii.85.
[97] Allen, p. 47.

the Psalter has made us very familiar, headed a group that disputed Moses' leadership and Aaron's priesthood.

Their approach is a typical challenge to authority: self-appointed spokesmen backed by an influential group ('well-known community leaders'), claiming to represent the whole assembly ('every one of them'), and taking the moral high ground ('the LORD is with them'; Num. 16:1–3). There is even an element of comedy in a deeply tragic affair, with tit-for-tat accusations flying to and fro: 'You have gone too far!' – 'No, *you* have gone too far' – 'Isn't it enough for you that . . . ?' – 'Isn't it enough [for *you*] that . . . ?' (Num. 16:3, 7, 9, 13). Typical also is the way that a towering menace, which not once but twice comes within a whisker of destroying the entire nation (Num. 16:20–21, 44–45), suddenly comes to nothing, rather like the fifty-verse chapter in Numbers which, as the psalmist points out, grows from and is reduced to the one little word 'envy'.

The envy of verses 16–18 is a development of the craving of verses 13–15. That was 'I want', this is 'I want what you have': not something just like it, but the thing itself, so that I have it and you don't. It could be anything; in this case it was authority. Moses might have looked into the self-righteous faces of the Reubenite brothers and his own kinsman Korah, and thought, 'You don't know what you are asking' (Matt. 20:22; Mark 10:38). To say nothing of the authority not being his to hand over, it was a burden to him, and often he would gladly have laid it down. The conspirators could not see that at all. Sin has such tunnel vision!

But for God, who in the previous instance had given his people what they wanted, this was the sticking point. Like it or not, in this case they were going to have what *he* wanted.[98] Moses and Aaron were vindicated, and the troublemakers went down, as the AV says, 'quick into the pit'.[99]

5. In the desert: idolatry (106:19–23)

As the psalm moves towards its midpoint, the sins it presents move from one that relates to oneself and one that relates to other people, to one that relates to God. Exodus 32 tells, and Deuteronomy 9 retells, the story of how the Israelites *worshipped an idol cast from metal.*

The attitude, if not the action, is part of our own experience. They shut their eyes to the facts: they made the golden calf 'at Horeb, of all places',[100]

---

[98] Motyer, p. 556.

[99] Num. 16:30 AV; meaning, of course, 'alive into the pit' (33 AV).

[100] Allen, p. 54.

where they were in the midst of the most stunning corporate encounter with God in the Old Testament. Second, *they exchanged their glorious God for an image.* Jeremiah (2:11) repeats the charge, and for Paul (Rom. 1:23) it typifies basic human sinfulness, for the golden calf was not a representation of the true God, as some suppose, but a replacement for him. And third, in taking not the Creator, but something he had created, to be the most important thing in their world, they *forgot the God who saved them* by doing *great things in Egypt.* His miracles there had shown his supremacy over the gods of Egypt, that is, the powers of nature. And here was Israel choosing as her god not even the sun, whom the Egyptians called Re or Aten;[101] not even the earth or its rivers or its mountains, Nile or Hermon (or Sinai); but a mere animal, which everyone knew would die if there were no grass to eat. When people abandon the God of Scripture, it is astonishing what foolish alternatives they propose.

It need hardly be said that the Lord would have none of it. The first two sections of the psalm highlighted his covenant love (vv. 1 and 7); each of these six central episodes, as it transpires, will portray him as a God of judgment. His people had betrayed their title as his *chosen ones* (5), and he would destroy them. Yet in the event he did not; for Moses, alone now worthy of that title (23), *stood in the breach* to turn aside his wrath. The scenario stands there in Scripture to show how grace works, and is played out comprehensively by Christ, the greater Chosen One, at Calvary.

6. In the desert: grumbling (106:24–27)

A number of other Old Testament scriptures converge in this fourth episode. It is chiefly concerned with Numbers 13 and 14, where the Israelites' route through the desert has brought them within striking distance of the Promised Land. Spies sent to reconnoitre come back with a report whose effect is described here. Though undeniably a *pleasant land*, the occupying of it looked like being more trouble than it was worth, so Israel retreated into her tents and sulked.

The wording of verse 25 connects it with Moses' review of the whole journey forty years later. Deuteronomy 1:27 has the 'grumbling in the tents' phrase, and the same chapter draws attention to the two divine oaths which we find also in Numbers, the first promising the land to Israel

---

[101] The pharaoh Amenophis IV, who championed a monotheistic worship of the sun and called himself Akhenaten in its honour, lived within a century or so of the exodus.

and the second denying it to that particular generation of Israel (Num. 14:21, 23, 28, 30; Deut. 1:8, 34).

It is Numbers 14:29 which dooms the latter to *fall in the wilderness* (v. 26 here). The further doom, that they *fall **among the nations*** and are scattered *throughout the lands* (27), comes from the Lord's threats of punishment for the disobedient set out in Leviticus 26:33 and 38, referring to later generations by then settled in the land: *their descendants*, as the psalm says. Thus the solidarity of the nation down the centuries is taken for granted. It is underlined by Paul's rounding off his list of Israel's follies in the desert with this one (1 Cor. 10:10). Execution there and then for some, he reminds us; others who would die in the course of the next forty years; many dispersed among the nations during the centuries that followed, as the psalm indicates; and we ourselves advised to take warning (1 Cor. 10:10, 5, 11).

We realize that the psalmist's order is not chronological. Moving hither and yon across the exodus narratives, he has focused first on the sinners' own cravings, then on their envy of others, then on their abandonment of God. Here he probes more deeply. What was happening when the first opportunity God gave for entering Canaan was refused? The AV and RV tell us plainly: the people would not go forward into the *pleasant land* because they 'believed not his word'; they stayed obstinately in their tents and grumbled, because they 'hearkened not unto the voice of the LORD'. Every other sin arose from their unwillingness to take seriously what God said. Those who reject his word reject him.

7. In the desert: apostasy (106:28–31)

The background to these verses is Numbers 25. Once we know the story, the two proper names here, a place and a person, make the psalmist's point for him.

Peor was a hilltop in Moabite territory (Num. 23:28). Arriving in the area, Israel was within sight of the Promised Land (Num. 27:12); this is chronologically the last of the six episodes, forty years later than the worship of the golden calf.

There were people living around Peor. Back to civilization at last! Here, perhaps with some relief, the travellers found culture and society, a renewed contact with the real world. Peor was a contrast to the desert, where (sometimes to their discomfort) there had been no-one but themselves and Yahweh.

Moabite society had beliefs as well as structure. It was religious. The golden calf may have reminded us of Chesterton's dictum that when people no longer believe in something, they believe, not in nothing, but in anything. But here at Peor was something again: a system of beliefs equivalent to, and a good deal more comforting than, the tiresome faith of Yahweh – comforting with the comforts of the whorehouse (Num. 25:1–3).

Long before Jesus' generation heard the words 'Take my yoke upon you' (Matt. 11:29), Israel had known that that was the call of Yahweh to her. But those who at Horeb had turned away from the Lord, and who at Kadesh had despised his word, now at Peor *yoked themselves* instead to the *lifeless gods* of this alien ideology.

Phinehas was Aaron's grandson, himself a future high priest of Israel. His involvement in these events is at first glance curious. The Lord in anger punished Israel with a plague, and the intervention of Phinehas checked it; but he intervened by himself punishing a flagrant example of Israel's sin (Num. 25:6–9). Why should his killing of one guilty Israelite stop the Lord killing many more?

'He was as zealous for my honour among them as I am,' explained the Lord (Num. 25:11). There were after all some in Israel, and within the nation's leadership, who still cared about righteousness as God did. But the fact that the zeal of a Phinehas should be needed showed how many in Israel thought otherwise.[102]

8. In the desert: rebellion (106:32–33)

The final episode goes back to Numbers 20, to the second of two places both called Meribah, or 'Quarrelling', and both of them scenes of a water shortage. On the earlier occasion, near the beginning of the forty-year journey, God had told Moses to strike the rock, and when he did, water gushed forth (Exod. 17:1–7). Now, near the end of the journey, again 'there was no water' and again the people 'quarrelled with Moses' (Num. 20:2–3). This time God's command was different. 'Speak to that rock,' he said, 'and it will pour out its water.' Perhaps from Sinai onwards he had been educating Israel in the symbolism of the rock, which became one of

---

[102] *Credited to him as righteousness* (31) is almost the same wording as Gen. 15:6. The difference is that God counted Phinehas' deed as what it actually was, an act of righteousness, whereas he counted Abram's faith not as if it were righteousness, nor as a substitute for righteousness, but as something in virtue of which he would reckon him righteous.

his own great titles, frequent with the psalmists and the prophets[103] and climaxing in the New Testament teaching of 1 Corinthians 10:4 and Matthew 16:18.

Moses, the meekest of men (Num. 12:3), had been pushed too far. Exasperated beyond endurance, he cried, 'Listen, you rebels, must we bring you water out of this rock?' and 'struck the rock twice with his staff' (Num. 20:8–11).

If his sin was not so much his anger, or even his disobedience, as his cavalier treatment of a divine symbol, we can understand his punishment. 'Because you did not trust in me enough to honour me as holy in the sight of the Israelites, you will not bring this community into the land I give them' (Num. 20:12). He had publicly treated holy things – God, his word, his symbol – as disrespectfully as his rebellious people were doing.

And why should the psalmist end his indictment of a past generation, designed as a confession for the present generation, with this incident? Is it not plain that the sin he is concerned with is not that of Moses, but that of the rebels who drove Moses to it? The sin confessed here by all who use this psalm is not the public folly of a leader, but the part others may play in causing it. The last of these warnings from the wilderness (1 Cor. 10:11) is about the sin that makes someone else sin, so roundly condemned by Jesus (Matt. 18:6–7).

9. In Canaan (106:34–42)

It was not the wilderness generation alone that was so persistently rebellious. The psalmist was at pains to show in verses 6–12 that Israel was just as rebellious before the brief believing and praising when she came out of the land of slavery across the Red Sea. He maintains likewise in verses 34–42 that she was no more obedient after she had been taken across the River Jordan into the land of milk and honey. This section of the chiastic pattern corresponds to that earlier one.

To make his point, he finds his sequel to the wilderness journey not in Joshua, the book that speaks very positively of the journey's completion and of the conquest that followed, but in Judges, the book after that. Once deprived of the charismatic leadership of Joshua, Israel's natural sinfulness reasserted itself. The narrative of Judges has as negative a tone

---

[103] Ps. 18 (four times) and thirteen others; Isa. four times, especially 44:8. See also Deut. 32 (five times); Hab. 1:12.

as the psalmist could wish for, and the book's first two chapters are repeatedly echoed here.[104]

Worse things figure in these verses than even Judges recounts. The psalmist speaks as the Old Testament prophets often do, when they depict what might be called a 'range of mountains' view of the future. Peaks which a traveller, or a map-reader, will find to be a long way apart, some near and others remote, appear to a spectator in the distance to be close together, part of the same range. Looking back, of course, not forward, since this is history and not prophecy, the psalmist sees the moral scenery of the past in the same way. The distant skyline of the time of the judges is very like the nearer one of the time of the kings. The bad things of those earlier days are repeated and intensified in these more recent days. There is a wholesale adoption of pagan beliefs and customs, including human sacrifice, even the sacrifice of one's own children.[105] There is a subjection to enemies in the land that eventually becomes deportation from the land.[106]

It is a fearful mercy which warns people that however low they may have sunk, they are quite capable of sinking considerably lower! Here at the end of Book IV, the first Exodus Collection, the psalmist gives Psalm 106 to his contemporaries, and to us, as a sobering penitential close to the book's comprehensive reminder of the story of redemption. For the story concerns the redemption of *sinners*, and this psalm sets out to show that sinfulness is as real in the people of God as in the rest of humanity; that it is always there, not during the wilderness wanderings only, but both before and since; and that it is no mere nuisance that may be shrugged off tomorrow if we don't get round to it today, but a compulsion that is to be feared as an ever-tightening grip.

But that is not the last word.

10. Remembrance and praise (106:43–48)

As the Lord kept his original promise to give the land to Israel, even though he made one generation forfeit it, so he would preserve the remnant of Israel beyond the exile, even though he destroyed her as an independent nation.

---

[104] Cf. Judg. 1:21–36 (v. 34); 2:10–13, 19 (vv. 35–36); 2:14–15 (vv. 40–42); 2:17 (v. 39).

[105] Cf. Judg. 11:30–40; 2 Kgs 17:14–16 (vv. 35–36); 16:3; 17:17; 21:6, 16 (vv. 37–38).

[106] Cf. Judg. 2:14; 3:8, 12; etc.; 2 Kgs 17:1–6; 24:1 – 25:21 (vv. 40–42).

The plea at the beginning of the psalm, that the Lord should remember both the individual and the community to which the individual belongs (4), is echoed here, therefore, with confidence (45). He has remembered them – these verses seem to speak of the exile and the restoration[107] – and will remember them again.

So the outer ends of the psalm also correspond. Verse 48 may be a doxology designed to close this collection of psalms, but at the same time it completes this particular psalm, forming an inclusio with verse 1. *Praise the LORD . . . his love endures for ever; from everlasting to everlasting . . . Praise the LORD.*

Covenant love, then, has the last word. Israel will be able to say in the end, like the Scottish hymn writer,

> With mercy and with judgment
> My web of time he wove,[108]

realizing with hindsight what in her better moments she has always believed, that it is mercy that hems the entire fabric.

---

107 Cf. 1 Kgs 8:50; 2 Kgs 25:27–30; Ezra 1; Neh. 2:1–9; Dan. 1:9.
108 Anne Ross Cousins, 'The sands of time are sinking'.

Book V
(Psalms 107 – 150)

Psalms 107 – 110

4. A further Exodus psalm and the third David Collection

The last and longest of the five books of the Psalter is also apparently the least organized. In our time, most hymn books group their contents under theological headings: 'God, the Father, the Son and the Holy Ghost; Man, his needs and moods; the Church, its privileges and services', as Manning puts it.[1] Hardly any now imitate John Wesley's 1780 *Hymns for the Use of the People called Methodists*, which are 'ranged . . . according to the experience of real Christians'. A few are severely practical, arranging their hymns alphabetically. The Psalter, though not averse to using the alphabet for its acrostic psalms, is not quite like any of these. In this respect, though not in much else, its compilers seem to be in sympathy with the editors of the *English Hymnal* of 1907, a book in which almost the largest single section is a catch-all entitled 'General Hymns'. But what a feeble heading that would be for this final part of the Psalter!

There is no denying that it contains few groupings of psalms as large or as obvious as those in earlier books. It is not, however, a mere miscellany, and the arrangement suggested here aims partly to recognize such classifying as the compilers did intend, and partly to make sequences of individual psalms more manageable.

Those with which Book V opens are a case in point. Since three of them are headed by the name of David, small though the group is we may call it

---

[1] Manning, p. 11, contrasting this with Wesley's method.

the third David Collection. The three have little else in common; in fact it may be the distinctiveness of each that first strikes the informed reader. Of them, 108 is notable as a straight duplication of material found elsewhere in the Psalter, 109 as perhaps the most shocking of the imprecatory psalms, and 110 as the psalm most often quoted in the New Testament.

On the other hand, 107 could belong to the previous book, the first Exodus Collection. It is yet another historical review of the Lord's dealings with his people, showing resemblances to 105 and 106, though painted with an even broader brush. The doxology of 106:48, though traditionally taken to mark the end of Book IV, differs from those at the end of Books I, II and III, and may have been meant to close only the psalm, not the sequence of psalms.

At all events, it is with the splendours of 107 that Book V begins.

Psalm 107

With its vividness and its inspired blend of repetition and variety, this celebration of the 'steadfast love of the LORD' (43 NRSV) begs for a singable metrical version worthy of the original. Sadly, I know of none. In choirs and places where they sing, we may at least hear (and even join in) the singing of it to Anglican chant, or to the psalmody of Joseph Gelineau.

It is the long inner section, verses 4–32, rather than the psalm as a whole, that is likely to stick in the mind when one first gets to know it. With that section we shall begin, returning later to its introduction and conclusion.

1. Four vivid word-pictures (107:4–32)

'The same in the other': that, says C. S. Lewis, is the principle of 'all pattern, and therefore all art'. He is talking in the first instance about the rhyming of traditional Western poetry, a pair of words with the same ending and different beginnings, and about the parallelism of Hebrew poetry, 'the practice of saying the same thing twice in different words', usually in two successive lines of a poem.[2]

On a slightly larger scale, we find 'the same in the other' in the four stanzas in verses 4–32. Each has a refrain in the middle, with people crying to the Lord and the Lord rescuing them, and a further one near the

---

[2] Lewis, p. 11.

end, which urges them to thank him. That is 'the same'. Why they cry, what he does, and how the stanza ends, is different in each case. That is 'the other'.

Here are people lost and perishing in the wide open spaces; people imprisoned, by contrast, in a very narrow place; people mortally ill; people in peril on the sea. In each case they pray, and their prayer is answered. The lost are found, the captives freed, the sick healed, the storm-tossed brought *to their desired haven.* Then in each case they are urged to give thanks for his covenant love and his wonderful deeds; after which two of the four stanzas say more about his love and his deeds, while the other two say more about their response of gratitude.

2. Early times (107:4–9)

There is much conjecture and no certainty about when and how the psalm was composed. Verses 4–9 may hint at Israel's return from exile (we leave aside for the moment vv. 1–3, which look like a clear reference to it), for the Lord's straight way through the desert is a familiar image from Isaiah's prophecy of the return in 40:3.

But a wandering *in desert wastelands . . . hungry and thirsty* sounds more like a much earlier time, the days of the exodus. In the narratives of those days, and in the psalms of Book IV which run parallel to them, there is no shortage of examples of God's people crying out to him (or more often against him) in their trouble, and being delivered from their distress.

They would not at the time have called his choice of route a *straight way,* which was what the seventeenth century would have understood by the AV's phrase 'the right way'. This was the right way, nevertheless, in the modern sense of the word also. The longest way round was the shortest way home, and it led to *a city where they could settle,* as the psalmist says twice over. If we imagine this stanza sung at the celebrations when David brought the ark to Jerusalem, the grand occasion to which 1 Chronicles 16 attaches three of the psalms from Book IV (1 Chr. 16:8–36 = Pss 105:1–15 + 96:1–13 + 106:1, 47–48), there is no doubt that one city in particular would be in everyone's mind.

Such words would have been appropriate even earlier. Moses had looked forward, and Joshua could look back, to God's giving his pilgrim people 'cities you did not build' (Deut. 6:10; Josh. 24:13), and long before David's time they had established urban settlements all over what had been Canaanite territory. Although the book of Judges is full of dreadful things, there were between the conquest and the monarchy, between Joshua and David, long periods of peace and prosperity, as is evidenced by the greater part of the book of Ruth.

3. Late times (107:10–16)

In contrast to its predecessor, this stanza looks at first glance as if it belongs to the exodus, and then begins to seem more at home in a later time.

We have just noted that 106:48 may not originally have been meant as an ending to Book IV, and that 107 may have been the eighteenth and last psalm of the first Exodus Collection. There are similarities between 106 and 107, crossing the present division between the books. One of them is that those who have *rebelled against God's commands and despised the plans of the Most High* here (107:11) are also rebellious, and care nothing for God's counsel, there (106:7, 13, 33, 43); and in 106 they are definitely the exodus generation.

Yet for all that, verses 10–16 sound more like the exile seven hundred years afterwards. For these people their suffering is the result of rebellion against God (10–11), which the Babylonian captivity was; the Egyptian captivity was not. Verse 16 describes the Lord's opening of this prison in exactly the terms of Isaiah's prophecy (45:2) about the ending of the exile. By no means had all the deported Israelites been literally imprisoned in Babylon, but some had (2 Kgs 25:27; Jer. 52:11). It was that generation for whom these verses would have been most meaningful and heartfelt.

4. Low times (107:17–22)

Most of the psalm, for most people who would have sung it in Old Testament times, could have been a series of easily understood metaphors for stressful situations. Since, however, Israel in her early days had experienced literal wanderings in a desert, and with the downfall of the monarchy literal captivity and (for some) literal imprisonment, might the pen-picture of verses 17–22 likewise be something more than a metaphor?

What we would be looking for would be some instance of illness, an epidemic, perhaps, rather than individual cases. As with the imprisonment of the previous stanza, it would be due to sin (17); these are the *fools* whose folly, as we are by now well aware, is not stupidity but wilful rebellion against God, as in the second stanza.[3]

Such an event is not hard to find. At the beginning of Israel's nationhood, rebellion with this result occurs on a national scale, not once but three times. At the beginning of the monarchy a personal sin of the king has similar consequences. In each case the community or the individual is at a low spiritual ebb. In the latter case, David, we are told, 'counted the fighting men' of his kingdom, a military census presumably intended to boost his self-confidence, and then 'conscience-stricken . . . said to the Lord, "I have sinned greatly"' (2 Sam. 24:10). His repentance could not prevent the Lord's sending a plague in which thousands died. The former, even more of a case in point, is Israel's threefold punishment by plague during the wilderness journey, recounted in Numbers 11:31–35; 16:41–50; and 25:1–9. These are three of the six examples of unbelief, of 'folly', that the last psalm set before us (106:13–33). If it is one or more of them that is in mind here, we have another tie that binds 107 to the Exodus Collection in Book IV.

5. High times (107:23–32)

The fourth stanza is something of a puzzle. Earlier psalms have shown God's people coming to terms with the terrors of the sea, much greater for Israel than for a maritime state like Tyre. Even so, the experience of storms at sea is not a prominent feature in the historical narratives of the Old Testament, unlike desert wanderings and captivities and plagues.

Do we have to turn to the prophets instead, and moreover to an atypical one like Jonah, to find a background for verses 23–32? The two scriptures do have much in common, except that Jonah did not exactly get to his *desired haven*!

Seafarers, if not storms, are nonetheless noted once or twice in the histories, on each occasion at a time of high endeavour, unlike the low times when Israel angered God and was stricken by plague. Traditional reluctance to embark on the *mighty waters* was put aside when Solomon at the height of his power built and sent out a fleet of great trading ships (1 Kgs 9:26–28; 10:22). Their home port was Ezion Geber, by Elath on the Gulf of Aqaba. Jehoshaphat, that great and good king, set about a similar

---

[3] Most versions concur in the translation *fools*. The rsv/nrsv has 'sick'; the stanza is clearly about sickness without this unnecessary change.

project at the same place, though in his case it came to nothing (2 Chr. 20:35–37). The account of the long and prosperous reign of his descendant Uzziah notes first among his achievements that 'he was the one who rebuilt Elath' (2 Chr. 26:2), presumably to re-establish a merchant navy there.

The regular schedule of Solomon's ships would inevitably have involved their crews from time to time in the experience described here in the psalm. At any rate, those for whom it was eventually written knew enough about such things for the stanza to make sense to them.

6. The gamut of history

If these first singers were picturing as they sang real-life situations of which they knew, it must have been from some late historical vantage point that the psalmist had surveyed the wonderful deeds of God. He had, as it were, set out to 'climb where Moses stood, / And view the landscape o'er',[4] and the greater part of the Old Testament story was spread before him.

The higher the hill, the broader the panorama. He and his contemporaries would look back not only to but beyond the exodus, and we Christians know of many further wonderful deeds in the second part of the Bible, for 'only together with us would they be made perfect' (Heb. 11:40). Hagar and her son wandering in the desert, doomed to die of thirst, in Genesis 21; Samson, imprisoned because of his own wilfulness, in Judges 16; Miriam, stricken with leprosy on account of her foolish presumption, in Numbers 12; Jonah, whose storm at sea is after all the obvious Old Testament illustration of the fourth stanza – Psalm 107 gives us a line on how to read every such story with profit. In each case there is a cry to the Lord out of trouble, and a rescue from distress even when the sufferer's sin is the cause of it: this is a wonderful deed, pointing us to his unfailing covenant love, and deserving of our praise.

The wanderings of New Testament days are largely those of the apostle Paul, and the imprisonments also, not that they were due to any wrongdoing of his. He too encounters sickness due to sin, among the Christians at Corinth, and the account of his experience of a storm at sea is even more exciting than that of Jonah's (see 2 Cor. 11:26–27; Acts 16:22ff.; 1 Cor. 11:28–31; Acts 27). Again in every case dependence on the Lord leads to deliverance by the Lord.

---

4 Isaac Watts, 'There is a land of pure delight', referring here to Deut. 32:48–49.

7. The gamut of experience

The singers of the psalm are not thanking God for what he has done for somebody else, for the psalmist says, *Let **them** give thanks.* It seems to be assumed that there will be members of the congregation who can say, 'Yes, I was lost and the Lord found me', or 'I was trapped and he freed me.'

There is more to this than meets the eye. First, it is conceivable that some may have been through just such an experience as one or other of these stanzas describes. They will praise God for having done for them exactly, literally, what he did for others long ago. Testimonies encourage!

A less obvious implication has a wider application, reaching out to touch those whose lives have been more humdrum. A sense of solidarity with our ancestors, such as recent psalms have been taking for granted, gives us a stake in what God did for them. 'Were you there when they crucified my Lord?' Yes, I was. And when Israel came out of Egypt, I was there; and when the exiles came back from Babylon, I came too. Because the church of God has been found, freed, healed and rescued, then as a member of it, so have I.

And what happened both literally and in a deeper, spiritual, sense can equally be used as a metaphor now. We sing with William Williams, 'Guide me, O thou great Jehovah, / Pilgrim through this barren land'; with Charles Wesley, 'My chains fell off, my heart was free'; with Henry Lyte, 'Ransomed, healed, restored, forgiven'; with Anna Waring, 'The storm may roar . . . / But God is round about me.' We know that these things can be true for us, not in some vague mystical way but as metaphors for real experiences. We may note in passing that while the four stanzas have many echoing repetitions, the *Some . . . some . . . some . . . some* of verses 4, 10, 17 and 23 is not in fact one of them. That gives the impression of four groups of people, each with its own special experience. Rather, the psalmist is saying that any or all of us could use any or all of these metaphors, since we are all part of the great assembly for which all of them are true.

We may note one further point of style. The opening verses of each stanza have the wanderers and the seafarers in trouble through no fault of their own, while the others are sick or in prison through their own fault; the pattern is ABBA, innocent/guilty/guilty/innocent. The closing verse of each stanza, on the other hand, underlines the divine blessing in the first and second and the human response in the third and fourth; the pattern is AABB, and the two patterns combined cover every permutation.

Innocent or guilty, see how God loves you! Guilty or innocent, see how you should respond!

8. Prosperity and calamity (107:33–40)

What is the relation between this passage and the four word-pictures? Even if the psalm originally consisted of them alone, as some suggest, the longer version was understood by the compilers at least to make a coherent whole. Two kinds of background help to integrate it. The Lord's bringing the *hungry to live* in a city where they settle and prosper (36–38) refers plainly to the first picture, and presumably to the exodus and the conquest. It seems to be followed by a decline in their fortunes (*oppression, calamity and sorrow*, 39) – the exile, and the second picture? – from which in due course he restores them (41).

Then there are connections between this passage and scriptures beyond Psalm 107. As well as echoes of Deuteronomy and Job (Deut. 28:1–5; 29:22–23; more closely, Job 12:21, 24), we find close parallels with Isaiah 41:18; 50:2; and other prophecies of the restoration of Israel.

It is Isaiah who elsewhere gives us a clue to the purpose of verses 33–40. In the startling AV translation of Isaiah 45:7, the Lord says, 'I make peace, and create evil.' The evil cannot of course be sin or wrongdoing, so the NIV tries to be less misleading with 'prosperity' and 'disaster', and the NRSV with the archaic but attractive 'weal' and 'woe'. It is, as another Isaiah scripture says, God's 'strange work' to bring about disasters (Isa. 28:21), but he has no hesitation in doing it when necessary.

The eight verses of our present passage should be taken not as a narrative of past events, but as a further series of pictures. This time they are rather like those of the Bayeux Tapestry, which we used to illustrate the oddities of Hebrew verb tenses in Psalm 18.[5] The tenses in verses 33 and 35 are imperfects, as if to say, 'Look, here is the Lord turning rivers into a desert; now here he is in this picture turning the desert into pools.'

Each pair of verses is such a picture. In the first, good things turn bad, to punish the wicked. In the second, bad things turn good, to bless the needy. In the third picture the blessing is shown again, now in detail. *Then* – if the NIV is right to supply the word 'then', it means not what the same people experienced next, but what we see next – the punishment is the subject of the fourth picture.

---

[5] See pp. 1.54–56.

The passage turns out to be a regular chiasmus –

calamity (33–34),
    prosperity (35–36),
    prosperity (37–38),
calamity (39–40) –

and makes the emphatic point that the Lord is behind both the weal and the woe. It is his people, needless to say, who are in view through the whole psalm, those who sooner or later ought to be thanking him for his covenant love. It is they who need to grasp that both good things and bad things do happen, and that the Lord is in control throughout.

9. A word to the wise (107:1–3, 41–43)

Verb. sap., as they used to say: *verbum sapienti*, a word to the wise – *Let the one who is wise heed these things* (43). What we have just found in verses 33–40 brings to light one more feature of the four big pictures in verses 4–32. When we have noted that, we shall be in a position to see the point which above all others a wise reader will heed in this psalm.

The pattern of those earlier stanzas is even richer than we may have thought. Was it their own fault that these people were in trouble? The opening verses of the four stanzas say, No, Yes, Yes, No: ABBA. How are their thanks rounded off? With a stress, say the closing verses, on Blessing, Blessing, Response, Response: AABB. Now we ask, Do they see the Lord as the bringer of their final prosperity only, or of their initial calamity also? And the answer is, Prosperity, Calamity, Prosperity, Calamity: ABAB. So here we have a truly comprehensive set of permutations!

Yet above this complex chord of theology and experience, one dominant note sounds. We may be lost, trapped, diseased or overwhelmed. It may be our own fault or it may not. The Lord may seem to us kind or cruel. Good things happen and bad things happen. But ultimately *God is good*. What we return to in the end is a picture of him lifting *the needy out of their affliction* and increasing *their families like flocks*. His love, covenant love, sets the tone in the first verse, and expects our appreciation in each of the four main stanzas; and the last verse crowns the psalm with *the loving deeds of the* Lord. This is what a wise person will *ponder*, and here the word is in the plural, gathering together all the great acts of covenant love.

One final point. The first three verses of 107 repeat 106:1 ('Give thanks to the LORD, for he is good; his love endures for ever') and answer 106:47 ('Save us . . . and gather us from the nations'). In fact with those verses 107 seems to join its two predecessors in spanning the history of God's people from the conquest, when 'he gave them the lands of the nations' (105:44), through the exile, when he made them 'fall among the nations' and scattered them 'throughout the lands' (106:27), to the restoration, when *he gathered [them] from the lands, from east and west, from north and south* (107:2–3).

Although the psalmist may be celebrating the end of the exile, his words have a far wider resonance. They take us right back to Genesis, and the promise to Abraham that 'all nations on earth' would be blessed through him (Gen. 18:18; 22:18; cf. 12:3). They take us right on to Revelation, and the vision of a countless multitude 'from every nation' gathered before the throne of God in heaven (Rev. 7:9).

The exodus and the thousand-year story that grew out of it were the classic exposition for God's Old Testament people of his wonderful deeds and unfailing love. The Christ-event, and the worldwide spread of the good news of it, are their fulfilment for us, his New Testament people. This is what the wise will ponder (43), and what the redeemed will tell (2).

Psalm 108

Arriving at this psalm after working steadily through the previous hundred-odd, we may well have the feeling that we have been here before. Does this not duplicate something somewhere else in the Psalter, as 53 very nearly duplicates 14?

Yes, it does; it reproduces parts of two earlier psalms, in fact – half of 57 and two-thirds of 60.

1. An old enmity reawakened

As with 60, the last four verses explain what 108 is about. Here are armies and enemies, the hope of victory and the fear of defeat, and Edom named as the antagonist whose *fortified city* Israel wants to capture.

This was an enmity that went back a long way, to the rivalry between the brothers Jacob and Esau, the ancestors of the two nations. In the histories of the Old Testament we learn of repeated hostilities during the period of the monarchy, from the reign of Saul in the eleventh century BC to that of Ahaz in the eighth (1 Sam. 14:47; 2 Chr. 28:17). In the prophecies, one final incident later than any of these is the sole subject of the book of Obadiah, which condemns Edom for standing aloof, in the famous security of her mountain fastness,[6] and gloating over the Babylonians' destruction of Jerusalem in 587 BC.

In the Psalms, this same incident will be referred to in 137:7. More important for our present purpose, however, is the earlier appearance of 108:6–13 in the form of 60:5–12. That psalm was linked by its heading with one of David's military campaigns.[7] Evidently the later use of this prayer has to do with some subsequent clash, when there was again a sense that all had not been well between God and his people (11), and yet this time a confidence also that he would come to their aid (1–5, taken from 57:7–11). Of such conflicts recorded in the reigns of Jehoram, Amaziah and Ahaz (2 Kgs 8:20–22 / 2 Chr. 21:8–10; 2 Kgs 14:7 / 2 Chr. 25:11–12; 2 Chr. 28:16–17), perhaps that of Amaziah's fits these circumstances best. This will still be a David psalm, however and whenever it may be adapted.

2. An old promise remembered

The prayer for help centres upon what God has said, concerning not only Edom but the peoples and territories of the region in general (6–9). All prayer, not least when God's people are under pressure, must be an appeal to his word. Times may change, but what God has 'spoken in his holiness' (7 RV) remains inviolable and true.

The proper names in these verses, as we saw in 60, point to places east and west of Jordan (7), and tribal districts north and south, as well as on both sides of the river (8). This was God's land even while the Canaanites lived there, and is still his now that he has given it to Israel. So are the lands of the Moabites, Edomites and Philistines (9). All these peoples are under his control, and each fulfils a role in his scheme: those who recognize him, one of honour, and those who do not, one of subordination. We are well aware of all this from 60:5–8.[8]

Such was the plan to which the holy God had committed himself from the outset, and which he would infallibly carry through. Such was the

---

[6] *Sela'*, 'The Rock', in Mount Seir, where the later city of Petra can still be visited. See p. 1.217.

[7] See pp. 1.215–216.

[8] See p. 1.217.

promise which another generation of Israel was now remembering as it found itself in a like situation.

Not so like, however, that the sixtieth psalm was appropriate just as it stood. An old prayer was refashioned to suit new circumstances; or rather, a new prayer was made out of parts of two older ones.

3. An old prayer refashioned

We should dismiss all thoughts of an unscrupulous mechanic welding the front end of one crashed car on to the back end of another! For one thing, the adapter has combined two 'back ends', prefacing the final two-thirds of 60 with not the first but the second half of 57. For another, he must have realized that they fitted together extraordinarily well. The resulting poem has as satisfying a poetic structure as either of the earlier ones.[9] For a third, there is nothing wrong with either of the discarded 'front ends'. It is simply that each begins its psalm in the shadow of 'disaster' and 'desperate times' (57:1; 60:3); while 108, whatever sobering experience it may be recalling in verse 11, is a thoroughly positive psalm, which as a whole celebrates God's covenant love and faithfulness (4).

Many commentators place it in the days after Israel's return from exile. Not that Edom was then a threat to the returned community, so far as we know (though her treachery in 587 would not have been forgotten); such a view has to imagine such a threat. But those circumstances would certainly sharpen two observations to which the rewritten psalm should give rise in any case. One is that the praises of a past generation can repeatedly come up as fresh as ever, the harp of verse 2 awaking even after years of silence in a foreign land (137:2–4). The other is that the claim of God's people to the whole land – meaning, in a figure, the whole earth – is as real as ever, even when her territory seems tiny. For as verse 4 reminds us, the changeless truth is that his faithfulness *reaches to the skies*, and his covenant love even higher.

Psalm 109

The imprecatory, or cursing, psalms are to be found 'all over the Psalter', as C. S. Lewis observes, hot with the 'spirit of hatred' that seems so alien to the spirit of Christ. We became aware of such embarrassing fierceness

---

[9] See Allen, p. 68.

in 7, and had to come to terms with it in detail in 35, and again in 58 and 69.[10] So 109 is by no means the first example; but, says Lewis, it is 'perhaps the worst'.[11] Having to confront the problem afresh, in a lengthy psalm, will recall those earlier considerations and suggest some new ones.

Rather than anticipate the difficulties of 109, as we did with 58, we shall work through it twice, first to remind ourselves what it says and then to ask what it means.

1. Accusation (109:1–5)

The psalmist is surrounded by enemies, and he cries to God for help. Such an appeal we have seen often enough, though less often this particular kind of enmity. In the first David Collection, the attacks of wicked men regularly involved armed force and threats of physical violence. The language was that of the hunt and the ambush. Here it is that of *lying tongues* and *words of hatred*, deceit and accusation; *they have spoken against me.*

We might say, Is that all? Sticks and stones may break my bones, but hard words cannot hurt me!

No, it is not all, and for four reasons. First, these tongues are lying, and it does hurt to have people assert, and no doubt to have other people believe, things about you that are not true. Second, as well as having no basis for their allegations, these enemies have no reason for their attacks. Why are they doing it? Out of pure malice, it seems. Third, so far from having done anything to provoke them, he has given them his friendship and the support of his prayer (which is probably the meaning of 4b). They are repaying *evil for good.*

Fourth, and most significantly, when he says *they accuse me,* it is no mere gossip or even slander that he fears. If we may after all anticipate just the opening of the next section, it does seem from the language of verses 6–7 to be a formal accusation in some kind of court of law.

2. Imprecation (109:6–15)

On the face of it, verse 6 appears to follow on from verse 1. The same person speaks, the same person is spoken to: it is the psalmist crying to God, first *Do not remain silent,* then *Appoint someone evil.*

---

[10] See pp. 1.21–22, 1.110ff., 1.208–209ff., 1.245–246.

[11] Lewis, p. 23.

We shall return later to consider the change from *they* in the first section to *he* in the second. Whoever *he* is, he is the object of the imprecations of these ten verses. And what terrible curses they are! The neat form of a chiasmus in no way inhibits the speaker's passionate indignation. With a blistering attack 'like the heat from a furnace mouth', to use Lewis's phrase, the object of it is cursed five ways: with regard to

> his personal guilt (6–7),
> > his personal punishment (8–9),
> > > his possessions (10–11),
> > his children's punishment (12–13),
> his parents' guilt (14–15).

When the psalmist thus wishes – prays – that not only this person, but also his wife and children, may suffer, and that his parents' sins may go unforgiven, it deeply offends even our liberal sensibilities, let alone our Christian principles. The New Testament tells us plainly, 'Bless those who persecute you; bless and do not curse . . . Do not repay anyone evil for evil . . . Do not take revenge' (Rom. 12:14, 17, 19). Yet here, it seems, are curses that surpass even the vindictiveness of Psalm 69:22–28.

3. Retribution (109:16–20)

One reason for recoiling at the fierceness of this onslaught is that it seems out of all proportion to what has provoked it. Granted, the provocation was as we have seen something more than mere *words of hatred* (3). It was apparently a groundless, motiveless betrayal of friendship, which actually led to legal proceedings. But even then the reaction of verses 6–15 seems excessive.

Less so, however, when verses 16–20 reveal what the psalmist's former friend (or friends) was really like. We now find what the psalmist understood himself to be doing. He was asking for a speedy end to the life of one who had *hounded to death the poor and the needy and the broken-hearted*. He was cursing one who himself *loved to pronounce a curse*. He was asking for the total elimination of one who had become totally saturated with evil. Since this enemy had chosen to wrap himself in malice, let it become his straitjacket.

If the imprecations of the previous section do express rage, then, at least it is not uncontrolled rage. Rather, according to a rigid code of retribution the psalmist is asking that his enemy may receive precisely what he deserves. Let him be well and truly dosed with his own medicine.

4. Supplication (109:21–25)

The psalmist sees this happening, we realize from verses 6–7, by due process in a court of law, in which some kind of presidency (*leadership*, 8) and the role of accuser have both been held by his opponents. Now let them find themselves on the receiving end of just such a process, with just such a judge appointed – *appoint* (6) has the same root as *leadership* – and just such a prosecuting counsel.

But you, Sovereign Lord (21) – where have you been in all this? True, all the psalmist's imprecations throughout the last fifteen verses were in effect a prayer addressed to God, and if they came true, would be *the Lord's payment to my accusers* (20). But there has been little sense of the Lord's presence in the cut-and-thrust of the courtroom. Now in this section the language suddenly becomes, so to speak, *religious*. Instead of the bitter tongue, verse 24 shows us the wounded heart. Instead of 'Do something to him', we hear 'Do something for me.'

Why? First, for the sake of *your name*; because of who you are, and what you have shown yourself to be. *Love* here is the covenant love of the covenant Lord Yahweh. We may see an inclusio framing the whole of that long acrimonious passage within the two personal appeals of verses 1 and 21, for the *Sovereign Lord* is the *God whom I praise*.

Second, for the sake of my need; because for all the fierceness of that sustained denunciation, for all the adrenaline rush, I am in fact *wounded* and *shaken*, *my knees give way* and *my body is thin and gaunt*. My courtroom battles will in themselves achieve nothing unless you act.

5. Expectation (109:26–31)

'Nothing unless you act' – but you *will* act! The psalmist's final appeal is that the Lord should save him in accordance with his covenant love, and therefore he has every confidence that he will be saved.

He expects that he will be blessed and that his enemies will *be put to shame*. That is, the evils they have wished on him (17–18) will not happen, whereas those he has wished on them will.

He expects furthermore that this will take place in such a way that they will recognize the Lord's hand in it (27). Not only his enemies, but also the *great throng* who praise God the Lord together with him (here is the larger inclusio, v. 1 and v. 30), will be witnesses to it.

And he expects it in this life, too. The confidence that the Lord will 'reward everyone according to what they have done' (62:12) is related in the New Testament to 'the day of God's wrath, when his righteous judgment will be revealed';[12] but God's Old Testament people, with a less precise picture of what the next life would hold, certainly hoped for some such righting of wrongs in this life.

So, startlingly, the private religious world of verses 21–25 is brought into the public arena of verses 1–20. The *wandering beggars* and *ruined homes* of the one are directly related to the activity of the Sovereign Lord in the other.

6. Who is 'he'?

Before we go back to the beginning for a second, more probing consideration of the psalm, we should clarify a question raised earlier. In verses 1–5 and 20–31 *they* are the enemy; in verses 6–19 *he* is being cursed. Why the change from plural to singular?

Neither the Hebrew nor the older translations use quotation marks, so in them the psalmist appears to be the speaker throughout. When he says, *let **him** be found guilty* (7), he is either regarding his opponents as if they were all one person, or saying, 'Let each of them be found guilty', or (most probably) focusing on their leader, one who is in some position of authority, as verse 8 indicates.

On the other hand, for some translators and commentators a quotation begins at verse 6. It is the enemies who are speaking, not the psalmist, and they say, 'Let an accuser stand at *his* [i.e. the psalmist's] right hand.' If then *they* proceed to curse *him*, the major embarrassment of the psalm is removed. Such 'unchristian' sentiments, so out of place from his lips, are only to be expected from theirs.

But there are problems with this view. As a fabricated condemnation of the psalmist, the passage seems unnaturally protracted and extreme, even for these unlovely people. More objectively, verse 20 (which is certainly his, even if the previous fourteen verses are not)

> takes the whole preceding section and turns it back on the heads of the enemy . . . Although some of the apparent harshness may be removed from the mouth of the biblical writer, it is not removed from his mind. All that appears in verses 6–19, the writer wishes upon the enemy.[13]

---

[12] Rom. 2:5. Paul goes on to quote Ps. 62:12 in the following verse.
[13] Shepherd, p. 31.

And we have to reckon with the fact that the words *may another take his place of leadership* are applied in the New Testament to the replacement of Judas as an apostle (Acts 1:20b = Ps. 109:8b). The apostolic church understood this second section, like the first, to be spoken by the righteous against the wicked.

In our rereading, therefore, we shall assume that the curses are what they seem to be, namely the words of the psalmist, and a nettle that has to be grasped.

7. Verses 1–5 again: how should God intervene?

This first section, though almost entirely taken up with the psalmist's complaint about the assault on his integrity, is introduced as an appeal: 'God, answer me.' Verses 2–5 fill out the reason why he wants an answer.

It is obvious what he hopes God will say: 'You are in the right, they are in the wrong.' But how exactly does he want him to say it?

This is the God of Moses and Elijah, who when he chooses no longer to *remain silent* can speak in highly dramatic ways. His voice answers Moses on Mount Sinai amid smoke and earthquake and with the sound of a trumpet, and everyone trembles (Exod. 19:16–19). When he answers Elijah on Mount Carmel, fire comes down from heaven and everyone falls prostrate (1 Kgs 18:37–39). Perhaps the psalmist is looking for something similar, especially if he is (as the psalm's heading suggests, and as the New Testament seems to agree in Acts 1:16–20) the great king David, as eminent a personage as these two famous prophets?

Well, no. Whatever the kind of court in which he finds himself arraigned, he seems to want things to be put right in the same context. So the following passage will indicate. The AV transferred the trial to a supernatural court by making verse 6b read 'let Satan stand at his right hand'; but the word in verse 6 is no different from that in verses 20 and 29. The psalmist is asking for his enemies to be accused by the same kind of prosecuting counsel as they have mobilized against him, and to be found guilty by the same kind of court. The divine intervention for which he prays is a correcting of the normal processes of law after a miscarriage of justice, not some frightening display of the paranormal.

8. Verses 6–15 again: what should the sentence be?

When verse 7 says *let him be found guilty*, then, 'the judgment is "this-worldly". There is no hint of "otherworldly" judgment or eternal damnation.'[14] And if the psalmist is right in what he reckons the appro-priate sentence for his enemy, it is for a 'this-worldly' court to impose it. He should not, for he is the plaintiff. God need not, since it is for just such a purpose that he has put the administration of justice into human hands.

If this man is convicted, it seems reasonable to the psalmist that he should suffer both the death penalty and the sequestration of his property. Many today disapprove of capital punishment, but at least the psalmist is not asking for something crueller. What he does ask for is largely a matter not of sadism but of realism; if the guilty man's life is to be cut short, it follows that his wife and children will be bereaved; if his property is seized, it follows that they will be impoverished. The sin of his parents is men-tioned not to blacken their character but to show that this was an inherited sinfulness (Exod. 20:5), though one that he chose to live with.

What we may still find hard to take is verse 12: *May no one extend kindness to him or take pity on his fatherless children*. Thereby hangs a tale, to which we shall return. That apart, it has to be recognized that the penalty asked for, though extreme, is not intemperate, but measured; a matter not of hot rage, but of cold calculation. It is, to use Brueggemann's phrase, 'that the guilty one should be *socially nullified*'. As with Korah, Dathan and Abiram in Numbers 16, and Achan in Joshua 7, this man together with the family unit of which he is the head should be eliminated from membership of God's people.

9. Verses 16–20 again: what was the charge?

How did the psalmist see the kind of penalty he was demanding in verses 6–15? In a word, as retribution. That was what verses 16–20 made clear. An eye for an eye, a tooth for a tooth. He simply wanted his enemy to suffer as he had made others suffer.

To this three responses may be made. First: for many, this is in itself one of the offensive features of the psalm. It expresses, says Kirkpatrick, 'the spirit of a dispensation' (he means the period of the OT) 'in which retribution was a fundamental principle'.[15] The 'eye for eye, tooth for tooth' teaching of the law, in Exodus 21:24 and many other places, has now, he asserts, been replaced by the non-retaliation teaching of the gospel, in Matthew 5:38–42.

---

[14] Brueggemann, p. 270. Brueggemann's treatment of Ps. 109 is very illuminating.

[15] Kirkpatrick, p. 652.

But second: the personal ethic of non-retaliation and the public administration of justice are two separate issues. New Testament and Old speak with one voice on the latter. As we have just noted, the New endorses the teaching of the Old, that God at his final judgment 'will repay each person according to what they have done',[16] and itself teaches that in the meantime the human judge on the secular bench does 'not bear the sword for no reason', for it is his or her responsibility 'to bring punishment on the wrongdoer' (Rom. 13:4). Our psalmist's complaint is more than a personal one. He is appealing for a public judgment (6–7) on a public scandal (16–19) and expects to be publicly vindicated (27, 30).

Third: the desired retribution is at a very deep level. A loose end left from the last section was the seemingly unwarranted verse 12: *May no one extend kindness to him or take pity on his fatherless children.* We may not like the sentiment, but it does relate directly to verse 16: *For he never thought of doing a kindness, but hounded to death the poor and the needy and the broken-hearted.* We are concerned here with more than the rights and wrongs of retribution, for *doing a kindness* is a woefully inadequate translation of what the psalmist wrote. The word in both places is *ḥesed,* love, or (better) covenant love, and it leads us to the heart of the psalm.

10. Verses 21–25 again: why should God intervene?

Here and in the next section the psalmist turns away from the public arena, as it were, and into the private place of prayer. The atmosphere is quite different. The tone changes from cursing to pleading.

But there is one common factor. As in verse 21 (and again in 26) he approaches God and addresses him by his covenant name, Yahweh, he prays, first, 'Deal well with me . . . out of the goodness of your *covenant love,* deliver me'; then, 'Help me . . . save me in accordance with your *covenant love.*'

Brueggemann points out the crucial connection between the four occurrences of this key word, in verses 12, 16, 21 and 26.[17] For the psalmist, the covenant love of the Lord, enshrined in his name and illustrated in all his dealings with his people, is the bedrock on which alone life can safely be built. The psalmist is *poor and needy* (22); that is his

---

[16] Rom. 2:6, showing that the *lex talionis,* the law of retaliation (Exod. 21:24; Deut. 19:15–21; etc.), reflects the justice of God's own character. The Latin term comes from the words *qualis/talis* – of what kind [the crime], of such a kind [the punishment].

[17] Brueggemann, pp. 275–278.

claim on the Lord; because of it he can look confidently for the Lord's covenant love.

But this covenant love is not for the individual only. It brought Israel out of Egypt, and made her a nation; *and it was meant to be reflected in her national life*. Remembering that, we can understand the sense of indignation in this psalm when the enemy, whatever personal injury he may have done the psalmist, turns out to be a man in a *place of leadership* (8) who has caused many besides him to suffer, and to suffer in precisely this way. There has been not a thought of covenant love in *his* dealings with the poor and needy (so v. 16 parallels vv. 21–22); rather, he has hounded them to death.

In a phrase which Paul will use in New Testament times, such heartless people as this man have made themselves 'foreigners to the covenants', and accordingly it is only right that they should be 'excluded from citizenship in Israel' (Eph. 2:12). So 'may no-one extend covenant love to him' (12).

11. Verses 26–31 again: where does God stand?

We have already seen that the psalmist wants God to intervene not in some miraculous way, but simply by making the processes of law work justly. Now we can see the reason: public life, particularly among God's own people, ought to operate on the same principles on which God himself operates.

God, the Lord of covenant love, will see that it happens, and these verses explain how he will do so. The psalmist was the needy individual, and therefore the beneficiary of God's love, in the previous section; so he is here in verse 31, which completes the psalm with a memorable picture. Near its beginning, at the right hand of the accused man it describes his accuser standing. But here at its end that position is taken not by an accuser but by a defender: [*The* Lord] *stands at the right hand of the needy, to save their lives from those who would condemn them*. We cannot help but be reminded of the New Testament *paraklētos*, the 'one called alongside to help'. In John 16:7 av he is the Comforter, in 1 John 2:1 rv the Advocate, the one text speaking of God the Spirit, the other of God the Son.

The expectation of this final section of the psalm is that both friend (30) and foe (27) will be well aware, when the Lord comes to his servant's help, what is happening in his personal life. And if the psalmist was contending for something parallel to happen in the public life of his nation, is it not our responsibility likewise to work to such ends?

Psalm 110

To the modern reader, Psalm 110 is full of puzzles. To the early church, it was full of treasures; a dozen books of the New Testament quote from it or allude to it, some more than once. One way to approach the puzzles is to turn a blind eye, temporarily, to the treasures – to try to see what the psalm meant when it was written, as if we were unaware what the New Testament would say about it, and how immensely influential it was to become.

1. What the psalmist said first

Whoever he was, whether David or another, he was a prophet as well as a poet. This is the word of the Lord, in verse 1 and again in verse 4. Confusingly, in most English versions, Lord speaks to Lord! As we know, in Hebrew the two words are quite different, and denote on the one hand the psalmist's God, Yahweh, and on the other his Master, or Sovereign. This second *Lord*, together with all that the psalm says about sceptre and rule, the crushing of kings and the judging of nations, must be a great monarch; and with his capital on Mount Zion, he must be a king of Israel.

God's first word to him certainly fits the whole pattern of Israelite king-ship. Verse 1 depicts a king who rules not in his own right but as viceroy to the true king, who is God. The histories agree: the kings in Jerusalem sit on 'the throne of the LORD', 'the throne of the kingdom of the LORD over Israel' (1 Chr. 29:23; 28:5). Psalm 2 has shown the Lord installing his king, his 'son', on Zion, his 'holy mountain' (Ps. 2:6–7), and many an Israelite king follows the same pattern by making his own son joint ruler with him in what is called a 'co-regency'.

2. What the psalmist said next

God's second word to the king has to do particularly with the place he has given him for his capital city. David had already been king for seven years when he left his base at Hebron and 'marched to Jerusalem to attack the Jebusites, who lived there'. He 'captured the fortress of Zion . . . and called it the City of David' (2 Sam. 5:6, 7, 9).

Although the Jebusite inhabitants of Jerusalem had long since been enemies of Israel, there was still a mystique about the place that went back hundreds of years, to the time of Abraham. He, already a powerful chieftain, fresh from a great military victory, came face to face with someone even greater, in the person of the then king of Jerusalem. To this man, in homage, Abraham gave a tenth of the spoils of battle. From him he received – what resonances the words have! – bread and wine, and a blessing; the city's name at the time being Salem, and the king's Melchizedek, so that he was both king of 'Peace' and 'king of righteousness' – and, Scripture tells us, not only a king but also a priest, 'priest of God Most High' (Gen. 14:17–20; Heb. 7:1–10).

The tradition persisted. The name, if not the character, was still there when Joshua, taking possession of Canaan, found among his opponents 'Adoni-Zedek [Lord of righteousness] king of Jerusalem' (Josh. 10:1). Did David, becoming first Israelite king in Jerusalem, succeed to that tradition? The Lord, through the prophet-poet, said that he did, and we see in him all four of its aspects. There was righteousness in him, for he was a man after God's own heart (1 Sam. 13:14); then Solomon, 'peace', was the name of his son and successor, and also the tenor of Solomon's reign. Third, he was seen as embodying the kingship as no-one else did, before or after, in those Old Testament times. And the fourth aspect of the tradition, the priesthood?

We leave that question, for the moment, hanging in the air.

3. What the teachers of the law said

So far, it looks as though Psalm 110 could be not simply about a king of Israel, but about one particular king, namely David. Just as we have found several psalms which seem to relate to the events of 2 Samuel 6, when David brought the ark to Jerusalem, so this one could relate to the events of 2 Samuel 5, when he first moved there himself.

Even if this had once been believed, by New Testament times it was a view no longer held. This is clear from two points that are made by a passage in the Gospels. The psalm is quoted in a debate between Jesus and the Pharisees, recorded by Mark, by Luke and most fully by Matthew (Matt. 22:41–46; Mark 12:35–37; Luke 20:41–44). From this conversation it emerges first that the 'teachers of the law', as Mark calls them, that is, the Pharisees and scribes, understood the psalm to be by David; and if it was spoken by him, it could scarcely have been spoken to him. It emerges, second, that they believed the person to whom it *was* addressed to be the Christ, the coming Messiah. It says things about God's king which were simply not fulfilled in David's reign, let alone in that of any of his successors.

The first prophetic word, verse 1, is expanded by the psalmist in a way that does reflect David's military successes. Verse 2 has the royal sceptre, the rule from Zion, and the unity between the Lord and the king – the sceptre is held by the one and stretched out by the other! – that we recall from Psalm 2:6–9. Verse 3 bids fair to be one of the most difficult verses in the Psalter, as the differences between various translations will show, but 'the general picture emerges . . . of a host of volunteers rallying to their leader in a holy war'.[18] As the morning mysteriously brings forth the dew, so the king is miraculously refreshed and renewed.

The expansion of the second prophetic word, verse 4, is difficult in other ways. One kind of problem arises if verses 5–6 are understood to speak to the king about the Lord, but disappears magically if we take the psalmist to be speaking to *the* LORD about the king: 'My lord the king is at your right hand, Yahweh' (v. 5, as v. 1); 'he will be refreshed and renewed' (v. 7, as v. 3b).[19] But now we find (6) that his success in battle is to be worldwide, and that has never yet happened. Nor of course has he become a priest, let alone a priest for ever. That is the other problem.

4. What Jesus said

We return to Matthew 22:41–46, where after a series of questions directed to him Jesus turns the tables by putting one to his questioners. It concerns this psalm. The Messiah is to be a descendant of David's, as he and they agree. 'How is it then', he asks, 'that David, speaking by the Spirit, calls him "Lord"? For he says, "The Lord said to my Lord . . ."' and so on.

The question is a real one for the Pharisees (not that they can or will answer it) because they and Jesus are agreed not only that the Messiah will be descended from David, but also that the psalm is about the Messiah, and *by David*. The many modern commentators who dispute this last point explain Jesus' words in one of two ways. Either (they say) he accommodated himself to the view that David wrote the psalm, knowing

---

[18] Kidner, p. 394.

[19] If we carelessly assume that v. 5 means '*Yahweh* is at your right hand, *O King*', we are forced to ask (1) why *Lord* refers to the king in v. 1 but to God in v. 5, while (2) God is everywhere else in the psalm called Yahweh; (3) why, when the king is at God's right hand in v. 1, they have changed places in v. 5; (4) why the subject of the verbs in v. 7, who is (as all agree) the king, has changed without warning from being God in vv. 5–6. A change in the vowel pointing of *Lord* in v. 5 is all that is needed to make everything fall into place: in vv. 2–3, *You* = my Lord, the king; throughout vv. 5–7, *You* = the LORD, God. See C. A. and E. G. Briggs, *Psalms*, ICC (Edinburgh: T. & T. Clark, 1906), pp. 378–380; E. J. Kissane, 'The Interpretation of Psalm 110', *Irish Theological Quarterly* 21 (1954), pp. 103–114.

himself that it was not so ('If, *as you believe*, David is speaking here'), or else he actually shared this allegedly mistaken view.

The first of these notions might make sense if Jesus were simply challenging the Pharisees to follow through the logic and the implications of their own belief, regardless of whether it were true. His aim, however, is not to score a point, but to make one. Matthew has just been describing how Jesus, riding into Jerusalem on Palm Sunday, was hailed as 'the Son of David' (21:9). It was an appropriate greeting, but a phrase misunderstood by both enemies and friends. David, first and greatest of the line of Israel's kings, was to have a descendant who would be – what? Another one like him, a patriot, a general, a politician, a monarch on the old oriental pattern, on a par with the Herods, even the Caesars, of this world? No; and the point was that it was *David* who was looking into the future, and speaking, awestruck, of a descendant of his who would be his Sovereign, one on an entirely different plane, to whom he would look up as his people looked up to him. The point turns on the fact that *David* was speaking thus. No wonder Jesus asserts so solemnly that David is 'speaking by the Spirit' when he 'calls him "Lord"'.

5. What the apostles said

A dozen allusions elsewhere in the New Testament are nearly all to verse 1, understanding the *lord* who is at God's right hand, his enemies under his feet, to be of course Christ. There is also a handful of actual quotations, in Acts and Hebrews.

Of the latter, Acts 2:34–35 is another reference to verse 1, and like Matthew 22:41–46 attributes the psalm to David. The words of Peter here are in some ways even more convincing than the words of Jesus there. Even if Jesus was going along with an erroneous view of the Pharisees for the sake of argument, that cannot be said of Peter. He is not having to accommodate himself to anyone; on the contrary, this is the day of Pentecost, he is filled with the Holy Spirit, and what he declares are the plain facts of the biblical gospel. Furthermore, his quotation too assumes David to be the author: it is the David who did not himself 'ascend to heaven' (indeed, whose 'tomb is here', 29) who said that his illustrious descendant would do so.

Hebrews 1:13 is yet another quotation of verse 1. What is new in Hebrews is its repeated quoting, and thorough expounding, of verse 4. The 'priest for ever, in the order of Melchizedek' is the author's theme from

6:20 at least to 8:2, and in some respects right on to the end of the letter. The dimension he adds to all the many New Testament references to verse 1 is that the Christ who is seated 'at the right hand of the throne of the Majesty in heaven' (8:1) is seated there as both king *and priest*.

6. What we say

What we should say about this 'prophecy in song' is what David's contemporaries would surely have said about it, except that the One it foretells was for them a hope but has become for us a reality. From David's time onwards it was meant to foster in Israel a vivid expectation that perhaps the present king's son, or if not him then perhaps his son's son, might be the One: a scion of David's house to whom God would say not only 'You are my chosen King' (1) but also 'You are my chosen Priest' (4), thus reviving from Genesis 14:18 the ancient Melchizedek tradition of Jerusalem.

Some did hold on to this hope. Even when, centuries later, the royal line had long since disappeared from sight, there was always within the nation a remnant waiting expectantly for the consolation of Israel, the redemption of Jerusalem and the kingdom of God (Luke 2:25, 38; 23:51); and when Jesus came, such people recognized him as the One who was to embody all this, the Christ.

So of course do we. We see, first, that in Christian terms verses 1 and 4 are what God the Father says to God the Son. Then after the Son's enthronement as King, the psalmist speaks *to* him (2–3): 'Yours is the majesty, the ever-fresh vitality, and the devotion of your people.' And after his appointment as Priest, the psalmist speaks to the Father *about* him (5–7): 'His is the power, the ever-renewed vigour, and the victory over his enemies.'

The words of Psalm 110 may not be common currency in Christian songs and hymns. But their very unfamiliarity may give us a new slant on how to express the praises of Jesus our Priest-King, as refreshing as the dew of the dawn or a drink from the brook beside the way.

Psalms 111 – 119

5. Three acrostics and the first Hallel

The next nine psalms are a set of praise songs flanked by acrostics. To group them like this serves the practical purpose of making Book V seem less fragmented, but they are in any case more than just a miscellany. As we shall see, this is not the 'General Hymns' section of the Psalter.

One thing is obvious when we compare the three alphabetical psalms here with the four previous examples of the form, all in Book I (9 – 10, 25, 34 and 37). The acrostics of Book V show it first at its most concise, and then at its most expansive. With only ten verses, 111 has just twenty-two lines, one for each letter of the Hebrew alphabet. The same is true of 112. At the other extreme, 119 has twenty-two eight-verse stanzas, with the same letter beginning all eight verses of a stanza.

The six praise songs framed by these acrostics, 113 – 118, are known as the Egyptian Hallel (*hallel* means 'praise'). They were traditionally used at major festivals, Passover in particular: hence the title, from 114:1, 'When Israel came out of Egypt'. They would have provided the hymn sung by Jesus and his disciples before 'they went out to the Mount of Olives' at the end of the last supper (Mark 14:26).

Hallel in its more familiar form *Hallelu Yah* ('Praise the Lord') is a word found in nearly all the nine psalms of the section. Its placing, at the beginning of a psalm, at the end, at both ends, or at neither, seems random, the more so when we find the Septuagint translators sometimes shifting it from the end of one psalm to the beginning of the next. But all becomes clear if we regard these hallelujahs not as topping and/or tailing individual psalms, but as linking them to one another, like the couplings of railway carriages. One 'train' consists of five successive psalms, from

110 in our previous section to 114 in this, each coupled to the next by a 'Praise the Lᴏʀᴅ'; the other consists of four, from 115 to 118, coupled in the same way; and both have been preceded, we realize, by yet another, similarly though not identically linked, that starts back in Book IV, namely 102 – 107.

The absence of a coupling between 114 and 115 suggested to some of the old translators that these two psalms were a single 'carriage' rather than the ends of two separate 'trains'. The latter is the truer picture; quite apart from the marked difference between them, the historic use of them requires a break, since it was, by ancient custom, between the singing of 114 and that of 115 that the Passover meal was eaten.

Psalm 111

In an echo of Book I, where 9 and 10 are the first pair of acrostic psalms, the compilers now place two more a little way in to Book V. In this case, 111 and 112 are separate, regular acrostics, not the two halves of a single and irregular one.

1. Sound and sense, sense and spirit

The acrostic method is in some ways the equivalent of rhyme, except that (1) the sounds that matter are those at the beginning of lines, not those at the end, and (2) the repetition of them is precisely what it does not have, since all twenty-two are by definition different. But the basic framework is nonetheless a sequence of sounds.

As for a sequence of thought, we might have assumed that at best we should get from 'this artificial conceit . . . a string of unmatched pearls . . . without any kind of systematic arrangement'.[1] In fact we have discovered in Book I that both the sounds and the sense of an acrostic can be arranged systematically. Our modern punctuation imposes on the text a sentence structure which the author did not necessarily intend; visualize this psalm without it, and you can see an inclusio that brackets verses 2–7a, followed by another bracketing verses 7b–10b. Though a mere semi-colon separates them in the ɴɪᴠ text (and in the following outline), there should really be a paragraph break halfway through verse 7:

---

[1] Weiser, p. 698.

I will extol the Lord (1);

> his works . . . his works (2–7a);
> his precepts . . . his precepts (7b–10b);

to him belongs praise (10c).

Besides this, we should remind ourselves that sound and sense can be aids, not hindrances, to the spirit of worship. When liturgical prayer and praise are memorable, they come in for repeated use, and while that brings obvious dangers, it brings great benefits too. Like a familiar pair of shoes, familiar Scripture and the songs it gives us will get us along the road without the pinch and chafe of newness at every step.

2. The works of the Lord (111:2–7a)

Great are the works of the LORD, meaning, when the Psalter first spoke of them, all his creatures in heaven (8:3) and on earth (8:6–7). That could be what 111:2 is celebrating. Even the Exodus Collections, which concentrate on certain historical events and use the same word to describe them (106:13 NRSV), use it more often in this broader way to describe creation and the natural world (Pss 102:25; 103:22; 104:13, 24, 31; 107:24).

But here too the chief theme is the great days of Moses. While the backdrop may be the universal and ceaseless work of the Creator, the events being recalled here in memory and in liturgy are the *deeds* and *wonders* of the Redeemer (3–4a). This is the Psalter's language for what God did at the time of the exodus (Pss 78:4, 11, 32; 95:9). We can see how this part of 111 as well as the psalms of the Egyptian Hallel would suit the commemoration of Passover.

The next three lines (4b–5) speak of God's care of his people through the wilderness journey. He made his name and character known in word – the psalmist quotes Exodus 34:6 – and in deed, as he provided for their physical needs. He asked no more from them than they had received from him: the unwearying devotion expressed by the repeated *remember*, here in verse 5 as it was in verse 4a.

At last he brought his people into the Promised Land. That was the final demonstration, for that time, of *the power of his works* (6–7a). It might seem odd to describe his work in creation in moral terms, as something *faithful and just*. His work in redemption, however, is placed firmly in that kind of context. It is bound up with his promise and his covenant.

This God does what he does because he has said he would. He has made his name known, and proves in experience to be indeed that sort of God. In the words of the original revelation to Moses, 'I AM WHO I AM' (Exod. 3:14).

3. The precepts of the Lord (111:7b–10b)

Here too the days of Israel's redemption from Egypt are in view (9), and the *precepts* are the law given at Sinai. As with God's works, so now with his words, the psalmist knows that they are all of a piece with those of earlier and of later times. God spoke at creation, and to Adam, and to Abraham, and repeatedly throughout the Old Testament. All of it, whether law or promise, might be summed up, together with the word spoken to Moses, as a declaration of 'how things are to be'.

This highlights an important aspect of the *faithfulness and uprightness* which belong as much to God's words as to his works. The latter, his *wonders*, resound down the centuries. The exodus is ever *to be remembered* (4) in the great Old Testament festivals; something very like it happens again when Israel returns from exile, as we saw in 107; and at Calvary, supremely, what God does is faithful to that basic pattern of redemption. The former, his *precepts*, are even more obviously unaffected by the passing of time. They are valid, not in a static but in a dynamic way, not just repeatedly but continuously: they *work*, and they never fail to work.

It stands to reason, therefore, that *all who follow his precepts have good understanding.* Since this is how the divine system is always operating, it is they who make it their business constantly to align themselves with it who will find themselves most at home with it.

This God is to be extolled, say the opening and closing verses of the psalm, not only now but always (10c), not only by each individual but by all the people of God together (1). The psalmist personally sings his praises *with all my heart.* He also loves to do so in an actual flesh-and-blood fellowship – to quote the NEB, 'in the company of good men' (and women!). And he never fails to recognize *the assembly*, the church as a whole. The vast majority of that greater company he does not (yet) know by name. But once more the limited view of the Old Testament is expanded by the New, in this case by the splendid vision of Hebrews 12:22–24, of the 'angels in joyful assembly' and 'the church of the firstborn' who acclaim in the heavenly realms the works and words of God.

Psalm 112

English readers may notice that 111 and 112 have the same number of verses, the same number of lines, the same distribution of lines to verses, and a good many of the same words. A Hebrew reader would instantly see the alphabetical pattern in the twenty-two initials of each. Clearly the two psalms are related.

1. A reflection

Like the Psalter's first acrostic, Psalms 9 – 10, these two resemble the hinged panels of a diptych. The outline of 112, and in some ways its content as well, correspond to those of 111. We might even think of it as a mirror, each section of it reflecting the section of the previous psalm opposite to it, as we shall see.

Its construction is perhaps less stylish. There have been attempts to find a sophisticated poetic shape alongside the simple alphabetical one, but they have not convinced many scholars. Rather, our psalmist is, in a slightly different sense, reflecting; and his train of thought in 112 seems to be guided by his meditations on 111. At first *those who fear the Lord* are described here in much the same terms as they were there, but with great perception the psalmist then begins to speak of them also in the kind of language which there was actually applied not to men and women but to God.

Perhaps this is after all a diptych rather than a mirror, the left-hand panel being a portrait of the Lord and the right-hand one a portrait of the believer. Yet so alike are they that we might be excused for thinking one a reflection of the other.

2. A spectrum

We may take the first eight verses in pairs. They describe the character and expectations of the people of God, and as a prism breaks up a beam of light, so they distinguish four aspects of them.[2]

a. Individual and family (112:1–2)

Stating the psalm's theme as *those who fear the Lord*, the first verse of 112 grows out of the last verse of 111 ('The fear of the Lord is the beginning

---

[2] The headings are those suggested by Motyer, p. 561.

of wisdom'). But it is when we set verses 1–2 alongside the opening verses of the earlier psalm that we begin to see new things. The same people are described in both psalms, and identified with *the upright*. In 111 they delight in the works of the Lord, like every believer whose eyes are open to the wonders of creation; whereas in 112 they delight in the words of the Lord, and that not just as a fascinating study, but as a ruling passion, for they are *commands* to live by. And then, as if by some spiritual sleight of hand, it is no longer a case simply of loving or even of obeying the Lord, but of reflecting him. *Great* and *mighty* are the first words in the two *gimel* lines, as if one were saying, '*Great* are the works this God has made' (111:2a), and the other, 'Their children will be *mighty* in the land' (112:2a).

b. Fortune and misfortune (112:3–4)

So it is likewise when 111:3–4 survey what we might call God's house, whether that means the world he has created (the 'temple' of 29:9) or the church he has redeemed (the 'temple' of 1 Cor. 3:16). Those verses speak of his glory and majesty. The corresponding verses in 112 look at the house of righteous people, and see wealth and riches. (We have already faced the problems of such a scripture, which seems so often belied by experience; this is the broad, and in the last analysis the true, picture of the one whom God blesses. We note that 112:4a does allow that they will not be exempt from misfortune.) Even more striking than the respective splendours of the two domains is our psalmist's wording for the *waw* line in 112 (3b). Since *waw* means 'and', there were no constraints on his choice of its second word or its theme. Yet he chose to reproduce 111:3b word for word: to assert that what is true of God is true also of God's people – *their righteousness endures for ever.* So too with verse 4b: gracious and compassionate is the Lord; gracious and compassionate are the righteous.

c. Generosity and security (112:5–6)

In 111:5–6 God is the provider of food, for Israel's wilderness journey and for all other circumstances; the giver of a place to live, when he leads his people into Canaan and at all other times. The people of God in 112 will therefore be *generous* too. The wisdom of Proverbs, which recognizes that in worldly terms wealth does bring security (10:15), also acknowledges that in a deeper sense the generous person is never diminished by giving it away (11:24). They who learn to give freely as God has given freely *will never be shaken*. He remembers, they are remembered, *for ever* (111:5b; 112:6b).

d. Threat and trust (112:7–8)

'Steadfast' begins the *samekh* line in 111 (8a), and the thought colours all four lines of its section. It binds together the last line of the 'works of God' passage (they are 'faithful and just') and the first of the 'precepts of God' passage (they are 'trustworthy' and 'established for ever', faithful and upright). For the *samekh* line in 112 the same word is used, though the NIV translates it *secure*.[3] Here, however, it is the human heart, not the divine word, which is secure. But the psalmist's point is that the one is implied by the other. It is *because* God's word is unshakeable that the believer's heart is unshakeable. And here 112 underlines what was hinted in verse 4a, that the people of God are not exempt from trouble. To say that they *have no fear of bad news* does not mean that for them the news is always good. It means that when bad news does come they can overcome their fears (so 8a JB). *Triumph*, gloating, in verse 8b is probably not what the psalmist intends; rather, although believers certainly do have enemies, they can confidently expect one day to see the back of them.

3. A contrast

The constant references to and fro between the two panels, the Lord's portrait and the believer's, appear to end at this point. The two verses that complete the psalm are a summary of the rest, and also a reminder of Psalm 1, which began so like this one (*Blessed are those*) and ended with the contrast between the way of the righteous and the way of the wicked.

Verse 9a sums up the practicality of the life of faith in terms of the well-doing of verse 5, and foreshadows the apostolic definition of pure religion, 'to look after orphans and widows in their distress' (Jas 1:27).

As James continues in that passage, it is equally required that one 'keep oneself from being polluted by the world', and with this verse 9b agrees. Arriving at the *tsadhe* line, the psalmist cannot resist starting it with the word for *righteousness*, which begins with that letter, and quoting 111:3b, 'his righteousness endures for ever', a second time.

Verse 9c foresees the future honour that awaits the righteous, while verse 10 amplifies what the last line of Psalm 1 said about the wicked.

---

[3] *Steadfast* in 112:7b represents a different Hebrew word.

Their chosen way 'leads to destruction' – the same word as the present psalm's *come to nothing.*

As the righteous will see the end of the wicked (8), so the wicked will see the vindication of the righteous. If both are to witness this final reversal of fortune, it sounds as though the psalmist is expecting a final judgment beyond the end of history, and thus reminding us of another element in the Old Testament view of a future life.

The dominant thought with which 111 and 112 leave us is that of the reflection of God's character that he looks for in the life of his people. It points back to the Genesis story, when 'God created mankind in his own image', and on to the creation of the new humanity, 'like God in true righteousness and holiness', and in due course to that of the new world: 'We know that when Christ appears, we shall be like him, for we shall see him as he is' (Gen. 1:27; Eph. 4:24; 1 John 3:2). What is happening in the present time is what Paul teaches in 2 Corinthians 3:18: 'We all, who with unveiled faces contemplate the Lord's glory, are being transformed into his image.' In the New Testament as in the Old, this is not a matter of some mystical experience, but of an entirely practical love for, and obedience to, God and his word, which his Holy Spirit owns and uses.[4]

Psalm 113

The further we go through the Psalter, the more familiar are the building blocks from which much of it is constructed. Yet always new combinations, and new components, shed new light on the prayers and praises of the people of God. This, commonly thought of as the first of six psalms that make up the Egyptian Hallel, is a case in point.

1. Psalm 113 as poetry

With simple words the psalmist weaves an intricate tapestry. The very first verse of the Psalter introduced us to parallelism, lines that state similar thoughts in different words ('walk in step with the wicked . . . stand in the way that sinners take . . . sit in the company of mockers'), and we have seen it often since. Here is its converse, lines using similar words to express different, though related, thoughts. Other poetic devices, too, are

---

[4] 'The process . . . is not mystical but educational . . . The content of the education is the gospel of Christ' (Paul Barnett, *The Message of 2 Corinthians*, BST [London: IVP, 2020], p. 65).

in evidence. A schematic version of the psalm, in three stanzas of three verses each, will show how artfully it is put together.

> Praise, you servants of the Lord,
> praise the name of the Lord (1).
>> The name of the Lord be blessed,
>>> from now to evermore (2),
>>> from east to west,
>> be praised the name of the Lord (3).
>
> Lifted above all the nations is the Lord,
> above the heavens his glory (4).
>> Who is like the Lord our God,
>>> who rises high to sit (5),
>>> who stoops low to look
>> on the heavens and on the earth (6)?
>
> He raises from the dust the poor,
>> from the ash heap he lifts the needy (7).
> He seats them with princes,
>> with the princes of their people (8).
> He sets the barren woman in her home
>> as a happy mother of children (9).

Inelegant it may be, but such a translation clarifies what the psalmist is getting at. In the first stanza, the repetition of 'from . . . to' links verses 2 and 3. The second is framed by 'above/above' in verse 4 and 'on/on' in verse 6. In the third, verses 7 and 8 have the double parallel of 'from/from' and 'with/with'. Verse 4 is connected with verse 7 by 'lifted' and 'lifts', and verse 5 with verses 8 and 9 by the word translated as 'sit/seats/sets'.

What picture is this careful patterning intended to create?

2. Psalm 113 as theology

The first and last stanzas take up from the previous two psalms the theme of the relationship between the Lord and his people. The opening verse, as more than one commentator points out, sees him making himself known to them, and them in glad response giving themselves to him. That is the force of *name* in verse 1c and *servants* in verse 1b.

Centuries ago that transaction was first made, but its effects have been and will be felt 'from' then 'to' the end of time. In a seemingly unimportant place it happened, but the God of the despised people who lived there is in fact the God of the whole world, *from the rising of the sun to the place where it sets*, and he *is to be praised* by all.

Opinions differ about the second stanza. They turn on the 'heaven and earth' phrase in verse 6b. One view is well expressed by John Keble's 1839 paraphrase: 'Exalting still his holy place, / Low bending still his eye of grace, / In heaven above' (where he sits), 'in earth below' (to which he stoops). Another sees a parenthesis in the middle of the chiasmus: 'Who is like the Lord (seated so high, stooping so low) in heaven or earth?' The JB translation makes a different point, and I think the right one; in it verses 4–6 are all about the transcendent greatness of God, and not until verses 7–9 shall we see something still more wonderful, his saving grace:

Who is like Yahweh our God? –
enthroned so high, he needs to stoop
to see the sky and earth![5]

It is in the third stanza that we celebrate not just his stooping to look, but his coming to save. He is a God of redemption, of rescue, who comes to save the poor and needy *from the dust, from the ash heap,* and to seat them *with* princes, *with the princes of his people.* See what he is doing, and see 113 developing the theme of 111 and 112. As he is, so his people shall be. He who is lifted high above all will lift them too. He who *sits enthroned* will seat them *with princes.*

After this, is not verse 9 an anticlimax? Why does the psalmist suddenly change the scene from revolution and royalty to contented domesticity?

Old Testament Israel took one thing for granted that we may sometimes forget. Her poor and needy might never find themselves literally seated with princes, but having no mental picture of crowns and thrones in the world to come, they would certainly see such practical gifts as that of motherhood to the barren woman to be the kind of princely blessing promised in verses 7 and 8. What God would do for his people in general, he would do for this person in particular (*settles = seats*). Whatever he

---

[5] The JB translators have been unwittingly betrayed into a rhyming jingle: 'Yahweh our God, enthroned so high / He needs to stoop to see the sky'!

187

might or might not have in store for a future life, he was, they were sure, a God who could touch their present lives with glory.

3. Psalm 113 as history

It is easy to see how apt this psalm would be for Passover. The exodus was the classic instance of God's lifting up of the needy. The barren woman's becoming *a happy mother of children* was a graphic metaphor for the rescue of Israel from hopelessness into new life, even to the point of her being settled in a new home (as in 107:7 or 111:6).

But then verses 7–9 are a very clear echo of the song of Hannah (1 Sam. 2:1–10), from the days of the judges. They also recall words from the first psalm of this book: 'He lifted the needy out of their affliction and increased their families like flocks' (107:41). That psalm suits the circumstances of the second great rescue, Israel's return from the Babylonian captivity. So this one too may be celebrating a deliverance later than that of the exodus.[6]

Lesser gods might be thought to have helped their individual devotees, but praise for an incomparable God (5) implies a rescue on the grand scale. No other god has done for an entire nation what this one has done for Israel. Even so, the reference to Hannah's song, and the actual wording of verse 9, are a reminder that the Lord does also act on behalf of the one as well as the many. Sarah in Genesis 21 and Elizabeth in Luke 1 are examples of the literal fulfilment of the promise of verse 9.

As for the general principle of God's action on behalf of the humble, the New Testament endorses it in two perhaps unexpected ways. It is thus, we learn in 1 Corinthians 1:27–30, that he undermines the self-confidence of the world. Why does he choose 'the lowly things', 'the despised things', 'the things that are not'? 'To nullify the things that are, so that no one may boast.'

And it is thus, we learn in Ephesians 2:6, that he assures the church of her present and future salvation. Using the very words of our psalm, he has 'raised us up with Christ and seated us with him in the heavenly realms'. We cannot miss the parallel between what the Egyptian Hallel celebrated, and the consequences of the dying and rising of 'Christ, our Passover' (1 Cor. 5:7).

---

[6] Goulder (*Return*) takes this entire sequence of psalms – not only 113 – 118, but a longer one, which might extend even from 105 to 119 – to have been compiled for use at the first Passover following the completion of the rebuilt temple in 516 BC (Ezra 6:19–22).

Psalm 114

In the Prayer Book it still has the Latin title *In exitu Israel*, and behind that lies the first line of the ancient Greek version, *En exodō Israēl*. However right it may have seemed to us to call the seventeen psalms of Book IV an Exodus Collection, and however many others have celebrated the theme, this is the Exodus psalm par excellence.

1. Psalm 114 as poetry

Many psalms, most recently 113, have confronted us with the complexities of Hebrew poetry. In contrast, 114 is one of the clearest and most straightforward. Its sixteen lines form eight verses, each of them a couplet whose lines are parallel in meaning. They make four stanzas of four lines each, and the whole divides into two chiastic halves:

> A people made to serve God (1–2);
>> the waters repulsed, the mountains shaken (3–4).
>> The waters repulsed, the mountains shaken (5–6)?
> A world made to serve God's people (7–8).

With its simplicity goes a sense of exhilaration, even glee. There is something like the giddy picture of verses 4 and 6 in the Prayer Book version of 68:16; but there the tone is very different. In a context of what is meant to be stern rebuke, 'Why hop ye so, ye high hills?' does perhaps leave something to be desired.[7] In 114:6, it is not nearly so inappropriate to ask the mountains why they skip, given the high spirits of this psalm. For high-spirited it is; the traditional minor-key chant that has long been inseparable from it in Anglican circles does it no service at all.

2. Psalm 114 as theology

Commentators can make unnecessarily heavy weather of the first two verses, debating when and why the psalmist would have used the two names Judah and Israel. Since his theme is the exodus, God's bringing of *Israel . . . out of Egypt*, it is simply the nation as a whole that is in view. He has rescued *from a people of foreign tongue* a people who will be distinctively his, and speak his language.

---

[7] The old translation of 68:16 is inaccurate. 'Why gaze in envy' (NIV).

The summary above has the ambiguous phrase 'A people made to serve God'. Does that imply compulsion? Yes, in a sense. God is to be introduced in verse 7 as Adonai, Sovereign, and the next psalm is going to remind us that whatever pleases him, that he does (115:3). But the words do imply creation. He has made a people, and he has made it in order that it shall serve him. Judah and Israel are parallel terms for the one nation, which is both his sanctuary and his dominion: 'a holy people who worshipped him as their God, and a vassal people who owned him as their King'.[8]

In verse 3 the entire story is contained between the events at either end of it, the two crossings, forty years apart, of the Red Sea and the River Jordan. Verse 4a describes the most significant event during those years, the earthquake at Mount Sinai when 'the Lord descended on it' (Exod. 19:18). Verse 4b may refer to the same thing, or perhaps to the quaking of the Canaanite hill country as the second crossing brought Israel towards a second demonstration of the Lord's power (Josh. 2:8–11).

Why was it, ask verses 5–6, that the waters were repulsed and the mountains shaken? It was of course because Adonai, their Sovereign Lord, was making himself known. Only now in verses 7–8 is he named. The psalmist would not have been best pleased with the NIV's pedantic insertion of *God's* in verse 2. Everybody knew perfectly well who was behind all this, and in case they had forgotten, the compilers had seen to it that 113:5, and the linking 'Praise the Lord', would have reminded them. Our poet deliberately put off identifying the divine Cause until verse 7, when the gleeful question had been put.

Earth in verse 7 is another debated point. It could mean 'land'. Perhaps this really is Canaan trembling at the threat of invasion, even if verse 4b is not. But probably the question is not a real one. In Hebrew the same word has both meanings, and both meanings are true here. Israel would find that God was sovereign, Adonai, in Canaan as in Egypt, and in the land between. For her, in Charles Wesley's words,

> The sea is turn'd to solid land,
> The rock into a fountain flows.[9]

---

[8] Allen, p. 105. Cf. Exod. 19:5–6: 'If you obey me fully . . . you will be for me a kingdom of priests and a holy nation.'

[9] Charles Wesley, 'When Israel out of Egypt came'.

For her descendants, both by race and by grace, he would prove to be equally sovereign in lands of whose existence she at that time had not the slightest idea.

3. Psalm 114 as praise

Other psalms, most of all the one which will follow the Egyptian Hallel to complete this group, highlight what happened at the centre of the exodus story, Israel's meeting with God at Sinai to receive his living word. To that crucial event 114 refers only indirectly. Instead it sets forth for the praises of God's people two tremendous facts that are inseparable from it.

To bring them to Sinai God has brought them out from among *a people of foreign tongue.* Centuries later he will threaten their descendants with another captivity, among another people 'with foreign lips and strange tongues' (Isa. 28:11), if they rebel against the plain truth of his word. It is central to their distinctiveness that they learn 'God-talk': not (heaven forbid) some anachronistic 'language of Zion', but a new way of thinking as well as speaking. If they – if we – are his sanctuary and his dominion, then both mind and mouth must be kept from the world's language of folly and greed and inanity and self-importance and deceit. The church is to be 'the pillar and bulwark of the truth' (1 Tim. 3:15 NRSV).

But this it shall be. If 114 is about anything, it is about God's power to accomplish his purpose. And as we praise him for giving us a new heart, and therefore a new tongue, we praise him too for showing how he controls all things to bring about his purpose. Why do the waters flee and the mountains quake? Because they see a people for whose benefit God directs them and everything else. Our one-line summary of verses 7–8, 'a world made to serve God's people', is ambiguous like that of verses 1–2, and it, too, is true in both its senses. Whether it is the rock of the wilderness, or the land of Canaan, or the earth as a whole, with its blessings and its challenges alike, God makes his world serve his church. It is even true to say that he made it for that very purpose. Here we are brought to know him and trained to serve him, and the exodus is our pattern.

Psalm 115

'*Non nobis, Domine,* / Not unto us, O Lord, / The praise or glory be / Of any deed or word.' Kipling based his powerful and solemn lines on the Latin title, the opening words, of 115. What the original author had gone on to say was not quite so straightforward.

1. A less than obvious structure

Verse 1 sounds at first like a modest disclaimer following some Israelite success in war or diplomacy. On the other hand, the question put by verse 2, *Where is their God?*, gives the opposite impression; the Lord has apparently let his people down, and this is the jeering of their pagan neighbours, however loyally they try to retort that he *is in heaven* (3).

The longer passage of tit-for-tat scorn for the pagan gods in verses 4–8 could have come from one of the prophets. Isaiah 44:9–20 and Jeremiah 10:3–5 say the same sort of thing. The rest of the psalm consists of several groups of verses in twos and threes; it is not always easy to see how they hang together, or who would say what when the psalm was used liturgically.

A curious historical sidelight shows how 114 and 115 have at times been thought of as a single psalm. After the battle of Agincourt in 1415, an old chronicler tells us, the victorious English king Henry V commanded *In exitu Israel* to be sung, and all to kneel when they reached the line *Non nobis, Domine*.[10] But the two are in fact separate, and very different, not least in their respective structures: that of the first clear and simple, and that of the second very far from obvious.

2. A fivefold mirror

The mix of disquiet and boldness at the start of our psalm would make sense both at the time of the exodus and in the days of the return from exile. In each case, trepidation at finding there were powerful enemies still to face was balanced by confidence because of what God had already done.

Into the same circumstances fits an inclusio which frames the psalm, and which was used by Timothy Dudley-Smith to connect all four verses of his fine paraphrase of it.[11] 'Not to us be glory given, / But to Him who reigns above' represents verse 1 of the psalm, and 'Not the dead, but we the living / Praise the Lord with all our powers' represents verses 17–18.

---

[10] Raphael Holinshed's *Chronicles*. Shakespeare uses the incident (*Henry V*, IV.viii.129). Ps. 114, celebrating the end of an old life and the beginning of a new one, was traditionally sung for the dead and dying. Ps. 115 expressed humble gratitude for what was perceived as a God-given victory.

[11] Like the best hymn writers of the past, Dudley-Smith shows how the gist of a psalm can be revealed, not obscured, by the disciplines of rhyme and metre, and shames the shoddiness of much Christian songwriting.

These are defining negatives, such as are set over the gateway to the Psalter in Psalm 1: what we believe, how we live, is *not* this, *but* that. Such a defining of the people of God was one aspect of both the exodus and the return: over against the peoples from whose lands they had come, and those into whose lands they were moving, this was their distinctiveness.

The second section, verses 4–8, describes at some length what the gods of these pagans cannot do. And if the second-to-last section were taken to be verses 12–15, it would correspond to this one not only in length but also in theme, since it describes what the God of Israel can and does do. He too is *not* this *but* that.

There remains a central section, verses 9–11. Apparently we have in each verse the words of two voices (or two choirs): one speaks to the assembled worshippers, the other speaks about them. The meaning of *All you Israelites, House of Aaron* and *You who fear [God]* is uncertain.[12] Holding that this set of psalms was designed for use at the first Passover after the completion of the new temple in 516 BC, Goulder links the phrases with Ezra 6:19–22. Perhaps the three groups here are those mentioned there: (1) the people 'who had returned from the exile', (2) 'the priests and Levites' and (3) of the few who had been able through the exile to hold on to an Israelite field or two, though not to a pure Israelite faith, those who had now 'separated themselves from the unclean practices of their Gentile neighbours in order to seek the LORD'.[13]

It is fair to say, then, that divided in this way the psalm does reflect the original Passover, and may also reflect this particular later one.

3. A commitment to a distinctive God
With verses 9–11 as their pivot, the five sections of 115 might be summed up like this:

Not to us, but to the Lord (1–3);
    what their gods cannot do (4–8);
        the Lord and his people (9–11);
    what our God can and does do (12–15);
not the dead, but we the living (16–18).

---

12 Suggestions besides that mentioned in the text include laity/priesthood/everyone, or laity/priesthood/converts from paganism, or everyone/priesthood/inner circle of true believers.

13 Goulder, *Return*, p. 171.

Whether after the exodus, or after the restoration, or after any life-renewing experience, the people of God often have to cope with the cold douche of verse 2. They may know, and others may recognize, that God *in heaven* presides over all, and 'has done great things for them' (126:2), yet there will be many with whom this cuts no ice, and whose disdain they still have to face. At such times, how tempting it is to retort by pointing to the church – its achievements, its importance – rather than to the Lord and his despised message, the 'foolishness' of 'Christ crucified' (1 Cor. 1:21–25).

For none of this world's gods can do what our Lord can do. The repeated *not* of verses 4–8 is more than merely ridicule of inanimate objects that are supposed to be alive and powerful. As Alec Motyer points out, even if they or their modern equivalents have mouths, eyes, ears, noses, no-one receives from them any spoken revelation, or moral oversight, or response to prayer, or propitiation through the 'appeasing fragrance' of sacrifice.[14] You never feel a loving touch from their hands, or sense their footsteps alongside yours. They can make a lot of noise, though? No, not even that; their devotees do, but no sound comes from the gods themselves, for they do not exist.

So, people of God, turn again to the Lord! And the threefold rejoinder in verses 9–11 is oddly encouraging as one choir sings it to the other; we might be overhearing a guardian angel saying matter-of-factly to his fellow, 'They have nothing to worry about, of course; he is after all their help and their shield.'

The word *bless*, five times over, binds verses 12–15 together and comprehends all that the false gods cannot do, and that the Lord can and does do. Both in Joshua's time and in Ezra's, the *help and shield* of verse 11 were the immediate needs of God's people while their new life became established. He has a special care for newborn believers and new-planted churches. Then the blessing of 'increase' (NRSV) and *children* in verse 14 was a long-term promise to Israel, ensuring her continuance. Just so the continuing life and growth of the church is also in his hands.

Verse 16, which Dudley-Smith turns into a neat little chiasmus ('His is heaven, earth is ours'), is more than a statement about the respective realms of God and humanity. It reminds us of the Old Testament understanding of death which we had to face as far back as 6:5: 'Among the dead

---

14 See Motyer, p. 563. Cf. Isa. 1:20; Ps. 113:6; Ps. 6:8; Gen. 8:21 JB.

no one proclaims your name. Who praises you from his grave?' We of course know that in the world to come our praise, like our knowledge and our service, will be not less but far more than it is now. But one thing the restricted view of the Old Testament saints can teach us. It concentrated their minds wonderfully, and encouraged them to make the very best of their time here below. It would be shameful if the hope of heaven led God's New Testament people to despise the daily opportunities for worship provided by this earthly life, which *he has given to the human race* for just that purpose.

Psalm 116

As with 115, there are fine things here, but no very obvious train of thought to hold them together. Two facts, however, we do know from the outset, one from Jewish tradition, the other from the text itself.

1. The starting point

As part of the Egyptian Hallel, 116 is a psalm for a festival, and therefore for corporate worship. We have pictured Jesus and his disciples singing one or more of the set at the last supper, and we know that this was a regular custom in the homes of their people at Passover. The psalm itself speaks of a much larger gathering *in the courts of the house of the* LORD (18–19). A major event of the kind would have been the Passover of 516 BC, the first in the newly rebuilt temple. That in turn would have recalled the still greater assembly in the days of Josiah ('none of the kings of Israel had ever celebrated such a Passover as did Josiah', says 2 Chr. 35:18).

Yet at the same time we cannot miss the individualism of this song. *I, me, my*, figure in practically every verse of it, reminding us of an earlier king, Hezekiah, who framed the similar psalm of Isaiah 38:9–20 round his own personal experience. To go back further, many of the psalms of David speak in the same personal way; indeed, some of them are echoed in this one, as we shall see.

How did such a seemingly private poem come into public use? Michael Goulder laughs at the idea that it was 'a hack job . . . "Berekiah, do you think you could do us a thanksgiving psalm suitable for recovery from sickness, childbirth, prison, libel, etc.? About twenty verses."'[15] Rather, he

---

[15] Goulder, *Return*, p. 176. Ps. 116 is used in the Prayer Book's service for thanksgiving after childbirth.

suggests, it was composed specially for the events of 516. The anonymous poet has the assembly speaking with one voice as *I*, and *my* unspecified *distress and sorrow* (3) represents the exile, now over.

On the other hand, there is no reason why an individual should not have written of his own sufferings, and his deliverance from them, in such a way that his poem lent itself to corporate use. In modern hymn books we find examples of the private poetry of George Herbert and John Keble, to name but two, thus taken over for public worship.

2. There and back

Repetitions of words or phrases here and there in the psalm suggest that it may not be as shapeless as it seems at first. The psalmist calls on the Lord in verses 2 and 17, speaks of death in verses 3 and 15, and celebrates God's goodness in verses 7 and 12. A familiar pattern begins to emerge. The division into two separate psalms that we find in Greek and Latin psalters (1–9 and 10–19) comes just where we should expect the midpoint of a chiasmus. That, in fact, is what we have. Nine verses take us out to that point, then the rest bring us home again.

The repetitions are not always exact. Death has the psalmist entangled in cords in verse 3, but we see him freed from chains in verses 15–16. He is now *delivered . . . from tears* (8) whereas he was *greatly afflicted* (10). But then the landmarks you pass on the outward journey are naturally seen from a slightly different angle on the return journey.

We may set out the chiasmus like this:

I call on him through all my days (1–2);
  snared by death, I call on him (3–4);
    to his goodness I testify (5–7);
      a bright prospect (8–9).
      A sober retrospect (10–11);
    to his goodness I respond (12–14);
  freed from death, I call on him (15–16);
I call on him among all his people (17–19).

3. The way there

Verses 1–2 start with a sentence that resembles 18:1, the only other psalm to begin so. It is the first of many reminiscences of David psalms in this one. In fact the Hebrew text says not *I love the LORD*, but simply 'I love', much as 1 John 4:19 says 'We love because he first loved us.'[16] In someone who has learnt to love in that absolute way, the *cry for mercy* of verse 1 is likely to be simply one aspect of a lifelong practice of crying out in prayer to God, in praise of God, or in proclamation about God (the *call* of v. 2 can mean all three);[17] the psalmist has grasped what a loving relationship with God really implies.

The cords and snares of death in verses 3–4 also echo Psalm 18 (4–6). *Anguish* means a narrow place, a tight spot, and recalls other David psalms too (4:1; 31:7). The tense of the Hebrew verb in verse 4 suggests to us that in such straits the psalmist called repeatedly, and even in English we can hear the directness and simplicity of his prayer: *Lord, save me!*

And the Lord did (5–7). Equally simple is the psalmist's testimony: *When I was brought low, he saved me.* Another kind of simplicity is less admirable; verse 6a is about naïve, gullible people, such as 'roam the pages of Proverbs drifting into trouble'.[18] How good the Lord is, caring even about those whose affliction is their own silly fault!

His goodness, moreover, goes beyond the benevolent smile and the soothing word, for he is able and willing to *act*. In verses 8–9 he has brought his servant back into what David called 'the land of the living' (27:13), and has, again in David's words, 'delivered [him] from death and [his] feet from stumbling' (56:13). How real the psalmist's distress was we may judge from the words he has added to the quotation: *me from death, my eyes from tears, my feet from stumbling.* It is another expression of his love that he looks forward to the bright prospect of a *walk before the Lord*, in fellowship with him.

4. The way back

The poem turns for home, as it were, with verses 10–11, a sober retrospect over recent events. We find another verb like that of verse 1, lacking an object: there *I love*; here *I trusted.* What exactly follows it? Does the psalmist mean, 'I trusted *even when* I said I was greatly afflicted', or '*even though* I said', or '*because* I said', or '*therefore* I said'? Each is possible, and each gives a different slant on the passage. In opting for the fourth, the AV (and older versions of the NIV) agrees not only with the Greek Old Testament's

---

16 Cf. Anderson, p. 791.
17 Cf. Allen, p. 112.
18 Kidner, p. 408.

understanding of the text, but also with the apostle Paul's when he quotes it in 2 Corinthians 4:13; and with this interpretation, as Roy Clements points out, the 'peevish soliloquies' become 'piercing insights'. In my crisis, says the psalmist, 'I discovered I was . . . a real believer . . . That faith . . . enabled me to verbalize my distraught emotions . . . to God. I told him . . . how miserable I was' (10b), 'how hurt I had been' (11b). Trusting God, he could shed all pretence and say just what he felt.[19]

His response to God's goodness (12–14) is to *lift up the cup of salvation*.[20] He means that all the blessings God wants him to have, he will make his own; he will *call* – that is, pray, praise and proclaim – as in verse 2; and he will pledge himself publicly to God's service.

Those upon whom the Lord sets his 'covenant love' are his 'saints', because being loved by him they respond in kind (the two terms are related). The psalmist's has been just such a response, and now in verses 15–16 he restates it. *Freed* from one bondage, he binds himself to another, to that of the Lord 'whose service is perfect freedom'.[21] Verse 15 means not that the Lord is looking for martyrs, but that to him it matters a great deal whether his servant lives or dies; hence the psalmist's rescue on this occasion.

The conclusion, verses 17–19, does two things. In returning to verses 1–2, it reiterates the psalmist's eagerness to *call on* the Lord, but now, repeating the words of verse 14, he wants to profess his devotion to him *in the presence of all his people.* The Old Testament knows of no private faith which is not also in some way public. And the psalm itself shows the same two faces. Without any awkwardness, a poem describing one man's suffering and deliverance goes public, as it were, and is recognized by the church as entirely appropriate for use *in the courts of the house of the LORD.*

Psalm 117

Although the brevity of this psalm is unique, its theme, a call to all nations to praise the God of Israel, appears in every book of the Psalter.[22] It is not hard to see the aptness of such a universal call in a group of psalms used at Passover. Affliction, then rescue from it, songs that hark back to the

---

[19] Clements, pp. 154–155.

[20] 'Take' (AV/RV) rather than *lift up* (NIV/NRSV). Everywhere else in the Psalter (11:6 RSV; 16:5; 23:5; 75:8) the cup is something given by God, not offered to him.

[21] The Prayer Book's collect for peace, in Morning Prayer.

[22] E.g. 22:27 (I); 67:3, 5 (II); 86:9 (III); 98:3 (IV); as well as this one (V).

exodus and that celebrate similar more recent saving acts of the Redeemer, from both a national and an individual point of view – all this could not help but have the widest of implications.

In Scripture, the duty of the nations to praise God is not always related to the experiences of Israel. As their Creator, all peoples owe to God 'life and breath and everything else' (Acts 17:25); therefore they owe him their praise as well. At the far end of history, he will reveal himself also as their Judge, and then most assuredly every knee will bow to him (Isa. 45:23; Phil. 2:10).

But in the meantime it is as Redeemer of this nation, Israel, that he expects recognition from the rest. There are a backward look and a forward look in verse 2, as well as in verse 1. It is not that his love, his covenant love, belongs to the past, and his faithfulness to the future, for both extend in both directions; Isaac Watts's paraphrase speaks of his 'eternal . . . mercies' and of his 'eternal truth'. Rather, it is Israel's past and future that inspire this tiny yet magnificent song. When Israel says *great is his love*, she is thinking of what he has done for her: 'I am the LORD your God, who brought you out of Egypt' (Exod. 20:2). When she says that his *faithfulness . . . endures for ever*, she is thinking of the unknown future creeping up behind her, as we saw in Psalm 48, confident that he is to be trusted through all the years to come.

But she can speak as she does in verse 2 because he has made himself known as her Redeemer; and it is the connection between that and the call of verse 1, the little word *for*, that makes Psalm 117 so astonishing. 'Praise him, *all you peoples*, for great is his love towards *us*.' When *you* grasp what he has done for *us*, when you see what the Passover and the exodus, in Christian terms the cross and the resurrection, mean, you will see that he alone deserves your allegiance too.

Yet again the Psalms come out with this uncompromising claim, which flies in the face of so many modern -isms. This Lord, and none of the other gods, is real. This fact, and none of the rival opinions, is true.

And how shall they hear this? Ah, that's another question. For the moment let Watts rephrase for us our call to the world and our confidence in the Lord:

From all that dwell below the skies
Let the Creator's praise arise:
Let the Redeemer's name be sung
Through every land, by every tongue.

Eternal are thy mercies, Lord;
Eternal truth attends thy word;
Thy praise shall sound from shore to shore
Till suns shall rise and set no more.

Psalm 118

This striking psalm completes the Egyptian Hallel. It resembles the one that begins Book V, and indeed the one before that (106 and 107), in that the verse which opens and closes it – *Give thanks to the* LORD, *for he is good; his love endures for ever* – opens each of them too. As we have seen, 106 forms a pair with 105, and that also begins, 'Give thanks to the LORD' (see NRSV); all three are linked, like the Hallel psalms, by the words 'Praise the LORD'; and the break between Books IV and V is less definite than it might seem.[23] So perhaps the compilers intended a group of fourteen psalms, 105 – 118, analogous to earlier groups of similar size, designed for use in the course of a festival week. We shall see how 118 might fit into such a framework.

1. A many-sided psalm

Like some other psalms of its length, its structure is complex and not very obvious. We hear, for example, a variety of voices. Often the psalmist speaks, but he also provides words for others to speak. Is it a congregation? Or a choir? Or two choirs alternating? Who are the individual and the two groups represented by *he, we* and *you* in verse 26? It seems to be a liturgy; is the psalmist leading it, or someone else?

And who is the psalmist anyway? To ask that is to open up another cluster of questions. The anguish and the rescue of verse 5 are very like those of 116:3–8, the experience of an individual, with snatches, here as there, of Davidic psalms from Book II. Verses 10–12 suggest that this is no ordinary individual, but a king, in conflict with national enemies; a king, however, later than David, in a time when Israel seemed to stand alone against *all the nations*. So perhaps an Israelite leader after the days of the monarchy, like Ezra or Nehemiah? If so, the anguish might mean the exile, and the rescue the return. And in that case, when the psalmist says *I cried*, he might be putting words into the collective mouth of the whole people of Israel.

---

[23] See pp. 2.154, 2.179.

There is a third way in which the psalm is many-sided. Four or five of its verses, and through them the poem as a whole, are seen in a number of places in the New Testament to have profound Christian significance. That too we shall want to explore.

One thing that unifies 118 is that it is clearly a liturgy, intended for use in the Jerusalem cultus on some special occasion, such as one of the great festivals. As it forms the climax of this group of Hallel psalms, Passover is no doubt the most likely.

2. Liturgy: i

An introductory voice declaims the words, familiar from earlier psalms, with which this one will also end (1). Verses 2–4 call the assembly to praise the Lord, and no doubt the assembly, presumably the same three groups as in 115:9–11,[24] responds with the threefold repetition of verse 1b.

The One (whoever he may be) then testifies, again with formal repetition, to his personal deliverance by the Lord (5–7), and it could well be that verses 8–9 are again a congregational response. In verses 10–14 his second testimony is in the same style, but has shifted to the level of international politics. Though it does sound like it, the deliverance is not necessarily a victory in battle; neither the return from exile nor the original exodus had involved that. But it did mean a vicious thrust from his enemies that would have felled him,[25] but for the Lord's help. We may take it that in verses 15–16 the congregation responds again (perhaps with v. 15a as a bidding by the worship leader, like the first lines of vv. 2–4): *The Lord's right hand has done mighty things!*

After this third united cry of the many, the One likewise speaks a third time, in verses 17–19. Egyptian slavery, Babylonian captivity, and many lesser afflictions between, had seemed like a death sentence; yet the bitter truth that these were chastenings from the Lord carried with it the comforting message that he who inflicted them could reverse them. It is as one who has received God's mercy, rather than as one who has achieved God's standards, that he expects the *gates of the righteous* to be opened for him.

These we must imagine as the literal gates of the city, or of the temple. This is a processional liturgy. The One, and all who are with him, form the procession which has now arrived at those gates.

---

[24] See p. 2.194.

[25] V. 13 nrsv mg. ('You pushed me hard') follows the Heb., with singular pronouns standing for both the One (or Israel) and his enemies. nrsv text and niv follow lxx.

3. Liturgy: ii

Not everyone has been walking with the crowd. Inside there are gatekeepers, Levites, for whose lines this is the cue. *Open for me the gates of the righteous*, cries the One. *This is the gate of the LORD*, they reply; 'the righteous shall enter through it' (20 NRSV). And again the implied challenge is met, not by a claim that this One does have the required righteousness, but by a prayer of thanksgiving to God: *you have become my salvation* (21).

We can only guess to whom it would fall to say the momentous words of verse 22: *The stone the builders rejected has become the cornerstone.* The gatekeepers, perhaps, with a rejoinder from the whole assembly in the *us/our* lines of verses 23–25. That would parallel verse 26, which is about the One *who comes in the name of the LORD*, and is spoken by those inside to those outside (*From the house of the LORD we bless you* – the *you* is plural). Verse 27 looks like a further exchange of the same kind: *The LORD . . . has made his light shine on us*, says the congregation; *Join in the festal procession*, say the gatekeepers.

Finally (28–29) the One addresses to God a prayer of thanksgiving and praise, and he or another – the voice that spoke verse 1, maybe – repeats the opening call to worship.

Before moving on to the background and the meaning of this remarkable psalm, we should try to make sense of its most difficult sentence, verse 27b. Three of the main Hebrew words here have at least two meanings each, and therefore produce several permutations. The more usual meanings would give, 'Bind the procession with cords.' But 'bind' could be 'join/begin/order'; 'procession' could be 'sacrifice'; 'cords' could be 'boughs/branches'.[26] A suggestion which takes all the words in their commonest sense is that the enthusiastic procession as it throngs through the gates is 'bound', that is, 'bounded', by cords – guide-ropes – towards the altar.[27]

4. When did it happen?

The background of Psalm 118 is as complex as its structure. There are cathedrals in England which took generations to build, and where guides

---

[26] 'Bind' is used in 1 Kgs 20:14 of 'marshalling troops for battle' (Cohen, p. 393). 'Bind the sacrifice with cords [and bring it] to the altar' (cf. Kidner, p. 416) is another suggestion; we are not to picture anything being 'bound to the horns of the altar' – the preposition means 'up to', 'as far as'. 'Branches' would be connected with Lev. 23:40 (and cf. Matt. 21:8).

[27] Cf. Goulder, *Return*, p. 184.

can show you still the evidences of each successive style of architecture – Norman, Early English, Decorated, Perpendicular. So it is here. We hear the testimony of David the fugitive, escaping from a tight corner ('anguish') and now at large again ('a spacious place') – these words from 31:7–8 are exactly those of verse 5. He is unafraid of what people can do to him, and looks in triumph on his enemies; 54:7 and 56:11 are taken up in verses 6–7. In the imperfect verbs of verses 10–12 we are back in 2 Samuel 8, with the picture of David the king striking down surrounding enemy nations. The background of verses 19–20 is the royal procession of 2 Samuel 6, when David brings the ark to Jerusalem, and the Davidic psalms 15 and 24 ('Lift up your heads, you gates . . . that the King of glory may come in').

Toward the poem's close, in verses 23, 25 and 29, we hear the prophesying of Jeremiah, full of a confidence that belies his reputation for gloom, even though he speaks in gloomy days when the Davidic kingdom is sliding to ruin. He believes the Lord will yet save his people (31:7), for nothing is too marvellous for him (32:17, 27, literally), and 'there will be heard once more the sounds of joy and gladness . . . "Give thanks . . . for the LORD is good; his love endures for ever"' (33:10–11).

Sure enough, this is precisely what happens when the first returning exiles lay the foundation of a new temple (Ezra 3:11). A contemporary prophet speaks of the completion of it, from foundation stone to capstone (Zech. 4:7–9). In the words of verse 17 of our psalm, Israel *will not die but live*, the unshakeable, permanent dwelling-place of God in his world.

So we shall not be too wide of the mark in picturing all this historical background, layer upon layer, each as real and vivid as the next, combining at the Passover of 516 BC, as Ezra 6 describes it. For to Passover the psalm surely belongs, and its roots are in the exodus. What lies behind verses 14–16 and 28 is the song of Moses:

> The LORD is my strength and my defence;
>   he has become my salvation.
> He is my God, and I will praise him,
>   my father's God, and I will exalt him . . .
> Your right hand, LORD,
>   was majestic in power.
> Your right hand, LORD,
>   shattered the enemy.
> (Exod. 15:2, 6)

Behind verse 27 is the blessing of Aaron: 'The LORD make his face shine on you' (Num. 6:25).

5. What does it mean?

Whether in the early days of the second temple Psalm 118 would in fact have been chanted in the dramatic form suggested above, and if so, who in particular would have taken the role of the One, we do not know. By the time of Christ the Hallel was in use at each of the great festivals, being sung at Passover both in the temple when the sacrificial lambs were offered, and later at home over the Passover meal; and even the former involved a simpler, responsive style of chanting.[28]

But in 118:25–26, it seems, all would have joined; and moreover the words would have been used as a regular exchange of greetings between Jerusalem people and visitors arriving for the festival. Parts of these verses were the very words of two such crowds on the first Palm Sunday, as (in more senses than one) the final Passover drew near: 'Hosanna!' (meaning 'Save, we pray'), 'Blessed is he who comes in the name of the Lord!' (Mark 11:9; John 12:13). In this case there was no doubt at all who 'he' was.[29]

Moving outwards from that crucial point, we begin to see how the whole of the psalm was coming true before their eyes. The next day he would take his enemies back to verses 22–23 of it, *The stone the builders rejected has become the cornerstone*, and make it crystal clear that what had happened to Israel – so often in Old Testament times rejected, yet vindicated by God – was about to happen to him. He was himself the Stone, the true Israel. He was the Righteous One, entering the gate (20). Once he had suffered for their sins, he and all his people would *not die but live* (17). Once he had risen, he would claim authority over *all the nations* (10–12). His love endures for ever (1, 29).

The future may often seem to us very dark. The darkness is nothing, though, compared to that which he faced at that Passover festival; and if he emerged from it in triumph, and we are one with him, then so shall we. We can take verse 6 for our own, as the writer of Hebrews did, and 'say with confidence, "The Lord is my helper; I will not be afraid. What can mere mortals do to me?"' (Heb. 13:6).

[28] Alfred Edersheim, *The Temple* (London: RTS, 1874), pp. 191–193; *The Life and Times of Jesus the Messiah* (London: Longmans, 1901), vol. 2, pp. 367–368.

[29] And perhaps 'branches' is right, after all, in v. 27.

Psalm 119

The most obvious feature of Psalm 119, after its extreme length, is its division into twenty-two equal stanzas, each headed by a letter of the Hebrew alphabet. It is in other words not only far and away the longest of the psalms, and the longest chapter in the Bible, but also the most elaborate of the Psalter's acrostics. In the first stanza, the initial word of each of the eight verses begins with *aleph*, the first letter of the alphabet; in the second stanza the initial words all begin with *beth*, and so on throughout.

It may be intentional that a group of nouns referring to the poem's main theme, the word of God, is also eight in number. Each noun occurs on average twenty-two times, and the eight verses of any given stanza will contain most if not all of them. Helpfully, the NIV is on the whole consistent in translating these nouns as commands (or commandments), decrees, law, laws (a different word, meaning judgments or rulings), precepts, promises, statutes and word. We shall compare their shades of meaning when we get to the *Heth* stanza, where they all appear once each.

As far back as Psalms 9 and 10 we had to come to terms with the artificiality of acrostic poems. Both on that and on the theme of this particular one, C. S. Lewis has perceptive comments. Unlike some other psalms, he says, 119

> is not, and does not pretend to be, a sudden outpouring of the heart . . .
> It is a pattern, a thing done like embroidery, stitch by stitch, through
> long, quiet hours, for love of the subject and for the delight in leisurely,
> disciplined craftsmanship.

He goes on to speak of that subject, the word of God, which (as the eight nouns tell us) is here thought of primarily as law – not irksome, restrictive rules, but God's way for his people to be happy. Undoubtedly the psalmist

> felt about the Law somewhat as he felt about his poetry; both involved
> exact and loving conformity to an intricate pattern . . . The Order of the
> Divine mind, embodied in the Divine Law, is beautiful. What should a
> man do but try to reproduce it, so far as possible, in his daily life?[30]

---

[30] Lewis, pp. 52–53.

Together with the form and the theme of 119, we should briefly consider its position. As in earlier parts of the Psalter, Michael Goulder's grouping of the psalms relates to week-long festivals at Passover and Tabernacles. A seven-day liturgy, with two psalms per day (evening and morning, with the day starting at sunset) and an extra one for the final evening, would require fifteen psalms. An eight-day liturgy would require seventeen, as in Book III (73 – 89). Goulder suggests that in their original form Books IV and V consisted of no fewer than four sets of fifteen (90 – 149), with 150 as a conclusion to the whole Psalter.[31] For him, 119 rounds off a Passover liturgy, which certainly included 113 – 118 and on his theory began with 105. It looks forward from that festival, which celebrated Israel's rescue from the old life in Egypt, to the next one, the feast of Weeks, traditionally linked with her arrival at Sinai and her receiving of the law, which set the course of her new life. Although this is only theory, it would be hard to imagine a more suitable occasion for the use of a very remarkable psalm. 'Clearly no one who relies on the law is justified before God' (Gal. 3:11), but once I have been justified by grace and redeemed from Egyptian slavery by the blood of the Lamb, I shall *delight in your commands* and *meditate on your decrees* (47–48). That is what this many-faceted poem enables us to do.

1. *Aleph* (119:1–8)

The first thing to notice about Psalm 119 is that it begins, and each of its first eight verses begins, with the letter *aleph*. This is not theological or spiritual frivolity. The Psalter itself begins with the same letter, because it begins with the same word 'Blessed' ('ašrê).[32] As there, so here, we may be struck by this emphasis on blessing – that that above all should be what the Lord wants for his people.

Equally striking is the fact that this sets the tone for a psalm about *God's word*. He is a God who speaks, and our blessedness is bound up with our attitude to what he says.

Perhaps more striking still is one particular word in this stanza. Of the eight terms we have already noted, the first to appear is *law*. Is this not strange, set alongside blessedness? Our modern world is one which both

---

[31] Goulder, *Return*, with a wealth of reasoning.

[32] *Aleph* is not the vowel A in *'ašrê* – that is a coincidence – but the almost unheard consonant indicated by the 'light breathing' sign, the 'right half ring' symbol (').

relishes lawlessness and strangles itself with legislation. How can *law* make us *happy*?

We need to understand the term as Bible people did. It does indeed mean legislation, the sort of thing we find in Leviticus or Deuteronomy. But more than that, it means all the first five books of Scripture, including the history of how God revealed himself in those early days; in fact it comes to be a label for the entire Old Testament.[33] It means something like 'directions' – a guidebook, a handbook; still better, 'the instruction a careful father gives to a loved child'.[34]

So 119:1–3 is the positive side of the negatives of 1:1. The law shows how not to 'walk in step with the wicked or stand in the way that sinners take or sit in the company of mockers'. Rather, it shows how to be *blameless*, that is, a person of integrity.[35]

After these three verses, every one of the remaining 173 (with the sole exception of v. 115) is addressed to the Lord, in praise or prayer. Verses 4–8 at once shift the ground from what Brueggemann would call the 'orientation' of Psalm 1, the simplified black-and-white view of two companies, righteous and wicked, to the disorienting facts of experience. I have to admit to the Lord that though he expects diligent obedience from me (4), he doesn't always get it (5). I do know what shame is (6); I am only a learner in the school of righteousness (7); and I could not blame him for giving up on me (8). Reality begins to bite.

2. *Beth* (119:9–16)

The psalm's first and most frequent term for the word of God, *law*, does not figure in *Beth*. Instead we find the two terms which *Aleph* omitted. The NIV usually translates them *word* and *promise*, though occasionally, as here, the latter also appears as *word* (11). The former frames this stanza with an inclusio in verses 9 and 16 – *living according to your word, I will not neglect your word* – and within the frame all the other terms (except *law*) are contained.

The *young person* of verse 9 is the person so often addressed in the book of Proverbs: 'Listen, my son'; 'My son, do not forget'; 'My son, pay attention' (1:8; 3:1; 5:1). Whether or not the psalmist is himself young, he puts himself

---

[33] Cf. John 15:25 (quoting the Psalms); 1 Cor. 14:21 (quoting the Prophets).

[34] Motyer, p. 566, connecting the word with its use in Prov. 3:1 ('teaching', NIV).

[35] See p. 1.3.

in the position of the 'son' in Proverbs, and shows what is meant by *living according to* [*the* LORD'S] *word*.

It is a very practical matter. The emphasis is not so much on the Lord's nouns (*your word* and its equivalents) as on the psalmist's verbs (*I seek*, and a series of similar declarations). First and foremost it is a matter of the will (10), less because that is the regular meaning of *heart* than because *seek* means a deliberate directing of it towards God, and *stray* means a deliberate walking away from him. Then (11) the great defence against temptation to sin is, as God might say to us in the words of Proverbs, to 'store up my commands within you' (2:1; 7:1).

And the more the better; though the psalmist is commending not the miser's love of mere quantity, but the connoisseur's appreciation of value, and still more the enthusiast's eagerness to share his or her pleasure. What God says to him, he will say to others (13).

The pleasure is there in verse 14 too. He rejoices, not because he thinks he ought to, but because he realizes what a treasure he has in God's word. So he will meditate and consider (15), delight in and not neglect (16), these good things.

At the heart of the stanza are a blessing and a plea (12) from one who wants to praise God, and who having learned much wants to learn more, as in verse 7 in the *Aleph* stanza. And at either end (9 and 15), giving the stanza another inclusio besides the *word/word* one, the psalmist testifies that the purity of his own way depends on his regular considering of the ways of the Lord.

3. *Gimel* (119:17–24)

After the humble realism of *Aleph* and the zeal of *Beth*, an element of stress comes into the psalm with *Gimel*.

It is not immediately obvious. Verses 17–18, bringing together the *law* and the *word* which figured at the start of the two previous stanzas, are very positive in tone. Some modern reactions to these two terms would surprise the psalmist. For him, submission to the word is a recipe not for frustration, but for revival; what he finds in the law is not a cramping of one's style, but a stretching of one's vision. He does recognize, though, that people are unlikely to see it that way until their eyes are opened!

His conviction is put to the test in verses 19–20. At this point the psalm moves out into the world he lives in, with its trials and its pressures. Wisdom writings like this one arise generally in a settled society, not in a period of *Sturm und Drang* (emotional unrest), as we first noted in earlier psalms, particularly 37. The psalmist's troubles here are not those of Babylonian invasion, as in 74, or Egyptian slavery, as in 90. He is not in exile, a stranger in a foreign country. He is having to come to terms with an even more disorienting fact, one that 39 and 105 have brought to our attention: right here in his own country, he is a stranger – *a stranger on earth.*

God's people have always needed to be reminded of this. Every day we walk familiar roads; this is our home town, our home country, we say. Yes and no, says God. This is my world, and you are here as *gērîm*, expatriates. 'The land is mine and you reside in my land as foreigners and strangers' (Lev. 25:23).[36] And that means you observe the laws and manners of your host country. We begin to see why the psalmist, *a stranger on earth*, cries, *Do not hide your commands from me.* He needs God's handbook for the duration of his residence in God's world.

What creates problems for him, and underlines his need of such a handbook, is the fact that though this really is God's world there are plenty of people in it who do not behave as if it were (21–22). On all sides he sees the arrogant and the accursed, and their *scorn and contempt* for God's principles. He is bound to be affected, and fears being infected, by all this. He does not have to be abroad for *rulers* to slander him, as the great ones of Babylon slandered Daniel (Dan. 6:1–16). Verses 23–24 remind us that right here at home there are powerful and influential people (the same word is used of Israelite 'leaders' in the time of Ezra and Nehemiah; Ezra 9:1–2; Neh. 9:32ff.) who reject God's law and vilify those who hold to it. Hence the constant need for the resolve, repeated from the end of the last stanza, to meditate on and to delight in that law.

4. *Daleth* (119:25–32)

Are we by now sufficiently in tune with the psalmist's mind to guess how he might set about composing the next stanza? We know his theme is the word of God. We know his aim is to show how it relates to the life of the believer. We know his chosen format is the acrostic, which at this point requires of him a stanza of eight verses each beginning with the Hebrew equivalent of the letter D. We can try reading his thoughts.

Dābār would come instantly to his mind, the *word* itself – of the eight law nouns, the one he has already used at the beginning of both *Beth*

---

[36] See pp. 1.134, 2.138.

and *Gimel*, though not of course as their first words. Here it could start every line!

Well, no, perhaps not; he seldom uses any of the eight more than once or twice in any one stanza, and certainly not several times. But another possibility is *derek* ('way'), which, though not one of the eight, fits the theme well. This he decides he will use, and for no fewer than five of his verses (the NIV slightly disguises the fact; the NRSV, and still more the RV, makes it clear).[37]

So his own *ways* introduce this *Daleth* stanza (26), and from verse 27 to verse 32 'the way of thy precepts', 'the way of falsehood', 'the way of faithfulness' and 'the way of thy commands' (RV) form a shapely chiasmus.

The poem is meant for use, not just ornament, and two more words which in Hebrew begin with D are ready to hand to express the psalmist's feelings. He is *laid low* (25 – 'downhearted', perhaps?) and *weary* (28 – 'drooping'?). It is a fact, not just a game with letters, to say that the stress he felt in *Gimel* has become real distress in *Daleth*.

The introductory verses 25–26 put in a nutshell how he copes when so desperately in need of being raised and renewed. He prays, and he finds a response in the word of God. He spreads everything before the Lord, for nothing is too trivial or too shameful to talk about with such a friend, and the rest of the psalm shows how the Lord opens up to him *the way* things are to work out.

A sequence of prayers begins at verse 27: *Cause me to understand, strengthen me, keep me, be gracious to me, do not let me be put to shame.* A sequence of resolves gradually overlaps it: *I have chosen, I have set my heart, I hold fast, I run.* All are based on the assurances God's word has given him.

There is one more repetition, almost impossible to bring out in translation. The D-word of verse 25 reappears in verse 31. When the psalmist is so down, and 'clings to the dust', the way up is to 'cling to your decrees' instead (NRSV). Are you stuck in the mire? Then get stuck into the Scripture![38] What will result is the setting free of the heart that in earlier psalms – 18:19; 31:8 – has been translated as a bringing out into a 'spacious place'.

---

[37] Repetition in the Heb. text underlines the point and clarifies the structure; by preferring variety, some modern translations dissipate the effect and confuse the structure.

[38] V. 31 AV actually says, 'I have stuck unto thy testimonies.'

5. *He* (119:33–40)

We are well aware that there is a great deal more to praying than merely asking God for things, as a child might – 'Do this', 'Give me that.' Petition is, even so, a proper and important aspect of prayer. While this longest of the psalms consists of prayer almost from start to finish, petition figures only a dozen times in the course of its first four stanzas. The *He* stanza redresses the balance. Every verse asks the Lord to do something for the psalmist. This letter of the alphabet lends itself to such praying, because an initial *he* can indicate a 'causative' verb in Hebrew: 'Lord, please cause *x* or *y* to happen.' Whether or not the first word of any particular line is of this sort, these eight verses are full of petitionary prayer.

Gimel showed the psalmist struggling with what W. E. Henley called the 'fell clutch of circumstance', and *Daleth*, looking inward, expressed his low spirits in that situation. Now, in *He*, he recognizes his own short-comings, the effects of the human weakness and sinfulness that were hinted at in *Aleph*.

Rephrasing the prayers will bring out what the Lord is being asked to do. 'Make me see the way of your decrees' – so we might translate verse 33. The *way*, frequent in the previous stanza, is here too, though hidden from us in some translations. What hides it from the psalmist is the sinner's natural inability to see spiritual truth. That is something the Lord must deal with, as in verse 18 (*Open my eyes*).

'Make me understand' (34): some aspects of the law I should keep wholeheartedly, if only I could grasp what they were saying. So 'make me go down the right path' (35), for once on it, I know I shall *find delight* in it.

On the other hand, there are things about the law that I understand only too well, and in those I need you to 'make me *want* to go' down a path away from the *selfish gain* I should prefer (36). 'Make my eyes turn away' from such worthlessness, and 'make my life new' according to your way (37).[39] 'Make your promise good'; it is when things happen as you say they will that your opponents will learn to reverence you (38). Conversely (39), 'make their contempt of no effect'; despite what they say, *your laws are good*.

So the psalmist rounds off his petitions by repeating that of verse 37b. A shopping-list prayer, maybe, but what shopping! These are things that only the Lord can provide, and only in his word are they to be found. He

---

[39] So most manuscripts, translations and commentaries; NIV *word*.

is honoured by our asking for them. Only he, declares the psalmist, can thus 'give me life' (40 NRSV).

6. *Waw* (119:41–48)

For a second-rate poet no other stanza in the psalm would be as technically easy as this one. An initial *waw* means 'and'; eight verses about anything at all could be strung together with a *waw* at the beginning of each, and the job would be done.

But as Spurgeon points out, when the word 'and' begins a verse it 'acts as a hook to attach it to the preceding verses'. The psalmist takes the form seriously, and makes it serve his purpose. Even the stanza as a whole is attached with an 'and' to all that has gone before. 'There you have the first forty verses of my psalm,' he says, '*and* in view of them . . .'

The *Waw* stanza, then, is a sequence in which the prayer of each verse is connected with the one before. Or rather, everything is connected with everything else; for sometimes the 'and' looks forward (meaning 'That implies also that I *will do* such-and-such'), while at other times it looks back (meaning 'That implies also that I *have done* such-and-such').

In addition, the psalmist's thought has two aspects, the word in his heart and the word on his lips. In private, he tells the Lord, I *meditate on your decrees*; in public, I am prepared to *speak of your statutes before kings*. The inward and the outward, together with the network of causes and consequences that we have just noted, are bound together in a glittering web. So since there is really no beginning to this seamless robe, we have to start *in medias res*, as the psalmist does, with the first of eight 'and's.

– And all I have written so far (he is just saying to the Lord in v. 41, as we eavesdrop on a prayer already in progress) implies of course that I want a repeated experience of your salvation, of your covenant loves – in the plural, please! And that will mean (42) that I have an answer for the unbeliever, as the word I have trusted proves to be true.

And that in turn implies that I can ask you with confidence (43) never to leave me without an apt testimony on my lips. And as your word is made known to others, I need hardly say that it will also be governing my own life (44); and I know that for me your law will be not restricting but liberating (45).[40]

---

[40] Again, the 'spacious place' of v. 32.

And that will tie in again with the testimony just mentioned; I shall find myself able to speak of your truth to anyone, even the most daunting (46)! And this springs from the delight in your law, and the love for it, which are my theme throughout (47), and points on to a continuing reverence for it, and meditation on it, which I shall certainly accord to it (48).

Here is the full-orbed picture of the person of the word. Every aspect is related to every other by the ubiquitous 'and'. Were any missing, the picture would be incomplete. As if to illustrate the point, when we check on the familiar recurring terms for 'law' we find here for the first time all the eight on parade, two of them (*word* and *commands*) even repeated in successive verses.

7. *Zayin* (119:49–56)

Remember, *zākar*, is the word that comes to the forefront of the psalmist's mind for the *Zayin* stanza. It provides the initial Z for three of his eight verses.

Bible people would be nonplussed by our curious modern preoccupation with the future, or rather by the notion that we need to find out somehow what the future holds, and that we do so by turning our backs on the past. Among the psalms, 119 is by no means the first to touch on the matter, as it does in this stanza. We may recall, for example, the attitude of 48, so unfashionable and so sensible, that it is the past, not the future, which we can know and learn from. The further back you look, the further ahead you can see.

One reason why Scripture takes this approach is that the God of Scripture is always active and always consistent. When therefore in verses 49–51 the psalmist asks God to remember, he is thinking of what God has done repeatedly in the past; he grasps what that says about God's character, and about the kind of thing he can be expected to do again in the present and the future. A considerably more reliable forecast, be it said, than any we are likely to find in our newspapers from astrologers, meteorologists or politicians!

As we have learned, in Scripture remembering is less a matter of memory than of action. The psalmist is asking God 'to act in conformity with an existing commitment'.[41] The three verses use three of the eight law-words in just this sense. The Lord's *word* is a basis for confident hope:

---

[41] Allen, p. 136.

once spoken, ever valid (49). His *promise* ensures that new life will always spring out of suffering (50). His *law* is a constant; no mockery, however unrestrained, will deflect the psalmist from it (51).

In verses 52–54 it is the psalmist who remembers, focusing again on three of the eight words. *Laws* (52) are not the same as the *law* in verses 51 and 53. As we shall see in the next stanza, they are the judgments pronounced by a judge; though the effects of such rulings, 'judgments' in the sense of punishments, may also be in the psalmist's mind. He is comforted to know that as in ancient times, at the flood and the exodus, at Babel and Sodom, so too today evil will not go unpunished. The Lord's *law* may continue to be rejected, which makes him angry (53); but the Lord's *decrees* continue to make him joyful, through all the ups and downs of life in an alien world (54; *lodge* is related to *stranger* in v. 19).

Once more in a final couplet (55–56) there is remembering, and once more we see the psalmist's reverence for God's *law*, this time linked with his *precepts*. The last verse is difficult; perhaps it means not *This has been my practice*, but 'This has been my *reward*, that I obey your precepts', rather as in Jesus' parable of the talents the 'reward' of service is more service (Matt. 25:21, 23). From all he has said, he does see a life centred on the word as something deeply rewarding. And it is *in the night*, when it is not so easy to see things clearly, that he finds he can anticipate the future with confidence by remembering what God has said in the past.

8. *Heth* (119:57–64)

Two great Old Testament words beginning with *heth*[42] must have jostled for attention when the psalmist reached this stanza. He began its first verse with the word for 'portion', *ḥēleq*, and its last with the word for 'love', *ḥesed*, and thus its theme was practically chosen for him: the believer's deep personal relationship with the Lord and his word.

Portion often means the share of land the Lord allocated to each Israelite family when his people took possession of Canaan (cf. Josh. 15:13; 18:5ff.; 19:9). Possession is perhaps too strong a word, for the land continued to be his, as it always had been, and in fact they were only tenants. Still more accurately, they were resident aliens (like the *stranger* of v. 19), with no rights, and entirely dependent on him.

---

[42] *He* is the equivalent of H; *heth* (*ḥêt*) has the sound of 'ch' in 'loch' or 'bach'.

The position of the tribe of Levi dramatized that of the whole nation. The Levites were not even given land; the Lord told them, 'I am your share' (Num. 18:20). In practice they were supported by the gifts of those to whom they ministered (cf. Deut. 18:1–2); but the point was made that for them, and by extension for all God's people, to have the Lord was to have everything. In the GNB version the stanza begins, 'You are all I want'; much as Paul would say, concerning God's gift of his Son, 'How will he not also, along with him, graciously give us all things?' (Rom. 8:32).

Love is the covenant love that brings about this relationship and guarantees its permanence. We shall return to it at verse 64.

Since this is the first stanza to display all the eight law-words once each (*Waw* had them all, but with one or two repeats), it is a good opportunity to note their shades of meaning. *Word* is the most general of the eight. As God is everything I need, so I pay attention to everything he says, in whatever form he first spoke it, in whatever way I now hear it (57). *Promise* also means something spoken; it too is sometimes translated 'word' in the NIV, and here too he expects me to respond with my whole heart to a grace that touches my whole life (58).

Statutes reminds us that God has made the covenant with us on his own 'terms' (as Allen renders it throughout), and that it witnesses[43] to the kind of God he is. It is one of the terms of the covenant that I should bring my life into line with his (59). *Commands* – the word, *miṣwâ*, is probably familiar to us from the Bar Mitzvah ceremony, when a Jewish boy becomes a 'son of the law' – means simply 'orders', and is about doing what you are told. It gives no leeway for prevarication or *delay* (60).

Of the eight, *law* is used first (1) and most frequently (25 times) in Psalm 119. We noted in the *Aleph* stanza that it means directions, or instruction. Verse 61 reiterates the surprising point that it brings freedom, in contrast to the entanglements of evil. *Laws* (62) is a different word, and means judgments or rulings, as we have recently noted. The psalmists often look forward eagerly to the Lord's coming to judge; in the darkest times (*at midnight*) they know that his decisions sooner or later sort things out. *Precepts* (63) is a matter of close attention to detail. It is a host of small particular things about another person, as well as a sense of spiritual kinship, that say to the believer, 'Bible truth is appreciated there; that is someone who fears the Lord as you do.'

---

[43] Hence 'testimonies' in AV/RV/RSV; and cf. the related word in (e.g.) Lev. 5:1; Deut. 17:6–7.

It is very fitting that the last of the eight, *decrees*, should appear in the last verse of the stanza. This is not just because it is the one that in Hebrew begins with *heth* (though it is), but because the *heth*-word that actually starts verse 64 agrees with it so well. *Decrees* are permanent, as it were carved in stone. The corresponding verb is used in Isaiah for the inscribing of God's words as 'an everlasting witness' (30:8), and for the engraving of his people's names 'on the palms of [his] hands' (49:16). What better word than *huqqîm* to link with the message of *hesed*, unchangeable covenant love, with which the word of God fills the earth?

9. *Teth* (119:65–72)

Since the whole psalm is saying what a good thing the word of God is, we should not be surprised at the dominant thought of this stanza. 'Good' in Hebrew begins with *teth* (*tôb*), and takes pride of place in five of the eight verses. The first two say in effect 'Good you will do to me' and 'Good judgment teach me'; the last two, 'Good it was for me' and 'Good is the law'; and in between, verse 68 has the word twice: 'Good you are, and good you do.' And once more God's word is mentioned in every verse, and everything is related to it, even though it is directly described as being itself *good* only in verse 72.

It is Scripture that both promises and conveys the good things that the Lord intends for his servant (65). They include knowledge, which is an excellent gift, and good judgment (the ability 'to distinguish good from evil', Heb. 5:14), which is even better; but the psalmist has his priorities right, for he sees that both depend on something more important still. That is faith in Scripture; and when Scripture is defined as *your commands*, to believe them means of course to obey them. So first you must trust and obey, and then you come to know and to discern (66).

The middle section of the stanza introduces a contrasting second subject, affliction (67–70). How do God's good words square with our bad experiences? We may remember the verses at the midpoint of the Psalter that implied a major question about the same *teth*-word: 'Surely God *is* good to Israel? But I nearly lost my foothold! How could he let that happen to me?'

The disoriented cry of 73:1–2 is reoriented in 119:67–70. The arrogant are here as they were there, being allowed by God to cause trouble for the godly. *Smeared . . . with lies* has a thoroughly modern ring. But our psalmist knows that when things are easy for him he tends to stray from the path, whereas trouble sends him back to the word. God *is* good, and what he does is good.

In the last two verses of the stanza we find that an appreciation of his word, his *decrees* and his *law* (repeated from vv. 68 and 70), is actually enhanced by the psalmist's bad experiences. *It was good for me to be afflicted so that I might learn your decrees* (71). No wonder the psalmist says, 'Good is the law from your mouth.' In whatever form he heard or read it, it seemed – as it can still seem to us – alive, dynamic, newly spoken by the mouth of the Lord. That, he tells us, 'means more to me than a fortune in gold and silver' (72 NEB).

10. *Yodh* (119:73–80)

The *Yodh* stanza draws together threads from much earlier psalms.

Here for the first time in 119 God is celebrated as the Creator, as in 33, and particularly as the Creator of humanity, as in 8. *Your hands made me*, the psalmist begins. When he continues *and formed me*, he uses not the word for 'form' in 33:15 (to mould or fashion), but the one that 8:3 applies to the making of 'the moon and the stars, which you have *set in place'*. It is as though God were saying in that psalm, 'There, that's a moon', and in this one, 'There, that's a man.' He has 'made me what I am' (73 NEB).

And human beings, established in their own special place in the created order, are unique. What sets them 'over the works of [God's] hands' (8:6) is not that they are reasoning or tool-using creatures but that they can have *understanding to learn [God's] commands* (119:73). Only those whose lives are aligned with the word of God exemplify humanity as he meant it to be.

Whether by accident or design – probably the latter, as I suggested in introducing this psalm – the stanza that describes the complete human being also displays the complete set of eight law-words, one per verse, as only the *Heth* stanza has done up to now. In another way also *Yodh* resembles *Heth*. Both look back to the very beginning of the Psalter and to the two companies of 1:6, the righteous and the wicked. *Heth* has *the wicked* on the one hand and *all who fear you* on the other (61, 63). In *Yodh* they are the God-fearers and the arrogant (74, 78, 79). Why does the psalmist speak of them at this point?

It is because he is taking up a further theme that figured often in the early part of the Psalter, that of affliction. The *Teth* stanza has just introduced it to this psalm (67, 71).[44] Affliction is either permitted or actually sent by God for a purpose. The verb is the one used in Deuteronomy 8 for

---

[44] *Suffering* in v. 50 is a different word.

the Lord 'humbling' his people during their exodus journey in order to test them and teach them. Here, the psalmist is willing to accept such treatment because he believes that it really expresses the Lord's faithfulness (75). This does not only mean that the Lord, faithful to his covenant love and his promise (76), is testing and teaching the psalmist himself. In faithfulness to the same principles the Lord intends also 'the encouragement of the godly and the confusion of the proud'.[45] He sets before them (remember 8:3 – 'When I consider [what] you have set in place'?) one who in trust and obedience has learned how to cope with affliction. That is a miraculous witness to his grace and power. By their reactions to it the two assemblies may be defined: those who recognize God's work in a human heart, and those who do not.

11. *Kaph* (119:81–88)

In five successive stanzas the psalmist has spoken of his ill-treatment at the hands of those who dislike and oppose him. In *Waw* he is taunted (42), in *Zayin* mocked (51), in *Heth* bound (61), in *Teth* smeared (69) and in *Yodh* wronged (78). Here in *Kaph* he is still being molested by the arrogant, and still there are no grounds for their attacks (85–86, as in 69 and 78).

A *kaph*-word comes to hand opportunely to take the psalm even deeper into this experience of trouble. It is the verb that begins each of the first two verses of the stanza, *kālâ*, translated *My soul faints* and *My eyes fail*; it is also the verb (though not the first word) in verse 87a, **wiped . . . from the earth**.

It sets the tone for the most heartfelt of the beleaguered psalmist's prayers so far. He is saying, literally, 'Lord, I'm finished', for that is the meaning of *kālâ*. He is at the end of his tether. A dried, cracked wineskin, past the end of its useful life – that is what he feels like. There comes a point at which the tormented soul can no longer tell itself, as it could in *Teth*, how good for you affliction can be. There comes a state of mind where it could not care less how confounded the wicked might be, or how encouraged the godly, by its splendid example. It could in *Yodh*; but those days are gone.

At such a time, the psalmist maintains, there remains always one thing that distinguishes the righteous from the wicked, something deeper than their antipathy towards each other. Verse 85 does not mean that to *dig pits*

---

[45] Kirkpatrick, p. 716.

is *contrary to [God's] law* (though it is), but that the whole mindset of the people who are doing it runs counter to what God has said. In contrast, amid all the turmoil of his distress the psalmist can say truly that he still hopes in the word, seeks the promise, remembers the decrees and looks for the judgments;[46] follows the law, trusts the commands, keeps the precepts and obeys the statutes. All the eight are here again, but they are eight aspects of a single fact: namely that God has spoken. Just that one hand to hold in the darkness, just that one thread to follow through the labyrinth – it would be nice to have extra helps, and not merely the voice of God; but as Bunyan's Pilgrim found, 'the way is the way, and there's an end'.

12. *Lamedh* (119:89–96)

There is both contrast and continuity between *Lamedh* and the stanzas that lead up to it. Their negative tone gives way here to a positive one; but the background is still described in the same terms, *affliction* at the hands of *the wicked*, and a plea that God would save his life (e.g. vv. 61, 71, 88). Now, however, although without God's help he *would have perished*, by God's help he has not. Although the wicked still threaten him, his life has been *preserved*. The imagery of the narrow and the wide, which we first came across in 18:6, 19, suits him exactly: 'In my distress [straits, narrows] I called to the Lord . . . He brought me out into a spacious [wide] place.'

It may be part of the psalmist's design that such a change should come at this point, halfway through the psalm. One of the old commentators suggests that the first eleven stanzas work towards *Kaph*, which says in effect 'Has the Lord brought me thus far only to abandon me?', while the remaining eleven carry forward the confident statement of *Lamedh*, 'His word is reliable, and he will complete his work in me.'[47] However that may be, *Lamedh* is itself divided into halves, with the same Hebrew word, *lĕʿôlām*, beginning each – very obvious in the original, though awkward in translation: '*For ever*, O Lord, your word is fixed'; '*For ever* I will not-forget your precepts.'

The midpoint of the stanza, the break between the two halves, is the turning point of a chiasmus concerning the Lord's word:

---

46 'When will you *judge* those who persecute me?' (84 nrsv).

47 J. F. Thrupp, quoted by Spurgeon.

The vastness of its scope (89–91),
    and what it has done for me (92);
    what it has done for me (93–95),
and the vastness of its scope (96).

The way that creation works, throughout space and time, demonstrates the power of God's creative, sustaining word (89–91). Whether it is his laws that endure, or all created things that keep going according to those laws (scholars differ), everything operates as he tells it to. The fact that all things serve him (91) has a very practical and comforting spin-off, evidenced by a question asked and answered in one of Thomas Toke Lynch's hymns:

Say not, my soul, 'From whence
    Can God relieve my care?'
Remember that Omnipotence
    Has servants everywhere.[48]

So the word that directs both the structure of the universe and the processes of history is the same word that preserves and sustains the Lord's servant (92–96). It does not save him out of a world still vexed by scoundrels, but it does save him in it.

Perfection in verse 96 is a thought-provoking, ambivalent word. 'Perfect' means complete, finished – and finished means finite, and therefore not at all perfect as an infinite God is perfect! But the following of the commands of God takes us beyond the limits, and the limitations, of this world. If all people were to serve him, as *all things* already do, they would find in that service (as the Psalter often observes) perfect freedom.

13. *Mem* (119:97–104)

If *Lamedh* showed an upturn in the psalmist's fortunes, *Mem* is even more positive. There are no traumas or trials here. Perhaps because of that, there are no petitions either; in contrast to *He*, where every verse is a plea, the prayers in *Mem* ask for nothing, but consist entirely of testimony and praise. It is the first such stanza in the psalm.

---

[48] T. T. Lynch, 'Say not, my soul'.

And the eight words for *law* – at any rate the seven of them that it uses – are not its background but its subject. It is actually *about* the word of God. In whatever form that word was known to the psalmist, it has come to us in the form of Scripture, and from our point of view it is of the practical use and value of Scripture that he speaks.

It is difficult to detect a clear shape in the *Mem* stanza without being over-ingenious. Is the repeated *how* (97, 103) some kind of marker? Do the three comparisons of verses 98–100 bind them into a subsection? Is *path/ path* an inclusio round the second half? As a whole, however, the stanza does plainly tell us of something – in fact five things – that the word of God does for the people of God.

First, it delights them: *How I love your law!* (97); *How sweet are your promises* (103 in the 1979 NIV). C. S. Lewis helps us to see how law, not just promises, could be sweet as honey (19:7–10). He suggests that the idea represents the contrast between the faith of Israel and the disgusting pagan religions that surrounded it. So today 'Christians increasingly live on a spiritual island; new and rival ways of life surround it in all directions and their tides come further up the beach every time.' We need to value all the more a satisfying biblical ethic 'which in a more Christian age we might have taken for granted'.[49]

Then it accompanies them constantly (97–98). Of course, to be able to *meditate on it all day long* they need to know it. For the heart to be able to love it, the mind has to think about it and the memory has to store it. The days of learning by rote are not quite past, as any stage-struck youngster is aware, and that is the only realistic way to be able to say of God's words [*They*] *are always with me*.

Third, it equips them (98–100). 'Enemies excel in policy, teachers in doctrine, and ancients in counsel,' said Thomas Manton,[50] explaining that the ordinary believer who knows the word is better equipped than clever, learned or experienced people who do not.

Next, the word directs God's people. Here as elsewhere, the Bible's teaching on guidance has far less to do with signs and pointers than with being right with God, and keeping that way. The sense of verse 104 is established by the parallel verse 101: *understanding* has to do with

---

[49] Lewis, pp. 55–57. The truth of Lewis's observation in 1958 has if anything become plainer in the intervening years.

[50] The seventeenth-century Puritan commentator, as quoted by Spurgeon. (He preached, and published, no fewer than 190 sermons on Ps. 119!)

obedience, not brains; the *wrong path* is the *evil path*, not simply the incorrect one.

Finally, it puts them in touch with God himself. The psalmist is in no danger of worshipping the book rather than the Lord of the book. Practically everything he says about the word of God in this psalm (172 verses out of 176) is addressed to God, and here in verse 102 he recognizes that whatever he has learnt from God's law, it is God himself who has been teaching him. The 'word of God' is no mere label to attach to a book; it means God speaking.

14. *Nun* (119:105–112)

Mem has been an interlude, with the psalmist shut away briefly from the pressures of the outside world to enjoy fellowship with the Lord and his word. Affliction (107) and malice (110) beset him once more in *Nun*. More important than these, and actually enhanced by them, is the stanza's main theme, the psalmist's resolve to outface such challenges. He is confident in the power of the word; indeed he deliberately commits himself to follow it. We note the oath confirmed in verse 106, the devotion of verse 108, the determination of verses 109–110, and the heart set on obedience in verse 112. This is Bunyan's Mr Valiant-for-Truth:

> One here will constant be,
>   Come Wind, come Weather.

A sequence of four metaphors runs through the stanza: *My feet, my mouth, my hands, my heart*. Each is associated with another metaphor of a different kind, as we shall see.

There are in fact four metaphors in the first verse alone. If asked what they mean, we might answer, 'Illumination on my way through life', only to realize that we are still using metaphors. *Light on my path* is simpler, *a lamp for my feet* more specific. The psalmist would see in his mind's eye not a lamp post or a lampstand, but a lamp that he himself would carry, as we would arm ourselves with a torch on a dark road; for verse 106, like the rest of the psalm, is about taking action.

As feet on the path are related to the light of a lamp, so in verses 107–108 the mouth is related to another concrete metaphor. The word the NIV translates by the abstract notion of *willing praise* normally means offerings of cattle, sheep or goats. From his mouth the psalmist gives God a goat! Willing praise was of course what such freewill offerings expressed. That would be the proper response from one who knows from experience both suffering and the renewing power of the Lord.[51]

There is no oddity about the idea of taking one's life in one's hands. Several Old Testament passages seem to be the source of a phrase that has come into regular English usage (see Judg. 12:3; 1 Sam. 19:5; 28:21; Job 13:14). Along with it, in verses 109–110, comes the image of a snare set for the psalmist. The obvious means of avoiding traps laid by the wicked would be to stay at home; but he has committed himself to the way of the law and the precepts, and at whatever risk he will pursue it.

In verses 111–112, the two metaphors are the heritage and the heart. The former, like *willing praise*, pictures something much more concrete than we might think, namely the land God promised to Israel (Exod. 32:13). What the psalmist is saying, in this graphic way, is that 'the Torah', God's law, God's word, is for him 'a whole promised land of joy',[52] and that he is utterly committed – for *heart* means 'will' – to the keeping of it.

15. *Samekh* (119:113–120)

This stanza has a clearer shape than many, with two halves mirroring each other. It is with the Lord and his word that the righteous belong (though the wicked do not), and here the psalmist prays to be kept; so the first four verses. Then verse 117 answers to verse 116, verse 118 to verse 115, and verses 119–120 to verses 113–114.

Like the many other chiastic walks out-and-back-again that we have noted, this is by no means a pointless exercise. It pictures on the tiny canvas of an eight-verse stanza a theological principle that holds good also on the broadest possible scale: the return to a starting point which is the same yet not the same. The author of Ecclesiastes speaks of this circularity in sun, wind and water ('to the place [they] come from, there they return', 1:7) and in human life ('the spirit returns to God who gave it', 12:7), thus, incidentally, making his own book likewise end where it began. But this view of life could not be further removed from the hopeless circularity of Hinduism, for in biblical theology the pilgrim makes progress, and his or her coming home to God is the consummation of it.

---

[51] As in the 1979 NIV, 'renew' rather than *preserve*.

[52] Allen, p. 143.

So here there is a progress from the love and hope of verses 113–114 to the love and awe of verses 119–120. The psalmist's hatred of the double-minded, at the beginning of this stanza, grows out of the single-minded resolve he has just shown in the last one. In the only verse in the entire psalm addressed to someone other than God (115), he distances himself, as one who cares about keeping God's word, from those who have no such care themselves, and who would make it unnecessarily hard for him.

Then in verse 116 an elementary fact is borne in on him afresh, and at once he turns back to God. Determination 'in keeping of thy commandments' is all very well, but 'through the weakness of our mortal nature we can do no good thing without thee';[53] so he has to plead for God's help to *sustain* him in his resolve.

At this point the chiasmus turns, and begins to retrace its steps with the prayer that God will *uphold* the psalmist (117). He realizes in verse 118 that his own distancing of himself from *evildoers* in verse 115 was only an imperfect reflection of God's final judgment on those who *stray from [his] decrees*; with complete knowledge of all the facts, and with perfect justice, the Judge will rule that those who do not want him shall not have him.

The psalmist, aware of his own frailty and sinfulness, is thus reminded that there is no room for arrogance in his claims to hate double-minded people and to distance himself from evildoers. He is one himself. Verse 119 does not express pride; it sounds, in the context, more like panic – 'You would be within your rights to discard me, along with all the wicked, but deep down, Lord, I do love your statutes.'

It is the closing verse that suggests we read the psalmist's return journey in this way. He loves the Lord and his word still, as he did at the beginning, but now he does so with fear. And let us not assume complacently that that 'merely means reverence'. Verse 120 is about the shudder of dread; 'for our "God is a consuming fire"' (Heb. 12:29).

16. *Ayin* (119:121–128)

The arrogant, who appeared frequently in the first half of the psalm and then for a while were lost to view, are back with a vengeance. We cannot miss the fact that they are once again oppressing the psalmist.

---

[53] The Prayer Book's collect for Trinity 1.

With an eye to language as well as content, we may also notice verse 122 as one of the few that do not contain any of the eight law-words. In the NIV, verse 121 looks like another of the same kind, but in fact it includes the word usually translated *laws*, though used here in an unexpected way ('I have acted with *judgment*'). It is noticeable too, on reflection, that verses 123–128 seem to use six of the eight more precisely, less interchangeably, than is the case elsewhere. Each shows a particular facet of the word of God, 'word' itself being the one term that is not used here.

One thing which is of course hidden in English is the psalmist's choice of *ayin*-words to begin his verses. One of them is ʿāsâ, translated 'do/deal/ act'; another is ʿal-kēn, 'therefore' (not 'because') twice at the end of the stanza. With these words italicized, the eight verses begin something like this:

> *Acted* I have with judgment;
> ensure my well-being;
> my eyes fail.
> *Act* according to your love;
> I am your servant;
> it is time for you to *act*.
> *Therefore* I love your commands,
> *therefore* I approve your precepts.

As two triplets and a couplet, this *Ayin* stanza makes good sense. If that is the structure the psalmist intends, he seems to be saying: 'I have acted with judgment, and righteously; but evil, not good, comes of it – so please, Lord, stand for me against my enemies. I have done what the word rules (121), but I am still looking for what it promises (123).'

So he asks the Lord to do what he himself cannot do. 'Act according to your covenant love, Lord; deal with me, not just with my enemies or my problems, for I still need to be taught what the word decrees (124), and to understand the terms it lays down (125). It is time for you to act, Lord, for your word, the "law" in its broadest sense, is being flouted (126).'

'Therefore', either because the law is being broken, or because of the entire situation described up to now (which amounts to the same thing), 'therefore let me declare where I, at any rate, stand. I am glad to have the word tell me what to do (127), and I accept that at every point what it commands is right and what it forbids is wrong (128).'

None of us, including the psalmist himself, fully lives up to this high claim. But each of us knows, and the Lord knows, whether we want to do so. That is the crucial thing.

17. Pe (119:129–136)

What the psalmist has said in *Ayin* about his oppressors, about his distress at their breaking of God's law, and by contrast about his own love for God's commands, is all carried forward into *Pe*. Our old friends inclusio and chiasmus reappear in the first two and last two verses of this stanza: obedience / the light of the word // the light of the Lord / disobedience. Framed by them is an appeal containing a number of pleas to the Lord (131–134).

We should notice three things about the psalmist's language. For the last time in the psalm he uses all eight law-words. This is not evident in translation – 'laws' (*mišpāṭîm*) seems to be missing, and verse 132 seems to be the place it is missing from; but in fact it is there, though in the singular, lurking behind the phrase *as you always do* (i.e. 'as your law is').[54] A God who binds himself by his own laws to have mercy on his people – what a basis for the appeal of these central verses!

Then two of the psalmist's choices of initial *pe*-words are of great interest. Like 'terrific' or 'brilliant', *wonderful* (the NIV's translation of *pele'*, 129) currently means little more than that one thinks highly of whatever-it-is. But the word of God really is a wonder, something supernatural, and the sense of its power underlies much of this stanza.[55]

The first word of verse 130 could be ambiguously translated as 'opening'. Of two very similar Hebrew words, one (*petaḥ*) means *an* opening, an entrance or door; the other (*pātaḥ*) means *the* opening up of something. Here the Hebrew text has the latter. So the unfolding or explaining of the word of God brings light,[56] and the light is, according to verse 135, the shining face of God; for there is no separating God from his word. At this point our psalm, like so many others in the Psalter, harks back to the classic blessing promised to God's people in Numbers 6:22–26.

In his light, which the opening of Scripture reveals to us, we see how desirable are the commands that it conveys to us (131), and how certain is

---

54 The same sort of thing has happened in *Ayin*, in v. 121 NIV: *I have done* **what is ... just**.

55 Similarly, the word of God is 'terrific' and 'brilliant' in the original sense in vv. 120 and 130.

56 Cf. 'explain' (a related word) in 49:4 GNB.

the promise of mercy that it offers (132). We see how our way can be directed, not just *according to* it, as if it were simply God's pattern, but *by* it (133),[57] for it is God's power, and can set us free from the reign of sin. And we can see how obedience to it is the purpose of God's redemption of his people (134).

Tragic indeed it is, as the first and last verses of the stanza say plainly, when a word so truly wonderful is so widely disregarded.

18. *Tsadhe* (119:137–144)

With what relish must the psalmist have arrived at this stanza! The *tsadhe*-word that begins three of its verses, and appears twice more besides, practically chose itself. He would have found himself entirely in tune with that greatest of Old Testament scholars, the apostle Paul; with the greatest of his writings, the letter to the Romans; and especially with the way it sets out to expound the central message of all Scripture, the gospel of Christ – 'the power of God that brings salvation to everyone who believes', for in it 'the *righteousness of God* is revealed' (1:16–17).

Righteous (*ṣaddîq*) is the Lord, says *Tsadhe*'s first verse, and righteous are his statutes, says its last. In much the same way *Pe* brought together the light of the word and the light of the Lord in verses 130 and 135. When in Romans people are made righteous, they are made what they ought to be, and that puts in a nutshell the meaning of the word. So if in verse 137 the Lord is righteous, then he is what he ought to be, and if in verse 138 he has laid down his statutes (the terms on which his covenant is based) in righteousness, they too are what they ought to be. They and he will tally. He 'expresses and conveys himself in his word . . . The "match" between the two is perfect.'[58]

We may readily grasp the theology, but the practicality is something else. How does this word of God fare in the real world?

The wholesale ignoring of it is a great grief to the psalmist (139). Like Lot in Sodom, he is 'tormented in his righteous soul by the lawless deeds' around him (2 Pet. 2:8). So ought we to be, when we see on all sides both the sins of the self-serving and the follies of those who in government or administration claim to be serving others. But he is himself

---

57 So the Heb. text, followed by few translations but many commentaries.
58 Motyer, p. 571.

totally persuaded of the value of the righteous word, however little the world cares about it. He has *thoroughly tested* it and means to live by it (140).

What then does it matter if people despise him and his peculiar views (141)? Over against the current fashions, short-term answers and quick returns to which they have yoked themselves, he has got hold of a 'righteousness [which] is righteous for ever' (142 RSV).

Even when *trouble and distress* come upon him, and he is no longer a spectator but a sufferer (143), he is fortified by the same conviction. He loves God's commands; they represent a law that will outlast all these evils, because it is 'righteous for ever' (144 RSV, repeating 142). And the word that speaks it is a word of life. Let me understand it, he says, *that I may live.* If the life it gives is life as it ought to be, how can that not likewise last for ever?

19. *Qoph* (119:145–152)

Against the background of Psalm 119's constant preoccupation with the word of God, two related themes dominate this stanza, one its first half and the other its second half.

Once more the psalmist is in trouble. He calls to the Lord, the kind of cry that pleads for a response: *answer me* (145), *save me* (146). He promises that if the Lord does respond he will find him, the psalmist, obedient to his word. We are not to see this promise as an attempt to strike a bargain with God. Deep down, every believer wants to keep his statutes: 'In my inner being I delight in God's law,' says Paul in Romans 7:22. The statutes are as we know the terms of his covenant, and naturally his covenant people want to be 'on good terms' with him. Distress should bring this desire to the surface.

It makes the psalmist forestall the dawn (147), even forestall *the watches of the night* (148), with his prayer and his meditation on the word. We may have formed the good habit of setting time aside for such things before the working day begins, but here is one who goes beyond that. If my job involved coming on duty in the small hours, he tells the Lord, even then I should be up that much earlier to seek you first.

It is not that such devotion is needed in order to persuade an un-interested God. (We remember the parable of the persistent widow and the unjust judge in Luke 18:1–8.) Verses 149–152 make it plain that the psalmist is confident his cry will be answered willingly.

First, he can rely both on the Lord's love and on his laws (149). The former is covenant love, and according to that, God has covenanted to hear his people's voice. The latter is still more remarkable, for the laws he has laid down govern him himself, as we saw in connection with verse 132; according to them, he has bound himself to bless his people. In a similar way the letter to the Hebrews highlights in the story of Abraham 'two unchangeable things in which it is impossible for God to lie': his promise and his oath (Heb. 6:18) – the one entirely reliable in itself, yet confirmed, as if confirmation were needed, by the other.

Second, the psalmist can rely on the Lord's nearness (150–151). If his enemies are near to him and far from God, does that mean that he is deep in enemy territory, and at their mercy? Well, from one point of view they really are far from God, for they are far from his law; but they do not realize that however they may distance themselves from him, his writ runs everywhere, his dominion is universal, and where his distressed servant is, there he is also.

So third, the psalmist can rely on the Lord's constancy (152). Powers of evil may claim, and may seem, to be permanent, but like so much else about them this is an illusion. Nazism was meant to last a thousand years, and died in twelve; Russian Communism rose and fell within the lifetime of my parents. 'All people are like grass,' says the prophet, and so are the systems their wickedness sets up; for 'the grass withers', whereas 'the word of our God endures for ever' (Isa. 40:6–8; cf. 1 Pet. 1:24–25). Far back in the past the psalmist learnt this, and however far he looks into the future it will always be true.

20. *Resh* (119:153–160)

It seems likely that three lines of thought were converging when the psalmist composed the *Resh* stanza.

The ungodly appear often in Psalm 119. They are not simply part of the scenery; the psalmist reckons them his enemies. Here they are the *wicked* (155) and the *faithless* (or treacherous, for they break faith with people as readily as with God; 158), and in between (157) he speaks of *the foes who persecute me*.

The prayer *Preserve my life* is something else that comes often to the psalmist's pen in this psalm, most recently in *Qoph* (149). Now suddenly, in *Resh*, he uses it three times over in a single stanza (154, 156 and 159). In other versions, and in other places in the NIV, the word is translated as 'revive', or 'restore life', or even 'give life'. It does not, however, begin with *resh* in Hebrew, and so is here for the sake not of the stanza's structure, but of its theme.

A *resh*-word that relates both to theme and to structure is the one that begins verses 153, 158 and 159 – *rāʾâ*, translated 'look' or 'see'. It is this that brings the stanza into focus. The group of psalms rounded off by 119 is a Passover sequence, certainly of six (113 – 118), possibly of fourteen (105 – 118). If then the psalmist is here asking that the Lord will give him a new lease of life in rescuing him from his enemies, and has the Passover story fresh in his mind, what more natural than that he should couch his prayer in exodus language? So he asks God to come and look at his troubles, as he came and looked at the plight of the Israelites in Egypt, and to redeem him, as he redeemed them, from the clutches of those who like the pharaoh of Egypt are both wicked and faithless (cf. Exod. 3:7–9; 6:6; 5:2; 8:8, 15; etc.).

Resh speaks as though the powers of good and evil (the Lord's great compassion, 156, and the psalmist's many foes, 157) were evenly matched; *great* and *many* are the same word. It is not so, but that is the way it seems. This repetition completes a word-pattern that brings to light a helpful chiasmus.

> Look, and give me life (153–154)!
>> The wicked care nothing for your word (155);
>>> yet there are many compassions,
>>>> so give me life (156)!
>>> Still, there are many foes (157);
>> the faithless care nothing for your word (158);
> look, and give me life (159–160).

As always, everything is related to the word and the law of God. Yet again the psalmist models for us the kind of praying which is based solidly on Scripture, and shaped by one of its key passages.

21. *Sin* and *Shin* (119:161–168)

We have often seen in this psalm how the shape of a stanza, the choice of its initial words and the repetition of others can help to bring out its meaning. In this respect the *Sin/Shin* stanza is a puzzle. The initial words of its eight lines are all different, except for the repeated *obey* in the last two verses: seven different words then. In these seven words the two forms of their initial letter, distinguished in Hebrew by the position of a dot above it, might have shown some symmetry, but in fact do not: we find the eight verses divided two, three, one, two, between alternating *sin* and *shin*. *Love* for the law appears three times, but irregularly, and not, it seems, with an eye to clarifying the structure.

So perhaps this stanza is meant to be kaleidoscopic rather than architectural. What does unify it is, once again, the law of God, and not now as the background but as the focus of attention. Successive verses picture the psalmist's attitude to the law from one angle after another.

Whatever distress he may feel at his rough handling by *rulers*, leading members of his own Israelite community who ought to know better, what really makes him *tremble* is the word of God (161). As we saw in verse 120, there are truths in it that are genuinely terrifying, and have to be held in balance with its hugely desirable treasures (162). To develop a real love for it is to develop a corresponding distaste for the illusions and the perversions of truth in which the world deals (163).

The psalmist has so let himself be captivated by the rightness of what God says that repeatedly he finds himself praising God for it (164). Presumably he did not have the luxury of being able to drop everything for seven formal times of prayer each day, and is encouraging us rather in the constant 'practice of the presence' during our ordinary daily occupations. A second time he speaks of love for the law (165), which brings with it a sense of blessed security; for the better we love the word of God the less likely we are to stumble into the snares of temptation.

There is nothing stoical, let alone impatient, about the psalmist's 'waiting' in verse 166. It has a confident expectancy such as we find in 104:27, where the same word is used: 'All creatures *look to you* to give them their food at the proper time.' It is matched by a corresponding eagerness about his side of the relationship, which is to follow the Lord's commands.

In verses 167 and 168, the repeated *shin*-word *obey* (*šāmar*, better translated 'keep') makes them a kind of rhyming couplet, with the 'rhyme' not ending but beginning the lines. This is perhaps intended to complete the stanza by drawing its threads together. The making of Psalm 119 may have been the patient toil of long, quiet hours, as Lewis says, but that does not mean the maker was placid and unemotional. Trembling and joy, hatred and love, praise and peace, expectancy and doggedness, all are summed up in these closing verses. To hold to the word of God, its precepts and statutes, is to tell him how warm is our love for him and how awesome is his knowledge of us.

22. *Taw* (119:169–176)

Where the previous stanza contained no petitions, this one contains little else. It was appropriate that before the psalm ended it should include a testimony or creed, and that is what *Shin* has provided. What this final stanza reminds us of is that we are never beyond the need of prayer.

Many facets of prayer, in fact, are set before us in *Taw*, just as its predecessor showed many facets of a profession of faith. So the two stanzas are alike in their variety, though they differ in their subject.

They differ also in their construction, as a piece of jewellery differs from a heap of gems. Here the eight verses are grouped in four couplets, and further into two pairs of couplets. We might say that the prayer of the first half, verses 169–172, is 'Lord, hear', and that of the second half, verses 173–176, is 'Lord, act.'[59] The stanza's four subdivisions might be headed 'Lord, hear my prayer', 'Lord, hear my praise', 'Lord, act to help me', 'Lord, act to restore me.'

The value of learning to use all these verses, each with its reference to the word of God, as prayers of our own must be inestimable. 'Lord, hear my prayer for *understanding according to your word*' (169): I need to know the right things, in the right spirit, at the right time and for the right purpose. 'Lord, hear my prayer for *deliverance according to your promise*' (170): I ask that in the way you know is best, you will order my outward circumstances just as you can order my inward thoughts.

'Lord, hear my praise for your *willingness to teach me your decrees*' (171): you have made me see what really matters, the truth graven in stone – crudely, the 'bottom line'.[60] 'Lord, hear my praise for the *righteousness shown in your commands*' (172): when you tell me to do a thing, you won't always say why, but I know it will be always right and never arbitrary.

'Lord, act to help me, because *I have chosen your precepts*' (173): as an act of will I have aligned myself with what you have laid down. 'Lord, act to help me, because *I delight in your law*' (174): I realize that the choice was

---

[59] So Motyer, p. 572.

[60] See on v. 64, and Isa. 30:8 (the 'everlasting witness').

not simply my decision, but that you have worked in me to make me love what I should otherwise think unlovely.

'Lord, act to restore me, because *I am sustained by your laws*' (175): apart from them there is no life worth living. 'Lord, act to restore me, because *I have retained your commandments*' (176): your word truly is in my heart, even though *I have strayed like a lost sheep*. I may know enough about you to write a psalm 176 verses long, but for all this industry and theology, for all this art and skill and grasp of the word, I am as 'prone to wander, Lord', as the next sheep is.

That phrase comes from the eighteenth-century hymn 'Come, thou fount of every blessing'. Robert Robinson, its author, himself strayed far, even after long service as a pastor to others. What grace it is that recognizes the frailty of a far greater 'servant', the author of this magnificent psalm, and brings him back repeatedly, by the word of God, to the word of God.

Psalms 120 – 134

6. The Songs of Ascents

It is a fact, not a guess, that the next fifteen psalms belong together, for each one carries the heading 'A song of ascents'. But there has been a variety of guesses as to what that heading signifies. Its key word can certainly mean 'goings up'; it is also the regular word for 'steps' or 'stairs'.

Does it refer to the type of poetry we find in Psalm 121, where 'help' steps up, as it were, from verse 1 into verse 2, and 'watch/slumber' from verse 3 into verse 4? Few psalms in the group, however, are actually like this. Are they then a liturgy for a choir ranged up a flight of fifteen stairs, such as we know existed in the Jerusalem temple? Some clues point in that direction, but the evidence is flimsy (cf. Neh. 9:4).

One of the two likeliest theories is that these are psalms for pilgrims 'going up' to God's sanctuary for one of the great festivals. Just as both Korah Collections begin with psalms full of longing for the house of God in the hearts of people who are far away from it (42 – 43; 84), so this set begins with misery in Meshek (120) and ends with joy in Jerusalem (134). The verb 'ascend' (though not the noun 'ascent') is used in this sense of Samuel's parents going up annually to Shiloh in 1 Samuel 1:3, of the tribes going up to Jerusalem in Psalm 122:4, and of the nations going up to the mountain of the Lord in the vision of Isaiah 2:3.

The other theory notes that in the book of Ezra exiles returning from captivity in Babylon are repeatedly said to 'go up' to Jerusalem, and Ezra's own 'journey' (7:9) is literally his 'going up', his *aliyah*, the noun in our psalm headings. In fact the 'ingathering of exiles to their ancestral homeland' is precisely what the modern Israeli understands by the word:

five Jewish *aliyoth*, waves of immigration, between 1882 and 1939, then a more or less continuous 'going up' ever since the founding of the state of Israel in 1948.

In all probability, then, these psalms relate in one way or another to people in biblical times going up to the house of the Lord in Jerusalem. Nearly all of the fifteen share family likenesses, in their brevity, their repetitions, their homely parables and their love for Zion. With a great festival as background to them, we may see other things that bind them together. And if we were right in guessing that it was one particular festival, the feast of Tabernacles in 445 BC, presided over by Ezra and Nehemiah, we might find in the 'songs of goings up' an underlying unity still more significant.[1]

Psalm 120

The fifteen songs seem to form five sets of three. For the most part the keynotes of the psalms in each set are distress in the first, power in the second and security in the third.[2]

Here as elsewhere in the Psalter the author's purpose in writing a psalm was not necessarily the same as that of a compiler grouping it with others. This first Song of Ascents sounds like a very personal cry of distress, afterwards adapted for rather different use in public liturgy.

1. My distress: the individual's poem

I cry, and the Lord answers, says the psalmist in verse 1. Verse 2 is the cry: he is beset by antagonists, and in his trouble he calls for help. Verses 3 and 4 are the answer. He is not spitting venom at these enemies – for all we know they may be quite unaware of his words – but having committed himself to the Lord in prayer, he is simply declaring a fact: this is how the Lord has said he will deal with such people.

Behind the curious wording of verse 3 is the common Old Testament oath which Saul, for example, used in 1 Samuel 14:44 NRSV: 'God do so to me and more also.' Well then, says the psalmist, since it seems you have sworn to get me, 'what will he do to you, and what more besides?'

---

[1] See Goulder, *Return, passim.*

[2] Motyer, p. 572.

He knows the answer. The enemy 'has shot his arrows of slander', as Kirkpatrick puts it, 'but a mightier than he, even God himself, will pierce him with the arrows of judgement'.[3]

The psalmist could not literally have lived in Meshek and Kedar simultaneously, for they were a long way apart. One was remote and presumably unfriendly; the other was near and definitely hostile. They were probably metaphors for his local enemies, much as when people complain today about living among vandals it is not the fifth-century inhabitants of North Africa that they have in mind.

2. Our distress: the assembly's psalm

Someone at some stage saw how apt this very personal poem would be as the opening psalm of a liturgy for public worship. If not a confession of sin, 120 is certainly an admission of need, like 42 – 43, 84 and 90, which introduce similar groups.

The conjecture that it heads a collection designed for the feast of Tabernacles, and in particular for the one in the year 445 BC, when the walls of Jerusalem were rebuilt after the exile (Neh. 6:15; 7:73 – 8:18), is something more than guesswork.[4] We know that Ezra, as religious leader of the restored community, gave public readings of the law of Moses daily throughout the festival. It would be entirely appropriate for the temple musicians to compile a new fifteen-psalm liturgy for the occasion, the 'Songs of Ascents' (not 'ascent', for there had been other 'goings up' from Babylonia and Persia before Nehemiah's[5]).

And Nehemiah himself, as governor, had been keeping a record of events, which would one day stand alongside the law of Moses as Scripture. The suggestion that that too might have provided public readings like Ezra's may seem a guess too far. But the distress of Psalm 120:1 parallels that of the disheartened remnant in Judah, and that of Nehemiah in Persia when he heard of it, in Nehemiah 1:3–4. Like the psalmist, he turned to the Lord in prayer. When he *went up* to join them, he found that he and they were in the thick of Psalm 120, living *among the tents of Kedar*

---

[3] Kirkpatrick, p. 735, echoing Spurgeon's comment on 64:4, 7 (see p. 1.227). 'Glowing coals are a metaphor for Divine judgements,' he continues (referring to 140:10), for one who 'has kindled the fire of strife by his falsehoods'.

[4] The possibility is worked out in detail in Goulder, *Return*.

[5] Following the traditional dating, Zerubbabel's was in 538, Ezra's in 458, Nehemiah's in 445. The new temple was begun in 520 and completed in 516.

with a vengeance, people *of peace* assailed by the *deceitful tongues* of those who were *for war.*[6]

Later songs also seem to reflect his narrative. Such a background to the Songs of Ascents helps us to sing and pray them as New Testament people in an equivalent situation. We may use them individually, like pilgrims who have been far from God and want to come back to him. But we may also use them like a company of the redeemed, brought out of captivity, building the city of God among people who reckon the world is theirs. They resent our intrusion into what they see as their territory, and consider us undesirable aliens. If they cannot remove us they aim at least to neutralize us.

In a sense we *are* foreigners, as the New Testament clearly teaches, and as the Psalter has periodically reminded us. But where we are, there is Jerusalem; and even if it is surrounded by the tents of Kedar, this is where we stay, and this is where we build.

Psalm 121

The second Song of Ascents is one of the best-known and best-loved poems in the Psalter. Singable metrical psalms are not so thick on the ground that we can readily dispense with John Campbell's version of it,[7] a faithful paraphrase which dared to correct the AV ('the hills, from whence cometh my help') for the benefit of Victorian congregations:

> Unto the hills around do I lift up
> > My longing eyes,
> Oh! Whence for me shall my salvation come,
> > From whence arise?
> From God the Lord doth come my certain aid,
> From God the Lord, who heaven and earth hath made.

While each of Campbell's four verses covers two of the Bible verses (and does it well), the psalmist may in fact have intended a division into three: verses 1–2, 3–5 and 6–8.

---

[6] Among the enemies in Neh. 2:19, 'Geshem the Arab' was actually king of Kedar, and 'Sanballat the *Horonite*' may in fact have come from *Haran* in northern Babylonia, in the general direction of Meshek, and the location of a famous temple of Sin, the moon god, from whom his name derives.

[7] Timothy Dudley-Smith's 'I lift my eyes to the quiet hills' is a meditation on only three or four of the eight verses.

1. A regular 'going up'

An individual speaks, and is spoken to; the *you* is singular as well as the *I*. But he seems not to be alone, for unless he is talking to himself in verses 3–8 (as in 42:5, 'Why, my soul, are you downcast?'), they are spoken by another voice or voices. There is of course no reason why solitary believers should not thus encourage themselves. But if this is a 'going up' to a festival, it could well be a company of pilgrims that is singing – each on his or her own account, as it were, for the first two verses, and to one another for the rest.

Is the psalmist thinking of the hills as a refuge or as a menace? 'Either way, he knows something better.'[8] He looks away from the dangers they may hold, and beyond the safety they may promise (we shall consider both shortly), to the One who made them and everything else besides. God the Creator and his keeping power are the theme of the psalm.

Twice in verses 3–5 he is named as Yahweh. Three times he is called the One who *watches over*; the noun 'guardian' would be a good translation. And five times *you* – the author, the singer, the listener or reader – are assured of his guardian care: *He will not let your foot slip.*

The three final verses reflect the shape of the previous three. Yahweh twice, the verb 'guard' (translated *keep* or *watch over*) three times, *you* or *your* five times;[9] and perhaps the day and the night of verse 6 were the background to verse 3 – your steps guarded during your waking hours and a wakeful Guardian while you sleep. With regard to verse 6, people have always known about sunstroke, and long feared the possibility of being 'moonstruck' too; but the believer is guarded against 'fears both rational and irrational'.[10] Perhaps the psalmist simply means that he need fear no evil either in daylight or in darkness.

But that, we protest, is unrealistic. It is not true to experience. The disoriented question of 73:1–2, at the midpoint of the Psalter, raises its head again, the question of one who did find his foot slipping in spite of God's assurances. Rereading our psalm as a song not just of the ascent to a festival, but of the ascent specifically to Tabernacles in 445 BC, will suggest an answer.

---

[8] Kidner, p. 431.

[9] 'Your coming and *your* going', v. 8.

[10] Allen, p. 154.

2. A specific 'going up'

Suppose that those who were chanting the second Song of Ascents were not in the process of going up to Jerusalem, but had already arrived there, to celebrate Nehemiah's going up earlier that year and all that had followed it. Suppose the psalm were a response to a second reading from his account of these 'mighty acts' of the 'Sovereign Lord', as 71:16 would describe them. What would 121 mean in the context of, say, Nehemiah 1:11b – 2:9?

The hills of verses 1–2 might be *both* a menace, most obviously as the haunt of outlaws and robbers, *and* (apparently) a refuge. They had repeatedly been the location of 'high places' where false gods were worshipped, and probably never more so than during the 150 years since the Babylonian invasion. Most of Israel had been exiled then, and the land repopulated with foreigners of other religions from all over the Babylonian Empire. To such a multicultural society, much like our own, the high places offered answers to problems, remedies for ills, protections, insurances, quick fixes of all sorts. But Nehemiah, away in the even more godless land of Persia, had 'prayed to the God of heaven' (2:4), a far greater deity than the gods of the hills. He could now testify, 'The gracious hand of my God was on me' (2:8). So the assembly gathered around him also looked away from the hills to *the Lord, the Maker of heaven and earth.*

They could be addressing verse 3 to Nehemiah – *He will not* (or perhaps 'May he not') *let your foot slip* – and then answering themselves as Nehemiah might answer: 'Indeed, he won't! He hasn't!'

Like our modern 'gods', the deities of the high places were far more likely to harm you than to help you, and since they undoubtedly included the sun god and the moon god (see Job 31:26–28; Isa. 24:23),[11] this may be an added meaning to verse 6. The Nehemiah connection helps us to understand what it means to be kept from all harm (7), that is, from evil, as we regularly ask in the Lord's Prayer. His book makes plain that while still in Persia he was not exempt from distress, and in Jerusalem he was not immune from vexation and danger, but through it all the power of God had kept him. The going out and coming in of verse 8 have many dimensions. Believers are guarded as they go to work and as they come home, in every venture and every return to base, at every departure and arrival, at birth and at death. The going down into captivity in 587 was a going out,

---

[11] See p. 2.237 n. 6.

and the goings up to Jerusalem that culminated in Nehemiah's return in 445 were a coming home.

Both in the great movements of history and 'in the common things of life, / Its goings out and in',[12] the Lord guarantees to guard his people, *both now and for evermore*. It is 'hard to decide which half of [the phrase] is the more encouraging: the fact that it starts "from *now*", or that it runs on, not to the end of time but without end'.[13]

Psalm 122

Besides Campbell's version of the last psalm, we may still sing Watts's version of this one. Like the noble lord (Campbell was the ninth Duke of Argyll), the humble pastor paraphrased the entire text that the Psalter set before him, though much more freely.

Watts's hymn celebrates the gathering of Christians for worship:

> How pleased and blest was I
> To hear the people cry,
> 'Come, let us seek our God today!'
> Yes, with a cheerful zeal
> We haste to Zion's hill,
> And there our vows and honours pay.

Our own first question must be, What did Psalm 122 celebrate in Old Testament times?

1. The coming to the city (122:1–2)

Pilgrim songs these fifteen may be, but we can hardly imagine the singing of them spread over the course of a pilgrimage to Jerusalem, since here the pilgrims are, at the beginning of only the third song, already arrived in the city. We can hardly imagine, either, that the suggestion to go there (1) was hailed as an unexpected good idea, since such journeys were normal, indeed obligatory.

What we could properly imagine would be the use of the psalm, early in one of the great festivals (similar Zion psalms figure a little way into

---

[12] Horatius Bonar, 'Fill thou my life, O Lord my God'.

[13] Kidner, p. 432.

other sequences of this kind; cf. 46; 48; 76; 87), practically any time from David's onwards. There is no reason why *Of David* should not mean 'By David', at least in embryo, with his original wording updated if and when necessary.

The joy of setting out and the thrill of arriving are unmistakable in these two introductory verses. With what added emotion would they have been sung after the exile! From 516 BC there had been a rebuilt *house of the Lord* to go to; in 445, for the first time in nearly 150 years, Jerusalem had walls and gates through which to pass in order to go to it.

The house of verse 1 and the city of verse 2 provide an inclusio for each of the main sections of the psalm (3–5, 6–9). Both begin with the city (3 and 6) and end with the house, though in two different senses (5 and 9): Jerusalem / the house of David, Jerusalem / the house of the Lord our God. The first concerns the building of the city, the second the blessing of it.

2. The building of the city (122:3–5)

When Miles Coverdale, in the Prayer Book version of verse 3, wrote 'a city that is at unity in itself', he seems to have pictured citizens living in harmony. That is really the concern of verses 6–9; here, *closely compacted* simply means a literal coupling together or joining up. The continuous fortified walls of Jerusalem were notable even before it became an Israelite city, and when it did, they were strengthened by David (1 Chr. 11:4–9). After the exile their restoration was Nehemiah's primary aim.

The two verses that follow are likewise 'closely compacted', in a tight little chiasmus:

Many tribes;
praises according to statute;
thrones for judgment;
one ruler.

God's statutes and judgments ('laws'), two of the eight law-nouns of Psalm 119, are central to the city's structure, or rather, fundamental to it. They expect God's direction of his people, through the word of his appointed ruler, to be accepted. They expect his people's response to him to be one of obedience and praise. That, his word tells us, is what Jerusalem is *for*.

When Hubert Parry's magnificent choral setting of Psalm 122 is sung at the coronation of a British monarch, the point of it is presumably understood to be something like this: 'I was glad when they said unto me, Let us on this significant occasion bring the life of the nation within the ambit of the church.' The meaning of the psalm in its own time was a great deal more straightforward. Nation and church were one. Still today God's nation and God's church are one; wherever they meet, there is Jerusalem, and by his statute and judgment the purpose of their meeting is to receive his word for the direction of their lives, and to respond with the praise of their lips.

There can scarcely have been a more poignant setting for Psalm 122 than Nehemiah's Jerusalem. Did the third reading from his book – say, 2:10–18 – precede the third Song of Ascents? In Ezra, to 'go up' always means to return from Babylon. But with a tingle of anticipation we now hear of a new kind of ascent, very concrete and literal. The new governor, having already returned from exile, is telling us of his secret, solitary reconnaissance of the city's ruined fortifications: 'I *went up* the valley by night, examining the wall' (Neh. 2:15). 'Let us rebuild,' he said, and they did; and now 'the walls have been rebuilt, the ruined houses repaired, the gaps and vacant spaces filled up; the city once more presents an aspect of unity, continuity, solidity, widely different from the dilapidated condition in which Nehemiah found it'.[14] Now not only the governor but also, as of old, *the tribes go up* to the city of God.

3. The blessing of the city (122:6–9)

What now lies ahead for the city and its people? What should they work towards, and what are they to pray for?

Certainly its security, and therefore their own. As distress was the keynote of 120 and power that of 121, security is that of 122. The psalmist has already celebrated the city's outward defences; now, as he says *Pray for the peace of Jerusalem*, he uses three times the word *within* – as well as peace preserved by her walls, he sees the need for peace fostered within them. It is here that he is speaking of the need for the church to be (in the Prayer Book's words) 'at unity in itself'.

As he encourages God's people towards something deeper than formal unity, so he wants something deeper than liturgical prayer. *Pray* in verse 6

---

[14] Kirkpatrick, p. 740.

means not 'Say your prayers', but, simply and bluntly, 'Ask.' We know from the conflicts that still lay before Nehemiah, not with foreign armies but with opposition within the borders of Judah, how important it is to plead with God for that kind of peace in the church.

The new governor made his position plain. As verse 8 says, he had come *for the sake of* [*his*] *family*, who had brought him the challenge, and of the *friends* in Jerusalem who needed his leadership (Neh. 1:1–3). The third instalment of his memoir began with powerful people in the land being 'very much disturbed that someone had come to *promote the welfare* of the Israelites' (2:10). He would be using exactly the same Hebrew phrase if he joined in singing verse 9 of the psalm: *I will **seek your prosperity***.

How can the church fail to see its priorities when it reads Psalm 122? Very easily, alas. Another, 'going up to Jerusalem' many years later, would weep over the city: 'If you, even you, had only recognized on this day the things that make for peace! But now they are hidden from your eyes.'[15] Fortunately his plans for his people's peace cannot in the end be thwarted, even by such blindness. The prayers of the psalm are going to be answered.

Psalm 123

For a short psalm with a good deal of repetition, 123 raises more questions than one might have expected. Why the unusual address in verse 1, to him *who* [*sits*] *enthroned in heaven*? Are the slaves of verse 2 looking to the master's or mistress's hand in expectation of a gesture of command, or (to speak realistically) in fear of a blow or in hope of a handout?[16] How does the enduring of contempt, in verses 3–4, fit into the picture?

1. In broad outline

As the first of another set of three, this is a psalm of distress, as 120 was. Verses 3–4 tell us so. Proud and arrogant people, who are used to having things their own way (that is the tenor of the words), are first dismissive and then angry if their position comes under threat. Their spite and scorn have reached the pitch where those they so dislike, the psalmist and the people he represents, are crying out for mercy: not to them, but to the Master in heaven.

---

[15] Luke 19:28, 42 NRSV. Jesus is quoting from the LXX of Ps. 122:4, 'Ask for the things that make for peace.'

[16] All three possibilities are suggested (if more genteelly) in the commentaries.

The comparison between these who pray to God and the slaves in the little parable of verse 2 is probably, then, that both are looking for help. Of course God's people should always be eager to obey the hand that directs, and willing to accept the hand that disciplines, but they are also ready to trust it as a hand that helps and provides.

If moreover the arrogant are powerful, it is no wonder that the psalmist appeals over their heads to the One supreme in heaven. The slave's eye looking to the master's hand illustrates our looking to God for his merciful help. Covenant loyalty works both ways: if we are responsible to him, he for his part is responsible for us.

2. In sharp detail

A real-life situation makes this general truth sharper and clearer. So aptly have the last three psalms related to the rebuilding of Jerusalem that we are not surprised to find the One who sits *enthroned in heaven* in 123:1 spoken of as 'the God of heaven' a number of times in the books of Ezra and Nehemiah (Ezra 1:2; Neh. 1:4–5; 2:4, 20; cf. 9:6). Furthermore, the providing, protecting hand of God, also frequent in Ezra, has been mentioned in each of the first three instalments of Nehemiah's story that we have supposed as readings to go with the Songs of Ascents (Neh. 1:10; 2:8, 18).

And now a fourth section of the story falls into place alongside Psalm 123. It begins, as the third did, with the hostility of Sanballat and his associates, and forms a reading of similar length to the others, if we omit the lists of chapter 3 and run on from 2:19–20 to 4:1–6. Here is this excerpt from Nehemiah's memoir, summarized so as to bring out the words it has in common with the psalm: 'Our enemies greeted with *ridicule* and *contempt* the news that we had started to rebuild the wall. I retorted that the God of *heaven* would give us success . . . Sanballat was greatly incensed, and poured *ridicule* on us . . . Hear us, O God, for we are treated with *contempt*.'

So the psalm's three elements, the heavenly throne, the master's hand and the unendurable hatred, fit convincingly together. Where real power and real malice are pitched against a righteous cause, the people of God know what to do. They keep patiently on with the task before them; but even more important, they look constantly in prayer to the One who alone is both pledged to uphold the right and able to frustrate the wrong.

Psalm 124

'If God is for us, who can be against us?' Paul's unanswerable question in Romans 8:31 echoes Psalm 124, along with many other Old Testament scriptures, and gives us two viewpoints from which to consider it.

1. Who can be against us . . .

'Everything is against me!' complained Jacob at one particularly frustrating point in his life (Gen. 42:36). It is of course people, not things, that may set themselves against us, and many of them have been ranged against the Israelites for whom the psalmist is speaking here. His own people have been *attacked*, and *anger* has *flared*, to frightening effect (2–3).

Four pictures convey how great Israel's danger had been. First, the danger of being swallowed alive (3): by death, perhaps, or by some mythical monster? Since the other illustrations are all real and literal, though metaphors of course as the psalmist uses them, this may be another of that kind, but the most awesome of the four – an earthquake like that which 'swallowed . . . all those associated with Korah . . . alive' in Numbers 16:32–33. After it, diminishing in scale but increasing in torment, come flood (4–5), the fangs of wild beasts (6) and *the fowler's snare* (7).

In David's time – we note this is a David psalm – the Philistines posed just such a threat, and the flood metaphor was turned back against them: 'As waters break out, the LORD has broken out against my enemies' (2 Sam. 5:20).

Once again, however, the many correspondences between the Songs of Ascents and the book of Nehemiah suggest that we look to that end of Old Testament history for a setting. The name of the villainous Sanballat heads the next episode of the story (Neh. 4:7–23), as it did the previous two. 'Angry' at the progress of the walls' rebuilding (the word in Neh. 4:7 is that used for *flared* here in v. 3), he and his friends plot to attack and destroy the Jews and their work. 'Who can be against us?' Why, all who are not themselves God's people and who see their stake in the land threatened by those who are.

Isaac Watts, whose England was not so secure that it could forget the Gunpowder Plot to blow up Parliament a hundred years earlier, entitled his version of this psalm 'A Song for the Fifth of November'!

2. . . . if God is for us?

It was Israel, that is, the patriarch Jacob, who had said back in Genesis, 'Everything is against me!' His descendants in Nehemiah's Jerusalem were beginning to say the same: the workforce can't cope, the job is too difficult, the enemy is all around us (4:10, 12). No, no, declares Nehemiah: 'Our God will fight for us!' (4:20). And the psalmist's opening lines use exactly the same turn of phrase. He has a solo voice declaim, 'If the Lord had not been *for us*', and then he wants everyone to join in: 'Let Israel say' (unlike its illustrious but peevish ancestor), 'If the Lord had not been *for us*, we should indeed have perished – but then our help is in the name of the Lord!'

This is the testimony of believers who have found themselves not simply threatened but actually trapped (7). But somehow, not by their own doing, *the snare has been broken*. God has done it; if 123 was a distress psalm, 124 is a power psalm. In that is our confidence. How could the God who created all things (8) be defeated by a bird-catcher's snare? Still more, as the New Testament will add, how could the God who redeemed us by the gift of his Son 'not also, along with him, graciously give us all things?' (Rom. 8:32).

Psalm 125

This psalm, like its predecessor, looks forward at one point to the New Testament. Each seems to colour Paul's thinking at a climactic moment in one of his letters. As 'God for us' in Romans 8:31 echoes 124:1–2, so 'Peace . . . to the Israel of God' in Galatians 6:16 echoes 125:5b.[17]

The psalm as a whole looks back. Its three nearly equal sections relate first to earlier Songs of Ascents, second to the historical records of the return from exile, and third to the Psalter's introduction in Psalm 1.

1. A simile (125:1–2)

In 124 we found both metaphor (the enemy attack *was* a torrent of raging waters) and simile (our escape *was like* that of a bird from a snare). While metaphorical language is found throughout the Psalter, the Songs of Ascents speak more in similes. Believers *are like* Mount Zion (1), and the Lord surrounds them *as* the mountains surround Jerusalem (2).

---

[17] 128:6b is identical.

As we noted back in 48:2, the pre-eminence of Zion is spiritual, not physical. In literal terms, the hilltop on which Jerusalem stands is lower, not higher, than the tops of the surrounding hills. This is the down-to-earth picture language of 125:1–2. *Those who trust in the LORD . . . cannot be shaken*, but the reason for that is something even more sure than their faith, something (like the ring of hills around Zion) greater and higher, namely his grace.

Security, then, is the keynote of 125, the third in this set of three, corresponding to 122 in the first set.

2. A reassurance (125:3)

Though the encouragement of verses 1–2 would be appropriate to any occasion, the reassurance of verse 3 is especially apt if the collection was designed for Tabernacles in 445 BC, and if this psalm followed a reading from Nehemiah 5.

If we imagine the Israelite community of the time enthusiastically united under Nehemiah's inspiring leadership, we imagine wrongly. His fifth chapter tells us of strife, dissension and injustice within it; but also of the effectiveness and integrity with which he dealt with such things. He held the *sceptre* as governor of Judah, duly appointed by the Persian king Artaxerxes I.

He had, more importantly, been appointed by God. God would not let *the sceptre of the wicked* – the power of the local grandees whose noses had been put out of joint by Nehemiah's arrival – *remain over the land allotted to the righteous*. Nothing would be more likely to corrupt God's people than the prospect of Nehemiah's failure and the reasserting of the rule of the ungodly. It won't happen, says the psalm. God's chosen one is in charge, and he, as his book tells us, will turn the 'outcry' (5:6) into praise (5:13).

3. A principle (125:4–5)

How like these closing verses are to those of Psalm 1! 'The LORD watches over the way of the righteous, but the way of the wicked leads to destruction.' If back at the beginning of the Psalter that seemed naïve, the old orientation which was doomed to be disoriented by hard experience, it is not so here. God's people have by now been through the mill; when the exile comes to an end the Sanballats of this world emerge; when Sanballat is dealt with there are evils even within Jerusalem. But *in the end*, for those who are right with God things will turn out right, and for those who prefer to be *crooked* rather than *upright* there will be no future.

Psalm 126

More explicitly than any of the other Songs of Ascents, this one is related to Israel's return from exile, if the NIV (margin) of 126:1 is correct. The translation 'When the LORD brought back the captives to Zion' is, however, debatable. The psalm's message is not quite so obvious.

1. Something clear, something obscure

It is clear from verses 1 and 4 that the psalm is about restoration of some kind. It is clear also that it falls into two equal halves; they open with similar wording (the NIV and NRSV have the restoring of fortunes in both),[18] their second couplets are similar (laughter/mouths // tongues/joy-songs in v. 2; sowing/tears // joy-songs/reaping in v. 5),[19] and both end with joy. We are reminded of the diptych, the double picture made of two hinged panels answering to each other, that the shape of Psalms 9 – 10 suggested to us.

But how are these two halves related?

That is less clear. It looks at first glance as if verses 1–3 are about a past restoration and verses 4–6 are about a future one. Probably, however, only one restoration is in mind: presumably the return from the exile. Some hold that from the psalmist's point of view this is still in the future. The first half of the psalm is a hopeful vision of an event that has not yet happened. It is, so to speak, in quotes. The second half is a prayer that one day author and singers alike will be in a position to utter the first half as a song of praise: 'Restore us, so that we shall be able to say, "He has restored us!"'

Much more likely is the view that this one almost incredible restoration – *we were like those who dreamed*[20] – has already happened. A great deal remains to be done, though, and the prayer of verse 4 is for more blessing of the same sort. Allen's title for the psalm is 'God can do it again'.

---

[18] Two slightly different Hebrew texts account for the differing translations.

[19] In the original each of these is a little chiasmus.

[20] Cf. Peter released from prison: 'He had no idea that what the angel was doing was really happening; he thought he was seeing a vision' (Acts 12:9).

2. Something quick, something slow

One reason why this second interpretation seems right is that it is exactly what happened to Israel at the end of the exile. Each of the goings up from the land of captivity to the land of promise was a memorable event in which the Lord was restoring the fortunes of the nation. Looking back to it, people rejoiced; looking forward from it, they were driven to their knees in prayer. They could see that as with the original going up from Egypt, there was much to give thanks for, yet there remained, as it were, very much land to be possessed (cf. Josh. 13:1 AV).

It was in his sixth chapter that Nehemiah could at last say that he had 'rebuilt the wall' (6:1). The work was completed just a few weeks before Tabernacles, the feast of Ingathering (15). Two chapters later (8:13–18) the festival arrived, and Israel was able to *reap with songs of joy*, as our psalm puts it; but for the moment Nehemiah was still having to *sow with tears*. Did the completion of the work make the enemy give up? Far from it. Sanballat and Geshem simply redoubled their efforts to destroy the governor and his work.

How the faithful in Israel must have longed for blessing to come like a flash flood, such as the winter rains brought to the southern desert (v. 4 of the psalm), to sweep away these incessant frustrations! This is not really a poem about joy; it is the first of another set of three, and a 'distress' psalm. But it does present a picture of hope and realism, the picture in its closing verses: the steady, persistent process of the farmer's toil and the seed's growth. Floods are not what farmland wants – they do more harm than good; better that the furrows be watered with tears! Our part is the persevering. We look to the Lord to do the restoring.

Psalm 127

The name of Solomon in this psalm's heading may not be telling us its author, but it does point us in the direction of other notable facts about it. As another Song of Ascents (the other phrase in the heading) it may well relate, as the rest of this collection seems to relate, to that other great man who ruled in Jerusalem five hundred years after Solomon, the governor Nehemiah.

1. The Solomon connection

There is a hint here of facts and events in Solomon's life, and more than a flavour of the wisdom writings so closely associated with his name. The psalm consists of neither prayer nor praise addressed to the Lord, but of observations about sensible godly living, like the book of Proverbs. *The LORD* and *the house* brought together in verse 1 may make us think of Solomon's temple (though they are probably not meant to), and the last words of verse 2 would remind a Hebrew reader of Solomon's other name, Jedidiah, 'loved by the Lord'. If rather than giving *sleep to those he loves* God is giving them some different thing 'as they sleep',[21] we may recall Solomon's dream at Gibeon, when God promised him wisdom and many other blessings (1 Kgs 3:5ff.).

The message of the psalm moves away from the passages where Proverbs sets before us good and bad behaviour, to those where it says, 'Trust in the LORD with all your heart, and lean not on your own understanding' (3:5). All the honest hard work in the world is *in vain*, says the psalmist, *unless the LORD* rather than you yourself is the person you rely on.

We are nonetheless in Psalms, not Proverbs, and this is a poem. Its two parts are not as disjointed as they may seem. Equal in length, like the two halves of 126, they have links both of sound and of sense: the first is about *bônîm* (builders) and the second about *bānîm* (sons), and 'both parts proclaim that only what is from God is truly strong'.[22] The second of a set of three, 127 is a psalm about the power of God.

2. The Nehemiah connection

Whatever its original date, author and purpose, it could not have a more appropriate setting than Nehemiah 6:15 – 7:5. With the completion of the new city wall in 6:1–2, we saw that Sanballat and Geshem, far from being resigned to defeat, were goaded into renewed plotting. That came to nothing; perhaps they lost confidence at last (6:15) once the city gates were in place (7:1). Yet still intrigues continued, for their accomplice Tobiah was sitting at the centre of a web of family links and subversive correspondence with 'many in Judah'.

Nehemiah kept his head, appointed a trustworthy leadership team in both temple and city (7:1–3; *Unless the LORD watches over the city, the guards stand watch in vain*), and saw very clearly what the next task must be. And here is the cue for our psalm. The reading moves towards its close with the words of 7:4: 'The city was large and spacious, but there were *few*

---

[21] V. 2 JB; so GNB, NASB. Both translations are awkward (if what he gives is not sleep, the verb has no object), and some scholars propose an entirely different word in place of *sleep*.

[22] Kidner, p. 441.

people in it, and *the houses had not yet been rebuilt.'* The singers take up the theme: *Unless the* Lord *builds the house, the builders labour in vain,* and similarly, *Children are a heritage from the* Lord – without him there is neither place nor people.

To some Solomon's name may have suggested that verse 1 was about the temple. I think not; the house is the house – your house, my house. We are concerned with the homes of the city. And about jobs, about going to work and coming home, about food, about sleep. Verses 1–2 are the psalmist's version of Christ's words about anxiety over the practical necessities of life: 'Seek first his kingdom and his righteousness, and all these things will be given to you as well' (Matt. 6:31–33).

And not only the house, but the people and especially the family: can we today recapture the value of that? We can picture Tobiah's henchmen trying it on with some godly Israelite, only to find the sons of his youth, full-grown now that he is middle-aged, looming up behind him – a couple of stalwart *arrows* ready at his hand to confront his 'enemies in the gate' (nrsv), and a quiverful more where they came from!

But without the power of the Lord none of this can happen. 'Apart from me you can do nothing' (John 15:5).

Psalm 128

Of the fifteen Songs of Ascents, this completes the third group of three. For the third time the need of Israel has been expressed (126), then the power of God (127) and now her consequent security (128).

1. Another diptych

As well as the theme of the psalm, its shape and no doubt its setting also are linked with those of the previous two. Each of them divides into two equal parts, and in each case the halves correspond, like the two facing panels of a diptych. Noting that 128 uses two different words for 'blessed', we might set out verses 1–3, with their various repetitions, like this:

> Happy the one who fears the Lord!
> Happy are you;
> > like a fruitful vine your wife,
> > like olive shoots
> > > your sons.

Verses 4–6 follow suit:

> Blessed the one who fears the Lord!
> Blessed are you;
>> see Jerusalem's prosperity,
>> see in your lifetime
>>> your grandsons.

This is again very much the language of the wisdom books. The fear of the Lord and his blessing are matters of daily life, to do with house and family, work and food, as in 127. Not that these psalms are taking us back to the uncomplicated world of 1 and 37, where good is always rewarded and evil punished. By this point in the Psalter, and (if the Nehemiah connection is right) by the time of the return from exile, the composers and singers of these songs had long since lost any naïvety they may once have had. Experience had taught them that Psalm 1 often seemed wrong; deeper experience had taught them that it was always right in the end. If they had been disoriented, they had also been reoriented. There really would be blessing for God-fearers (vv. 1 and 4) and peace upon Israel (6); but such grace does not come cheap.

2. Another episode

In the book of Nehemiah, the governor's personal memoir is interrupted after 7:5 by nearly six chapters of other material, before his first-person narrative resumes at 12:31.[23] But the first two verses of chapter 11 may be his own; they do follow on smoothly from 7:1–5. That was where Psalm 127 fitted so well, as we have seen. We could imagine the public reading of those verses of chapter 7, about a city of ruined houses and a tiny population, being followed by an announcement: 'Now the choir will sing the anthem "Unless the Lord builds the house" ' – and (the anthem would add) unless he provides the people to live in it!

Then Nehemiah 11:1–2 describes how one-tenth of the population of every other town in Judah agreed to move into the city, to boost its numbers in the short term. Everyone 'commended all who volunteered to live in Jerusalem', perhaps in the words of Psalm 128: *May the* Lord *bless you from Zion.*

---

[23] Or perhaps 12:27.

The long-term prospect is also in view. People are needed to defend the walls, but of course the walls are there primarily to defend the people – to protect the community as it becomes established, and so has the opportunity to raise families for the future.

Some commentators assume that a blessing like that of Psalm 128 would have to be pronounced by a priest, in the Jerusalem temple. It must be part of the cultus, the liturgy, they would say. A setting in Israel soon after the exile helps us to see things less rigidly. Of course the temple and its worship were immensely important; its rebuilding had taken precedence over everything else, nearly a century before. But there were many Israelites who for decades had had to keep in touch with God without its aid. The institutions of priesthood and kingship had been thoroughly dismantled. Now, with the return, the leaders of Israel were a governor instead of a king, and a priest who was much better known as a scribe or teacher of the law. I think Nehemiah and Ezra would heartily endorse the use that Christians make of songs like these, when we sing them for one another's encouragement and don't wait for a properly appointed person in a properly appointed place to assure us of the Lord's blessing.

Psalm 129

If we set 129 alongside 124, we can see at once that in structure they are twins. In each psalm the first half has an opening line sung apparently by a solo voice, with the congregation repeating it as they join in (*let Israel say*). Then follows a distressing picture of the ordeals from which God's people have recently been rescued. In each psalm the second half describes, again in picture language, the frustrating of Israel's enemies, and proclaims the name of the Lord in its closing verse.

The likeness extends to the type of picture language the two psalms use: metaphor in their first halves, simile in their second halves. In the case of 129 this means the furrows of verse 3 and the grasses of verse 6.

1. Long furrows

In verses 1–4 the description of Israel's suffering is doubly metaphorical: her oppression is a (not literal) flogging, and the flogging is in its turn a (not literal) ploughing. Unpleasant experiences of this kind have been her lot since her *youth*; Hosea 11:1 speaks of the nation's 'childhood' in Egypt. On her flogged back (metaphor 1) ploughmen have made very long furrows (metaphor 2) which extend throughout her history, and still hurt even after the return from exile, with the persistent enmity of Sanballat and his friends.[24]

But she can say *The LORD . . . has cut me free from the cords of the wicked* (4). The cords relate more readily to metaphor 1, as what ties up the victim of a flogging, than to metaphor 2, as something to do with oxen ploughing; but either way the real power of Israel's oppressors has been broken. *The LORD is righteous*, and keeps his covenant by rescuing his people. They are, as J. B. Phillips famously translated 2 Corinthians 4:9, knocked down but never knocked out.

On that positive note we move on to verses 5–8.

2. Short grasses

As in 124 the enemies' hostility *is* a torrent (metaphor) and our escape *is like* that of a bird from a snare (simile), so now in 129 they *are* ploughing furrows, while their fate is to *be like* grass.

Grass in the general sense includes all cereals – hence the reaper of verse 7 – and the picture of grass on the housetops relates to the layer of dust, of wind-blown soil, which would accumulate on a flat roof and in which seeds might lodge and take root. Never with much of a root, however, and such grasses, whatever they were, would never grow tall enough to be worth reaping (cf. Matt. 13:5–6). In contrast then to Israel, unaccountably surviving centuries of oppression, one after another her enemies come to nothing. (Vv. 5–8 may be a prayer, but they are also in effect a prophecy.) The sixteenth-century French Reformer Theodore Beza used yet another metaphor to say the same thing to King Henry of Navarre: 'Sire, it is the lot of the Church of God to endure blows and not to inflict them. But may it please you to remember that the Church is an anvil that has worn out many hammers.'

Verse 8 ends the psalm with a blessing. It is ironic, because the psalmist's point is that the enemy will *not* be blessed like this. Parallels suggest that it should be printed not as a double blessing, as in NIV and most modern versions except JB, but as two separate blessings, one which will not be said (8b) and one which is said (8c): 'No-one will bless them; but *we* will bless *you*.' In Ruth 2:4 just such a greeting is divided in two, while here in

---

[24] Goulder's list of Nehemiah readings skips at this point to 13:4–14. It is not clear how much of that passage could have been written before Tabernacles in 445, and how much of it belongs to a date at least twelve years later (13:6–7).

the Psalms 124 ends with similar confidence, and 125 and 128 end with a similar blessing.

If the dates fit,[25] all this could well refer to Nehemiah's enemy Tobiah. With his Israelite contacts and family connections, his unending intrigues, and the base he had contrived to set up in the very temple, he kept ploughing his vexatious furrow even after Sanballat and Geshem had been vanquished (Neh. 6:17–19; 13:4–9). Though an Ammonite, he had an Israelite name ('The Lord is good'!); but the blessing of Israel's God was what he would not get.

Most trying of *all who hate Zion* are people like this who feign to belong to her, and who carry on a persistent campaign of destructiveness from within the church. Encouragingly, where the previous psalms of distress (120; 123; 126) do not get beyond the plea for help, 129 recognizes the liberating power of God (4) even from such foes. But how the church needs to be on its guard against them!

Psalm 130

The Christian world knows well how John Wesley was converted one May evening in 1738 in a London meeting house, listening to a reading from Luther's preface to Romans. It is less well known that in St Paul's Cathedral that same afternoon he had heard, and been deeply moved by, Psalm 130. The cry of the psalmist was his cry; the word of the apostle was God's answer.

1. A great need and a great God

Verses 1–2 are a cry out of great need. Interestingly in view of the historical setting we are supposing for the Songs of Ascents, when in verse 2 the psalmist asks God to be *attentive* he uses a word found hardly anywhere else except in Nehemiah (the same is true when in v. 4 he looks for God's *forgiveness*).[26] But any believer might utter such a cry, when deep in any kind of affliction. Though we may have thought instantly of the depths of despair, they are not the only depths. The 'flood' that 'would have engulfed us' in 124:4 was an attack by enemies, and here in 130:1 the *depths*, like Hamlet's 'sea of troubles', could be our experience in a hundred different ways (cf. Ps. 69:2, 14–15; 88:6ff.).

---

25 See n. 24 above.
26 Neh. 1:6, 11 ('attentive'); 9:17 ('forgiving').

But we have a great God (3–4). Not at once, we notice, the God of hope, or of peace, or of all comfort, of whom the New Testament speaks (Rom. 15:13, 33; 2 Cor. 1:3); he is first a God concerned with sin and forgiveness, a moral God. The liturgical question of 24:3, as to 'who may stand' before such a God, here becomes the agonized question of a guilty sinner.

The New Testament has told us how a God who hates sin can also forgive it. The psalmist has grasped the fact, though he perceives less of the method than we do, knowing the Old Testament sacrifices but not yet the sacrifice of Calvary. But he does realize that, as Spurgeon puts it, 'none fear the Lord like those who have experienced his forgiving love'. All our worship starts from the place where we confess our sins and lay hold of the One who is the atoning sacrifice for them, as 1 John 1:8 – 2:2 reminds us repeatedly.

2. A great desire and a great effect

In verses 5–6 the psalmist's desire for God is expressed at first simply as *I wait for the LORD*. Each phrase is then amplified. *I wait* means that 'my soul waits' (NRSV). This is the real me, eagerly expectant. This is no mere formality. And to wait *for the LORD* means that I put my hope *in his word*. If he is to become real to me, it will be as he speaks to me and makes himself known.

For us that means of course a wholehearted attention to the living voice of Scripture. No wonder the psalmist likens himself, and us, to watchmen awaiting the morning. For us in the Bible, as for him in the earlier revelations of God that were to be summed up in it, there is the assurance that sooner or later light will certainly dawn.

Verses 7–8 bring together more than just the Lord and his forgiven servant. Here in verse 7, as in verse 4, Yahweh is, so to speak, not alone: with him are three constant companions, Forgiveness, Covenant Love and Redemption. Wherever he is, there they too will be found. And the psalmist also is not alone: with him come the rest of his people, for they too may be redeemed from all their sins.

The incident of Nehemiah 13:15–22 could date from the three or four Sabbaths between the setting up of Jerusalem's new gates (7:1–3; 13:19) and the beginning of Tabernacles. Both the people and their leaders were responsible for the Sabbath-breaking that it describes. The whole community needed cleansing. But *full redemption* covers the unrighteousness of all, repeated backsliding, and every sin.

Psalm 131

'One of the shortest psalms to read,' Spurgeon called it, 'but one of the longest to learn.' And there is something inherently odd about a claim to have learnt humility: 'He who ventures to esteem it his Proves by that single thought he has it not.'

Still, these three verses do depict attitudes that every believer should cultivate. To be careful not to rate others low and ourselves high; to recognize our limitations; to have grasped, like a child weaned from the breast, that even without what we thought we needed, we are still loved and cared for; to have a confidence in God which will be as sure tomorrow as it is today – these are lessons worth learning.

Where 129 reckoned that long furrows had been ploughed over the body of Israel since its youth in Egypt, the perspective of 131 telescopes that thousand-year history. It sees the nation as a child still only just finding its feet even after the exile. The community of Nehemiah's time, like the church in so many places today, had to come to terms with its loss of status and its precarious position. The time of the goings up from Babylonia was a time of growing up for Israel.

Perhaps it is Nehemiah himself in whose mouth these words would be most striking. Are they a riposte to the huffing and puffing of the offended establishment in Jerusalem? The reforms of 13:23–29 could well have led to accusations that the governor was getting above himself. Again, it is possible he had both carried them out and written them up in time for that first great feast of Tabernacles. Then leader and worshippers together, with the reading and the psalm together, could celebrate the grace of God that enables strong leadership to be exercised with a humble spirit. The fierceness of Nehemiah 13:25 and the quietness of Psalm 131 combined in the same person? Surely not! Ah, but in that lies one of the great challenges of Christian service.

Psalm 132

Very different from the rest of the Songs of Ascents if only by reason of its length, 132 was presumably included among them for some special reason. It is not labelled as a David psalm or a Solomon psalm, as some of them are, but those names will shed considerable light on it.

1. A David psalm

The first half of it, verses 1–9 at least, is about David, and about an important event in his reign. Once he had made Jerusalem his capital, he was eager to bring the ark of God there too. The story has been the background to earlier psalms, notably 24 and 68.

Here, verse 1 speaks of the trouble David took (not 'endured')[27] in making Zion the religious as well as the political centre of Israel. Verses 2–5 seem to combine with his fetching of the ark, in 2 Samuel 6, his desire to house it in something better than a tent, in 2 Samuel 7. The psalmist heightens the importance of this point, which in Acts 7:46 the New Testament also notes, by having David promise it with the exaggerated language of a vow.

So first David says, 'Let us bring the ark of our God back to us, for we did not enquire of it [literally, 'seek it'] during the reign of Saul' (1 Chr. 13:3). Then in verse 6 other voices join with his as they do now seek, and find, and fetch the ark, which has been for many years at Kiriath Jearim.[28] They have a better place for it (7–9). Their prayer recalls the liturgy of Numbers 10:33–36, used by Moses during Israel's desert journeys. Forty times in those days (see Num. 33) God had moved the pillar of cloud and fire to show where the ark should rest, and therefore where the travellers should rest, and now it, and they, come to their final *resting place*. For Zion is where both palace and temple, both kingship and priesthood, are to be. David and his Lord, Israel and her God, are not to be separated.

2. A Solomon psalm?

Though there are other analyses, a division of the psalm into verses 1–9, 10–16 and 17–18 makes very good sense.[29] The two main sections have eighteen lines each, and once again we have a diptych. At point after point the two panels correspond, from the swearing of an oath in verses 2 and 11 to the prayer of verse 9 and the promise of verse 16. Set the two passages side by side, and see.

---

[27] Cf. 1 Chr. 22:14 NRSV: 'With great *pains* I have provided for the house of the LORD.'

[28] 1 Sam. 7:1–2; 2 Sam. 6:2–3. Kiriath Jearim means Forest Town, and the phrase *the fields of Jaar* (Ps. 132:6) means the 'wooded district' around it. In 'We heard of it [i.e. the ark] in Ephrathah' (NRSV), Ephrathah means either (1) Bethlehem, David's home town ('when I lived in Ephrathah, we knew where the ark was'); or (2) the Ephraimite area where Shiloh, the ark's previous home, was situated; or (3) Kiriath Jearim itself, an Ephrathite place like Bethlehem (1 Chr. 2:50–51).

[29] Allen opts for a different analysis, but his own very detailed list of parallels seems to point rather to this one.

In the second section the anointed king must be not David but Solomon, or one of his successors: *For the sake of your servant David do not reject your anointed one.* Verses 8–10 are quoted in 2 Chronicles 6:41–42 at Solomon's dedication of the temple. But the later occasion is seen in the light of the earlier. First in each section the psalm prays for David (1) or his successor (10). Then an oath is sworn, by David to the Lord (2–5) and by the Lord to David (11–12). Two corresponding lines of the oath begin with *If* (4 and 12a),[30] and *till* in verse 5 is reflected in verse 12b, literally 'till ever and ever'. Verses 6 and 13 contain the only place names in the psalm. And although verses 8 and 14 (*resting place*) are not quite opposite each other, the parallel between verses 9 and 16, about the clothing of the priests and the singing of the saints, is a striking one.

To whatever later date it belongs, the second section is very like the Lord's response to David on the earlier occasion. David had wanted not only to bring the ark to Jerusalem, but also to build a house for it; God's response was that in a different sense he would build a house for David, and David's sons would rule in Zion for ever. That is verses 11–12. But verses 13–16 revert to what David had wanted to do. Yes, the Lord would have a house there too, and there, like David's descendants, he also would reign *for ever and ever.* We can hardly miss the New Testament echoes for those who 'have come to Mount Zion, to . . . the heavenly Jerusalem', who are 'seated . . . in the heavenly realms in Christ Jesus' and who there with him 'will reign for ever and ever' (Heb. 12:22; Eph. 2:6; Rev. 22:5).

3. A Nehemiah psalm?

After the exile, Nehemiah's dedication of the rebuilt walls of Jerusalem followed very consciously the David tradition (cf. Neh. 12:24, 36, 45–47). The temple had already been rebuilt, and he knew that God was once more among his people in Zion. We find these words in the brief final passage of his account of his momentous governorship: 'I purified the priests and the Levites of everything foreign, and assigned them duties, each to his own task' (13:30). The one task that had remained to him was to see that Zion's priests were clothed with righteousness; her saints certainly sang for joy in 8:16–17. So verses 9 and 16 of the psalm slot into the Nehemiah story.

---

30 V. 3 also. The *I will not* is literally 'If I do', i.e. '[May God punish me] if I do.'

If with other psalms of this collection 132 was resurrected, or even specially composed, for Tabernacles in 445 BC, there must have been two major questions (and perhaps their answers) in the mind of Nehemiah. First, where was the ark of the Lord? And second, where was the Lord's anointed king?

God's *footstool* in verse 7 means the *ark* of verse 8 (the only place in the Psalter where it is mentioned). It was the symbol of God's presence. But after the destruction of the first temple in 587 BC the ark was never seen again. So had the Lord abandoned his city? The whole thrust of the book of Nehemiah is that he had not. There could be, in other words, a real presence of God among his people even when there was no visible symbol of it.

As to the other question, not a few of the anointed kings of Judah had in the words of verse 10 deserved rejection. But in the days of Nehemiah, did a possible *anointed one*, worthy or unworthy, even exist? Zerubbabel, a hundred years before, had been a descendant of David, but nothing had come of that possibility, nor could have done within the Persian Empire. As for Nehemiah himself, though he was the outstanding leader of his time he would have ridiculed the idea that the crown should be his, even if Persia were to crumble. The kingdom was God's, and it was Nehemiah's privilege simply to rule it, not to reign over it. Like the Stewards of Gondor in J. R. R. Tolkien's saga, with their unadorned chair set below an empty throne, he governed 'in the name of the king, until he should return'.[31]

But the promise to David remained: *One of your own descendants I will place on your throne* (11). In Nehemiah's time, when Persia ruled the world, the assembly in Zion must have sung the epilogue to this psalm (17–18) with a frisson of expectancy at its graphic images of what was to come. The lamp for glory, the horn for strength, and the horn would 'sprout' for David (NRSV) – the word is the 'Branch' whom the prophets foretold (Isa. 4:2; Jer. 23:5; 33:15; Zech. 3:8; 6:12). We are not surprised to find Peter applying Psalm 132:11 directly to the risen Christ (Acts 2:30). Shame to clothe his enemies, splendour to crown his head: we still await the climax of the ark's long journey, and the last great going up.[32]

---

[31] J. R. R. Tolkien, *The Lord of the Rings*, vol. 3, pp. 26, 333.
[32] See on Ps. 68.

Psalm 133

You might be more hopeful of finding this psalm's brotherly unity in the extended families of Bible times than in the fragmented society of ours. Not that a large close-knit family is automatically happy and united; the Bible record itself tells us otherwise. But it is a canvas on which goodwill and hard work can produce an attractive picture of domestic harmony.

As a nation, Israel was most visibly united when people of every tribe converged on Jerusalem for the great festivals. At the first Passover of Hezekiah's reign a royal appeal brought worshippers there even from what was left of the breakaway northern kingdom. 'The hand of God was on the people to give them unity of mind,' says the Chronicler (2 Chr. 30:12). *How good and pleasant* a thing to celebrate with our psalm!

It fits equally well, if not better, with the 'goings up' to Judah after the exile. Nehemiah had to cope with a deeply divided community. His account of the dedication of the wall, once it was 'compacted together' again, as of old (122:3), might have been kept back till last in a sequence of fourteen Tabernacles readings, to accompany Psalm 133.[33] There in Nehemiah 12:27–43 he describes one final, literal 'going up', as two processions climbed to the top of the new wall, went round it in opposite directions, met on the far side, re-entered the city, and together moved into the temple for a united service of praise.

Brotherly unity has to be translated from a one-off liturgy like that into the practice of everyday life. This is what the psalmist likens to oil and dew. Aaron's anointing oil of verse 2 has a pervasive fragrance (cf. Exod. 30:25). The unusually heavy dew of Hermon is a boon to plant life.[34] For *people*, that is, the people of God, thus to *live together in unity* is *good* (like the dew) and *pleasant* (like the oil).

Does the life of our own church fellowship achieve this? Does it even seek it? The cynic might say that the quaint opening line of Watts's version of the psalm, 'Lo, what an entertaining sight', applies to the way things are, not to the way things ought to be, in the many churches that teem with farcical misunderstandings and squabbles. Aiming at real unity within a

---

[33] Assuming that the events of Neh. 12 preceded those of Neh. 8 – 10. Incidentally, a short reading with a long hymn (Neh. 13:30–31; Ps. 132) and a long reading with a short hymn (Neh. 12:27–43; Ps. 133) are the mark of a thoughtful planner of services. (With regard to fourteen readings, see below, on Ps. 134.)

[34] See Kirkpatrick, p. 771.

church is a much greater challenge than attending ecumenical events between churches.

And there was surely a further reason for the psalmist's likening this unity to oil that runs down, and dew that falls, the last two similes of the Songs of Ascents. Almost alone among the versions, the NASB brings out what must be a deliberate play on words: this penultimate 'song of goings up' speaks three times in three verses of the blessing of God 'coming down . . . coming down . . . coming down'. Not that human effort can ever compel a divine response; but where there is a wholehearted reaching up to some ideal of his, a corresponding blessing is on its way down. Just like (if the modern simile is not too incongruous) the counterpoise of the lift of which the words 'going up' and 'coming down' irresistibly reminded you!

Psalm 134

As well as being the last of this collection of fifteen psalms, 134 is the third of its last set of three. The repeated themes of previous sets, distress, power and security, have been left behind; this one is securely at home in Zion throughout (132:13; 133:3; 134:3).

Like its immediate predecessor, it has a keynote struck three times, though here too this may be obscured in translation: 'bless . . . bless . . . bless'. First God's people are called to bless him (in the NIV, *praise*), then they are promised that he will bless them. As Kidner well says, 'To bless God is to acknowledge gratefully what He is; but to bless man, God must make of him what he is not, and give him what he has not.'[35]

Opinions differ as to who the *servants of the LORD* are. Some take them to be temple staff – clergy, as we might call them – because they *minister . . . in the house of the LORD*. More probably they are, as the NRSV suggests, the whole assembly, all who 'stand' (rather than *minister*) in the temple precincts,[36] lifting up their hands in praise and prayer 'towards' (rather than *in*) the holy place.

As to when this final song might have been sung, few are prepared to say anything very definite. Goulder's theory, however, makes sense of these psalms here as at so many other points. On the supposition that 120 and 121 were to be sung on the first day of Tabernacles (evening then

---

[35] Kidner, p. 454.
[36] See the detailed discussion in Allen, p. 216 nn. 1c, 1d.

morning, since the day began at sunset), fourteen psalms, with fourteen related readings from Nehemiah, would cover the seven days. For one final gathering, on the evening that technically began the eighth day, those who had stood 'night after night' (NEB; *night* is plural) to listen and to respond would bless the Lord once more, and receive his blessing, in the words of 134.

He is Maker of heaven and earth (3). They know this from the creation stories of Genesis, and from the vanquishing of the powers of Egypt at the exodus. The returned exiles know it from the evidence of their eyes, as they have seen the great powers of their day overruled by his greater power (cf. Ezra 1:1ff.; Neh. 1:5; Dan. 4:17). As Maker of heaven and earth, he is 'infinitely able to fulfil this prayer'.[37]

But the blessing can come only from Zion, that is, from the place he has appointed, the true 'Zion' of Hebrews 12:22; not in our day Jerusalem, far less Rome or Canterbury, or even any local church building, but the gathering of his people at the feet of Jesus. 'There the LORD bestows his blessing, even life for evermore' (133:3).

---

37 Alexander, p. 528.

Psalms 135 – 145

7. The second Exodus Collection and the fourth David Collection

The largest remaining collection in the Psalter is the eight consecutive psalms that bear the name of David, 138 – 145. Why 135 – 137 are grouped together before it is a puzzle. In some ways they look back to the Songs of Ascents. Thus 135 begins and ends like 134, and might be an expansion of it; one Jewish tradition actually joined them together, and if 'Hallelujah' was meant as a coupling between psalms in the Egyptian Hallel it might be so here also. Then 136 in turn is obviously a close relation of 135; in fact the term 'Great Hallel' was applied sometimes to 136, sometimes to 135 and 136 together, and sometimes to all the psalms from 120 to 136. It would be reasonable, therefore, to think of these psalms along with the post-exilic 137 as a supplement to the Songs of Ascents.

On the other hand, we might equally reasonably reckon 150 to be a conclusion to the entire Psalter, corresponding to the introduction provided by 1 (and perhaps 2). If it were, there might be more fact than fancy in Goulder's theories about sets of psalms designed for use during week-long festivals. He does not propose this only in respect of Books III and IV, each furnishing seventeen psalms for an eight-day festival. On the supposition that Book IV was originally meant to cover seven days, not eight, it would consist of the fifteen psalms 90 – 104. Then 105 – 119 would be another fifteen; 120 – 134 are in any case the fifteen Songs of Ascents; and 135 – 149 would be a fourth and final fifteen, with 150 to round off the whole.

It is certainly fact, not fancy, that two of these fifteens, 105 – 119 and 135 – 149, run parallel. The earlier sequence begins with 105 – 107 reviewing the exodus from Egypt and the return from Babylon, and the later one begins with 135 – 137 doing the same. In each sequence a group of David psalms follows, then a set of Hallel psalms, and the Hallels lead up to 119 in the one case and 149 in the other.

For want of a better title, we might call the first three of this group an Exodus Collection, although (as in the earlier instance) it embraces Israel's liberation from Babylonian captivity as well as from Egyptian slavery.

Psalm 135

Like 105, then, 135 reviews the story of Israel, and sees it as the story of what the Lord has done for his people. Far from being a mere history lesson, though, it is a call to them to join in singing his praises.

1. A rich song of praise

It reads so easily that we may not at once notice two of its intriguing features. The first is its strong, carefully crafted structure. The following outline, with the twenty-one verses divided into three sevens and then subdivided 4 + 3; 2 + 3 + 2; 4 + 3, will bring this out:

Praise to our electing Lord (1–4),
    the 'making' God who gives life (5–7)!
        Pharaoh's servants have been vanquished (8–9);
            with the gift of the land (10–12),
        Yahweh's servants have been vindicated (13–14).
    The 'made' gods bring death (15–18);
praise to our indwelling Lord (19–21)!

A summary so terse must seem rather cryptic, and needs to be opened out a little. The Lord's servants (1) are all his people, as verses 9 and 14 will show; as in the corresponding verses at the end of the psalm, everyone is called to praise him. The *servants . . . who minister*, as we noted in 134:1, are not just the clergy! In verse 4, the reason for their praises is that long ago he chose them for his own; in verse 21 it is that now he dwells among them.

Such a God differs sharply from all others (5–7 and 15–18). The word for 'do' or 'make' appears twice in each of these sections. The 'gods' that people allow to run their lives are man-*made*; these same people have *made* them themselves. The Lord, by contrast, is the *Maker* and the *Doer*, the first cause, of everything. The word for 'wind' or 'breath' or (significantly) 'spirit' also appears in each of the two sections. The Lord fetches the wind that brings the rain that feeds the crops on which his people live, picturing the truth that he is the giver of life in a greater sense also. The gods have no breath, therefore no life, and *those who make them will be like them*; every such 'god' is a bringer of death.

The heart of the psalm describes the classic historical demonstration of all this at the time of the exodus. The false gods and those who trust them (*Pharaoh and all his servants*, 9, and *all the kings of Canaan*, 11) are vanquished. The God of Israel and those who trust him (*the Lord and his servants*, 14) are vindicated. Israel is delivered from Egypt and given the land of Canaan.

The coherence of the psalm is perhaps surprising when we first notice how familiar much of it is, and then realize that practically every verse recalls something somewhere else in the Old Testament. It is in fact a patchwork, a mosaic, but one extraordinarily well put together.

2. A subtle mosaic of borrowings

However well 135 may function as the first psalm of a festival collection, it also ties in undeniably with the preceding psalms. From the end of the Songs of Ascents we recognize the servants of verse 1 and the blessing from Zion of verse 21[1] (134:1, 3), and the 'good' and 'pleasant' of verse 3 (133:1). From the previous fifteen psalms come the concept of a historical review (105 and 106), the introductory Hallelujah verse (111; 112; 113), a great deal of 115, and a passage from 118 (see 115:2–13; 118:2–4).

Then the prophets Isaiah and Jeremiah speak as verses 15–18 do of man-made idols, and Jeremiah contrasts them with the One who *brings out the wind from his storehouses* (Isa. 40:18ff.; Jer. 10:1–13; 51:15–19). From the books of the law come verse 5, the words of Jethro in Exodus 18:11; verses 10–11, the stories of Sihon and Og in Numbers 21; verse 4's beautiful epithet for Israel, the Lord's *treasured possession*, in Deuteronomy 7:6 and 14:2; and verse 14, taken directly from Deuteronomy 32:36.

As Allen says, 'older materials are unashamedly recycled'.[2] Yet what emerges from the workshop is a fresh, finely structured, vigorous psalm

---

[1] NRSV rightly distinguishes 'praise' (1–3, 21b) from 'bless' (19–21a).

[2] Allen, p. 227.

of praise. The Lord has brought out the wind of inspiration from his storehouses, and the mosaic comes to life.

3. An enthusiastic statement of faith

Some modern hymn books include versified forms of the creed.[3] To my mind, none of them quite works. Carefully worded theological propositions, as such, do not lend themselves to singing. The fact is that the creed-makers were drawing maps of Bible truth, whereas the Bible writers had come from that country, and waxed lyrical about it.

So it is with regard to this psalm. Although a kind of creed, a statement of faith, it is something more than that, for it is also full of colour and drama, of praise and the pageant of history. And with regard to the one who put it together, he knew this territory at first hand. It was as familiar to him as it had been to those whose work he was quoting. In verse 5, for instance, he can take the words of Moses' father-in-law and make them very much his own: 'What Jethro knew, I also know' – the 'I' is emphatic.

This gives Psalm 135 an added value for the modern reader. What is explicit in it is the creed, in its Old Testament form, of every Bible believer. It looks back to God the Creator (5–7), forward to God the Judge (13–14), and at the heart of its faith to God the Redeemer (8–12). It surrounds these proclamations with praise (1–4, 19–21). But what is implicit is the fact that all this is as real and as vivid to our psalmist as it was centuries before to Jethro, and to everyone else from whom he has taken his materials. Not only is his God always the same, but his changelessness is a dynamic thing, not a static one. 'He who began a good work in you will carry it on to completion' (Phil. 1:6).

Psalm 136

One of the oldest English hymns still in use, John Milton's 'Let us with a gladsome mind', is based on this psalm. Together with the metrical version by Isaac Watts, 'Give to our God immortal praise', it enables Christian congregations to sing at least part of a psalm that would otherwise be a rare bird indeed in its visits to our Sunday services.

---

[3] E.g. John Henry Newman's 'Firmly I believe and truly' from the nineteenth century and Michael Saward's 'These are the facts' from the twentieth.

1. A companion to Psalm 135

Verses 17–22 reproduce 135:10–12 almost exactly, while in general terms the whole psalm follows 135 in celebrating the story of the Creator of the world who is also the Redeemer of his people. As we have noted, the two psalms form a pairing which resembles that of 105 and 106, both in its twofold historical review and in its position at the head of a series of fifteen.

Like 135, 136 is also a statement of faith. In fact its first word, *Give thanks*, though different from the 'Praise' and 'Bless' of 135:1–3 and 19–21, aligns it with its predecessor, since the meaning is 'Confess' – a confession not of our sin, but of God's greatness. So we have here another creed from Bible times, coming white-hot from the place where its facts were forged.

There are of course other differences between 135 and 136 besides the varied words with which they summon us to worship. This psalm does not contrast Israel's God with 'the idols of the nations' (135:15), or even mention them. Sihon king of the Amorites and Og king of Bashan figure centrally in 135 but near the end of 136.

The most obvious difference, however, is the refrain *His love endures for ever*, repeated in every verse of our psalm. This sets it apart not only from 135 but also from every other psalm in the book. In due course we shall give it closer attention.

First we must look at the way 136 has been constructed, and what the psalmist has put into it.

2. Its shape and content

As with some earlier psalms, this is more than just a string of beads, although the reiterated *His love endures* may make it look like that. It should be possible, though it is not easy, to find within the twenty-six verses groupings which are fewer and larger. Of a number of possible analyses the simplest is a division into eight sections, mostly of three verses, though each of the last two will be a verse longer.

The content, though, suggests something more complex, centred on a single verse (16) describing Israel's journey from Egypt to Canaan. Before this, six verses (10–15), divided three and three, are about God bringing his people first out of Egypt and then across the Red Sea. (Milton, taking 'Red' at face value, says in a line the hymn books omit, 'The ruddy waves he cleft in twain'!) After verse 16, another six verses, in this case divided two, two and two, tell of God's destruction of the Canaanite kings whose land was earmarked for Israel: 'Large-limb'd Og he did subdue / With all his over-hardy crew.'[4]

Framing all this are a six-verse introduction (4–9) and a three-verse summary (23–25). The one praises God as the Lord of heaven and earth (space) and of day and night (time). The other, speaking of this same Creator God, shows his wider creation provided for and his chosen people redeemed. Finally, as an outer frame the first three verses and the last one are our call to worship.

3. Its relevance

Although Yahweh is undoubtedly the God who did, and does, all these things, we may still ask how a psalm sung so infrequently can be used meaningfully in the church today.

Verses 23–24 suggest an answer. There the singers praise the One who *freed us from our enemies*. Either they are the returned exiles, seeing in their own experience a parallel to that of the exodus long before; or they are Israelites of any generation, looking back to the exodus and saying, '"We" were there in principle',[5] in the person of our ancestors. It is proper for all God's people, even today, to join in such praises.

It is instructive to notice what editors of modern hymn books make of Milton's version, a youthful tour de force (he was fifteen when he wrote it) of twenty-four stanzas, covering the entire psalm. It becomes a nose of wax, to be pushed into whatever shape pleases them. Some take a few stanzas from the beginning and end to make up a hymn about the creation only, which it is not. Others do include the lines 'He hath with a piteous eye / Beheld us in our misery',[6] but ignore the connection made by both author and translator with the events of the exodus and the story of redemption.

Watts rewrote the psalm in explicitly Christian terms, and defined the misery: the God of creation is the One 'who sent his Son to save / From *guilt and darkness and the grave*'. The Watts version thus brings out the permanent, present relevance of Psalm 136 (though even here the hymn books deprive us of the exodus connection).

But why not sing the original, the psalm itself? Why are we likely to hear it only ever at a cathedral evensong on the twenty-eighth day of the month?

---

[4] Milton again, of course, referring to Deut. 3:11.

[5] Allen, p. 234.

[6] Afterwards adapted, like much of Milton's original, to fit the 77.77 metre: 'Looked upon our misery'.

4. Its distinctive feature

For most Anglicans the honest answer would be (dare one say it) that they would find it so *boring*! By the time you have heard that distinctive refrain twenty-six times over, 'For his mercy endureth for ever', you may be forgiven for wondering whether the psalm is going to do the same.

It may help a little to streamline the words, with the NIV's *His love endures for ever*, or still better one of the Gelineau versions, 'His love has no end.' But the best approach is first to grasp what the refrain is saying, and then to imagine in what circumstances it might actually catch fire. 'His love has no end' binds into one the entire sequence of these facts of faith, repeatedly reminding us of its presence even between the phrases of a sentence. From the beginning of creation to the climax of redemption, from the first making of the heavens to the final inheritance of the saints, all is to be seen against the background of the love of God. That love is both indestructible, because it is covenant love, and boundless, because it endures for ever. As you look around at all that he has made, and follow through all that he has done, at every point the psalm is saying '*Covenant love did this.*'

In Charles Williams's novel *War in Heaven*, snatches of Psalm 136 come repeatedly to the lips of the little clergyman who is at the centre of the drama, as the forces of good and evil surge to and fro around him, and as eventually the latter threaten to overwhelm him. At the climax, when beyond all hope he is suddenly delivered from unimaginable evil and the powers of destruction are themselves destroyed, it is as if he sees in a vision, and hears in the words of this and similar psalms, what has really been going on.

> 'Let them give thanks whom the Lord hath redeemed,' a great voice sang, and from all about it, striking into light and sound at once, the answer came: 'for His mercy endureth for ever.'
>   'And delivered out of the snare of the enemy,' it sang again; and again an infinite chorus crashed: 'for His mercy endureth for ever.'
>   . . . And again all around him the litany wheeled like fire:
>   'He hath destroyed great nations: for His mercy endureth for ever:
>   'And overthrown mighty kings: for His mercy endureth for ever.'[7]

---

[7] Charles Williams, *War in Heaven* (London: Faber, 1930), p. 245.

One might reckon it a simple truth, couched in simple words. But with the words first learned by rote, and the truth of them then experienced again and again both in blessings and in troubles, God's servant finds them in time of real need a blazing affirmation that cannot be too often repeated.

Psalm 137

Psalm 137 is memorable for its evocative opening phrase, *By the rivers of Babylon*. Equally memorable, for different reasons, are its closing verses, about the babies of Babylon and their gruesome fate. That passage is hard to stomach, and not surprisingly the Anglican ASB liturgy decreed in 1980 that it 'may be omitted'. We shall come to it in its place, remembering that that place is at the climax of one of the most moving psalms in the Psalter.

The first three verses indicate a date for the psalm: these are the words of exiles returned from Babylon, recalling things that happened there during a time now happily past. Verses 4–6, and perhaps the rest of the psalm as well, are in quotation marks, as it were, as the exiles' response during that time to the demands of their tormentors.

1. The crime in question (137:1–4)

As with 136, the structure of 137 is neither obvious nor generally agreed. Verses 1–4 do seem to belong together with *We* as the subject, speaking of our exile *in a foreign land*. They also seem to have a chiastic shape, describing *us*

> in a foreign land,
>> weeping
>>> about Zion.
>>>> There, no playing of harps,
>>>>> despite our captors' demands;
>>>> there, no singing of songs
>>> about Zion –
>> *singing*
> in a foreign land?

We can imagine how incongruous, and how painful, the exiled Israelites would have found it to sing the songs of Zion in the land of their captivity. The reason was not simply that they missed the place. It was that so many hopes and promises were bound up in it, as we know from the songs of Zion we have already found in the Psalter. They would have felt rather as Abraham did when he was called to sacrifice his son, without whom God's covenant would be meaningless (cf. Heb. 11:17–19).

From a human point of view, Babylonia was not a bad place. Its 'waters', as the RSV and the Prayer Book call them, 'included a system of canals across the huge plain', which was green and prosperous. But it was 'a landscape alien . . . to natives of the hills and valleys of Judah'.[8] Nor could the exiles forget that these people whose unwilling guests they were had invaded their country and destroyed their capital. What they could not know was that the hostility between Jerusalem and Babylon was to become the symbol of the ultimate rift in the human race, between those who are for and those who are against God: as Revelation 17 – 21 puts it, adding further symbolism, between the bride of Christ and her rival the great prostitute – that is, between the church and the world.

2. The court in session (137:5–9)

The second part of the psalm also sets Jerusalem over against Babylon. The psalmist addresses each in turn. In between he speaks to the Lord, about a third party, Edom. The Edom verse is linked with the Jerusalem verses by the word *Remember*, and with the Babylon verses by the phrases 'Sons of Edom' (JB) and *Daughter Babylon*.

Remember also tells us that the psalmist is pleading a case in a court of law, for it is a legal term. He is addressing God the Judge in respect of the crime of which Israel has been the victim: the loss of Zion.

First, however, he speaks to that beloved city, now both distant and ruined. When he says it is unforgettable, we must understand why: it is the focus of all God's promised blessing, and for that reason *my highest joy*. To have destroyed *that*, of all things, is a crime beyond reckoning.

We begin to see why it is that when he turns to address Babylon he speaks so fiercely. His disconcerting word *happy* – *happy is the one who repays you* – anticipates Revelation 18:20, when the entire anti-God world system symbolized by the ancient city finally falls. 'Rejoice over her, O heaven! Rejoice, saints and apostles and prophets! God has judged her for the way she treated you.'

---

[8] Kidner, p. 459.

And what of Edom? *On the day Jerusalem fell*, we are told in Obadiah 11 that that nation, Israel's neighbour and close kin, 'stood aloof while . . . foreigners entered . . . you were like one of them.' Perhaps the Edomites were allied with Judah against the invading Babylonians until it became obvious who would win, and then sent envoys to say how eager they were to change sides, and how pleased they would be to see the fall of Jerusalem: *'Tear it down,' they cried.*[9]

Edom is an example of all who have to choose between the church and the world. 'Once to every man and nation / Comes the moment to decide, / In the strife of truth with falsehood, / For the good or evil side.' James Russell Lowell's lines go on to say what Edom was not prepared to do – to 'side with truth' and to 'share her wretched crust'. As then, so now, sooner or later Edom has to take sides, for in the end there is only Jerusalem or Babylon. Or rather (let the Sons of Edom take note) there is only Jerusalem: risen from death to witness on the last day, as Revelation tells us, the smoke of her rival's burning (Rev. 18:8–9, 18; 19:3).

3. The poetry of the Psalter

Although our own civilization is in no position to criticize that of 2,500 years ago for such cruelties as dashing infants against rocks, we can reasonably ask why they should be approved by the psalmist. Three observations may be made on this persistent question.

In the context of the Psalter's poetry, we have to face the fact that the psalmist did write the objectionable closing verses of 137, that the compilers of the book saw no reason to edit them out, and that generations of Hebrew worshippers were prepared to sing them. This is one of the psalms about which C. S. Lewis said, apropos of the suggestion that we should simply leave out the bits we don't like, that 'the bad parts will not "come away clean"', being often 'intertwined with the most exquisite things'.[10] Here and elsewhere the problem passages are an integral part of the poetic structure.

4. The metaphor of the courtroom

In the context of the courtroom metaphor, the psalm deals with an open-and-shut case. There is no question about the verdict: everyone knows

---

9 See Allen, pp. 236–237, quoting U. Kellermann.

10 Lewis, p. 24.

Babylon is guilty of the destruction of Jerusalem. The sentence, which is what concerns us, is the straightforward eye-for-eye retribution that the old law required (Deut. 19:16–21), deeply unfashionable though it may be today. Verses 8–9 are no different from the barbarities of the Babylonian invaders of Judah. We know also that verse 8 simply echoes what the Judge himself has said concerning the punishment of Babylon, in Jeremiah 51:54–56.[11] And savage though the psalmist's words may sound, he does leave the issue to the Judge. Even in Old Testament times the law of retribution was not for individuals to take into their own hands. In this the two Testaments agree: 'Do not take revenge,' says Paul, quoting Deuteronomy in Romans, 'for it is written: "It is mine to avenge; I will repay," says the Lord' (Rom. 12:19, quoting Deut. 32:35). For his part, the Lord as Judge will by definition do what is just and right: the *lex talionis*, an eye for an eye, is 'a statement of *equity*, expressed with typical Old Testament sharpness and gutsiness'.[12]

5. The history of Israel

Finally, in the context of Israel's history, this psalm is not about just another of the recurrent disasters that God's people have suffered down the years. It is about an event of the first magnitude. Like 105, 135 traced the story of the exodus; 106 did the same, but added a reference to the exile, which 136 also perhaps had in mind; now, like 107 (though in very different tone), 137 has as its setting an Israel rescued from exile. Both sets of psalms place exodus and exile in parallel. In other words, with regard to her great significance in biblical theology Babylon is on a par with Egypt. What happens to her is vastly more important than what happens to other enemies of Israel like the Moabites or the Philistines or the Arameans. It should not surprise us if extreme language like that used in Revelation of the spiritual Babylon is inspired in the psalmist when he condemns the historical Babylon, infants and all.

A curious fact emerges to reinforce this possibility. Although the psalm quotes the words of exiles living in Babylon, it was clearly written after their return to their homeland. We tend to assume that in verses 8–9 they look forward to the catastrophic fall of that great empire. But the very reason they were back in Judah was that Babylon had already fallen to the

---

[11] *Destruction, repays, done* (137:8) correspond to 'destroyer', 'repay', 'retribution' in Jer. 51:56.

[12] J. A. Motyer, in a private communication.

Medes and Persians, as recorded in Daniel 5. Furthermore, its world had ended not with a bang but a whimper; far from devastating the city, its new rulers made it a regional centre of their own. Is the psalmist then consciously looking beyond the Babylon of his day to some fearsome continuing spiritual reality that may have to be defied throughout history and that only the Lord's judgment will finally destroy?

It is but a step from there to Lewis's challenging exposure of the Babylonian evil that persists in all of us, and the necessity of dashing it against the rocks.

> I know things in the inner life which are like babies; the infantile beginnings of small indulgences, small resentments, which may one day become dipsomania or settled hatred . . . Knock the little bastards' brains out. And 'blessed' he who can, for it's easier said than done.[13]

Psalm 138

The eight psalms of the fourth and last David Collection begin with 138. If it is right to see here a larger group of psalms almost completing the Psalter with a week's sequence of fifteen (135 – 149), this collection is the core of it.

1. Testimony, expectation, confidence

In verse 1 the psalmist praises God *before the 'gods'*. We saw back in Psalm 82[14] the various possible meanings of the word; here it means what it says, the gods that are believed in by those who do not know the true God. Whether the psalmist is challenging them, or even defying them, or simply comparing them with a God who actually lives and acts, his praise is a testimony to what this God has done for him.

The name (God's nature) and the word (his revelation of it) have been made known, says verse 2, 'above everything' (NRSV).[15] One practical consequence is that in his love he responds to those who call on him, and in his power he makes them what they cannot otherwise be (3).

---

[13] Lewis, pp. 113–114.

[14] See p. 2.39.

[15] The Heb. of 2b, represented by the AV/RV 'Thou hast magnified thy word above all thy name', is peculiar. Most translations emend it slightly.

After the testimony of verses 1–3 comes the psalmist's expectation in verses 4–6 that one day this Lord will be recognized universally. All will hear his word and see his glory. The word and the glory are of course already realities: his own people are well aware that the God of the Bible is far above every other power, yet reaches further down, and with greater effect. He is not too remote to see the need of the lowly; and he 'can tell the haughty a mile off'![16]

The psalmist's present experience leads in verses 7–8 to great confidence for the future. The psalmist sees God as a God who by his very nature 'fulfils'. So the *works* he has already done on the psalmist's behalf are sure to be completed, reminding us again, as the end of 135 did, of the promise of Philippians 1:6. John Newton's lines also come to mind: 'His love in time past / Forbids me to think / He'll leave me at last / In trouble to sink.'[17]

2. 'Your love, LORD, endures for ever'

We may take the David of the psalm's heading to have been the author at least of an earlier version of it, if not of the poem as it stands. The contrast between the Lord and the gods in verse 1 could well reflect the victory in which David said, 'The LORD has broken out against my enemies', and the fleeing Philistines 'abandoned their idols' (2 Sam. 5:20–21). The temple in verse 2 does not have to be Solomon's; long before David's time the home of the ark at Shiloh was called the temple (1 Sam. 1:9; 3:3), and in any case David psalms in Book I use the word to denote the dwelling of God in its widest sense (Pss 18:6; 29:9).[18] *Greatly emboldened* in verse 3 suits David very well. *All the kings of the earth* in the psalm's middle section is not too grandiose a concept for the internationally respected monarch of 2 Samuel 8, or even the youthful visionary of 1 Samuel 17:46. The troubles and enemies in its last section are familiar both from the David stories and from the early David psalms.

Whatever its origin, we can see how the psalm would be unlikely to date. Set like a jewel in its final verse is the acclamation that has become very familiar in these psalms towards the end of the Psalter: *Your love, LORD, endures for ever*. Both 106 and 107, reviewing God's mercies to his people right through to the end of the exile, begin with it. It chimes in

---

[16] Goulder, *Return*, p. 234.

[17] John Newton, 'Begone, unbelief'.

[18] See p. 1.90.

every verse of 136. It is the song with which the returned exiles celebrated the founding of the new temple in Ezra 3:11.

Since 137 clearly seems to belong to those early days of the restoration, with the captivity over but not long over, the surrounding psalms (if they were indeed grouped together by design) presumably also belong there. We have seen reason to believe that such a group might begin with 135. It would then look back over an astonishing thousand years of history to marvel repeatedly, with 136, that 'his love endures for ever'; continue with 137, which dates the collection; and move on into a set of David psalms, taken perhaps from a much older collection, which in a different sense do not date at all. For here once more, in their opening number 138, and indeed at its climax, is the same old truth which by its very nature is always new: 'His love endures for ever.'

Psalm 139

Words like omniscience and omnipresence can be a useful shorthand for stating facts about God. With regard to Psalm 139, 'one of the summits of Old Testament poetry',[19] they are not perhaps the best words. It is such a personal and deeply felt expression of what the psalmist knows of God that we should want to describe it in simpler, more direct terms. As he might himself tell us, 'It is about how God knows me, how he surrounds me, how he has made me, and how he tests me.'

By the same token the simplest analysis of the poem is probably the best one. It divides readily into four equal sections, and the six verses in each section subdivide four and two.

1. How God knows me (139:1–6)

God's amazingly detailed knowledge of the psalmist (6) is set forth in a variety of ways in the first four verses. A series of verbs reads like an extract from a thesaurus: search/examine, know, perceive/understand, discern/sift, be familiar with. Rather like the A–Z of the acrostic psalms, pairs of words suggest how comprehensive God's knowledge is: whether I sit or rise, whether I travel or settle down – that is, whatever I do, he knows. He knows my thoughts from afar, my words before I utter them; he knows me *completely*.

---

[19] Kidner, p. 464.

Great wonder such knowledge may be, as verse 6 says, but small wonder that the phrase *You hem me in* in verse 5 should seem ambivalent! Is the psalmist feeling heartened, or is he feeling threatened?

From what he has said so far, it could be either; and it would depend on him which it was. There is only a step from one to the other – or rather the two steps it takes to perform the about-turn that the Bible calls repentance. So long as I am looking to my own self-pleasing and away from God, I shall feel his overwhelming knowledge of me as a threat. As soon as I turn from sin and back to him, it becomes a comfort.

Francis Thompson's long poem 'The Hound of Heaven', which as a schoolboy, in a world now vanished, I learned by heart, reflects this psalm. Perhaps verse 5 was in the poet's mind when at last he turned at bay to face his Pursuer, and realized that his 'gloom, after all', was the 'shade of His hand, outstretched caressingly'.

2. How God surrounds me (139:7–12)

Thompson's 'long pursuit' – 'I fled Him, down the nights and down the days; / I fled Him, down the arches of the years' – is still more in evidence in the second section. *Where can I flee from your presence?* The answer is, Nowhere. The heaven and hell of verse 8 in the AV are misleading, for the psalmist is not thinking of the next world; but he knows that in this world too he could not escape God either in the heights of the sky or in the depths of the earth. If verse 9 runs parallel, flight to the farthest east (the *dawn*) or to the farthest west (the *far side of the sea*) would be equally vain.[20] And perhaps even more scary than a God who pursues you to the ends of the earth is one who (as the psalm suggests) is already there when you arrive!

This whole approach takes it that the psalmist wants to get away from God, like the nineteenth-century poet, and indeed like the Old Testament prophet: when he was told to go to Nineveh, 'Jonah ran away from the LORD and headed for Tarshish', in exactly the opposite direction (Jon. 1:3). *Surely the darkness will hide me* (11) does have a hopeful ring to it.

But as the psalm goes on, it seems increasingly to be, not apprehensive, but appreciative of a God who knows everything and is everywhere. Just as the heading *Of David*, often dismissed, might mean nonetheless a

---

[20] To *rise on the wings of the dawn* (to 'take the wings of the morning', in the older English versions) is beautiful, but unclear: it could mean to 'race the light of the rising sun as it sweeps across the continent', as Clements graphically puts it (p. 172).

connection of some kind with the poet-king, so the heading 'Of Zechariah, in the Dispersion', found in one Greek manuscript of this psalm, might mean a song much loved by the people of the exile. In the darkness of distant pagan lands, with even, it seemed, *the light become night*, the ever-present Lord could make *the night . . . shine like the day* (11–12). Psalm 139 would sit well alongside 137 in a hymn book for the new temple.

3. How God has made me (139:13–18)

He has made me *fearfully and wonderfully*, says the third section. Though the exact translation of verse 14 is much debated, that is the gist of verses 13–16.

As with the first two sections, he is the 'Already' God. I cannot utter a word without his knowing it already (4); I cannot go anywhere without his being there already (8); I cannot even be what I am without his having already made me thus in my mother's womb (13). The womb is the *secret place* of verse 15a. Perhaps it is even what is meant by the *depths* of verse 15b:

> If there was ever a time when I was concealed in the darkness, out of your divine line-of-sight, then surely, God, it was during that ante-natal period . . . My own mother wasn't aware of my existence for a while. It was as if I was buried in some deep cave under the earth . . . But . . . it was precisely then . . . that I was most conspicuously the recipient of your care and attention.[21]

I was being *woven together* – 'intricately wrought', says the RSV – by a God who on that tiny scale was engaged in a task perhaps more like his original immense work of creation than anything else that he does.

He was *creating*. And he was creating not only life, but *a* life: in the astonishing words of verse 16, from the embryo (*my unformed body*) right on through *all the days ordained for me*. Not just from birth to death, but from conception to death, a human life is God's handiwork. Psalm 139 is his forthright 'No' to those who for reasons of their own would cut it off, by abortion at one end or by euthanasia at the other.

In the context, the countless thoughts of God in verses 17–18 are his thoughts about *me*, the incredible detail with which he has made me and

---

[21] Clements, pp. 174–175.

keeps me going, my body and mind, my psychology and emotions, my circumstances and relationships. Daily the psalmist awakes with that realization: 'New every morning is the love / Our wakening and uprising prove.'[22] And it may be that among the many 'second meanings' of the Psalter is the New Testament revelation that *all the days* of verse 16 will in fact go on into eternity; and that therefore the awaking of verse 18 looks forward also to the day of resurrection.

4. How God tests me (139:19–24)

This is one of those psalms that disconcert us with a sudden switch from the noble to the venomous, all the more perplexing because the psalmist himself seems to see nothing odd about the change of tone. To quote Lewis, he throws in verse 19 (*If only you, God, would slay the wicked!*) 'as if it were surprising that such a simple remedy for human ills had not occurred to the Almighty'.[23]

As with 137 and the Babylonian babies, we might think 139 much improved by the removal of the hate-filled verses in its final section. But things like the inclusio of *search/know* in verses 1 and 23 point to its being an integrated whole, and once more 'the bad parts will not "come away clean"'.

Pointers of another kind, suggesting a possible background to the psalm, may help to clarify its overall message. Verse 20 provides several. The threats of enemies remind us of early David psalms, as the darkness of verses 11–12 recalls the 'valley of the shadow' in 23:4. Jeremiah too was surrounded by enemies, and much here would express his convictions: 'You who . . . probe the heart and mind, let me see your vengeance on them . . . "Who can hide in secret places so that I cannot see them?" declares the LORD' (Jer. 20:12; 23:23–24; see also 11:20; 12:3; 17:10). Nehemiah, facing the hostility of an influential section of the Israelite establishment, would have uttered verse 20 with feeling, if its difficult Hebrew is taken to mean, 'They use your name, but their motives are evil; your towns[24] have been led astray by them.'

We have to thank one such traumatic time for the memorable psalm to which it gave rise! But at all those times, and especially in the early days

---

22 John Keble, 'New every morning'.

23 Lewis, p. 24.

24 So the Heb. text. 'Adversaries' is an emendation.

of the return from exile to which 137 seems to belong, God's people were called to identify with God's cause. Like Edom 'on the day Jerusalem fell' (137:7), they had to take sides. That is the point of verses 21–22, and the real thrust of the psalm as a whole. The psalmist's Maker has made him in his own image, and therefore a moral being. Will he side with the right or with the wrong, with God or with God's enemies? The rest of the psalm may seem to leave little room for human initiative, but here the choice is ours.

History is littered with examples both of those who tried to evade the challenge and of those who took it up but got it wrong. Hence the importance of verses 23–24. Only those whose hearts are open to God's searching eye, who have misgivings (*anxious thoughts*) about their own discernment, and who are all too aware of the possibility of something *offensive* in themselves, will be able to follow the Lord in *the way everlasting*. 'Search all my sense, and know my heart, / Who only canst make known . . . / Search all my thoughts, the secret springs, / The motives that control': the hymn based on these verses will repay our meditation.[25]

Psalm 140

The theme of conflict with 'mighty kings' in 135 and 136 is carried forward across the centuries to Israel's sufferings at the hands of Babylon and Edom in 137. As the psalmist speaks to God in the following psalms, it becomes the malice of 'my foes' in 138:7 and of 'your adversaries' in 139:20. The same conflict is the burden of 140.

1. The background and shape of the psalm

The kind of heading it shares with its close neighbours is rare in Book V, but frequent in Books I and II. The same is true of the *selahs* we find here. As for its theme, the host of enemies surrounding the psalmist with malice and threatening him with violence also points back to those early psalms and to the days of David.

As so often elsewhere, it is entirely possible that a psalm should have originated at the beginning of the monarchy, even from David himself, and have been republished much later as part of a new collection. Turns of phrase that did not come into use till long after David's time may simply

---

[25] Francis Bottome, 'Search me, O God, my actions try'.

represent the kind of updating we find in today's hymn books. Are we to assert that 'The heavens declare your glory, Lord' could not possibly be Watts's version of Psalm 19 because he would have written 'thy', not 'your'? The fact is, of course, that he did; 'your' is the work of his modern editor.

At the end of the exile another new era was beginning for Israel, and again those who like Nehemiah had been chosen 'to promote the welfare of the Israelites' (Neh. 2:10) had to cope with the malice of *evildoers* devising *evil plans in their hearts* (1–2). But whether the ringleader (the Hebrew has the singular, 'the evil man') is Saul or Sanballat, or any of a score of miscreants in Old Testament history, the psalm is one that God's people repeatedly need to make their own.

What seems the most likely structure in the poet's mind does not quite tally with the divisions suggested by the three *selahs*. It is broadly, though not strictly, chiastic. The journey out (1–5) is a prayer for God's servant to be protected, and the journey back (8–11) is one for God's enemies to be punished. Each is followed by two verses (6–7, 12–13) expressing the psalmist's confidence in the Lord first on his own account and then on behalf of God's people.

2. Lord, protect me (140:1–7)

Parallelism, to which our attention was first drawn in Psalm 6, appears at its simplest in this psalm in verse 12: *The Lord secures justice for the poor / and upholds the cause of the needy.* On a bigger scale, its first six lines (vv. 1–3) run parallel to the second six (4–5). 'Rescue me from evildoers,' says one passage, while 'Keep me from the wicked,' says the other; the metaphors of war and snakebite are in one, while those of snares and traps are in the other; and verse 1b is repeated word for word in verse 4b.

Whatever the occasion when these lines were introduced or reintroduced, some attack on the people of God was threatened. Its object was violence, and its method slander. How deliberate it was, the metaphors show: conflict fomented, snares set and hidden. How serious it was we may judge from the repetition, which underlines the peril of the time.

When in Romans 3:13 Paul quotes verse 3, *the poison of vipers is on their lips*, it is to help show that evils of this kind are endemic to human nature. So we should not be surprised to find them on all sides in our modern world, swamped as it is by communication, with the misuse of words a weapon ready to hand for the wicked. And let us make no mistake: now as then there are plenty of *violent* people around who really do intend evil, and who really do deserve the imprecations of psalms like 140.

This is a cry for help, then (6–7). But the psalmist bases his prayer on his relationship with the Lord (*You are my God*) and on his experience of the Lord (*you shield my head in the day of battle*).

3. Lord, punish them (140:8–13)

The chiasmus tracks back from the centre of the psalm, picking up from the outward journey the crooks and their crimes and asking God to deal with them as they deserve. The psalmist remembers always that vengeance belongs to God, so in prayer he renounces it for himself and puts it in God's hands.

First and foremost, in verse 8 he targets the wicked and the proud from the earlier part of the psalm. The reason they are proud is that they believe they can get away with their wickedness. This prayer the Lord will infallibly answer sooner or later; if not in this world, then with terrible clarity in the next, they will see that crime does not pay.

Verse 9 picks up the words of verse 7: as his head has been covered protectingly, theirs are to be covered with the trouble they have caused others. This is the iron law of retribution that runs throughout Scripture. Verse 10 with its cluster of metaphors corresponds to verse 5: these who deal in snares and nets and traps, for them await burning coals and fire and miry depths.

Tongues used in verse 3 to wound and kill will in the end talk in vain, for the slanderers of verse 11a, literally the 'man of tongue', will find themselves deprived of all security. The violent people who in verses 1–2 devised 'evils' will themselves be hunted down by 'evils' – the same word – in verse 11b.

To make plain once and for all that none of this is personal vindictiveness, it is completed by a final claim with which the most liberal could not quarrel. It is for the sake of the poor and needy, not for an aggrieved individual but for a society which groans under the cynical heel of such evildoers, that the Lord *will* do away with them.

For the psalmists and their times, of course, society meant God's society. The psalms are about the world, but they are primarily about the church. Even more important than the fight against social evil is the conflict with spiritual evil. There we really do need to learn how to pray this sort of prayer.

Psalm 141

The difficulties of Psalm 141 are of the kind that becomes obvious as soon as you set different translations side by side. At verses 5–7 an exposition based as this one is on the NIV could totally mystify a reader following in the NRSV. But the main thrust of the psalm is clear, and it has much to do with the spoken word.

1. Urgent words

The first two verses, where prayer is likened to an evening sacrifice, take us back to the earliest David psalms, where 4:4–5 suggests an evening prayer set between the morning prayer of 3:5 and that of 5:3. Of several related scriptures, a New Testament one most expressly echoes verse 2a: Revelation 5:8 describes 'golden bowls full of incense, which are the prayers of God's people'. Another, Hebrews 13:15, speaks of the 'sacrifice of praise'.

If we take these phrases to imply rapt meditation, we are wrong. We have here an urgent cry for help. The last two verses of this psalm arise directly from the parlous situation of the last one. Practically every word is found in 140:4–5, and the prayer that the wicked who have been scheming to entrap the psalmist should *fall into their own nets* echoes that of 140:10.

The same urgency may well colour all four verses from 7 onwards. As the text stands, this is the psalmist begging the Lord to do something about **our** bones. Amid the brokenness of the Lord's faithful people, he pleads, *Do not give me over to death.*

2. Guarded words

There seems to have been a stage in the conflict between the psalmist and his enemies when the battle lines were much less clearly drawn. Verse 4 suggests the possibility of their getting together over a meal. In fact he would have declined the invitation. 'Not for me the delights of their table', as the NEB translates his words. But there opens up before us a familiar world of social intercourse and polite conversation, long before any hostility is declared, when decent people may find themselves almost imperceptibly *drawn to what is evil.*

Lewis's *Reflections on the Psalms* touch on this situation in the chapter he calls 'Connivance'. 'How ought we to behave in the presence of very bad people' – not, he hastens to add, the disadvantaged, but 'very bad people who are powerful, prosperous and impenitent'? The temptation of 'an evening spent in such society' is to go with the flow, 'to condone, to connive at; by our words, looks and laughter, to "consent"'.[26] Most of us do not have the acumen, the boldness or the sanctity to see what is really going on and to say what really ought to be said on such an occasion. Best, then, to stay away.

In any case, both in those early stages and when the gloves are finally off, every believer needs to have the Lord guard his or her mouth and watch his or her words. Especially do we need to pray verse 3 when unguarded speech is exactly what our Enemy, a slanderer just as the psalmist's was (140:11), delights to pick up and use against us.

3. Well-spoken words

We have already noticed something of the obscurity of verse 7. Verses 5 and 6 are equally difficult; the translation of the NIV is as likely as any. As so often in the Psalms, the gist of the passage is plain enough even if the details are not.

The psalmist could do without the verbal attacks of his enemies, no doubt the same sharp-tongued, poisonous words that 140:3 deplores. Hard words from the righteous are a different matter. He can cope with tough talk, whether it is abrasive or gentle, if it comes from one he knows to be a person of integrity. Many years in church ministry have taught me that opinions are to be weighed, not counted! And when something negative does need to be said to us, we shall be wise to remember the well-spoken words of Proverbs 27:6, that 'wounds from a friend can be trusted'.

What the psalmist says about his opponents is considerably more negative. He is totally *against* their deeds, to the point of predicting their leaders' fate – *thrown down from the cliffs*, or, as we might say (or might once have said), ending up on the gallows.[27]

When that happens, he says, *the wicked will learn that my words were well spoken*. In practice, the observation 'I told you so' is not generally appreciated; but in the broader sense it has to be recognized that the

---

[26] Lewis, pp. 60, 62.

[27] *Cliffs* is sela', the Rock. This was the name of Edom's fortress-city (a link with 137:7? See on 60:8 and 108:10), and also one of the titles of Yahweh (18:2 and frequently). Here the NIV probably has the right meaning.

psalmist's clear-headed and forthright plain speaking is something his world, and ours, sorely needs.

Psalm 142

If we are in the midst of a collection of psalms that is to be dated by one of them (137) soon after the exile, it must be admitted that 142 seems somewhat out of place. By contrast, it would be very much at home in the time of David, as the heading proposes.

To quote with feeling the African-American spiritual 'Nobody knows the trouble I've seen' is to invite the retort from the psalmist that he has a pretty good idea of it. Few troubles that we might experience are not put into words somewhere or other in this short psalm. Three of its verses, however, show confidence amid the storm, and stand out like rocks in a surging sea.

1. My way (142:3)

David *in the cave*, probably Adullam in 1 Samuel 22 rather than En Gedi in 1 Samuel 24, could well have expressed himself in terms like these. There are many likenesses between 142 and the psalms of the first two David Collections, especially those from 52 to 59, whose headings place them too in the days when he was being hunted by Saul. The words of 57 in particular, also reckoned to come from *the cave*, echo those of this psalm, though much more cheerfully.

Exhausted and wretched, the psalmist is also alone. He has no 'fellow-creature's ear' to fill 'with the sad tale of all [his] care'.[28] So such energy as he has left is, in Cowper's words, 'to heaven in supplication sent', as he cries aloud to God (1–2).

But this God is the one who knows the way that brought David to the cave, and the way of escape from it. He does not let his people be tested beyond endurance, says Paul in 1 Corinthians 10:13, but always provides 'a way' through.

2. My portion (142:5)

Before the psalmist stretches a path that is no less hazardous for the fact that God knows all about it (3b); there are still snares to entrap him, as in

---

[28] William Cowper, 'What various hindrances we meet'.

140:5 and 141:9. Beside him, moreover, stands no helper (4). In terms of the David story, we are at 1 Samuel 22:1a, with the fugitive as yet alone in the cave of Adullam, before friends and family begin to rally to his cause in verse 1b. Specifically, he feels the lack of a helper *at* [*his*] *right hand*, 'where his protector would be standing if he had one'.[29]

But such a champion has in fact been standing up for David in the place where he can serve him best, namely his friend Jonathan. He is a committed advocate on David's behalf before a judge who is in a hanging mood, Jonathan's own father Saul (1 Sam. 20:24–34).

Even better than Jonathan is the Lord himself. He is not only David's permanent 'right-hand man', but also his *portion*. An early David psalm brings the two metaphors together (16:5, 8).[30] David's portion in every normal sense, his home and all that goes with it, seems to be lost to him. But he still has the Lord.

> Thou, O Christ, art all I want;
> More than all in thee I find.[31]

3. My hope (142:7)

For the moment waves continue to break over his head, and the confidence of verses 3 and 5 is swamped again. Perhaps we can feel with him the desperation and the inadequacy of verse 6. Perhaps we are no strangers to the contradictory sense of being both hemmed in and on the run, as David has Saul as a pursuer and the cave as a prison.

Yet the Lord who knew every step of his way and was himself his portion had set him among, and would one day set him over, a great company of people. He was not the isolated figure that he felt himself to be. Psalm 1 rises up again to remind him, and us, of the basic facts: 'Blessed is the one', the individual, whose 'delight is in the law of the LORD'; for over and above every individual blessing such a person is a loved and valued member of 'the assembly of the righteous'.

When the psalmist grasps once more that one day 'the righteous will *surround*' him (7 NRSV), the word is one which can be translated 'crown' (cf. Prov. 14:18). To be enthroned above our fellow human beings, which

---

[29] Kirkpatrick, p. 802.

[30] Cf. also the courtroom scene leading up to 109:31.

[31] Charles Wesley, 'Jesu, lover of my soul'.

was David's destiny, is not what most of us are destined for. But equally glorious is the prospect we do have, that the Lord will never fail to lead us, to provide for us, and to keep us in the loving fellowship of his church.

Psalm 143

As the last of a close-knit group of four psalms within the eight that form this David Collection, 143 is very much of a piece with those immediately before it, and therefore with the David Collections of Books I and II. Far less links it with the days after the exile, though the only other place where the phrase *your good Spirit* occurs is Nehemiah 9:20. Whatever its background, it is a prayer that emerges from deep distress.

There are hints of a chiasmus, with the appeal to the Lord's righteousness in verses 1–2 and 11–12, and *enemy* and *spirit* in verses 3–4 and 9–10. It is perhaps more productive to take it that the *selah* divides the poem in two, to move out towards that midpoint hearing the psalmist's cry from the previous psalms intensified, and to come back from it hearing his pleas multiplied.

1. The cry intensified (143:1–6)

Mercy is the theme of verses 1–2. We have heard the psalmist ask for it before, and we have heard him appeal to God's righteousness too – that is, ask God to do what ought to be done. But here he realizes that righteousness is two-edged. How if God were to do 'what ought to be done' not only with his enemy but also with him? He recognizes that no-one, including him himself, is righteous before God, and as Hamlet says, 'Use every man after his desert, and who should 'scape whipping?'[32] The New Testament sees in verse 2 a cornerstone of the doctrine of justification by faith (cf. Rom. 3:20; Gal. 2:16). This really is a cry for mercy: not just for help but for forgiveness.

Misery is the next theme. These psalms have been describing wickedness in many forms, and verses 3–4 show the effect on one man of all this accumulation of evil. Here is somebody who does know the trouble we've seen, for he himself is overwhelmed by troubles as bad or worse.

Meditation is the theme of verse 5–6. The psalmist is helpless before the bad things that are happening to him, and helpless too when he turns

---

[32] William Shakespeare, *Hamlet*, II.ii.561ff.

to God, for he knows that in his unrighteousness he has no claim on God's help, and can ask only for mercy. But in one respect he is not helpless. He has some record, in some form, of the deeds of God, such as we now have in Scripture. On that he can and will feed his mind.

2. The pleas multiplied (143:7–12)

The reminder of God's past dealings with his people and his world enables the psalmist to put into words a quick-fire barrage of prayers that fills the rest of the psalm. The Lord's hard-pressed servant may be sure of a response to any or all of them, for prayer based on God's revelation of himself is always answered.

An answer, and a speedy one, is the first thing he pleads for (7). That, though the psalmist may not yet see it, is already on its way – 'Before they call I will answer' is the divine promise (Isa. 65:24). Next he begs for a sight of the Lord's face, that is, an awareness of his presence. Sooner or later that also is guaranteed.

Every new day is in some sense a new start. We may recall the morning prayer of the very first David psalm, in 3:5–6, and be able ourselves to testify to the effect of asking last thing at night that we may wake to 'New perils past, new sins forgiven, / New thoughts of God, new hopes of heaven'.[33] The spiritual blowing away of the cobwebs will clarify *the way I should go* (8).

The prayer for rescue in verse 9 would represent something of a triumph of the imagination for David in his cave. He would be making of his wretched surroundings a metaphor for the welcome refuge he finds in God: *I hide myself in you*. In verse 10 the psalmist recognizes that he can neither obey nor progress unless God enables him. Indeed, he knows (11) that only God can preserve, or renew, his life; only God can rescue him from his troubles.

The psalmist's focus has moved in this psalm from his persecutors to himself. A certain amount of introspection – healthy, not excessive – has done him good. But the facts remain, and the psalm ends with a note of

---

[33] John Keble, 'New every morning'. Ps. 143:8 certainly looks like an evening prayer, and on the theory that Pss 135 – 149 form a collection for a week's festival, this like every other odd-numbered psalm in it would be for evening use. But the notion that *bring me word* has to refer to 'a divine oracle transmitted via a cultic official' (Allen, p. 281) is a different matter. One would like to know where the obligatory 'cultic official', beloved of some scholars, would have come from when the poem was first written (by David alone in the cave?). Why should not this 'word' simply mean fresh light shed on the psalmist's meditation on revealed truth (5)?

realism. His situation will not finally be put right till the enemy is dealt with. Covenant love, which is tough, not soft, will do this also.

Psalm 144

This is one of those psalms that seem remarkably familiar: 'I have seen you, or someone very like you, before,' we say. Two-thirds of it turn out to be a reworking of verses adapted from psalms far back in the Psalter. In the course of its publication history it appears to have gone through three editions.

1. First edition

There is more to its David connection than the heading that it shares with seven other psalms in this part of Book V. Its framework is provided by several verses from 18, one of the David psalms of Book I. That in its turn is connected with the history of David's reign in 2 Samuel, where chapter 22 reproduces it almost exactly, together with the introductory heading it has in the Psalter: 'David sang to the LORD the words of this song when the LORD delivered him from the hand of all his enemies and from the hand of Saul.'

Against the background of the reign of the great king, we may highlight four of the points that that earlier psalm makes. First, what the Lord means to David: he is his rock, fortress, deliverer, refuge, shield, stronghold (18:2). Then what he has done for David: he has parted the heavens and come down; with smoke, arrows, lightning, he has reached down from on high and rescued him from deep waters (18:9, 14, 16). Third, what he has made of David: he has trained his hands for battle (18:34). Fourth, what he has overcome on David's behalf: as David's Rock, he is exalted above all the power of foreign nations, giving victory to his chosen king (18:43–47, 50).

2. Second edition

These points from 18 provide a framework for the first eleven verses of 144. They are filled out by other lines that are equally familiar. Verse 3 (*what are human beings*) comes from 8:4; verse 4 (*They are like a breath . . . fleeting*) is adapted from 39:5. Both of these are David psalms from Book I. Verse 9 (the *new song* and the *ten-stringed lyre*) is from 33:2–3, and the same psalm provides verse 15b, *Blessed is the people whose God is the*

LORD (33:12). Though itself lacking the David heading,[34] 33 also belongs to the first David Collection.

In other words, 144:1–11 is another mosaic, a 'creative adaptation' of existing psalms.[35] The psalmist here does more than merely shuffle the pieces. The insertion of *what are human beings . . . ?* at verse 3 subtly alters the mood of the exultant opening quotation. Verses 5–8 turn the praise of 'He parted the heavens' into prayer: *Part your heavens, LORD. Hands* now appear three times, in verses 1 and 7, binding together the new structure: the psalmist's hands are trained for war, but in the end it is the Lord's hand alone that will rescue him from the enemies' hands.

So, experience tells him of the Lord's power (1–2), but also of his own weakness (3–4). Now he needs God to do again what he has done in the past (5–8). He repeats the praise (9–10) and the prayer (11).

Finally, with verses 12–15, past experience and present need are followed by future expectation. On the analogy of the first eleven verses, the rest of the poem might be adapted from a psalm or psalms now lost; an obvious similarity is between the family portrait of verse 12 and that in one of the Songs of Ascents (128:3). The prosperity of the countryside and the security of the city complete the happy picture.[36]

3. Third edition

As the second edition of Psalm 18, or rather as a new psalm based on it, 144 would have suited any of David's successors whose throne was under serious threat from hostile foreign nations.

From the exile onwards there was of course no more Davidic throne to be threatened. Yet evidently the psalm came back into use at the restoration, king or no king, in what we might call its third edition. Even if there is no truth in the idea of a post-exilic collection of fifteen psalms running from 135 to 149, the Psalter in its final form is post-exilic, and we have to ask what 144 is saying to those later times, and therefore to our own.

Perhaps something like this. Then and now, whenever God's people are under assault they do well to remind themselves of all that their *loving God* has done for them in the past, insignificant though they are. They can quite properly ask him to act in ways that even in modern times might be

---

[34] In the Heb. text; the Gk version (LXX) has it.

[35] Allen, p. 290.

[36] The translation of v. 14 is problematic; cf. NIV mg., RSV, etc., for other possibilities.

described as the rending of the heavens, a bolt of lightning, rescue from a sea of troubles. They know that his, and their, chief weapon is the truth of the gospel, to destroy the lies which (like Samson's hair) are the secret of the enemy's great strength. They are sure that nothing but good can result, even from the most disastrous circumstances, when God's people are taking refuge in the Rock.

Psalm 145

The last of all the David psalms fittingly completes the tally, and at the same time is an equally fitting lead-in to the five songs of praise that will bring the Psalter to a close. We cannot fail to be struck by the psalmist's artistic skill, his breadth of vision and the deceptive simplicity of his message.

1. Skill

As well as being the last David psalm, 145 is the last of the Psalter's acrostics. Verse 13b is not in most manuscripts of the Hebrew text, nor in the older English translations; if, as in the NIV, it is brought in from some of the other ancient versions, it supplies the *nun* verse which with the initial letters of the existing twenty-one verses makes up the Hebrew alphabet.

It is not the alphabetical scheme that makes the poem the tour de force that it is. As Allen says, the psalmist 'took the acrostic pattern in his stride and found it no obstacle to a coherent development of his message'.[37] He had as it were become a past master in the technique of tapestry-making, and could concentrate instead on the grand picture that would be made up of all those individual stitches.

Nor is this broad effect achieved by anything so obvious as a series of panels, that is, of stanzas of roughly equal length. Within the inclusio of the *aleph* and *taw* verses (*Praise your/his name for ever and ever* at the beginning and end), the poem's midpoint – structurally, not mathematically – is after verse 13a. 'I will praise you,' say verses 1–2, then in verse 3 comes the reason why. 'The generations will join me in praising you,' say the next four verses, and then two verses say why. In verses 10–12 'all will praise you', and verse 13a says why. From that point the sequence is reversed. Two passages each of four verses give the grounds for praise first

---

[37] Allen, p. 296.

(13b–16, 17–20), and the praise itself follows, completing the psalm with verse 21.

2. Breadth: i

Having taken a peep at the last verse, we already have an idea of how broad the psalmist's vision is going to be. He alone sings the opening verses; by the end he has been joined by the whole of God's creation – as Watts versified Psalm 72, 'Let every creature rise and bring / Peculiar honours to our King.'[38]

Not surprisingly, since the praise of verses 1–2 is that of one individual, and a mere human being at that, the contrasting fact that elicits it is the greatness of God. *Great* is the *gimel*-word that begins verse 3, *gādôl*, a stitch of exactly the right colour in just the right place.

In verses 4–7 the successive generations add their voices to the solo voice of the psalmist. Praising God's works in creation, they move on to his acts and his deeds and the glory shown in his work of redemption, passing, so to speak, from Genesis to Exodus. His unforgettable revelation of himself in Exodus 34:6 – this is at least the fifth time it has been quoted or alluded to in the Psalter (cf. 86:15; 103:8; 111:4; 112:4) – was in fact required to be passed down from *one generation . . . to another*. The quotation of it here coincides with the need for a *heth*-word at verse 8: '*Gracious* (*ḥannûn*) and compassionate, slow to anger and rich in covenant love, is the Lord.' In the end, not his people only but also *all he has made* (9) will have cause to thank him for his grace in redemption, as Paul explains in Romans 8:19–21.

Yes, all he has made will praise him, but his saints have the privilege of also making known the message of his kingdom (10–12). The praises of these verses are grounded in the fact of the Lord's kingship. With that the psalm began, four times over it is celebrated in this section, and at verse 13a the alphabet duly reaches the *mem*-word *kingdom*, *malkût*. Significantly, the words of this verse are found on the lips of Nebuchadnezzar in Daniel 4:3, in a book which, with the demise of the old Hebrew kingdoms, opens up an entirely new notion of what God's kingdom really is – a dominion that is primarily spiritual, and not bound up with a literal throne in an earthly Jerusalem: the first glimpse of a butterfly emerging from a chrysalis, or of a plant sprouting from a seed.

---

[38] Isaac Watts, 'Jesus shall reign'.

3. Breadth: ii

The inclusion of the *nun*-verse from the Greek Old Testament and elsewhere gives a symmetry and a connection between the next two passages.
First, verses 13b–16 are about God's general care for the world he has
made, and for its inhabitants. It is not his pleasure that any of his human
creatures should *fall* or be *bowed down*, and there is no reason why any
living thing should not have enough to live on.

Then verses 17–20 are about his special care for *all who call on him in
truth*. To them his nearness (18) is a matter not just of proximity but of
relationship: he is their 'next of kin'. Thus *the Lord . . . has compassion on
all he has made*, both his world and his church.

So as the earlier part of the psalm praises God as both Creator and
Redeemer, this part similarly speaks first of that which is his handiwork
and then of those who are his children. And reversing the previous order,
praise now follows the grounds for praise. Because the Lord is this kind of
God, the psalmist takes up his praise once again, but now accompanied
by the praises of all creation (21).

4. Simplicity

With his tongue in his cheek, as once before, Brueggemann says that 145
'may be regarded as a not very interesting collection of clichés'.[39] He
means that it could seem so to readers who see in it a naïve and unrealistic
view of the world. At the other end of the Psalter, the author of the first
psalm might seem to wear similarly rose-coloured glasses. The righteous,
a tree whose leaf does not wither? The wicked like chaff blown away?
A touch of reality will be a disorienting experience for such an unworldly
person. As Sidney Smith complained (with a snobbishness that was also
probably tongue-in-cheek) when some low-class neighbours moved in
next door, 'This is indeed a severe dose of the People' – the kind of thing
that might make the psalmist revise his complacent optimism.

But the author of Psalm 145 has worked through all that. It is not inex-
perience, but experience, that enables him to write as he does.

He has long since been reoriented, and has discovered on the far side
of trial and suffering and mystification that in the end this *is* how things
are. Yes, there is much evil in the world; but taking the long view, a single
half-verse – *but all the wicked he will destroy* (20b) – is all that it will

---

[39] Brueggemann, p. 10.

amount to in the end. So in C. S. Lewis's dream the vastness of hell became an infinitesimal speck down a tiny crack in the ground between two blades of grass, when seen from the standpoint of the ultimate fact of heaven.[40]

How to live as if all this were true, though?

Brueggemann points us to the Sermon on the Mount, and to Matthew 6:25–33. In the words of the hypothetical verse 13b, the Lord is indeed *trustworthy in all he promises and faithful in all he does*. It is those whose simplicity is not that of naïvety, but that of experience, who know that if they seek first the kingdom of God all these things will be added to them. 'The one with looking eyes and open hands and yearning desire', says Brueggemann (and we shall not misunderstand his provocative language), 'does nothing, produces nothing, earns nothing, manipulates nothing, possesses nothing – only gladly, trustingly receives.'[41] That is why Psalm 145 is a defiant song of praise in a world ridden by self-seeking and self-sufficiency.

---

[40] C. S. Lewis, *The Great Divorce* (London: Bles, 1945), p. 112.

[41] Brueggemann, p. 124.

Psalms 146 – 150

8. The final Hallel

'Praise the Lord', Hallelu Yah, begins and ends each of the last five psalms of the Psalter. The psalms of the first such 'Praise' collection were 113 – 118, the Egyptian Hallel, and the second was the Great Hallel, meaning either the seventeen from 120 to 136 or just the last one or two of them. The present group, then, is the third and final Hallel.

Though a distinct set, it does follow on very naturally from the David psalms that immediately precede it. The Lord's endless praise, his everlasting kingdom, and his care for the hungry and the burdened figure in 146 as they did in 145. Everything from the Songs of Ascents onwards might perhaps be intended as an integrated collection.

The tone of these remaining psalms is one of unalloyed confidence, with scarcely a shadow of past horrors. For such things *are* past; what we have here is no naïve optimism that has not yet noticed that they exist, but a mature, forward-looking faith that has faced them and knows they are being dealt with. Praise the Lord!

Psalm 146

Watts's paraphrase 'I'll praise my Maker' is a fine one.[1] His words will crystallize for us three aspects of the psalm.

1. I'll praise my Maker while I've breath

I *intend to* praise him every day of my life: that is the force of verse 2. This resolve is a mark of the mature believer. The psalmist puts his mind and

---

[1] It appears in modern hymn books with John Wesley's editorial alterations, which include the omission of the princes (v. 3) and the wicked (v. 9).

his will to the matter. His hallelujahs are not empty-headed repetitions, triggered by certain kinds of atmosphere or music. Nor are they songs for the good days only, when he is in the mood. He has learned to look for the facts behind the appearances, and to see the Lord at work in everything: the sun that is always shining, even if it is behind the clouds or on the other side of the world.

As so often, Watts adds a New Testament gloss to the Old Testament scriptures, and it makes up five-sixths of his first verse. What does it mean to me as a New Testament believer to praise God *as long as I live*? It means that not only for the duration of my earthly life, but also

> when my voice is lost in death,
> Praise shall employ my nobler powers;
> My days of praise shall ne'er be past,
> While life, and thought, and being last,
> Or immortality endures.

Surely, some will say, that was not in the psalmist's mind? Surely the words with which the previous psalm began, 'I will praise your name for ever and ever', must have been the words of Israel the nation, not those of any Old Testament individual? But the Old Testament itself teaches that the future holds more than that. Its people knew, as verses 2 and 10 together remind us, that somehow the individual's seventy years, *and* the continuing generations of Zion, *and* the everlasting reign of God, were all bound together in the 'bundle of the living' (1 Sam. 25:29). From Psalm 6 onwards we have found repeated pointers to what that might imply about a life after death.

2. The man whose hopes rely on Israel's God

> Happy the man whose hopes rely
> On Israel's God! He made the sky,
> And earth, and sea, with all their train.

The Maker of all things is the God of Jacob (5–6); all the power that made the worlds was channelled into preparing the way for that man, making him, remaking him with his new name Israel, and directing and redeeming and blessing his descendants.

And the God of Jacob is *our* help and hope. There is no-one else to rely on. All the princes of our world, all the people of power and influence, whether we revile them or revere them, in the end *return to the ground*, and *their plans come to nothing*. Briefly, in contrast to his pervasive celebration of life and of things that last for ever, the psalmist reminds us of the mortality with which Adam was cursed in Genesis 3:19: 'Dust you are and to dust you will return.' Though it is not easy to bring it out in translation, verses 3 and 4 of the psalm use the same words: *Do not put your trust . . . in human beings, who . . . return to the ground.*[2]

But our God is not like that. As Creator and Redeemer, the one whose greatness the last psalm was extolling, he is the same God today that he was in Bible times, and to that character he *remains faithful for ever*.

3. None shall find his promise vain

A solo voice it may be that in verse 2 sings *I will praise the* Lord, but this individual is no individualist. He looks around at, and identifies with, a big complex world full of an infinite variety of people. People, too, with an infinite variety of needs; but true to the spirit of these psalms, when he looks at the many evidences of evil in that world he sees them only in relation to the Lord, Maker and Saviour, who *remains faithful for ever* in his ability and willingness to do something about them.

His truth for ever stands secure;
He saves the oppressed, he feeds the poor,
    And none shall find his promise vain.

The Lord gives eyesight to the blind;
The Lord supports the fainting mind;
    He sends the labouring conscience peace;
He helps the stranger in distress,
The widow and the fatherless,
    And grants the prisoner sweet release.

This is not a naïvety that is going to be disoriented the moment it notices a beggar who has not been fed or a prisoner who has not been

---

[2] An earthling returning to earth (Allen, p. 299) would convey the effect, were it not for the unfortunate echo of the tinny voices of little green aliens.

freed. It is the certainty of a totally reoriented believer that in the end the Lord alone can (and will) put all these things right. Five times in verses 7b–9 his name rings out, and, as Brueggemann puts it, 'dismisses every other name': the Lord, not Baal; the Lord, not a powerful world leader; the Lord, not the free-market system nor a Western government; the Lord, not the church organization; the Lord, not my favourite political persuasion.[3] If it were not so, where should we be? But it is so. Praise the Lord!

Psalm 147

While the outstanding English metrical version of 146 has held its own for three hundred years, we find a hymn writer of our own time making 147 equally singable for us, in Timothy Dudley-Smith's 'Fill your hearts with joy and gladness'.

1. Another mosaic

Linking this psalm not only with 146 but also with the last of the David psalms, 145, is its celebration of the Lord as both Creator and Redeemer, who cares alike for his world and for his people. It has connections too with the psalms which, a little further back, the compilers placed between the Songs of Ascents and the fourth David Collection, namely 135, 136 and 137. These seem to belong to the days of the restoration, like 147:2, where the Lord builds up Jerusalem and gathers the exiles of Israel. The broken heart of verse 3 and the blessings of verse 13 might be a before-and-after picture of Nehemiah and the reconstruction of the city's walls and gates (cf. Neh. 1:4; 2:3; 3:3; etc.).

In fact much of the psalm seems to come from other psalms, and from Deuteronomy, Job and Isaiah. If 145 is a tapestry, 147 is another mosaic like 144, assembling fragments of quotations to create a picture which is familiar yet distinctive. Just as the psalmist adapts these other scriptures to make his psalm, so Dudley-Smith adapts the psalm to make his paraphrase. What in the text before us forms three sections he rearranges in four stanzas – very effectively, be it said, but still in a different order from the psalmist's. In the latter, each section begins with a call to praise our God, and ends with a contrast between his people and the rest.

---

[3] Brueggemann, p. 127.

2. The God who knows the stars (147:1–6)

As Redeemer, the Lord has brought home the exiles of Israel, the 'wounded souls' and 'humble hearts', as the paraphrase calls them. As Creator, he is the God who numbers and names the stars. Why would the psalmist bring these two facts together?

This aspect of God's control of his world had a double significance for his people. First, the stars represented Israel herself, partly because they symbolized the twelve sons of Jacob (Gen. 37:9ff.; cf. Rev. 12:1ff.), but more because of God's promise to Abraham in Genesis 15:5: 'Count the stars – if indeed you can count them . . . So shall your offspring be.' Abraham couldn't, of course; but God could, and could even name each one of them. This is the God who likewise knows every single child of his, scattered over the face of the earth and across the centuries of history, and will one day bring them all home.

Second, the stars also represented Israel's enemies. The worship of 'all the starry hosts' was a pagan practice originating, it seems, in Assyria and Babylonia, the great empires that had successively taken the northern and southern Israelite kingdoms into exile.[4] The God who numbers and names the stars has the measure of the pagan deities on whom his people's enemies rely. At the time of his choosing he shows them to be powerless, each empire crumbles in turn as he *casts the wicked to the ground*, and the freed exiles return.

3. The God who feeds the earth (147:7–11)

In his commentary Craigie recalls puzzling over verse 10 when as a boy he regularly wore a kilt. Was this very proper Scots fashion being condemned by the Prayer Book's words 'Neither delighteth he in any man's legs'?[5]

Fear not, Scottish readers, the psalmist is here talking about something completely different. Our God, he says, is not on the side of the big battalions, the cavalry (10a) or the infantry (10b) of Babylon or Assyria. He cares nothing for their armies, any more than he cares for their star gods. It is his own people, who fear and trust him, in whom he delights.

That is God the Redeemer. On the other hand, God the Creator is in this section the God of clouds and rain, who by means of them feeds the earth,

---

[4] Israel was infected by the worship of astral deities (2 Kgs 17:16, north; 21:3ff., south), though God had warned against it long before (Deut. 4:19). See also Jer. 19:13, and the Babylonian astrologers of Dan. 2.

[5] Craigie, p. 9.

in more senses than one. Again we ask, what is the connection between these two aspects of his work?

We might rephrase verses 8–9 in the style of a nursery rhyme: This is the God who brings the clouds, that drop the rain, that enriches the earth, that produces the plants, that feed the birds and beasts. All around his people 'Crowns and thrones may perish, / Kingdoms rise and wane',[6] but something else is going on regardless. The cycle of nature is an extraordinary dynamic process carrying on year after year, and surviving the most violent dislocations. It has a power different from and far greater than the power of armies or corporations or even philosophies.

This is the kind of power available to those *who put their hope in his unfailing love*. In terms the seer of Revelation would recognize, Babylon destroyed Jerusalem; yet now Babylon is 'thrown down, never to be found again' (Rev. 18:21), and lo! Jerusalem has risen anew. Or in terms not too unlike those of verse 8, the wreckage of the bulldozer rusts in the shed, while from the ravaged earth the grass springs yet again.

4. The God who commands the weather (147:12–20)

Like the end of 144, this third section of 147 looks at the community now settled both in and around rebuilt Jerusalem, and praises God for a strong city and a prosperous countryside. This too is the work of the Redeemer. When he rescues them from a wretched past, it is in order to give them a bright future; and however comfortably some of them may have settled down in Babylon, that future is in Jerusalem.

The work of the Creator in verses 15–18, though again to do with weather, differs from that in verses 8–9. Here a command goes forth from him to say, 'Let there be snow! Let there be frost! Let there be hail!', and it is so; then the word that sent the temperature plummeting raises it again, and the ice melts. Who said there should be a freeze? Who said there should be a thaw? The God who speaks in such a way that inanimate nature does what he wants it to.

This God has spoken a corresponding word designed for human ears. This one requires an intelligent response, and obedience to it brings great blessing. Where is it to be heard? It is the word *revealed . . . to Jacob . . . He has done this for no other nation*.

---

6 Sabine Baring-Gould, 'Onward, Christian soldiers'.

It is nevertheless a message for everyone; the question is, are the other nations going to hear it from the one nation that has it? As the many Zion psalms in the Psalter have made abundantly clear, and as the closing verses of 147 reiterate, only in Jerusalem will anyone from any nation ever find lasting security and prosperity. But only God's people know the way there. Are they making it known?

Psalm 148

Who that knows the Lord will not love to praise him with these psalms of the last Hallel? After Watts's paraphrase of 146 and Dudley-Smith's of 147, the English-speaking church is suddenly spoilt for choice when it reaches 148. We may of course chant it, or its big brother the Benedicite,[7] in liturgical versions old or new. We may say it congregationally in a Bible translation, or memorize it (or its little sister 145:10!) for private meditation. But in today's hymn books we have in addition at least four hymns based on it that are well worth singing.[8] To one of these we shall return, for a rather special reason.

But what about the psalm itself, as the psalmist wrote it?

1. A stanza of verbs, a stanza of nouns

We should take note of how the first of its two stanzas is put together, because the second will follow the same pattern. In the four opening verses the heavens, in all three senses of the word (where the angels sing; where the stars shine; where the rain clouds fly), are called on to praise the Lord, together with everything that might be thought of as being 'up there'. Then in the next two verses a reason is added: let them praise his name, because his eternal word of command made them and set them in place (5–6, recalling 33:9).

Not suffering from the modern preoccupation with mere size, the psalmist in his second stanza gives to what is 'down here', to our little world, more lines than he has given to the vastness of the heavens. For six verses (7–12) the earth, with all that is in it, is summoned to praise.

---

[7] The 'Song of Creation', from the Apocrypha, used in Christian liturgies (including the Prayer Book) from the earliest times.

[8] T. B. Browne's and Timothy Dudley-Smith's, both beginning 'Praise the Lord of heaven'; Michael Perry's 'Praise him, praise him, praise him! powers and dominations'; the anonymous 'Praise the Lord, ye heavens adore him'.

Then in the next two verses he again adds a reason, and here too he spreads himself: verses 13–14 have six lines, where verses 5–6 had only four. Let them, that is those who bring praises *from the earth* (7), praise his name, in this case precisely because of his name. It is, of course, Yahweh. The first stanza's praise, the reason for it, the second stanza's praise, and the reason for that, all begin with the name *the* Lord, and counting in the Hallelu Yah inclusio as well, it rings out six times in the course of the psalm. It is the name of the Redeemer; so as stanza 1 praises the law that creates, stanza 2 praises the love that redeems.

One further way in which the two halves mirror each other is the repetition of verbs in the first and of nouns in the second. In a sense, *Praise him, all his angels* (2) and *Praise the* Lord . . . *you great sea creatures* (7) reflect each other. But in the first, it is the imperative verb *Praise* which is one of a sequence of nine, whereas in the second it is the vocative noun *creatures* which is the first of no fewer than twenty-three.

2. Yet at the same time a chiasmus

It is worth noting these ways in which the psalmist shapes his poem in two stanzas, because attentive readers soon grasp that another pattern lies behind this one. From one point of view, stanza 1 progresses from verse 1 to verse 6, then stanza 2 goes back to the beginning and follows the same sort of path from verse 7 to verse 14. But then, as in a kind of optical illusion, our eyes refocus, and we realize that in another sense the sequence of verses 7–12 retraces that of verses 1–4 *backwards*, that is, from verse 4 to verse 1. These passages are the outward and homeward journeys of a chiasmus.

The effect of this is to open up for us the psalmist's measureless vision. Beginning *from the heavens* in the highest meaning of the word, he calls on the angels first; then on the denizens of the second heaven, the sun, moon and stars; then on those of the heaven nearest to us, the rain clouds. With verse 7 he has reached what we might today think of as the biosphere, that thin yet teeming layer in which all the globe's inhabitants live. So he begins this stanza *from the earth*, together with the sea and its creatures. Back goes the chiasmus, via earth's weather, then its denizens, mineral, vegetable and animal, to the human race in all its variety, high and low, great and small – the crown of God's creation, destined to be even greater than the angels (cf. Ps. 8).

The picture's grandeur, its comprehensiveness, is highlighted by the repeated *all* – all angels, all stars, all depths, all hills, all cattle, all nations. Even all rulers: for the notion that Bible religion is today the concern only of a small and eccentric minority is quite blown away by this stupendous summons. Everything and everyone, from the angels of God to the most powerful and godless of people, is to recognize the supremacy of Israel's Lord – the one who has made himself known to these alone, *the people close to his heart.*

3. A poem set for mixed voices

There is one other thing the chiastic pattern does for us.

The sequence of verses 1–4 moves from the most articulate to the least articulate. The angels can use words, and know with total clarity what they are singing about in the 'Holy, holy, holy' of Isaiah 6 or the 'Glory to God' of Luke 2. 'The skies' in which God 'has pitched a tent for the sun', so another psalm tells us (19:1, 4), 'proclaim the work of his hands', but not verbally. Even the clouds that bring the rain glorify God, but they do so simply by obeying the *decree* (6) that has made them what they are.

That is the point from which verses 7–12 start. Mountains too can praise him by simply being! Trees live and grow, animals move and feel (we notice the order, the progress from the inanimate to the animate), until once again we reach those of God's creatures who, like the angels, can actually put their praises into words.

The most familiar of the English metrical versions of this psalm is the anonymous 'Praise the Lord, ye heavens adore him'. It appeared in 1796 in a collection put together for use in one of the charitable institutions of the day, the Foundling Hospital in London. Only in the hymn's third stanza, which was not added till forty years later, do we find the 'young and old' of verse 12. Nevertheless that is where the homeward journey of the chiasmus ends. It began with the angels, and ends with the children; as if to say that at these two extremes you will find the most direct and articulate praises of God. The Gospel record tells us that our Lord came to his birth amid the songs of angels, and went to his death amid the songs of children (Luke 2:8–14; Matt. 21:15–16). There is something peculiarly apt about the fact that this psalm, of all psalms, should have been sung in this version first by an assembly of homeless, abandoned youngsters who had been reached by Christian concern, and who, we may hope, responded to it with childlike faith. In the words of a psalm at the other end of the Psalter (this one has already reminded us of it), 'From the lips of children and infants you ... have called forth your praise' (Ps. 8:2, as quoted in Matt. 21:16).

Psalm 149

Intentionally or not, 149 seems to grow from the picture with which 148 ends, the picture of an Israel strong, glorious, and 'close to his heart'. It might have been composed in the first instance for some military victory in the days of the kings. It would have been equally valid in the days after the exile, even though the strength and glory of Israel was then of a deeper and less obvious sort, as we saw in 147. But always there was an expectation of days yet to come when with a sense of fulfilment God's people would be able to say concerning scriptures like the present psalm, 'So this is what it was really all about.'

1. The saints (149:1, 5, 9b)

'Saint' in the Old Testament represents either of two Hebrew words. *Qādôš* means belonging to God, and therefore being distinct, and distinctive, as he is. *Ḥāsîd*, the one used in this psalm, means being loved by God with his covenant love (*ḥesed*) and so being devoted to him with a love of the same kind. The two senses converge in *hagios*, the New Testament's equivalent Greek word.

All God's people are saints. Nowhere does Scripture even entertain the idea of an aristocracy of holiness, whose members are spiritually a cut above the rest of us, recognized by being given canonization and a halo. If we are God's people, we are his saints; and we appear three times in 149. Only here in the Psalter is the word used so often, and in a short psalm it stands out: a marker, in fact, to divide the poem into two.

In verse 1 we, the saints (NIV *his faithful people*), gather to celebrate something new. The words take us back to the first Exodus Collection, where several psalms begin with 'Sing to the LORD a new song', as here (96; 98), or 'The LORD reigns', as verse 2 implies (93; 97; 99).

In verse 5 we rejoice on our beds! Whether this means that we cannot sleep for joy, or that we *can* sleep (that is, sleep in safety), or that the *beds* are couches on which we recline at a celebratory banquet, clearly something has happened that is worth celebrating.

In verse 7 we are honoured – and this really does seem strange – to *inflict vengeance on the nations*. We need to look to the two passages framed by these three mentions of the saints in order to make sense of them, especially the last one.

2. The King (149:2–4)

From early times Israel knew God as both her Maker and her King. At the time of the exodus he had made her a nation; following the conquest, although the judges were her leaders, he was her ruler (cf. Judg. 8:23; 1 Sam. 8:4–7).

But we should not be wrong in seeing here an added dimension to both great titles. On the one hand, each of the first three psalms of the final Hallel has praised the Lord as the Maker not just of Israel but of all things. On the other hand, only here in this group of psalms is he King, but the word is a link with the last of the David group (145:1), where his 'kingdom is an everlasting kingdom' (145:13). So he is more than the Maker and the King of Israel. He has been Creator of the world from its very beginning; he will be King of the universe to its very end.

So his delight in his people, his glorifying of *the humble*, that is, those who put their trust in him (4), points us to the stupendous vision of the future in Isaiah 60, which is filled with similar language. And that in turn points forward to the revelation in the Bible's last two chapters of God as Alpha and Omega, original Maker and ultimate King, and of the church radiant with his glory (Rev. 21:9–11; 22:13). For whatever special event Psalm 149 was first designed, we can scarcely help seeing these extra depths and heights in it.

3. The kings (149:6–9a)

The depths and heights help us to understand the fierceness of the psalm's second half. If in the prophecy of Isaiah we were to continue from chapter 60 into chapter 61, we should find there also, especially in its first few verses, many echoes of this psalm: the humble (the 'poor') crowned with beauty and blessing when the King reigns in Zion.

In this case the New Testament reference is to the gospel story. Jesus begins his ministry by proclaiming in the synagogue at Nazareth that he himself fulfils Isaiah's prophecy (Luke 4:16–21). But significantly, he stops short at 61:2a. His coming into the world brings 'the year of the LORD's favour'. Not until his second coming will 'the day of vengeance of our

God' arrive. Retribution for the *nations*, that is, for all who refuse to accept him as King and thus become his people, is threatened (and properly so) in Psalm 149:7 and in Isaiah 61:2b. It is in abeyance so long as the message of Christ is being made known. It finally comes home to roost in Revelation 19:1–3, where the saints praise God for the day of vengeance.

For the evil that stems from rebellion against God and plays havoc with his wonderful world must be destroyed sooner or later. The second psalm tells us that Messiah will 'dash . . . to pieces' the rebellious nations (2:8–9); here, the second to last psalm picks up a belief hinted at in a number of ancient scriptures, that in some way Messiah's people will be associated with him in this judgment.[9]

In the meantime, whatever the last judgment will be like and whatever the church's part in it, the conflict in verses 6–9a of our psalm is already a reality. So far from toning down its violent language, the New Testament backs it up. The fighting talk of 2 Corinthians 10:3–5 and Ephesians 6:10–18, and hymns derived from it like Charles Wesley's 'Soldiers of Christ, arise', show us the proper target of Christian aggression. Both sides in the religious wars of the past have misused this and similar warlike psalms; but that does not mean that they do not have a proper use. The powers of evil are abroad in our world, and it is for the church of God, with the praise of God in her mouth and the double-edged sword of Bible truth in her hands (Eph. 6:17; Heb. 4:12), to see that they do not have their way – that their plans are frustrated and their captives liberated. Where we know for certain the great Enemy is mobilized, most especially within ourselves, there let no quarter be given.

Psalm 150

So we come to the last psalm of the last Hallel. Its thirteen calls to praise (counting in the hallelujahs of the inclusio) bring Book V and the entire Psalter to a magnificent climax, not only rounding off, but also summing up, all that has gone before.

Hebrew readers would be aware of another repeated word binding the poem together. We miss it in our English versions, because it is hard

---

9 In particular Dan. 7:22 LXX/AV/RV; 1 Cor. 6:2; Jude 14–15 AV. See Gordon Fee, *1 Corinthians*, NICNT (Grand Rapids: Eerdmans, 1987), p. 233.

to translate consistently; but almost as frequent as *hallēl*, 'praise', is *bĕ*, rendered 'in' or 'for' or 'with'. We should catch the effect if the verb were not 'praise' but 'rejoice', for then we should be able to sing about rejoicing '*in* the heights of heaven', rejoicing '*in* God's acts of power' and rejoicing '*in* music', with three slightly different senses to the word *bĕ*, like the shifting lights in a prism.

1. In heights of heaven: in acts of power: in sounds of music

In his sanctuary God's worshippers gather: verse 1 speaks of the *place* of praise. Perhaps these are his people in the temple courts, looking up to the sky, where *in his mighty heavens* is gathered a far greater company – either the sun, moon and stars of 148:3, or the angels of 148:2, or both. Perhaps, though, verse 1 is about two kinds of heaven, first that of the angels and then that of the stars. So Henry Baker seems to take it in his splendid metrical version.[10] 'O praise ye the Lord! / Praise him in the height,' he begins – that is where the angels are; after that, the sky that came into being on the second day of creation, 'in brightness arrayed', is likewise called to adore its Maker.

His worshippers rejoice also in *his acts of power*: verse 2 speaks of the *theme* of praise. We are to praise him both for his greatness and for what he has done. We know well from recent psalms that both his creating work and his redeeming work are in view. The latter in particular has underlain his dealings with Israel as they are reflected in every page of the Psalter. And when the psalmists look back over Israel's history, and forward into the prophetic future, they fill verse 2 with meanings yet more spectacular. 'Ye sons of new birth,' Baker goes on, 'Praise him who hath brought you / His grace from above; / Praise him who hath taught you / To sing of his love.'

With yet a third sense of the word 'in', we rejoice in the sounds of music. Verses 3–5 speak of the *mode* of praise: 'O praise ye the Lord, / All things that give sound.' The passage points less to an exotic band like that which assailed the ears of Daniel's friends in Babylon (cf. Dan. 3:5ff.) than to the procession with which David brought the ark to Jerusalem. We have found many psalms that seem to allude to this, and the two accounts in 2 Samuel 6 and 1 Chronicles 15 describe priests with trumpets, Levites

---

[10] It is interesting that for this great poem both the leading British composers of their generation provided music still regularly used today: Charles Villiers Stanford's chant for the psalm, Hubert Parry's tune (*Laudate Dominum*) for the hymn.

with harps, lyres and cymbals, and 'tambourines and dancing' as in Exodus 15:20. One day we shall have something even better than organs and guitars and synthesizers.

Verse 6 is the psalmist's way of concentrating here in a single line what 148:1–14 detailed at length, and what 103:22 summed up as 'Praise the LORD, all his works everywhere in his dominion.

2. In conclusion

This psalm with which the Psalter ends is as brief and as deceptively simple as the one with which it began. To present either of them out of its context is to provoke puzzlement, if not outcry. The good prosper and the wicked perish, and everything will work out just fine, says 1; and the answer of 150 is, Praise God, so it does. And the perplexed Bible reader says, Yes, but does it?

So we must see these two psalms in their context. What has happened is that the intervening 148 have worked their way, often painfully, through all the 'Yes, buts'. They set forth the conflicts, burdens, mysteries and sufferings that both the individual believer and the assembly have to cope with, and all that God, as their covenant Lord, does for them on their journey of faith. In doing so, they help us to grasp what the first and last psalms are really saying.

Walter Brueggemann describes the progress from one to the other as a movement 'from obedience to praise'.[11] We have to begin by submitting to what God says; and what he says is, in outline, the simple facts set out in the first psalm.

But it does not take long for us to realize that living God's way is a great deal less easy than we thought. Things happen that seem to belie the simple truth we started with. We are disoriented (to use another Brueggemann term we have come across before), and that experience, together with the ways in which the Lord graciously reorients us to a new outlook, fills the rest of the Psalter. The single-minded praise of 150, which sees no evil, is not shutting its eyes to awkward facts. It is not naïve, even if we might have thought (wrongly) that the simplicity of 1 was naïve. It knows that all such things will in the end have been dealt with by God's *acts of power*, and in the meantime abandons itself in total trust to the Lord who has so revealed himself and his purposes.

---

11 Brueggemann, pp. 189–213.

There is no God like this God, let Israel now say. Indeed, in George Herbert's words, it is not to be Israel alone that says it, nor is it only to be said:

Let all the world in ev'ry corner sing,
    My God and King.
    The church with psalms must shout,
    No door can keep them out:
    But above all the heart
    Must bear the longest part.
Let all the world in ev'ry corner sing,
    My God and King.

Listen to God's Word
speaking to the world today

The complete NIV text, with over 2,300 notes from the Bible Speaks Today series, in beautiful fine leather- and clothbound editions. Ideal for devotional reading, studying and teaching the Bible.

Leatherbound edition with slipcase
£50.00 • 978 1 78974 139 1

Clothbound edition
£34.99 • 978 1 78359 613 3

The Bible Speaks Today:
Old Testament series

The Message of Genesis 1 – 11
The dawn of creation
David Atkinson

The Message of Genesis 12 – 50
From Abraham to Joseph
Joyce G. Baldwin

The Message of Exodus
The days of our pilgrimage
Alec Motyer

The Message of Leviticus
Free to be holy
Derek Tidball

The Message of Numbers
Journey to the Promised Land
Raymond Brown

The Message of Deuteronomy
Not by bread alone
Raymond Brown

The Message of Joshua
Promise and people
David G. Firth

The Message of Judges
Grace abounding
Michael Wilcock

The Message of Ruth
The wings of refuge
David Atkinson

The Message of 1 and 2 Samuel
Personalities, potential, politics and power
Mary J. Evans

The Message of 1 and 2 Kings
God is present
John W. Olley

The Message of 1 and 2 Chronicles
One church, one faith, one Lord
Michael Wilcock

The Message of Ezra and Haggai
Building for God
Robert Fyall

The Message of Nehemiah
God's servant in a time of change
Raymond Brown

The Message of Esther
God present but unseen
David G. Firth

The Message of Job
Suffering and grace
David Atkinson

The Message of Psalms 1 – 72

Songs for the people of God

Michael Wilcock

The Message of Psalms 73 – 150

Songs for the people of God

Michael Wilcock

The Message of Proverbs

Wisdom for life

David Atkinson

The Message of Ecclesiastes

A time to mourn, and a time to dance

Derek Kidner

The Message of the Song of Songs

The lyrics of love

Tom Gledhill

The Message of Isaiah

On eagles' wings

Barry Webb

The Message of Jeremiah

Grace in the end

Christopher J. H. Wright

The Message of Lamentations

Honest to God

Christopher J. H. Wright

The Message of Ezekiel

A new heart and a new spirit

Christopher J. H. Wright

The Message of Daniel

His kingdom cannot fail

Dale Ralph Davis

The Message of Hosea

Love to the loveless

Derek Kidner

The Message of Joel, Micah and Habakkuk

Listening to the voice of God

David Prior

The Message of Amos

The day of the lion

Alec Motyer

The Message of Obadiah, Nahum and Zephaniah

The kindness and severity of God

Gordon Bridger

The Message of Jonah

Presence in the storm

Rosemary Nixon

The Message of Zechariah

Your kingdom come

Barry Webb

The Message of Malachi

'I have loved you,' says the Lord

Peter Adam

The Bible Speaks Today:
New Testament series

The Message of Matthew
The kingdom of heaven
Michael Green

The Message of Mark
The mystery of faith
Donald English

The Message of Luke
The Saviour of the world
Michael Wilcock

The Message of John
Here is your King!
Bruce Milne

**The Message of the Sermon
on the Mount (Matthew 5 – 7)**
Christian counter-culture
John Stott

The Message of Acts
To the ends of the earth
John Stott

The Message of Romans
God's good news for the world
John Stott

The Message of 1 Corinthians
Life in the local church
David Prior

The Message of 2 Corinthians
Power in weakness
Paul Barnett

The Message of Galatians
Only one way
John Stott

The Message of Ephesians
God's new society
John Stott

The Message of Philippians
Jesus our joy
Alec Motyer

**The Message of Colossians and
Philemon**
Fullness and freedom
Dick Lucas

**The Message of
1 and 2 Thessalonians**
Preparing for the coming King
John Stott

The Bible Speaks Today:
Bible Themes series

The Message of the Living God
His glory, his people, his world
Peter Lewis

The Message of the Resurrection
Christ is risen!
Paul Beasley-Murray

The Message of the Cross
Wisdom unsearchable, love indestructible
Derek Tidball

The Message of Salvation
By God's grace, for God's glory
Philip Graham Ryken

The Message of Creation
Encountering the Lord of the universe
David Wilkinson

The Message of Heaven and Hell
Grace and destiny
Bruce Milne

The Message of Mission
The glory of Christ in all time and space
Howard Peskett and Vinoth Ramachandra

The Message of Prayer
Approaching the throne of grace
Tim Chester

The Message of the Trinity
Life in God
Brian Edgar

The Message of Evil and Suffering
Light into darkness
Peter Hicks

The Message of the Holy Spirit
The Spirit of encounter
Keith Warrington

The Message of Holiness
Restoring God's masterpiece
Derek Tidball

The Message of Sonship
At home in God's household
Trevor Burke

The Message of the Word of God
The glory of God made known
Tim Meadowcroft

The Message of Women
Creation, grace and gender
Derek and Dianne Tidball

The Message of the Church
Assemble the people before me
Chris Green

The Message of the Person of Christ
The Word made flesh
Robert Letham

The Message of Worship
Celebrating the glory of God in the whole of life
John Risbridger

The Message of Spiritual Warfare
The Lord is a warrior; the Lord is his name
Keith Ferdinando

The Message of Discipleship
Authentic followers of Jesus in today's world
Peter Morden

The Message of Love
The only thing that counts
Patrick Mitchel

The Message of Wisdom
Learning and living the way of the Lord
Daniel J. Estes